The Sociology of Law

The Sociology of Law:
An Introduction

Second edition

Roger Cotterrell LLD, MSc (Soc)
Professor of Legal Theory,
Queen Mary and Westfield College,
University of London

Butterworths
London, Dublin, Edinburgh
1992

United Kingdom	Butterworths, a Division of Reed Elsevier (UK) Ltd, Halsbury House, 35 Chancery Lane, London WC2A 1EL and 4 Hill Street, Edinburgh EH2 3JZ
Australia	Butterworths, Sydney, Melbourne, Brisbane, Adelaide, Perth, Canberra and Hobart
Canada	Butterworths Canada Ltd, Toronto and Vancouver
Ireland	Butterworth (Ireland) Ltd, Dublin
Malaysia	Malayan Law Journal Sdn Bhd, Kuala Lumpur
New Zealand	Butterworths of New Zealand Ltd, Wellington and Auckland
Singapore	Reed Elsevier (Singapore) Pte Ltd, Singapore
South Africa	Butterworths Publishers (Pty) Ltd, Durban
USA	Michie, Charlottesville, Virginia

First edition 1994, Reprinted 1986, 1989, 1990, 1993, 1995, 1996, and 1997

A CIP Catalogue record for this book is available from the British Library.

ISBN 0 406 51770 3

Cover Illustrations: Friedrich Karl von Savigny (*Great Jurists of the World* (1914) Little Brown & Co, Boston); Karl Marx (Marx and Engels, *Selected Works* (Vol 3) (1970) Progress Publishers); Emile Durkheim (Lukes, *Emile Durkheim: His Life and Work* Penguin Books Ltd); Max Weber (*Economy and Society* (1978) University of California Press); Karl N Llewellyn (Summers, *Instrumentalism and American Legal Theory* (1982) Cornell University Press); Talcott Parsons (*The Structure of Social Action* (1968) The Free Press, A Division of Macmillan Publishing Co Inc, New York); Jürgen Habermas (Heinemann Educational Books Ltd); Michel Foucault (*Politics, Philosophy, Culture–Interviews and the other Writings* (1988) Routlege & Kegan Paul Ltd); Niklas Luhmann (Raiser, *Rechtssoziologie* (1987) Alfred Metzer Verlag), Permission to reproduce these illustrations has been sought from the publishers.

Printed and bound in Great Britain
by Redwood Books, Trowbridge, Wiltshire

Preface to the Second Edition

Since this book was first published, the literature directly addressing its concerns has continued to grow rapidly. While an effort has been made to retain the integrity of the text as far as possible, alterations have been made throughout to take account of new material or changes of emphasis in interpretation, to update references and to take the opportunity to clarify some passages. As a result, all chapters contain substantial revisions, and most have much new writing and many new references to recent literature. In addition, the section of notes and further reading has been almost entirely rewritten to take account, within the framework of the book's themes, of new research published since the first edition. In revising the text I have also tried to bear in mind a wealth of helpful comments from reviewers of the original edition.

This edition retains the basic theoretical outlook of the original work. Some of the book's theoretical formulations, especially about legal ideology, have been found useful and built upon by other writers. Those formulations remain unchanged. I have, however, used some new passages in the last chapter to reflect further on commentary relating to the approach adopted in this book. More generally, despite the plethora of new research in sociology of law, the book's analytical structure still seems to me to be broadly appropriate as a framework in which to present sociological study of law today as an open, continually evolving and self-questioning, and yet reasonably systematic enterprise. I am still convinced that sociology of law should be thought of not as a discipline or sub-discipline within social science but as the effort and aspiration to develop a theoretically sophisticated, systematically empirical, and permanently reflexive outlook on law in society. Viewed in this way, sociology of law is compatible and allied with a diversity of contemporary critical movements in legal scholarship and social theory. And the vitality of current research activity in many countries seems encouraging for sociology of law so conceived. A sociological perspective on law—emphasising the need for ambitious theory to structure broadening understandings of experience, and also detailed empirical researches to reveal the diversity and complexity of local contexts of legal life—remains essential. It is a necessary underpinning of all efforts to construct order, solidarity and justice in a seemingly chaotic world, and a means of revealing some of the illusions that too often surround attempts to achieve this aim.

Roger Cotterrell
Queen Mary and Westfield College
March 1992

Preface to the First Edition

Over the past decade social scientific research in law has proliferated in Britain as elsewhere. Yet observational studies of 'law in action' originated many decades before. Also, despite the heavy, indeed almost exclusive, emphasis on analytical commentary on legal doctrine which has long been characteristic of Western legal scholarship, it is important to stress that rigorous theoretical and empirical study of law as a social phenomenon serving social ends has a long history. Law has two faces: as a mechanism of regulation of social life through distinct institutions and practices, and as a body of doctrine or ideas which can be logically or dogmatically interpreted and developed. This has ensured that in practice, if not always in theory, law has had to be treated as a matter of social experience as well as of abstract logic. Only in the law books can legal rules have a life of their own. Elsewhere their meaning and significance come from the way in which they are applied—if at all—to actual social situations and relationships.

Nevertheless, the changes which have occurred in legal scholarship in recent years are obvious and pervasive. The amount of empirical research on legal institutions—courts, legislatures, police, administrative agencies, etc.—has vastly increased. It has involved both academic lawyers and scholars from a variety of social science disciplines who previously might have regarded this research area as an exotic diversion but now treat it as a central focus of concern. In addition, the increasing attention to fundamental theoretical questions about the nature of law in society shows a serious quest for rigorous scientific explanation rather than merely for practical hints about social conditions helpful in implementing legal policy. It also marks the beginning of a long overdue confrontation between the new insights of contemporary social scientific research and the long-established traditions of jurisprudential inquiry. Jurisprudence—that collection of lawyers' speculations on their craft gathered and stored over the centuries—offers a vast treasure of insights into lawyers' outlook and into the functions of law in moulding thought and so influencing social behaviour.

The application to legal study of social theory—theory seeking to explain the structure of societies and the processes of social change—holds out the possibility of reformulating and reinterpreting many of the issues canvassed in the vast literature of jurisprudence. Developments in this country, as elsewhere, show a serious concern to develop a broad understanding of the nature of law in society drawing on the whole range of literature in modern social theory and connecting its insights with the results of particular empirical researches on aspects of law.

Much of what has occurred reflects a degree of dissatisfaction with traditional conceptions of law as a discipline. But this dissatisfaction has, itself, definite sociological causes which are discussed in this book. As an undergraduate student of law—a decade and a half ago—I was puzzled at the contrast between the great issues which I saw in and around the law—political and moral issues and fundamental questions of social policy—and the apparent triviality of many of the disputes that seemed to be the staple fare of legal argument. I could not then see that a sociologically important part of the mechanisms of modern law is to turn moral and political controversies into issues of purely technical regulation. Later, social science seemed to offer a way of understanding not only why and with what effects law took this form, but also why the containment of major issues in this way—for example, the substantial exclusion of explicit policy analysis from judicial processes in England—seemed to be breaking down. In one way or another much of this book is concerned with the gradual and fundamental transformation of modern Western law which such developments reflect. The transformation, carried forward in legislative change, is reflected in all the key social institutions of law including the judicial process, the organisation and practice of the legal profession, legal education and scholarship, and the numerous and varied agencies of law enforcement.

This book is intended as a general introduction to the sociological study of law. Its potential field is vast and therefore its aims are strictly limited. Its direct concern is only with theory and empirical research bearing on law in the contemporary industrialised societies of Western Europe and North America, the successor societies of those that typified what the classic social theorists of the late nineteenth and early twentieth centuries termed 'modern society'. Since the book is concerned only with the most general, sociologically significant features of this law it makes no attempt to be comprehensive in referring to the legal situation in these varying jurisdictions. On the whole, it concentrates on general concepts, theoretical issues and sociological hypotheses that reflect legal developments common to these advanced Western industrialised nations. But the important differences in legal traditions existing between Western countries are not sociologically insignificant and their importance in this context is reflected in the text. Since this book is written primarily for students of law and social science in Britain it naturally tends to reflect preoccupations in the sociological analysis of law formed by contact with the legal institutions of this country and present in the writing of British authors. It draws extensively, although certainly not exclusively, on English language publications which are likely to be reasonably accessible to students. And because empirical sociological studies of law are most extensively developed in a vast modern literature from the United States this book necessarily strongly reflects the developments achieved in that literature.

The book does not presuppose existing knowledge of law or of social science on the reader's part but it has been written in a form designed to enable it to confront lawyers' and law students' typical assumptions about law with the very different perspectives offered in sociological writings. It does not offer a 'history of ideas' and it refers only to the process of development of sociological studies of law where this is essential to its contemporary concerns. To keep the book within manageable limits certain fields are excluded. Thus my concern here is with law within states rather than between them, so international law finds no place as a subject for discussion. And the book makes no attempt to survey the extensive literature on crime, deviance, punishment and penal policy although much of the material in this volume is of direct relevance for criminological studies. The central concern is with law as legal doctrine and as the rule-sanctioned practices of legal institutions. Further, in a general introductory work of this kind it would be quite impossible to attempt to discuss—even in general terms—the whole range of institutions that, in contemporary Western societies, can plausibly be regarded as 'legal'. Here the material developed in the first five chapters, which discuss a variety of theoretical approaches to systematic analysis of law from a sociological viewpoint, is applied in Chapters 6, 7 and 8 to three major institutional aspects of law—professionalisation, adjudication and enforcement. The processes of legislation are not specially analysed, however, as a comparable discussion of them would lead deep into the field of political sociology as a whole. While many issues of political sociology are discussed in the first half of the book, particularly in Chapters 4 and 5, their further development has to be left to other writings in other contexts and would be out of place in a general introduction to sociological analysis of law.

The literature of this field is vast and rapidly growing. It is also extremely dispersed, being found in a proliferation of monograph publications and in law and social science journals of many kinds and from many countries. I have sought to keep the text as uncluttered by footnotes as possible. But I have also sought to provide a reasonably detailed guide to further reading on the various topics discussed in the text as well as a supplementary apparatus of notes. To try to fulfil both of these objectives a separate section of notes and further reading appears at the end of the main text. The text is organised and presented so that it can be read through without immediate reference to the section of notes. In this way I hope that the mass of literature will seem less bewildering to the newcomer to this field.

A primary concern in organising this book has been to steer a middle course between two extremes. On the one hand, the text does not set out to propound its own new and original legal theory but is concerned to describe and comment upon the varied theoretical positions and types of study that are its subject matter. On the other hand, I have sought to avoid a bewildering juxtaposition of inconsistent frameworks of analysis. Consequently the book attempts to suggest elements of a reasonably consistent analytical framework out of the materials and approaches it presents and to sketch and develop a consistent image of the nature of law in contemporary Western societies insofar as the material seems to me to make this possible. While I have not tried to disguise my own theoretical positions neither have I sought to elaborate them in full detail. A work such as this should ask the student to reach his or her own conclusions, not present a ready-made set. Consequently many questions remain unanswered, many leads are deliberately not followed up. Nevertheless, the book is intended as a contribution to the field of study it surveys. I have sought to advance the literature and not merely to describe it.

I am grateful to many people who in various ways made it possible for me to write this book. I owe much to Paul Hirst, Sami Zubaida and Susanne MacGregor who some years ago first helped me find my way in sociology and showed me what was important in it, and to Professor Bernard Crick's fine Birkbeck Department of Politics and Sociology which provided inspiration and support for an academic lawyer floundering in what was then alien territory. I cannot name all the friends and colleagues in Britain and abroad who by example, through discussion, and through their writings have deeply influenced my ideas on law in society. Suffice it to say that their names are scattered through the references in this book, and in a real sense it is intended as a tribute to their work in the sociological study of law. I am deeply grateful to my colleague Dr Michael Bryan who read through the manuscript in draft and made numerous helpful suggestions for improvement; also to Professor Roy Goode who provided detailed comments on particular sections. Neither, of course, holds any responsibility for the views expressed in the text or for errors remaining. I am grateful also to Queen Mary College for granting me sabbatical leave for a term to work on the book; and to the staff of Butterworths for their efficiency and patience.

The most important debt of all is to the members of my family who have had to live with my long-term preoccupation with this project. My children know the cost in terms of a father who too often had to remain undisturbed when he should have been available for their fun and their problems. And I cannot adequately express what I owe, in every aspect of the writing, to my wife Ann Cotterrell. As a practically-minded social scientist she read all of the book in draft and improved it in numerous ways through constructive criticism. As a computer buff she got me out of trouble when modern technology in the shape of my word processor started to show its limitations. In numerous other ways she provided support through the various traumas of authorship. For what seem to me obvious and excellent reasons this book is dedicated to those who having already shared a house with it for a considerable time can reasonably expect an early return to more normal life.

Roger Cotterrell
Faculty of Laws
Queen Mary College London
March 1984

Contents

Introduction: Theory and Method in the Study of Law

Suppose that a new piece of legislation comes into existence, created in the proper formal manner by an accepted law-making institution. What happens? Immediately lawyers set to work, digesting and comprehending the changes brought about by the new rules. The new law is probably published in some official form and finds its way into the libraries of law schools, lawyers and administrators. The body of legal doctrine—rules, principles and concepts of law—is slightly, or perhaps fundamentally, altered. The changes are registered in digests of legislation, legal encyclopedias, lawyers' updates or periodicals. But what then? Does anything else happen? Does the law somehow reach the world beyond this rarefied professional sphere? If so, in what way? With what effect?

Not every such law will even reach the courts of law because no case may arise to raise the issues with which the new law is concerned. Perhaps the matter which is the object of the law is not important in the experience of social life or, if it is, for various reasons the issues are kept away from courts. No one sees fit to raise them. Suppose, however, that the new law is invoked before a judge. Even so the court may refuse to apply it. It may be ruled irrelevant or interpreted in such a way as to remove some or all of its potential effect.[1] But suppose the court does apply the new law to the case under consideration. What effect will the judgment have on the conduct of life outside the courtroom? Very often, surprisingly little may be known by judges and lawyers about the law's potential or actual social effects. Perhaps even more surprisingly, rarely is any systematic attempt made by them to find out.

Practical questions such as these concerning the effects of laws have provided a major impetus for social scientific study of law. Yet they provide only a part of the justification for such study and not necessarily the most important part. The major justification is that law is too important a social phenomenon to be analysed in a way that isolates it from other aspects of society and makes impossible an understanding of

1 A well-known British illustration is the fate of the Sex Disqualification (Removal) Act 1919. Despite the apparently clear and wide terms of the legislation its words were not taken at face value but given a meaning in judicial interpretation which rendered the legislation of little effect. See e.g. *Price v Rhondda Urban Council* [1923] 2 Ch 372; *Viscountess Rhondda's Claim* [1922] 2 AC 339.

the complexity of its relations with other social phenomena, its 'reality' as a part of life and not merely as a technique of professional practice. 'Law permeates all realms of social behaviour. Its pervasiveness and social significance are felt in all walks of life' (Vago 1988: 1). One recent writer notes, echoing a theme of such earlier sociologists as Durkheim and Gurvitch, that 'the law in any social system is, in fact, a fundamental framework (a skeleton, if you like) of the nature of *all* its forms of association and institutions. If we know the law of any society, we have an excellent outline of the nature of the social system as a whole' (Fletcher 1981: 33). For another writer, the effort to understand law's significance 'takes us straight to the heart of... the major unsolved problems of social theory' (Unger 1976: 44). What is common to all such views is that analysis of law is seen as revealing, or having the potential to reveal, more than just law itself. If we understand law as a social phenomenon we understand much about the society in which it exists.

Lawyers' Conceptions of Law

Nevertheless, as every lawyer knows, law can be analysed in its own terms—that is, in terms of the internal logical structure of legal doctrine—at least if logic is tempered with dashes of expediency. What has sometimes been underemphasised by lawyers, however, is that 'pure legal analysis' is a highly problematic concept. The analysis of legal doctrine—the rules, regulations, principles and concepts set out in law books and authoritatively stated in legislation or deduced from judicial decisions—involves numerous decisions as to how far and in what manner logical analysis can be developed. Considerations of policy cannot be excluded from the analysis since legal doctrine is continually being shaped in the practice of courts and other agencies of interpretation by reference to assumed social purposes of law. Further, lawyers' analysis of law is grounded in an array of philosophical assumptions—for example, about the nature of responsibility, obligation, causation and the autonomy of the individual—which often necessarily remain unexamined. These assumptions have, however, increasingly become matters for examination as changes have occurred in the modern political and social context of Western legal systems. With the development of modern forms of legislation, purely 'legal logical' interpretation has seemed ever more problematic as law reflects and embodies policy more explicitly and as the scope and character of regulation changes.

None of this is intended to deny the validity of lawyers' pragmatic rationalisations of legal rules into more or less systematic form. This ordering activity is essential to professional legal practice. But the character of contemporary law—an immense, ever-changing network of legislative rules, judicial precedents, orders, regulations, powers and discretions—is such that these necessary rationalisations are inevitably partial and limited. They serve practical ends. They are part of the technique of orderly application of law; practical instruments in the enterprise of regulating conduct. Systematisation and generalisation of doctrine are tools to be used or put aside depending on the character of the task in hand. Serious problems arise only when it is assumed that the nature of law *in general* can be adequately explained—that comprehensive *theories of law* can be constructed—by logically organising and analysing legal doctrine without relating it to systematic empirical knowledge about the societies in which it exists and in relation to which its concepts acquire their meaning (cf. Cotterrell 1989: ch 8). Theory developed solely through rationalisation of and speculation on the rules, principles, concepts and values considered to be explicitly or implicitly present in legal doctrine can be termed normative legal theory. It constitutes a major focus of past and present legal philosophy. By contrast the empirical legal theory with which this book is concerned proceeds on the basis that an understanding of the nature of law requires not only systematic empirical analysis of legal doctrine and institutions but also of the social environment in which legal institutions exist.[2]

A Variety of Perspectives on Law

To say that law should be analysed empirically as a social phenomenon is one thing. But how should this be done? Is there a single 'social reality of law' to be discovered? A lawyer's professional outlook on law may well differ from that of a social scientist or from the varied conceptions of law that ordinary citizens in different ethnic, occupational or other groups hold. Furthermore, different kinds of social theory will portray law in different ways within the competing pictures of the character of modern Western societies which they present. Law thus has different social realities constructed from different vantage points. Yet some of these perceptions of law have more depth, more explanatory power than others; they take into account more—or more systematically gathered—empirical detail about law. Their theoretical analysis is more fully

2 This is an appropriate place to define the terms 'social institution' and 'legal institution' which appear throughout this text. 'Social institution' refers here to a system of patterned expectations about the behaviour of individuals fulfilling certain socially-recognised roles. Cf. Parsons 1954a: 231. In this sense we refer to, for example, marriage, collective bargaining, joint stock companies or money as social institutions. The term 'legal institutions' is often used in legal literature to refer to fundamental legal concepts such as property, trust or contract (see e.g. MacCormick 1974) which would be social institutions according to the above usage. In the following text 'legal institutions' refers specifically to patterns of official action and expectations of action organised around the creation, application and enforcement of legal precepts or the maintenance of a legal order.

worked out, more coherent, or more aware of and capable of incorporating or explaining rival hypotheses, competing theories or data relating to the social environment of law. A lawyer may have a far better grasp of the complex patterns of doctrinal development in the law than a sociologist possesses. A social scientist may be able to draw on knowledge of social institutions and social theory seemingly unrelated to law but which, properly interpreted, can illuminate the nature of legal developments in a way that might entirely escape the reflection that lawyers bring to bear on their particular professional experience.

The possibility of ultimately describing and analysing the social reality of law, as the embodiment of knowledge that transcends partial perspectives, is the possibility of *science*. That it remains only a possibility, an aim to work towards, and one that may never be realised is no reason to deny its importance. In the most general sense scientific method involves two elements: first, a clear and explicit recognition that all perspectives on experience are necessarily partial and incomplete[3] and, secondly, the serious (but necessarily never completed) attempt to overcome the limitations of partial perspectives through systematic collection, analysis and interpretation of the empirical data of experience. Knowledge of the social world is, however, affected by many considerations besides the disinterested quest for enlightenment. Indeed, the latter may be the least significant of the factors that have promoted social science in general and social research on law in particular. Yet the material discussed in this book should suggest that some progress has been achieved. Ultimately, however, progress in understanding the complexity of social life must require the breakdown of boundaries between intellectual disciplines; a further step in overcoming partial perspectives. For the moment it requires a willingness to confront the methods and preoccupations of particular disciplines with those of others, and to clarify the conditions under which such confrontations can take place (see e.g. Cotterrell 1986).

Sociology and Law

It may be asked why a specifically *sociological* perspective on law is justified and what such a perspective implies. In one sense law and sociology as forms of professional practice are similar in scope yet wholly opposed in method and aims. Law as a scholarly professional practice is concerned with elaboration of the practical art of government through rules. Its concern is prescriptive and technical. Sociology is

3 As a recent writer notes: 'We are always understanding and interpreting in light of our anticipatory prejudgments and prejudices which are themselves changing in the course of history. To understand is always to understand *differently*': Bernstein 1985: 139.

concerned with the scientific study of social phenomena. Its concern is explanatory and descriptive. The lawyer is essentially a man of affairs entrusted with part of the apparatus of regulation of social relations. The sociologist remains a relatively uncommitted observer. If these stereotypes are often belied in practice they nevertheless broadly point to differences in outlook which appear typical when the respective disciplinary statuses of law and sociology are self-consciously asserted.

Yet both law and sociology are concerned with the whole range of significant forms of social relationships. And in practice the criteria determining which relationships are significant are often similar, deriving from the same cultural assumptions or conceptions of policy relevance. Furthermore, both legal studies and sociological inquiries typically seek to view these phenomena as part of, or potentially part of, an integrated social structure. Thus, despite their radical differences in method and outlook law and sociology share a fundamentally similar basic subject matter. Law is a practical craft of systematic control of social relations and institutions. Sociology is the scientific enterprise that seeks systematic knowledge of them. An American commentator writes, 'Sociology is concerned with values, interaction patterns, and ideologies that underlie the basic structural arrangements in a society, many of which are embodied in law as substantive rules. Both sociology and law are concerned with norms, rules that prescribe the appropriate behaviour for people in a given situation. The study of conflict and conflict resolution are central in both disciplines. Both sociology and law are concerned with the nature of legitimate authority, the mechanisms of social control, issues of civil rights, power arrangements, and the relationship between public and private spheres' (Vago 1988: 2–3).

It is this common concern of law and sociology with the whole range of social relations which makes a sociological perspective on law potentially more *generally* fruitful than, for example, a perspective drawn exclusively from economics or some other discipline concerned with a particular category of human relationships. This is, of course, in no way to deny the utility of economic analysis in illuminating particular aspects of law. Legal relations are not, however, solely economic relations nor relations whose content and significance are necessarily explicable in exclusively economic terms. As the jurist Savigny noted, 'law is the totality of life, but seen from a specific viewpoint' (quoted in Timasheff 1939: 343; cf. Savigny 1831: 46). Sociology, alone among the social sciences, is similarly comprehensive. In its perspective, both law as a mechanism of social regulation and law as a profession or as a special field of knowledge and practice become equally objects of study to be explained in sociological terms.

It has already been suggested above, however, that progress in understanding the complexity of social life must eventually require a breakdown of boundaries between existing intellectual disciplines, or a systematic denial of the autonomy of disciplines. For the moment it is enough to say that a sociological perspective on law is not limited by the range of present or past concerns of sociology as a distinct academic discipline. Many theoretical and empirical researches to be discussed in this book have been contributed by writers who would not label themselves sociologists nor see their concerns as needing to be located within sociology as a distinct academic field. Interdisciplinarity has long been one of the more productive forms of intellectual non-conformity.

A sociological perspective implies here the kind of broad view expressed by the American historian H. Stuart Hughes. For Hughes, sociology is not 'the highly specialised and fragmented discipline with which we are familiar in the United States' (or in Britain, for that matter) but 'a more universal social theorising in the tradition of Montesquieu or Marx' (Hughes 1959: 22). Writing of three classic social theorists he notes: 'This was the notion of sociology held by Weber or Durkheim or Pareto. However finite the problems to which they might address themselves, what they were really after was the overall structure of society. And it is significant that they were all men of broad general education who came to sociology only after having received their original training in other fields' (1959: 22). A sociological perspective on law does not require that law should somehow be subsumed as part of academic sociology's territory but that it should be viewed with a 'sociological imagination' (cf. Mills 1959). Such an imagination constantly seeks to interpret detailed knowledge of law in a wider social context, consistently looks for the relations between legal development and wider social changes, tries to understand law as interacting in complex ways with the social environment it purports to regulate, and tries always to approach these matters systematically with a constant sensitivity to the need for specific empirical data and rigorous theoretical explanation.

If sociology has fallen from favour as a distinct academic discipline it is because simultaneously too much and too little has been expected from it. Too much has been expected in the sense that it has been assumed that the collection of quantitative data can somehow solve the social problems of the time. Yet this data is inevitably partial and problematic information gathered by means that cannot usually meet the tests assumed as relevant in natural science research methods. Against the background of this information political problems and value choices remain to be faced, not avoided. In the view of one eminent British sociologist the achievements of social science in general have typically been assessed from a 'vulgar and shallow technocratic point of view' (Rex 1979:14).

In other respects too little has been expected of sociology in the sense that a stress on immediate policy relevance and accumulation of quantitative empirical data has diverted attention from the significance of the sociological imagination as what might be called (at the risk of pretentiousness) a form of human self-consciousness. This kind of study ought to enable us to locate ourselves in relation to our social and cultural environment in a far wider, deeper sense than can be obtained through concentration on the accumulation of data for short-term policy ends.

The classic social theorists, Max Weber, Karl Marx and Emile Durkheim, whose insights about the character of Western societies inform the pages of this book, understood the analysis of social phenomena in this broad sense, although they were far from unworldly or impractical in their concerns. They sought answers to large questions about the nature and direction of social change, the conditions and forms of social order, the relationship between the individual and society. At this level sociological study has contributed much enlightenment, taking up persistent questions of social philosophy but seeking as far as possible to confront theory with empirical data in a serious manner, so as to escape the blind gropings of uncontrolled speculation. It is at this level that sociology can contribute most to an understanding of law (cf. Hayek 1982 I: 114). It offers not 'finished' knowledge—a body of technical, scientific prescriptions or diagnoses—but a continually broadening, self-critical effort to explore the conundrums presented by the empirical data of social life.

Compartmentalisation and its Dangers

It should be apparent from what has been said that the sociological study of law hardly forms a neat intellectual compartment—nor should it do so. Its boundaries are set only by the quest for understanding of the character of law as a social phenomenon. The term 'sociology of law', now often used to describe this area of study, is convenient until it is used to justify a rigid disciplinary compartmentalisation which can only hamper development of the field. One writer remarks, 'the sociology of law is but a sub-discipline of sociology and, as such, aims at the understanding of that discipline's particular subject-matter' (Wilkinson 1981: 67). Yet contemporary sociology as an academic discipline is marked by an immense variety of special concerns and theoretical and methodological approaches. Its character as a resource to be drawn on in the development of knowledge in particular fields—for example, legal study—is perhaps more apparent at the present time than its disciplinary integrity. Although among the classic social theorists Durkheim most strongly promoted sociology as the unifying central discipline of social science, he also clearly and continuously stressed its utility as a resource in the study of particular social fields.

As suggested earlier, the extension of knowledge beyond particular fields is likely to come through the *weakening* of disciplinary claims and not through their extension. Indeed, viewed in terms of the disciplinary concerns of sociology, 'sociology of law is, at the present stage of development, very loose and fragmented, and does not offer any consistent theoretical framework' (Los 1981:197). As a field of inquiry it is 'not marked by any special unity or internal coherence' (Campbell and Wiles 1976: 554). While these statements are perhaps too negative they are understandable insofar as they measure development in this field by established disciplinary criteria. The sociological study of law remains marginal to academic sociology. At the same time it coexists uneasily with the established discipline of law (which is, nevertheless, changing in important respects to accommodate the perspectives that social scientific research has introduced in legal study) (cf. Cotterrell 1990a). Paradoxically, this situation with its possibility of relatively independent development not wholly constrained by the preconceptions of established disciplines remains for the moment the greatest strength of sociology of law. Indeed, Carbonnier's term 'juridical sociology' *(sociologie juridique)* might be more appropriate for the field, implying not a branch of sociology but a study of society through law, and of law in society (cf. Carbonnier 1978: 19-21).

Legal Positivism

So far the term 'law' has remained undefined in these considerations and some of the most basic issues involved in conceptualising law sociologically are discussed in the first chapter. But it is important to note here a few quite general problems of method which arise as soon as the attempt to study law as an empirical social phenomenon is made. Law is often said to have a double-faceted character which can be expressed in various ways. Thus law consists of prescriptions—'ought propositions' specifying the way legal subjects ought to behave. Yet at the same time it constitutes a social phenomenon which only 'exists' if the prescriptions of conduct actually have some effect on the way people think or behave. Law is thus both prescriptive norm and descriptive fact. It is to be considered in terms of its validity and also its efficacy. It is *sollen* and *sein*—'ought' and 'is' (Schiff 1981: 154ff). This dualism is much discussed in the literature of jurisprudence. It is seen to pose problems for analysis since, although law appears as both prescriptive norm and empirical fact, 'these two categories logically exclude one other' (Castberg quoted in Schiff 1981: 155). In fact the rigid separation of these two aspects of law holds good only if a particular approach to analysis of law is adopted. This approach, which is really a philosophical conception of what constitutes valid knowledge and of how it is to be obtained, has been pervasive in both legal theory and social science and is known as positivism.

It would be impossible in the space available here even to begin to survey all the major ramifications of the positivist outlook in legal study and sociological analysis. Nevertheless, since much of the literature discussed in this book is either informed by positivist assumptions or (particularly in the case of phenomenological and related approaches) is written in more or less explicit criticism or rejection of them, some brief introductory remarks must be offered here. In essence, positivism is a philosophical position which asserts that scientific knowledge derives from observation of the data of experience and not from speculation that seeks to 'look behind' observed facts for ultimate causes, meanings or essences. What we observe is, therefore, what really exists—and, scientifically speaking, all that exists. Hence judgments of value, of what is good or bad, political or policy questions, questions about the ultimate nature of things which cannot be determined by generalisations from observation—all of these are unscientific. Because these matters are subjective, existing only in the minds of individuals, they are unanalysable by scientific means. In the strongest versions of positivism they do not constitute knowledge at all. Fact and value are thus rigidly separated. Science should be 'value free' in two senses. It should not, itself, make value judgments about what it observes. And it should not seek to inquire into the meaning or ultimate significance of the values held by those it observes. This is not to say that values cannot be studied but they can be studied only as the observable preferences and commitments of actual individuals, not as having significance or reality in their own right.

In the Anglo-American legal world, and indeed to a greater or lesser extent in most modern highly-developed legal systems, a positivist outlook on law is the typical outlook of lawyers and informs much legal scholarship and teaching. Law consists of data—primarily rules—which can be recognised as such by relatively simple tests or 'rules of recognition' (Hart 1961). A familiar such simple test is that the rules have passed through certain formal stages of a legislative process, or (less simple) that they can be derived from the *ratio decidendi*—the essential grounds of decision—of a case decided by a court having the jurisdiction and authority to lay down new rules in such a case. According to a positivist conception, these rules of law—possibly with some subsidiary legal phenomena—constitute the law, the data which it is the lawyer's task to analyse and order. In this sense, law is a 'given'—part of the data of experience. If it can be recognised as existing according to certain observational tests it can be analysed. The tests by which legal positivism recognises the existence of law or particular laws are thus analogous to those by which a scientist might recognise the presence of a particular chemical.

Some Limitations of Legal Positivism

Although, up to a point, this is an obviously useful way by which the lawyer or legal analyst identifies the subject matter of his or her inquiries it necessarily directs attention away from the idea that law consists of human processes. To treat the data of law merely as legal rules may be a static (and therefore inadequate) representation of a dynamic phenomenon: the reality of regulation as the continually changing outcome of a complex interaction of individuals and groups in society. Legal positivism seeks tests of the 'legal' which make it possible to identify the data of law, as far as possible without looking behind legislative rules to the process by which they were created, and without considering judicial attitudes or values. What is considered to be the justice or injustice, wisdom or efficiency, moral or political significance of a law is not essential to an understanding of it as long as rules of law can be clearly ascertained. Only when the 'data of law' are elusive—when the rules are not clear or their applicability to a new case is in doubt—must these 'non-legal elements' be considered.[4] Since, however, they are by definition external to law they are not necessarily considered systematically but are typically used more or less selectively as rhetorical ammunition in debates on legal interpretation.

Positivism is a primary modern philosophical foundation of legal professional knowledge, a form of knowledge which will be considered particularly in Chapter 6. Consequently, there are powerful professional reasons for maintenance of a positivist outlook in legal analysis. Yet it is significant that, as a philosophy of law, positivism has come under powerful attack in recent years. It has been charged that it ignores the role of values in law and the way in which law is established in interpretation (cf. Dworkin 1986: 37–43), that in treating rules as the given data of law it assumes a certainty and clarity in rules that is by no means apparent, that it cannot cope with the complex relationship between rules and discretionary powers of officials in legal regulation in complex contemporary societies, and more generally that it cannot provide an adequate basis for understanding processes of legal change. In this respect, critics of legal positivism refer to theoretical issues about contemporary Western law which are a major focus of sociology of law.

4 Although their relevance even in these circumstances is sometimes denied. A French authority writes: 'Extrajuridical arguments which do not assist in the solution of a case are among those which lend a merely sophistical appearance to a decision. To invoke considerations of economics, sociology or diplomacy is to confuse different kinds of arguments and to conceal the correctness of sound reasoning' (Mimin, quoted in Zweigert and Kötz 1987: 127).

Sociological Positivism Versus 'Interpretive Sociology'

Positivist method, in various manifestations, is also characteristic of certain types of sociology. However, it does not represent, by any means, a universal conception of the nature of sociological knowledge and of the means of acquiring it. Indeed, in much contemporary Western European sociology, positivist approaches are typically either overlaid with many qualifications and modifications or are explicitly rejected. While legal positivism remains strong in the legal systems of Britain, the United States and other Western states, sociological positivism has been widely challenged by flourishing competing approaches which have stressed the need for interpretive 'understanding' of social phenomena in terms of the motivations of social actors rather than mere observation of behaviour or measurement of attitudes.

Sociological positivism in its most explicit form is typified by Durkheim's famous injunction that we should 'treat social facts as things' (Durkheim 1982: 60, 161-2). In other words, social phenomena should be measured and analysed in basically the same manner as the natural scientist would measure and analyse substances and processes in laboratory experiments. Durkheim pointed out that, although many social phenomena—for example, the morale or cohesion of a society—are far too intangible to measure directly, it may be possible to discover indicators of these intangible phenomena in more directly observable matters. In his own studies, changes in the law and variations in suicide rates provided two such 'indices' of wider, more nebulous social phenomena. Of course, controlled experiments cannot usually be carried out in the social world in the same manner as in a laboratory although, for example, studies of jury decision-making have made use of 'simulated juries' replicating as far as possible the actual conditions of jury deliberations under experimental conditions. In fact, social science possesses a whole battery of fact-gathering techniques including sophisticated questionnaire survey methods, participant observation, and techniques of conversation analysis, which go some way to meet the claim that observational methods comparable in rigour with those of natural science cannot be used.

The often pointed-out flaw in a strict sociological positivism is that society is not a 'thing' external to the observer. At the same time as social facts appear as things constraining or influencing the actions and attitudes of members of a society they can also be seen as shaped or sustained by the interactions, motivations or beliefs of those same members. As a member of a human society the social scientist is implicated in—a part of—what he or she studies. For this reason, the conception of a totally objective attitude on the part of the observer is very problematic. As a 'social being', such an observer cannot put aside fundamental and perhaps unstated conceptions of social life which are an integral part of his or her personality.

In one sense, however, social science possesses a great methodological advantage over natural science. In social science the observer observes other human beings. Because of the possibility of empathy between observer and observed, between subject and object, the researcher has the chance not only to record behaviour and attitudes but also to understand the motivations of the social actors being studied; to understand social action as *meaningful* to those engaged in it. Because of this commonality of observer and observed the former can legitimately go beyond mere observation to interpretation. This is not to assume that all social action is rational but only that it may be useful to interpret it in terms of models of rationality or of typical expectations about conduct in situations such as those observed. The observer can, and perhaps should, thus attempt to make sense of social phenomena in terms of the outlook of the actors whose conduct constitutes these phenomena.

From this viewpoint sociology's concern is to understand social phenomena in terms of the subjective meaning of actors, rather than merely to measure observable regularities (Weber 1978: 8). As Max Weber, the classic exponent of this 'understanding' (*verstehende*) approach to study in sociology expressed the matter, social action—the basic subject matter of sociological analysis—is behaviour that is subjectively meaningful to the individual undertaking it and is directed towards, or takes into account the position of, other actors with whom the individual interrelates (cf. Weber 1978: 4). An emphasis on explaining how social phenomena are created in social action or interaction is in no way incompatible with a parallel concern with the mechanisms by which these phenomena control or influence the action of members of a society as long as it is recognised that some individuals or groups in a society may have more power than others to shape social conditions (see Merry 1990: 110–1).

That this 'understanding' approach is of the greatest importance as a means of explaining how social phenomena are constructed is illustrated by developments both in legal philosophy and in the sociology of law. The influential legal philosopher H.L.A. Hart introduces in his major work on legal theory (Hart 1961) the notion that rules are to be understood in terms of their 'internal aspect' which, broadly speaking, is the *subjective* meaning that rules have for those who understand concepts of legal obligation. In the sociology of law much writing now follows directly or indirectly Weber's methodological lead though often mediated through related philosophical conceptions. Law can be seen as consisting of norms—'ought propositions'—but these norms 'exist' in the experience and reasoning patterns of actual individuals. Hence law as embodied in behaviour and attitudes, as one of the determinants of social action, is a social fact. But at the same time it is a realm of ideas to be understood in terms of the subjective meaning of those ideas for individuals living within a legal order.

A very strict positivism remains aggressively championed in the sociology of law, most notably in the writings of the American sociologist Donald Black (1976; 1989). For him, law 'consists in observable acts, not in rules as the concept of rule or norm is employed in both the literature of jurisprudence and in every-day legal language' (Black 1972: 1091). The legal positivist's conception of legal data as rules is replaced by a sociological positivist conception of legal data as quantifiable observable behaviour. Law, defined as governmental social control, 'behaves' in various ways, increasing or decreasing in measurable extent. Thus the 'quantity' of law varies with the quantity of stratification (differentiation of individuals and groups into hierarchically ordered classes or categories) in a society. Lower ranks in a society have less law to call upon than higher ranks. Deviance of lower ranks against higher is more likely to be seen as serious than the converse. Law varies directly with culture. 'Where culture is sparse so is law; where it is rich, law flourishes' (Black 1976: 63). Law varies also with collective organisation in a society. The more organisational complexity and diversity, the more law. And so on. In Black's view it is not for the sociology of law to explain *why* law changes or 'behaves' in such ways but merely to observe and measure correlations between the behaviour of law and other measurable social phenomena. From such correlations predictions about the behaviour of law are said to be obtainable. In Black's most recent work, trends in the behaviour of law are held to justify predictions about law's future. They also inspire highly speculative proposals as to how sociological knowledge might be harnessed in legal and social practice (Black 1989). But explicit evaluation or interpretation is out of bounds. So is any political analysis of law or any consideration of the nature and ultimate significance of legal ideals.

Objectivity and Values

The view taken in this book is that the separation of science and values—not to mention the reduction of law to apparently motiveless behaviour—is impossible in any strict sense. Law is both fact and value. The ideals existing in law or projected on to it inform conduct and attitudes and cannot be left out of consideration. Equally, the values of researchers necessarily influence their own researches on such a subject. The safest scientific approach would seem to involve being alert to recognise that value judgments inform both the selection of problems for study and their analysis, to make them explicit where they can be isolated, continually to re-examine the facts that appear to make them plausible and to remain permanently willing to reconsider such judgments in the light of new arguments and new data. In a weak sense positivism is simply scientific method in its most general and uncontroversial form; that is, reliance on observed data as the basis for considered judgments and a refusal to speculate beyond what observed experience will justify as plausible. Only when positivist method restricts the subject matter of inquiry to a form in which broader understanding is likely to be curtailed by the erection of rigid boundaries between compartments of knowledge does it become dangerous and, in fact, a barrier to recognition of the complexity of law as a sociological phenomenon. In this extreme sense positivism, implying that what is not measurable is perhaps not knowledge at all, 'is an act of escape from commitments, an escape masked as a definition of knowledge... The language it imposes exempts us from the duty of speaking up in life's most important conflicts' and 'encases us in a kind of armour of indifference to... the indescribable qualitative data of experience' (Kolakowski 1972: 244).

Indeed, much that seems of great social significance about law cannot be 'measured', surveyed, or tabulated in the forms that positivist science approves. Observation—carried out in the most careful and rigorous manner possible—is merely an essential prerequisite of interpretation: interpretation of the social significance of what is observed, first, in terms of the meaning of the social phenomena for those individuals and groups whose actions and expectations constitute the phenomena, and, secondly, in terms of its significance for the concerns of those whom the researcher seeks to persuade through his or her researches. A broader conception of science than that of positivism makes it possible, in studying the variety of established approaches to sociological analysis of law, to recognise that law's many facets require analysis from different standpoints, using different methods. In the chapters that follow, something of the variety of outlooks and approaches that contribute to a sociological perspective on law in contemporary Western societies will be outlined and illustrated.

The literature of sociological study of law is a rich tapestry to which many have contributed and which was begun many centuries ago. The ideals of those who have written have been extremely varied. Some have sought a more just legal order; some have hoped for a world that would dispense with law altogether. Many have considered that understanding law meant understanding the great issues of politics and society. Some of the most influential social and political theorists have been legal scholars or trained in law, among them Bodin, Montesquieu, Bentham, Millar, Gumplowicz, Weber, Marx and Lukacs. Today this field is one of the liveliest foci of social research. For some researchers its justification, wholly or partially, is to improve law, to aid the legislator or the judge (e.g. Carbonnier 1978: 378-419) or, even, to facilitate 'social engineering', a more efficient organisation of society or a more efficient technology of government for realising collective welfare (e.g. Podgorecki 1974: 8, 31). Whether such aims are appropriate or realistic can be left for the reader to judge in the light of material discussed in subsequent chapters. For this writer, however, its primary objective is to increase understanding of legal phenomena, to contribute to the overcoming of partial perspectives, and so to contribute to wider understanding of the society in which these phenomena exist, and of the conditions and responsibilities of individuals in relation to each other as members of such a society. In this broad sense the objective of the sociology of law is to contribute to an understanding of the meaning and conditions of justice in society.

1 The Social Basis of Law

Whatever the wider significance of law in society, perhaps the most obvious characteristic of law as a cluster of institutions and professional practices in Western societies is its apparent isolation. A most tangible experience of this air of isolation of the world of law is to walk from the noise and bustle of London streets through the gates of the Inns of Court, into the leafy squares with their neat lawns where the barristers who serve the Royal Courts of Justice have their chambers and where the life of the law, in this narrow professional sense, goes on with a tranquillity far removed from anything happening beyond the walls that surround the Inns.

To many people law seems separate from other aspects of life. It appears as an arcane world of professionalism centred on a body of esoteric knowledge which is intimidating to the uninitiated in its bulk and obscurity. Laymen usually seek to avoid it. Few actually want to be involved in litigation. Few people other than lawyers discover the mysteries contained in the thousands of volumes of law reports and legal treatises. Legal experience is thought to exist in a different realm from social experience. Judges in England are popularly if often erroneously assumed to be as remarkable for their limited knowledge of life beyond the courtroom as for their mastery of what goes on within it.

This apparent isolation is closely related to and in part sustained by the professional autonomy of lawyers which varies in character and degree in different Western societies and has many ramifications. One consequence of it is that lawyers' typical conceptions of law, shaped and refined in their professional environment, have long had a self-sufficiency and comprehensiveness which have made them extremely resistant to different and perhaps opposed views of the nature and functions of law arising outside legal professional circles. The concern of this chapter is to outline some basic sociological assumptions involved in these typical conceptions of law and to suggest some of the important sociological questions to which they give rise but which they do not answer.

One of the most important characteristics of law seen from this professional standpoint has been its intellectual isolation. Law has been envisaged in such a way that as doctrine and professional practice it can be analysed and understood in terms of its own internal categories and without reference to the social environment within which it develops (cf. Goodrich 1987: 128). It is specifically in the modern Western societies with which this book is concerned that this remarkable conception of law has been most fully developed. As noted in the Introduction, it has been founded on the assumed rational doctrinal structure of law and underpinned by a positivist conception of legal science. In earlier times, the idea of law as an arcane field of special knowledge was blended with an assertion (considered to be without need of empirical demonstration or theoretical examination) of the roots of legal ideas in general culture (Cotterrell 1989: ch 2). Law was seen as a craft handed down by tradition and consisting of technical mysteries accessible only through the practical experience of apprenticeship. In fact, in the Anglo-American legal world this earlier craft conception of law has not entirely disappeared but rather been overlaid with modern professional conceptions.

Anglo-American legal thinking still remains strongly influenced by the traditions of the English common law—that is, of law developed pragmatically case by case through judicial decisions rather than elaborated from *a priori* general concepts or legislated in the form of codes or statutes. In the common law conception law grows like coral, through the slow accumulation of minutiae over the centuries, the encrustation of precedent. The rational strength of legal doctrine comes not from any systematic overall structure but from the accumulated wisdom of the judges preserved in the thousands of recorded cases which make up this coral kingdom. Today, when legislation created by elected assemblies constitutes by far the most important source of new law in Western societies, this older conception of law can hardly dominate. Yet in the Anglo-American legal world it expresses itself in lawyers' tendency to see judges as at the heart of the legal system, to view legislation with some reserve, and to laud the virtues of case law. Common law still remains a subsidiary source of new law in these jurisdictions and, more importantly, the concepts developed in common law remain a general foundation of legal reasoning within them. For this reason they remain known as common law systems in contrast to the civil law code-based systems of continental Europe.

Perhaps because lawyers' claims about the intellectual autonomy of law have, in general, been so tenaciously maintained without regard to developments in social science they are difficult to confront directly using modern sociological literature, most of which has adopted standpoints radically different from these orthodox professional conceptions. A useful strategy, then, is to consider some relatively early sociological perspectives on law which, because of the intellectual environment of their time, engage orthodox or traditional lawyers' conceptions on their own ground, bringing to light tensions or ambiguities in legal professional thoughtways, at the same time as they elaborate sociological assumptions contained within them.

Folkways and Mores

In his classic work *Folkways* (1906), the American sociologist William Graham Sumner indirectly provides a convenient sociological commentary on assumptions typical of common law thinking. Sumner sets out on what has been for many theorists the basic sociological quest: to explain the forces of social cohesion, the elements that contribute order and unity in societies. The boundless ambition of the book—to generalise about all societies and all human history—locates it firmly in a late nineteenth-century tradition. Certainly it draws on a vast range of ethnographic material from numerous societies. Sumner writes, 'If we put together all we have learnt from anthropology and ethnography about primitive men and primitive society we perceive that the first task of life is to live [i.e. to survive] ... Need was the first experience and it was followed by some blundering effort to satisfy it' (Sumner 1906: 17-8). The basic method for early man in attempting to solve the problems of survival was trial and error, a blundering utilitarianism. The ability to distinguish pleasure and pain is 'the only psychical power which is to be assumed' (1906: 18). The experience of pleasure and pain provided the test of success. But the historical struggle for survival went on in groups so that many seeking the same aim tended to come to similar opinions as to what was best, more productive of pleasure than pain. 'Each profited by the other's experience: hence there was concurrence towards that which proved to be most expedient. All at last adopted the same way for the same purpose; hence the ways turned into customs and became mass phenomena. Instincts were developed in connection with them. In this way folkways arise' (1906: 18).

The concept of folkways is at the heart of Sumner's thinking. They are the group ways of doing things, of solving problems. All 'the life of human beings in all ages and stages of culture, is primarily controlled by a vast mass of folkways handed down from the earliest existence of the race' (1906: 20). They are not conscious creations but 'like products of natural forces which men unconsciously set in operation, or ... like the instinctive ways of animals, which are developed out of experience' (1906: 19). The young learn them through tradition, imitation and authority. The folkways provide for all the needs of life: they specify the best way to make a fire, to cook meat, to greet one's neighbour, to raise one's children. They are uniform, universal in the group, imperative and invariable and as time goes on they become more and more arbitrary, positive and imperative. 'If asked why they act in a certain way in certain cases, primitive people always answer that it is because they and their ancestors always have done so' (1906: 18). In early society the folkways are sanctioned by fear of ancestors. The ghosts of ancestors would be angry if the living should change the ancient ways.

According to Sumner's account, however, other ideas eventually become attached to the folkways beyond that of their utility. Folkways are not noticed or consciously considered until long after they have become established. But eventually some folkways come to be seen as good for the welfare of the society. And the judgment of social welfare may eventually diverge from the relatively simple utilitarian judgment of pleasure and pain. The conversion of folkways in this manner requires 'some intelligent reflection on experience' and when the judgment of social good is added to folkways they become *mores*. 'When the elements of truth and right are developed into doctrines of welfare, the folkways are raised to another plane. They then become capable of producing inferences developing into new forms and extending their constructive influence over men and society.' They become 'the source of the science and art of living' (1906: 42).

Law grows, or should grow, out of the mores. It shades into them but is distinguished by being backed by state force. Folkways and mores change gradually as the conditions of life change but there is, in Sumner's view, little scope for changing them fundamentally through any conscious acts of legislation. 'Legislation ... has to seek standing ground on the existing mores and ... legislation, to be strong, must be consistent with the mores' (1906: 63). Thus social life has a dynamic of its own. Law, philosophy, religion and morality have no independent existence but are various reflections of that dynamic. They are deeply rooted in the processes of social development, yet virtually powerless to alter them. Thus 'rights' are the expression of the rules of mutual give and take in the competition of life which are accepted within the group in the interests of peace. They are never 'natural', 'God-given' or absolute in any sense. Morality is the sum of the taboos and prescriptions in the mores by which right conduct is defined. So morals are never intuitive but historical, institutional and empirical. Philosophy and ethics, too, are products of the mores and philosophy attempts the impossible when it tries to construe absolutes from the accidents of experience which shape the mores. After all, folkways and mores do not necessarily have a source that is rational according to modern conceptions. Some derive from mistaken inferences from experience, and from what Sumner calls the 'aleatory interest'—the rationally uncontrollable factor of good and bad fortune. 'The aleatory interest has always been the connecting link between the struggle for existence and religion. It was only by religious rites that the aleatory element in the struggle for existence could be controlled' (1906: 22).

What is patently absent from this account is any adequate conception of differentiation in society. Sumner is clear that the folkways and mores are rooted in the life of 'the masses'. A ruling elite can, to some extent, alter its own mores and exert influence by legislation or other means on those of the 'common man'. But the masses, 'the core of the society', are conservative, living by tradition and habit (1906: 54ff). And, since an elite will not want to stir up change in such a way as to upset its own privileged position, law will in any event be used more often to reinforce the mores of the masses than to reshape them. In any case, to the extent that law deliberately separates itself from the mores it weakens its social base and authority. Legislation against the mores is likely to be futile. 'We might as well plan to reorganise our globe by redistributing the elements within it' as try to reorganise society through law (1906: 95).

Sumner provides a sociological basis for common law assumptions about the deep social roots of law and the slow process of legal evolution. Common law thought does assume something like this slow emergence of law through a process of evolution of social norms. At the same time, Sumner offers a warning about modern forms of law. Legislation can and does diverge from the mores and to the extent that this occurs it threatens to become divorced from the sources of its authority and potentially ineffective. The legislator therefore needs to understand the nature of the complex social ties on which the cohesion of a society depends. More fundamentally, while 'for lawyers ... law is at the centre of things' (Bankowski and Mungham 1976: xii), in Sumner's massive picture of human history it is very clearly peripheral, a dependent variable, a sideshow in the main drama of social development. Its social significance is not a given but depends on social conditions which vary in different stages of social development in different societies and which law itself has little power to shape.

What Sumner does not offer, however, is an adequate account of how the folkways and mores of some groups or elements in a society may prevail over those of other groups, nor an account of the special role of law in maintaining social cohesion or social order. The attempt to found common law assumptions in sociological analysis leads to powerful assertions of law's lack of autonomy as a social institution. But it merely raises further questions about the nature of the forces that shape law.

Law and Culture

Savigny

In the context of Sumner's America, the kind of evolutionary theory that he provided reflected widespread conservative doubts about the emerging form of modern law. This law appeared as merely technical regulation taking little account—as the common law judges were supposed to have done—of community custom and sentiment. Sumner's theory takes its stand against the positivist lawyers and legislators emerging to supervise a planning or restructuring of social relations through law.

In other Western societies at other times the context in which defences of a pre-modern legal order were mounted was different, but these defences were no less significant in expressing perceived problems in law's relationship with social conditions. The late eighteenth and early nineteenth centuries saw the emergence of the first great European modern legal codes, most notably the French Civil Code of 1804. With them the modern idea of law as a comprehensive system of logically ordered and conceptually coherent doctrine, as opposed to a mere collection of customary rules or judicial precedent, became established in continental Europe. The German conservative statesman and jurist Friedrich Karl von Savigny was, in this context, one of the most eloquent defenders of the old legal world. To Savigny the proposed codification of German law at the beginning of the nineteenth century seemed disastrous primarily because it sought to fix in immutable principle legal ideas which, as an expression of culture, should be allowed to develop spontaneously. While Sumner emphasises the insensitivity and ineffectiveness of legal innovation through legislation if social roots of law are ignored, Savigny stresses the atrophying of natural processes of change in social rules when the state ignores those processes and seeks to fix legal doctrine in a comprehensive conceptual system. In a famous pamphlet of 1814, surely one of the most effective polemical tracts in the history of legal scholarship (it is reputed to have been highly influential in delaying the codification of German law for nearly a century (e.g. Patterson 1951)) Savigny set out the reasons for his opposition to codification and in doing so spelled out a theory of the social basis of law which was to have profound influence (Savigny 1831).

For Savigny law is an expression—one of the most important expressions together with language—of the 'spirit of a people' (*Volksgeist*). This deeply mystical idea at least involves the notion that law is much more than a collection of rules or judicial precedents. It reflects and expresses a whole cultural outlook. The spirit of a nation or people is the encapsulation of its whole history, the collective experience of the social group extending back through the ages of its existence. The law of such a people or nation written down at any given time is no more than a static representation of a process which is always continuing: the evolution of culture.[1] For Savigny, law is incomprehensible as a social

1 Taking culture in its widest anthropological sense as 'that complex whole which includes knowledge, belief, art, morals, law, custom, and any other capabilities and habits acquired by man as a member of society' (Tylor 1913 I: 1).

phenomenon except in the perspective of the history of the society in which it exists.

Legal development passes through the early stage of unwritten custom, followed by the writing down of customs as rules. The earliest known written codes of law, for example the Code of Hammurabi (Mesopotamia: *circa* eighteenth century BC), give all the appearances of more or less systematic collections of customary norms. Yet, as has often been remarked, with this writing down customary law lost its character as custom. It could be interpreted as rules. The reduction of law to written form reflected the rise of political authorities and the transformation of law from customary norms based on 'the relations of individuals arising out of chance circumstances' to 'an aspect of political power' (Lévy-Bruhl 1961: 53–7). In Savigny's analysis, from this stage of historical development law's sociological character seems to become ever more problematic. As society develops, the division of functions becomes more clearcut among its members and the development of classes and subgroups becomes more pronounced. Whereas in early society the *Volksgeist* is reasonably identifiable and capable of spontaneous expression through law, this becomes progressively less so for two reasons. First, divisions of function and class make it harder for the 'common consciousness' of the people to provide a sufficiently powerful impetus for the spontaneous creation of new law. Secondly, the forms of law themselves become more complex until they leave behind the common consciousness as far as the details and technicalities of the rules are concerned.

According to Savigny this situation gives rise to two major institutional developments: modern legislation and modern legal science. When spontaneous processes of law creation no longer operate effectively, legislative institutions are necessary. Legislation is important, first, to remove doubts and uncertainties in evolving law and, secondly, to enact settled customary law - but not in the manner of a code which denies the evolutionary nature of law by setting out fixed, final and comprehensive principles (Savigny 1831: 33, 152, 153; 1867: 31–6). Almost inevitably, however, legislative activities drift from their appropriate functions, like a ship dragging anchor. They become detached and remote. Somehow the legislator must be 'the true representative' of the *Volksgeist.* Yet, at the same time, as law drifts further away from its roots in community life and ceases to be a part of folk knowledge, its knowledge becomes the monopoly of a 'special order of persons skilled in law' whose job is to know and organise the rules of law. Law henceforth leads 'a twofold life' (Savigny 1831: 28; 1867: 36). In its broad outline it continues to live in the common consciousness of the people. In detail it becomes the sole preserve of lawyers (Savigny 1867: 36–40).

What clearer picture could be given of the dilemma of modern law as that dilemma has often been seen since Savigny's time: of law becoming more and more remote as it becomes an ever more sophisticated regulator of increasingly complex societies? Yet the notion of the 'spirit of the people' is impossible to analyse empirically—a purely mystical idea on which nationalist or racist sentiment can easily be hung—glossing over the political struggles involved in legal development with a simple conception of unified culture as a given and as a causal factor. Cultures 'are not unitary phenomena' (Tyler 1969: 4). 'Any large, complex society, with its multiplicity of social backgrounds and individual experiences, contains varying mores and attitudes within itself. On any given piece of legislation there will not just be supporters and enemies; rather there will be many points of view, ranging from unconditional support, through indifference, to unmitigated opposition' (Roche 1964: 353–4). And, as Savigny himself recognised, a culture is the product of complex social, political and economic processes. It is these which need to be understood if we are to make sense of their cultural expression.

Legal Ideas and 'Shared Understandings'

In discussing Savigny's ideas, however, the term culture has been used in its widest sense. More typically in modern sociological writing it refers to the complex of beliefs, attitudes, cognitive ideas, values and modes of reasoning and perception that are typical of a particular society or social group. In this sense culture constitutes shared understandings (Redfield 1941: ch 6), a common outlook reflected in numerous aspects of collective life. Taken in this way, an assertion of the relation between law and culture is more than opaque mysticism or vague truism. The American lawyer Lawrence Friedman has used the term legal culture to suggest the whole range of ideas which exists in particular societies—and varies from one society to another—about law and its place in the social order (e.g. Friedman 1985; 1990a). These ideas inform legal practices, citizens' attitudes to law and their willingness or unwillingness to litigate, and the relative significance of law in informing wider currents of thought and behaviour beyond the specific practices and forms of discourse associated with legal institutions. Variations in legal culture may thus explain much about differences in the ways in which seemingly similar legal provisions or institutions may function in different societies.

More fundamentally, it is extremely difficult to find any institutional or doctrinal element typically associated with modern Western law that appears to be *universal* in all cultures. The concept of 'reasonableness', on which Anglo-American law relies in interpreting behaviour and fixing responsibility, presupposes a complex range of cultural assumptions about reasonable modes of thought and action which may seem wholly unreasonable from another cultural standpoint (e.g. Seidman 1965). The fundamental modern Western concept of 'equality before the law' may appear incomprehensible in the context of a self-evidently 'natural' caste society (Cohn 1967: 155). Similarly such notions as 'negligence', 'defamation' as injury to reputation, and even 'crime' are alien to some societies (Abel 1981a: 54–5, 57, 65) as are the concepts of judge and court (Keedy 1951). All of this should warn against treating anything in legal language or institutions as self-justifying or natural. Everything about law's institutional and conceptual character needs to be understood in relation to the social conditions that have given rise to it. In this sense law is indeed an expression of culture.

Within Western societies important cultural differences can and do exist, with the result that attitudes to legal institutions and doctrine may vary considerably from one social group to another. In 1946 the United States Supreme Court found itself forced to rule on the legal status of polygamy as practised by American Mormons.[2] In effect the question of statutory interpretation for the court (whether an intention to marry polygamously constituted an 'immoral purpose') required a choice between the moralities of dominant and subordinate cultures, a choice made by the court in favour of the former. Culture conflict may thus highlight the value judgments and cognitive assumptions embedded in the law. Research has shown how important the culture of distinct ethnic groups within a society may be in determining their attitude to law and willingness to invoke it rather than to settle disputes by extra-legal means (Doo 1973). Research on the effects of 'transplantation' of laws from one society to another has suggested that the importation of foreign legal principles, even from societies of very different culture from the recipient society, may be successful as long as the laws concern instrumental matters (such as commercial practices) where there may be strong incentives to accept change. However, areas of social relations that reflect strong cultural values (such as family relations) are often shown by such research to be extremely resistant to the influence of imported legal principles reflecting different cultural assumptions (Lipstein 1959).

To this limited extent, then, Savigny was right. Law embodies important cultural assumptions and an important aspect of its influence in society depends on this. But the strength and significance of these assumptions varies from one area of law to another. What is involved is the question of law's relation to the way people think about the society in which they live, to the fundamental values they accept and to the way they interpret the data of experience presented in everyday life.

2 *Cleveland v United States* 329 US 14.

Yet these evolutionary theories of breathtaking range and generalisation provide only the vaguest hints of the complex nature of social change: in Savigny's case because social context is sketched only to give body to a polemic about law reform, in Sumner's because social change is seen as a natural process obeying the same fundamental principles in all ages and societies (though he distanced himself from the analogies with Darwinian theory popular in social science in his day (Hinkle 1980: ch 9)). Now, it is apparent that the variety of societies is such that evolutionary studies assuming broad uniform patterns of social development in all societies are at best simplistic (if suggestive), at worst grossly misleading. Nevertheless, a leading French writer on the sociology of law asserts that an evolutionary perspective constitutes at least the general climate in which sociological research on law proceeds because it affirms that law is always historically specific, never absolute in form or content, and always provisional and in the process of change (Carbonnier 1988: 10-1). And, in a quite different way, the concept of legal evolution has been invoked recently to refer to the emergence of general mechanisms that may regulate legal development or stabilise legal structures (Teubner 1988a).

Thus, Savigny remains interesting because he is acutely aware of law in transition. His writings look forwards and backwards. They suggest a future in which the divorce of rational modern law from the life of the society it purports to regulate may reach crisis point. At the same time they glorify the juristic skills of the past: not those of the modern legislator with technical and policy concerns but those of the distiller of abstract concepts from age-old doctrine—exemplar of a breed of German jurists to whom Savigny's work gave renewed inspiration during the nineteenth century but which passed into history with the turmoil of political conflict and social change reflected in twentieth-century legislation.

Ehrlich's Polemic Against Legal Positivism

By the last decades of the nineteenth century it was becoming apparent that the legal professions of Western societies would have to accommodate themselves to the fact that legislation was becoming the obviously dominant source of new law. The development of modern positivist legal theory originating in the writings of the English legal reformer Jeremy Bentham and his more professionally orthodox follower John Austin provided a set of concepts that were exactly what was required. They justified the intellectual autonomy of legal doctrine despite the fact that it could no longer be seen as rooted in the craft mysteries of common law but was increasingly handed to the lawyer ready-made as the enactments of an elected legislative body (Cotterrell 1989: ch 3).

In the Austinian theory of legal positivism laws are the commands of the sovereign—the supreme legal authority of an independent political society—typically expressed through legislation and supported by state sanctions. Judges are mouthpieces of the sovereign, their powers of law creation existing only by delegation from sovereign authority. Whatever the later refinements and developments of this normative legal theory, which do not concern us here, its general thrust is clear. All law derives directly or indirectly from the state, that is, from the supreme political authority of a politically organised society. It is recognisable as law through various formal tests which enable us to recognise that it 'really is' the sovereign's will (for example, the Act of Parliament is enacted by the proper procedure, the judge decides cases within the limits of the court's jurisdiction). Most importantly, it is recognisable as law because it is backed by the force of the state. Law itself provides for state sanctions—for example, fines, imprisonment, requirement to compensate the injured party through damages—to be imposed on offenders. Law so defined changed its content in a way that lawyers—except through influence on the legislature—could not directly control. Its form, however, could be specified by positivist legal theory and, because of this, legal doctrine could be seen as a systematic body of knowledge.

The price paid was a conception of the separateness of law from society very different from the view of law embedded in common law thinking and paralleled in Savigny's romanticism. While the common law approach necessarily located law in a web of cultural assumptions, legal positivism separated it as a distinct realm of knowledge and practice, 'purified'—to use the legal philosopher Hans Kelsen's terminology—of ethical, political, social scientific or historical considerations (Kelsen 1945).

As it became refined in Western legal thought and practice, legal positivism was challenged from inside and outside the legal profession. It was attacked for the narrowness of its view of law in the light of pressing moral and political issues, and also by conservative critics fearful of the accelerating pace of change in legal doctrine which a positivist attitude viewed with relative equanimity. The most important early sociological critique, however, came from Eugen Ehrlich, an eminent and prolific Austrian law professor. Ehrlich taught in a province of the Austro-Hungarian Empire which, after the First World War, became part of Romania. The central authority of the state in Vienna and Budapest must have seemed highly remote from the lives of the numerous diverse ethnic groups of the area in which he lived. Perhaps it was a consciousness of this which fuelled his belief that legal positivism's definitions of law made it impossible to understand law's reality as social regulation and included only those aspects of it that tended to have little relevance for the experience of most people.

The lawyer, Ehrlich writes, is concerned primarily with the legal resolution of disputes. Yet, over large areas of social life governed by law, disputes rarely occur and when they do they are often settled without recourse to institutionalised means of decision. The lawyer's typical concern is with the abnormalities of life, not the normalities. Furthermore, even in considering these abnormal cases lawyers are concerned not with the whole framework of regulation by which disputes are settled, but with a particular and limited kind of regulation, the rules that direct a judge or other official how to decide the case. Ehrlich calls these rules 'norms for decision' (*Entscheidungsnormen*). If we asked a traveller to describe the rules governing social life in a country he has visited, writes Ehrlich, he would tell us, for example, about marriage customs and the structure of family life and commercial practices, but he might have little to say about the rules by which law suits are decided. Lawyers tend to assume that the norms for decision legitimised by the state are rules of conduct as well but, in reality, they are rules that, it is thought by those who make and apply them, *should* govern conduct. Whether they do so is an empirical question to which the answer is often unknown. The rules actually followed in social life are the real 'living law' (*lebendes Recht*) which generally operates to prevent disputes and, when disputes arise, to settle them without recourse to the legal institutions of the state.

Thus Ehrlich makes the claim, which may be startling to the modern lawyer but is familiar to the sociologist, that law is far wider in scope than the norms created and applied by state institutions. Today the basis of this claim is the same as when Ehrlich wrote at the turn of the century. In contemporary Britain, for example, numerous institutions, organisations and social groups develop their own formal rules for self-regulation. This process is to a considerable extent incorporated in, and accepted by, the state's legal order, through a general supervisory jurisdiction of the courts and through enforcement of contracts within this legal order. Thus the state legal system oversees, for example, decisions of professional disciplinary bodies or the interpretation and application of rules governing trade unions. Commercial and industrial companies function on the basis of the rules contained in their articles of association which may be interpreted by the courts. Codes of practice in industrial and other spheres, collective agreements, constitutional conventions, rules of parliamentary procedure, codes governing or guiding the exercise of official discretion in various fields: all of these constitute regulatory systems of great importance. Although it may be necessary for the lawyer to try to distinguish these categories of rules and principles from law this is done for one reason alone: because it is necessary to take account of the rules that will be treated as binding on the court for which the lawyer is preparing a case or in which it is envisaged that a case may be brought. Rules governing jurisdiction and practice of courts determine what is law for lawyers. This is, however, quite arbitrary from the point of view of the effects of normative regulation. The 'formal' legal rules may be relatively insignificant.

Historically, the concept of law as a plurality of interlocking legal orders is essential to make sense of patterns of legal development. Not until relatively modern times in Western societies has a single dominating and comprehensive legal system, conterminous with the territorial reach of the state, come to appear typical. In earlier times systems of religious law applied by ecclesiastical courts, mercantile law of trading communities, and local or personal law of particular regions or categories of people could co-exist in a complex array of jurisdictions within particular territories. In many non-Western societies these features of law remain strongly present. In Western societies elements of them remain despite the typical centralisation of legal authority; and international and transnational legal obligations and institutions transcending state jurisdiction are of increasing importance. The relationship between law and state is clearly a complex one.

Is it not clear, however, that in contemporary Western societies state law dominates? Whatever doubts we may have about the comprehensiveness of positivist definitions of law, the law that they define is surely most important? For an answer we can return to Ehrlich's discussion. Undoubtedly, he writes, the modern state engages in very extensive legislative activity. Furthermore it controls the courts through which law is administered and the tribunals and agencies by means of which effect is given to its statutes. At a certain historically significant moment the state comes to monopolise the prosecution of offenders in criminal law. The force it possesses is widely believed to be capable of ordering society. Yet even in the law-making activities of the state vast areas of new law (for example, governing family and commercial relations) derive from the usages of social life and if we are to say state law 'dominates' what does this mean? For Ehrlich it dominates only in the consciousness of lawyers. The character of social life is such that state law is often an irrelevance in the real structure of social controls upon which order and harmony depend. It is this structure which needs to be examined.

Law as the Framework of Social Life

Modern forms of positivist legal theory have reacted against earlier varieties which stressed that provision of state sanctions—formally enforceable penalties such as fines, imprisonment or damages—in case of non-compliance is a vital mark of law distinguishing it from other social rules (see e.g. Cotterrell 1989: ch 3). Nevertheless, legal positivism assumes a close and vital connection between law and state sanctions. So much so that when lawyers talk about the sanctions of law they almost invariably mean those provided by the state.

It must be emphasised that to include, as Austin did, the threat or availability of such sanctions among the distinguishing marks of law does not entail a belief that people actually obey law because of these elements of force built into it. Few modern positivist legal theorists would make any sweeping claims about the role of state sanctions in securing the effectiveness of law in regulating behaviour. Yet, as Ehrlich understood the matter, state sanctions were virtually irrelevant in social life. It is obvious, he writes, that in the mass of legal relations and social associations in which people live, with few exceptions they quite voluntarily perform the duties that those relations and associations entail. 'As a rule, the thought of compulsion by the courts does not even enter the minds of men' (Ehrlich 1936: 21). They usually act out of habit, he notes, or else to avoid the social consequences of deviance. They seek to avoid quarrels, loss of status or loss of custom and goodwill in business dealings, or bad reputation—for example, for quarrelsomeness, dishonesty, unreliability or irresponsibility. Indeed the actual rules of conduct (for example, in codes of professional ethics or mercantile custom) may be different from or more stringent than rules enforced by the state. Ehrlich uses the example of duelling to show that pressures of social sanctions (loss of honour) may work in opposite directions to those of state sanctions (criminal punishment) and even prove stronger (cf. Kiernan 1990; Timasheff 1939: 160–5). He concludes that one 'might reasonably maintain that society would not go to pieces even if the state should exert no coercion whatever' (Ehrlich 1936: 71).

More recent writers have doubted that living law can prevail in a direct challenge to state law. Lévy-Bruhl claims that customary rules in modern societies governed by the law of powerful states are relatively fragile, lacking the strength and firmness (*solidité*) of 'official' law (Lévy-Bruhl 1961: 50). A British writer on the history of commercial adjudication argues that the evidence suggests that 'few systems for the adjudication of commercial disputes could be viable without the ultimate sanction of legal enforcement. Nevertheless legal enforceability is dispensable, albeit only in exceptional circumstances' (Ferguson 1980: 155: cf. Goode 1982: 973–5). Thus through a combination of circumstances in England in the nineteenth century, in effect 'the Stock Exchange had its own legal system with its own legal sanctions, every bit as coercive as the sanctions of ... [state] law' through the power to suspend or expel members (Ferguson 1980: 155). Equally, the power of professional norms in conflict with state legal norms is illustrated by the acute tensions which arise when a court seeks to force journalists to reveal the sources of their information.[3] The powerful rules of proper practice which appear essential to the occupational environment directly oppose the law's demands.

These varying examples should warn against wide generalisation, yet much evidence shows that extremely powerful systems of normative regulation distinct from the 'official' or lawyers' law govern important areas of social life with little or no reference to state norms for decision. For Ehrlich the key to understanding this is to recognise that all human life is lived in 'associations' (*gesellschaftlichen Verbände*), that is, formal or informal groupings of numerous kinds. Some associations, for example trade unions, business corporations and partnerships, are formally defined or regulated by state law. Some have legal personality, that is, they are recognised by law as distinct entities with rights and duties. The associations of social life also, however, include voluntary societies (for example, clubs), occupational groups, contractual bonds, social classes, political parties, ethnic groups, religious affiliations, the family, and the nation or state. Law is the inner ordering of these associations. It consists of the rules that assign to every member of the association his or her position within it and the rights and duties attaching to that position. Law is thus not something imposed externally but arises from the modes of thought that underlie the associations. So the *real* sanctions of law arise from the fact that in general no one wants to be excluded from the associations of life—from the ties of citizenship, family, friends, profession, church, business community, and so on. Refusal to conform to the norms leads to a weakening of the bonds that tie the individual to the social association.

State law—lawyers' law or the law applied in state courts by state officials—is the law of one association, the state, within this complex social whole. Yet, as the law of what Ehrlich sees for practical purposes as the widest association, it appears to have a special role. Two forms of law affect the social associations. As well as their 'internal' law fixing relations of members within them, they are protected from external attack by forms of state law, for example, providing for punishment of certain offences as crimes and defining the jurisdiction and procedures of state-controlled agencies such as courts. Laws that concern the state's existence (for example, relating to taxation and the military system) naturally depend upon state sanctions—the sanctions arising within the state as an association (cf. Klepper and Nagin 1989). More generally, Ehrlich recognises that state coercion is necessary against those whose social deviance is particularly serious. These, however, are a minority

3 *British Steel Corporation v Granada Television* [1980] 3 WLR 774. Contempt of Court Act 1981, s.10. Cf. Denning 1982: 246–52.

insignificant in comparison with the law-abiding majority. Typically they are individuals who have been excluded from the social associations through psychological, economic or other circumstances. It is only 'in the case of these outcasts that the widest association which includes even them i.e. the state, steps in with its power to punish' (Ehrlich 1936: 68). It would seem to follow from this that rehabilitation, whatever its difficulties and limitations, is the appropriate aim of penal policy.

It is apparent that Ehrlich's conceptions are characterised not only by important omissions—the concept of the state as an association, for example, glosses over a host of questions—but by serious confusions. No coherent theory of the relationship between living law and state law emerges from his discussion. On the one hand, society 'would not go to pieces' without the state: on the other hand, state law provides the external protection of systems of living law. The concept of social association is so broad and vague as to make it difficult to begin to grasp the variety of forms of social relationship and the structures of domination and co-operation within them. The great German jurist Otto von Gierke, the foremost historian of the relationships between law and forms of collective organisation, saw law in politically organised society as a continuous struggle between two categories of association, those based on domination (*Herrschaft*) and those based on co-operation (*Genossenschaft*) (cf. Gurvitch 1947: 72–4). Ehrlich also recognises that patterns of domination exist in the associations yet he tends to underemphasise this aspect of them (cf. Ehrlich 1936: 87ff). Consequently the concept of power and the relationship between law and power are not explored. The dominant image of the basis of social order which Ehrlich conveys is that of co-operation based on reciprocal obligation, a familiar image in social theory.

Within their limitations, however, Ehrlich's ideas offer a powerful challenge to lawyers' typical assumptions about the nature and scope of law and of its importance. To designate as 'law' in modern Western societies normative systems other than those of state law is to raise the hypothesis that the problems with which lawyers concern themselves—about the justifications of legal decision-making, the interpretation, development, generalisation and systematisation of rules, the relationship between rule and discretion and between justice and certainty in law—may be problems that arise in some form in many normative systems, not only in lawyers' law. In this sense 'legal' problems appear as central problems of social organisation and legal thought is not merely lawyers' thought but, in some sense, a part of the everyday means of solving problems in innumerable organisations, institutions and relationships within a society (Cotterrell 1983a).

Empirical Studies of the 'Living Law'

In practical terms, the function of the sociology of law as Ehrlich conceives it is to discover and analyse systematically the living law operative in different areas of social life, to develop criteria for measuring the extent of divergence between the norms of living law and the corresponding lawyers' law, and to use that measure to assess the effectiveness of lawyers' law. Later researchers worked out elaborate procedures for measuring and assessing the discrepancies between norms for decision and living law (Moore and Sussman 1931: cf. Northrop 1950). The fact of the matter, however, is that Ehrlich's concepts cannot provide a means of determining the appropriateness or otherwise of state law in any particular area. Whether state law or living law *should* ultimately prevail when the two conflict, or whether divergence is itself beneficial in certain respects, are matters of political evaluation.

Published studies showing the relationship between lawyers' law and the norms actually regulating particular areas of social life are now very numerous. Perhaps the most important of these, which fully bear out Ehrlich's assumption of the likelihood of wide divergence between norms for decision and living law, are studies of the use of contract and commercial law. In a classic study of business practices in Wisconsin, Stewart Macaulay, an American lawyer, discovered that business agreements were frequently made without knowledge of the relevant rules of contract law and that, in many cases, they would be invalid according to those rules if challenged in the courts. He also found that businessmen actively sought to avoid the use of law and lawyers in their affairs. 'If something comes up,' one businessman explained, 'you get the other man on the telephone and deal with the problem. You don't read legalistic contract clauses at each other if you ever want to do business again. One doesn't run to lawyers if he wants to stay in business because one must behave decently' (Macaulay 1963: 61). Perhaps the key words are 'if you ever want to do business again'. Macaulay found that business firms were much more willing to invoke the law against other firms regarded as newcomers to the business community and not fully accepted within it. Furthermore, where relations completely break down and there is nothing more to lose by invoking the law it can be a way of spreading losses, gaining compensation or keeping opposing interests in check. Later research broadly confirms Macaulay's findings but tends to emphasise specific uses of lawyers' law (e. g. Blegvad 1990). Thus, one British study found that, in the businesses examined, legal planning was used on particular matters: 'the contractual device can be made to lessen a particular risk or avoid it altogether, as when a seller insists on cash with order' (Beale and Dugdale 1975: 60; and see Vincent-Jones 1989: 173).

Thus, lawyers' law can be used as a lever in negotiation, a spur to the making of agreements designed to avoid all recourse to it (cf. Mnookin and Kornhauser 1979), or as a means of controlling risk. Invoking law is a particular strategy which may be appropriate under certain conditions, but these conditions probably vary greatly from one kind of business relationship or transaction to another. For large organisations the scale of business operations may be such that the cost of expert legal planning and protection, particularly in a climate of extensive state regulation of business, seems obviously justifiable given the risk of disruption which could ensue from legal difficulties (cf. Galanter 1983). Many modern empirical studies, however, carried out in a variety of jurisdictions, have confirmed that invocation of or reliance upon formal law is an unusual and exotic circumstance in many business situations. Whatever the complexities of assessing the relationship between business practices and lawyers' law we can say with some certainty that contract law operates in practice in a manner very different from that typically assumed in the law books.

In other fields of legal regulation similar evidence of wide divergence between the content of 'official' or state legal norms and the actual rules governing social behaviour has been discovered. A body of literature has been concerned with the 'private legal systems' (Evan 1990: ch 8) of various groups and of institutions such as schools or factories. The relationship between state legal norms and other social norms and patterns of behaviour has been explored in such fields as family law, industrial law and consumer law. Even lawyers' legal practice can be thought of as having its own living law. Certain areas of legislation and case law tend to be much better known by lawyers than other areas, more frequently brought to clients' attention, and more likely to be the focus of practitioners' specialisms. In a study of lawyers' practices with regard to consumer laws, Macaulay concluded that lawyers' interests and values affect the way they represent clients and that reforming laws, such as new laws favouring consumer interests, need to have incentives built into them to encourage lawyers to use them and advise their clients of them (Macaulay 1979).

As regards criminal law, the long-established field of criminology has provided a continuing social scientific commentary unparalleled for other areas of state law. The modern sociology of deviance, which developed out of earlier criminological research but has also drawn upon much wider currents of sociological thought, has placed much stress on understanding the rules that grow up within and govern 'deviant subcultures' - the ways of life and outlook of particular types of individuals, groups or communities sharing similar conditions and experience and judged as deviant according to the prevailing norms of the dominant culture. Hustlers, hobos, drug users, street gangs and dance band musicians are just a few of the numerous categories of people whose ways of life, upon which norms of lawyers' law may have little bearing, have been studied. These studies do not usually employ Ehrlich's concepts and derive from different theoretical sources, yet the style and objective of many of them are directly comparable with those of his sociology of law. The aim is often to promote an understanding of the rules of 'deviant' life on the part of those who follow the rules of 'straight' life. The studies often polemically assert the rationality of other ways of life just as Ehrlich's aim is to assert the continuing validity of other, non-state, forms of law. 'Interactionist' approaches in the sociology of deviance stress, in a manner reminiscent of Ehrlich's thesis, the formation of social rules in the process of interaction between individuals or groups, rather than through imposition from external sources (see Chapter 5). Further, the idea that 'deviant' is merely a label attached to some people's conduct by others who find it reprehensible or merely strange points to the relativity of normative systems: a relativity that might be considered the *leitmotiv* of Ehrlich's view of law.

Mere Polemic?

How useful is the concept of 'living law' itself as a guide for research? It seems to invite inquiries of seemingly boundless scope. In fact it becomes useful only if thought of as the *alter ego* of lawyers' law; the 'real-life' parallel to the rules written in the law books (cf. Gurvitch 1947: 121). It follows that living law—if it is not to be equated with the whole range of studies in descriptive sociology—can be studied only in relation to the categories established in lawyers' law. It is a concept devised solely for polemical purposes, by a lawyer concerned to organise the data of social life in a way that would directly challenge lawyers' conceptions and categories. Paradoxically, to achieve this the data had to be organised in terms of those conceptions and categories.

This view of society through a legal prism is hardly unique to Ehrlich. It applies to the sociologically oriented writings of many other scholars. To transcend it, it is necessary to look for sociological explanations of the development and consequences of the norms for decision and of the institutions by which they are created, interpreted and enforced. A particular modern manifestation of the tendency to see social life in legal categories is found in many examples of what have come to be called 'legal impact studies' (e.g. Lempert 1966). Their object is to assess the effects of particular legislation or judicial decisions on behaviour or attitudes. Since they appear to offer the prospect of amassing data of obvious legislative policy relevance they have sometimes been generously funded and have been quite prolifically produced. Thus, for example, the effect on behaviour of particular road traffic laws has been an important focus for research (e.g. Ross 1984; Hayden 1989).

Social data, in these kinds of studies, tend to be organised primarily in terms of practical concerns focused on the implementation of specific laws at a particular time and place. Insofar as particular statutes or judicial decisions rather than sociological variables relating to law or legal institutions provide the focus, the studies are often hard to relate in theoretical terms to each other and to other literature on law in society, although their potential as short-term policy guides is not to be denied. One critic has written: 'If impact analysis is to be useful, it should be a tool for a richer understanding of how legal rules fit into the social and political system. Documenting the proposition that law has an impact, without linking the findings to behavioural patterns and institutional change, is a dead end' (Rabin 1979: 991). Impact studies provide important evidence of the effects (or lack of effects) of laws. But their findings usually need to be put in a much wider context if they are to contribute to general sociological understanding of law.

There is another possible danger in formulating concepts to confront directly lawyers' assumptions about law. The reaction against lawyers' views of law may go so far that it blindly disregards much that is valuable in those views. Lawyers naturally think of law in terms of doctrine. An obvious reaction is to consider living law (and perhaps all law) solely as observable behaviour (cf. Black 1976; 1989), the reasons for such behaviour being less significant than the fact that it may diverge from that envisaged in the norms for decision applied by state courts. Ehrlich himself sometimes seems to imply such a view when he writes of the observations of a traveller in a foreign country of marriage customs and of the way contracts are made as suggesting the essence of living law. Indeed, Gurvitch criticises Ehrlich's 'excessive positivism' (a critic of legal positivism may nevertheless espouse sociological positivism) and his indifference to the 'spiritual elements' of social life and law (Gurvitch 1947: 122). But, although this kind of rejection of consideration of legal values and of the integrity of legal thought is typical of some sociological analyses and has been especially apparent in some behavioural studies of judges carried out by political scientists (see Chapter 7), there are many elements in Ehrlich's writings that suggest, as indicated earlier, an important part of his polemic as being to affirm the rationality of normative systems other than those of lawyers' law.

Thus the idea that the living law provides its own system of sanctions makes no sense except in terms of the subjective meaning which the living law has for members of the social associations regulated by it. The clearest illustrations of this are in the fields of industrial relations and commercial arbitration. A long tradition of thought in several Western countries, reflected in government policy in Britain and elsewhere for nearly three-quarters of a century until the early 1960s, assumed that the role of state law in regulating industrial relations should be kept to a minimum (e.g. Hasselbalch, Neal and Victorin 1982). This was explicable in terms of the complexity of rules and practices based on negotiated understandings between employees and management which structure this field, a *laissez-faire* climate in the formative era of modern industrial regulation, management and trade union perceptions of the nature of industrial relations and the balance of industrial power, and the assumed consistent bias of the courts against the interests of labour. Whether this assumption of bias is well grounded or not is irrelevant in this context (cf. Clark and Wedderburn 1983: 166–73). Effective social rules can presumably be built only on the basis of shared understandings or reasonably negotiated compromises, not on the basis of patent mistrust of the rulemaker (cf. Barker 1990: 175–8).

On the other hand, since industrial relations constitute a field of often bitter struggle between opposed interests, state law provides both a minimum framework of order and a weapon in this struggle (cf. Stone 1981). Just as contract law does not shape the reality of contractual relations but contributes elements that may be taken into account by negotiating parties in working out commercial agreements, so industrial law may perform a similar function with regard to industrial collective bargaining. This field, however, also provides a good illustration of the limits of autonomy of social associations. Industrial relations appear too central as determinants of other aspects of social and particularly economic life to be left subject to their own internal regulation. In most Western countries, including Britain over the past two decades, state law has been increasingly used to influence their character (Simitis 1987).

Commercial arbitration provides a different but related illustration of the significance of living law for those subject to it. Historically, in England, business interests sought to avoid using the ordinary courts for adjudication of commercial disputes because of the capriciousness of jury trial and the expense of using the judicial process (Ferguson 1980). Even more important, however, in modern times, has been the need for a system by which commercial disputes could be solved by expert arbitrators possessing detailed knowledge of the norms of commercial practice in the particular area of dispute. Hence the growth of an extensive system of commercial arbitration. By the beginning of the 1980s London arbitration bodies were handling about 10,000 disputes a year, the London Maritime Arbitrators' Association's members were dealing with about 4,000 arbitrations a year and 70–80 per cent of the world's maritime arbitrations, involving shipbroking and chartering disputes, were being held in London.[4]

4 See the sources cited in Ferguson 1980: 145–6.

The way the 'official' legal system has responded to these developments is interesting. In England, the Commercial Court adopted simplified procedures and uses judges with commercial experience, yet only about 100 cases a year are heard and disposed of by the court.[5] Judges were empowered under the Administration of Justice Act 1970 to accept appointment as arbitrators, the assumption being that their judicial expertise would be welcome if available in the more private and informal environment of an arbitration. The scheme has not proved popular within the commercial community and has been little used. Indeed, the state legal system has gradually adjusted to its substantial irrelevance in this field and 'atoned for this failure by making formal provision for its own circumvention' (Ferguson 1980: 147; cf. Blegvad 1990: 408–9). Thus since the 1850s the courts have enforced compulsory arbitration clauses in contracts preventing judicial proceedings being brought until the processes of arbitration are complete (Ferguson 1980: 147) and thanks to the severe curtailment of rights of appeal to the courts from arbitrators' decisions 'the arbitral award now has a greater degree of finality than a judgment' (Goode 1982: 972). It would be hard to find clearer indications of the strength of a system of normative regulation intended to operate with a substantial degree of independence from state law.

In one sense, however, Gurvitch's criticism of Ehrlich is apt. The concept of living law is used indiscriminately to refer to a vast array of normative systems. Yet the motivations that guarantee the integrity of informal business norms may be wholly different from those that maintain the cohesion of, for example, religious orders or the norms of family life. It may be impossible to explain the contrasting experiences of 'transplantation' of commercial and family law, the different outcomes of confrontation between lawyers' law and living law in these fields, as well as many other aspects of the relationships between normative systems, without recognising and explaining these kinds of differences in what Gurvitch calls the 'forms of sociality'. In this sense it is true that Ehrlich pays insufficient attention to the 'spiritual elements' in life and treats living law systems uniformly and positivistically merely as rule systems.

5 In 1991, 364 cases were set down for trial, of which 95 were heard and disposed of. However, proceedings in 2,034 cases were started. Official reports of the court's work imply that proceedings are often used as a way of judging the strength of opposing parties or gaining preliminary information prior to a negotiated settlement. Commercial Court Statistics November 1991 (mimeo) and e.g. 'The Commercial Court 1989-90' (statement on the work of the court by Hobhouse J., December 21st 1990, mimeo) para 7. I am grateful to David Bird, Clerk to the Commercial Court, for relevant information.

The Problem of the Concept of Law

Underlying all that has been discussed above is the fundamental problem that Ehrlich's approach to legal analysis poses. How is the object of inquiry—'law'—to be conceptualised? As has already been indicated, it is essential from a professional point of view for the lawyer to be able clearly to distinguish law from non-law. Ehrlich's approach deliberately denies this objective. Law is seen as an aspect of social life, not a separate compartment of it. Savigny's analyses proceed on a similar assumption. So do numerous modern sociological studies of law. The lawyer needs a test to specify what materials can be relied upon in legal argument before a court or in devising legal strategies which may one day be tested in litigation. A social science of law, however, while taking full account of these lawyers' tests of 'the legal' must seek not to close off inquiry, before it begins, by conclusively specifying the nature of the object of study in a definition. Sociology of law relies on 'working models' or open conceptions of law which are adequate to guide inquiry and are constructed solely for that purpose. They make it possible to formulate hypotheses about the character and functions of law but they may be modified substantially as inquiries are pushed further and the researcher's perceptions of law alter with new knowledge. There is, therefore, a fundamental difference between a *definition* of law, which legislates the way we are to think of it and, in effect, terminates inquiry, and a *model* of law, which is no more than a starting point for study, a peg on which to hang ideas, data and hypotheses. Open-minded inquiry requires merely provisional concepts. 'Who likes may snip verbal definitions in his old age, when his world has gone crackly and dry' (Bentley 1908: 199).

This does not, however, solve the problem of specifying an adequate working concept of law which makes it possible to think of law independently of other forms of social control, or, at least, as in some respects distinctive. For Ehrlich, law could be distinguished from other social norms only in vague terms. Law governs matters that 'at least in the opinion of the group in which it has its origin' are 'of great importance, of basic significance', and legal norms in contrast to other social norms can be stated in relatively clear and definite terms (Ehrlich 1936: 167–8). From such a viewpoint law is part of a continuum of social norms, and not a clearly distinct category.

In the literature of the sociology of law three broad approaches to conceptualisation of law can be recognised. The closest to the contemporary lawyer's typical concept is that associated with much Marxist writing which takes the view that law must be understood in terms of state power. Law is thus the regulation established, interpreted and applied by state institutions, but the extended definition of the state in some contributions to this literature (e.g. Althusser 1971; Cain 1983b) highlights the point that the concept of law as state regulation remains an open one until the extent of 'the state' as a concept is theoretically established. Nevertheless, in general, such an approach merely takes what the lawyer thinks of as law as its focus. A second approach recognises, like Ehrlich, the 'hypothesis of juridical pluralism' (Carbonnier 1988: 16ff) as appropriate not only to earlier or non-Western societies but also to contemporary Western industrialised societies. A third approach, intermediate between a thoroughgoing legal pluralism and a relatively simple working concept of law as state law, treats law as characterised by special institutional arrangements (for enactment or interpretation of social rules or development of legal doctrine, for adjudication or processing of disputes, or for systematic enforcement of social order) which are particularly but not necessarily exclusively associated with state activities.

Legal Pluralism

Of the approaches which do not merely accept the lawyers' law or state law concept, that of legal pluralism is typified by Georges Gurvitch's conception of 'layers of law' (Gurvitch 1947). Law, for Gurvitch, is the expression of order or harmony of different forms of 'sociality' or collective life. Accordingly its character varies greatly depending on the nature of the different forms of sociality it represents and the different kinds of societies or social groups it regulates. Law can be organised or unorganised, fixed in advance, created *ad hoc*, or purely intuitive. It may be—but is not necessarily—accompanied by provisions for external restraint (sanctions) (Gurvitch 1947: 44ff, 174–5). For the pioneer legal sociologist Leon Petrazycki (Petrazycki 1955), law is a psychic phenomenon consisting of associated feelings of right and duty ('attributive-imperative experiences'). It is categorised in four ways. It may be positive (based on established practice or definite formal provisions) or intuitive (not so based). It may be official (recognised by courts or other state institutions) or unofficial (not so recognised). N.S. Timasheff distinguishes 'state law' and 'social law' but considers that the former determines the limits of validity of the latter (Timasheff 1939: 302). However, all forms of law 'express one basic social phenomenon, that of the co-ordination of human behaviour by authoritative patterns' (Timasheff 1939: 3,1). The renowned American legal scholar Karl Llewellyn refuses to define law in his writings, claiming that 'legal' functions have to be fulfilled in regulating any stable social group of whatever size from a family to a nation (e.g. Llewellyn 1940). For Karl Renner, an important early contributor to sociological analysis of law, the conventions of industrial relations and the practices existing in economic enterprises are just as much law as the manorial law of feudalism (Renner 1949: 114–5).

These orientations are widespread in the literature. Sometimes, as in Ehrlich's case, a vagueness in the concept of law seems deliberately to have been introduced with polemical intent, to challenge lawyers' assumptions directly. In such cases the enterprise easily invites the criticism levelled at Ehrlich that this is 'megalomaniac jurisprudence' seeking to encompass everything with little discrimination (Allen 1964: 32; cf. Carbonnier 1988: 22–3). In the most sophisticated legal pluralist sociological writings such as Gurvitch's, however, elaborate legal typologies are often constructed and new insights into varieties of regulation can be obtained in a way that would not be possible with a narrower focus (cf. McDonald 1979: 50).

Law as Coercive Order

Many writers, however, have considered that law can be distinguished from other types of social control primarily in terms of the sanctions it uses. Thus for Max Weber, 'an order will be called *law* if it is externally guaranteed by the probability that coercion (physical or psychological) to bring about conformity or avenge violation, will be applied by a *staff* of people holding themselves specially ready for that purpose' (Weber 1954: 5; Weber 1978: 317). Although this concept of law emphasises special enforcement processes it still carefully avoids equating law with state law (1954: 17; 1978: 314ff). Some anthropologists, recognising the difficulty of distinguishing 'the legal' in stateless societies, have similarly located the distinguishing mark of law in its sanctions. Thus, for E.A. Hoebel, 'a social norm is legal if its neglect or infraction is regularly met, in threat or in fact, by the application of physical force by an individual or group possessing the socially recognised privilege of so acting' (Hoebel 1954: 28).

Conceptions of law such as these are plainly not co-extensive with the modern lawyer's typical positivist view of law. Their form, however, is such that, in societies in which a centralised state has developed to concentrate political authority in a single source and to monopolise the regularised use of force, law will tend to appear co-extensive with state enforced norms. What is lost in flexibility and in the possibility of a radical critique of the lawyer's concept of law is perhaps compensated for by a starting point for sociological analysis that realistically recognises that in modern Western societies many of the most important questions about law are questions about a highly professionalised set of practices, and about an aspect of the activities of the state. The danger of such an approach is that law tends to be seen *only* in these terms, that its social bases so clearly stressed in the approaches of the legal pluralists tend to be obscured, and that a sociological concept of law may be subordinated to and constricted by definitions created by lawyers and others for professional purposes different from those that guide social scientific analysis of law.

Dispute Processing

At least two other approaches are possible which give a certain realistic primacy to state law in considering law in contemporary industrialised Western societies but also preserve some of the breadth of the hypothesis of juridical pluralism. An influential modern focus of study, particularly in American literature, has been on dispute resolution or processing. In contemporary law the resolving of disputes is assumed to be a major function of courts, and the dispute processing focus reflects the court-centred approach to law typical of Anglo-American common law thinking. It also, however, reflects the influence of anthropological studies and a desire to find a focus of study which would facilitate comparisons over a wide range of societies with extremely varied systems of political, economic and social organisation (e.g. Abel 1973). In contemporary Western societies the most authoritative dispute processing system is assumed to be that of the state controlled courts. Yet the field of study is sufficiently wide to embrace other means, actual or potential, of resolving 'trouble cases' in these societies besides litigation, and also to include analyses of means of settling or containing disputes in societies or situations where anything resembling a modern law court is hard to find. If there is a fundamental criticism to be made of the dispute processing focus it is probably that it diverts attention from many equally or more important institutions, processes, conditions or consequences associated with contemporary Western state law. Law can be considered much more than the processing of disputes and the disputing focus cannot in itself provide an assessment of how central or peripheral dispute processing may be as an aspect of contemporary Western law.[6]

Law as Doctrine

The second of these alternative approaches focuses on the concept of 'legality' and takes the existence of rules as a central element of a working concept of law. The concept of rule implies the limitation of arbitrariness and a degree of normative control of official discretion. In some sociological approaches legality has been explicitly accepted as a *value* forming part of the essence of law (e.g. Selznick 1969; Skolnick 1975), the exclusion of arbitrariness through known rules being an

6 See further ch 7.

imperative of government through law. Thus the sociology of law, in this perspective, itself tends to adopt a moral stance since it takes the specific value of legality to be central to its concerns.

It is not necessary, however, to adopt a commitment to particular legal values in order to treat rules as central to a working concept of law. In its most open form this approach merely implies that law can be interpreted, learned and applied as a body of doctrine. Law thus consists primarily of social rules importing or implying certain cognitive and evaluative principles and concepts. As long as law is distinguished from social rules in general—for example, by specifying that legal rules depend upon the existence of definite institutions or procedures employed specially for their creation, interpretation or enforcement (but not necessarily for all three functions)—this is a useful concept of law in many respects. Since the notion of a rule is not as clear as legal positivism often assumes it to be, and doctrine can consist of many kinds of regulation, the problem of the nature of official discretion is not defined out of existence by a concept of law as doctrine. From the standpoint of the sociology of law the factors that determine how rules are interpreted in particular contexts are at least as significant as the content of the rules themselves.

Further, this view of 'the legal' does not too rigidly associate law with particular kinds of socio-economic order since social rules (although not necessarily the minimal institutional framework for creation, interpretation or enforcement which would allow us to recognise them as legal) are an ubiquitous feature of all societies and of all stable social groups. Neither does such an approach confine law to state law. Again, to see law, first and foremost, as doctrine makes it possible to explore ideological aspects of law directly. At the same time, in a sociological view, legal doctrine is not seen as existing for itself in a self-contained world of ideas. It is constructed in social action: in disputes; in political conflict; in the interaction between and organisation of courts, lawyers and law enforcement agencies; in business practice; and through the actions (or inaction) of citizens in invoking law in aid of their interests. In a sociological view legal doctrine has meaning and significance only in relation to the social conditions in which it is developed, interpreted and applied.

There is, of course, no single concept of law that will serve for all analytical purposes. However a book on the sociology of law must take a particular concept of law as its preferred organising focus. In this book a concept of law as institutionalised doctrine, as outlined above, is taken as the basis for discussion. Nevertheless, in considering in the following chapters major fields of contemporary theory and empirical research in the sociology of law it will be necessary to bear in mind, first, that a variety of concepts of law is adopted in the literature and, secondly, that even if a doctrinal focus is adopted this in no way removes the problem of explaining the nature of legal doctrine from a sociological perspective. Indeed much of the discussion in the remaining chapters of this book will be concerned, in one way or another, with this problem.

The approach adopted here allows us to recognise that state law must, for most practical purposes, be taken as the primary focus of analysis of law in contemporary Western societies. In these societies state law constitutes that category of social rules for which the processes and institutions of creation, interpretation and enforcement are most visible, formal and elaborate. In this sense state law is most obviously 'the law'. In the following chapters, therefore, the word 'law' will generally be used to refer to the social rules and related doctrine created, adopted, interpreted and enforced by state agencies as a framework of general regulation within a politically organised society.

A working concept of law is, however, only a point of departure and none of the possible directions of inquiry that sociological writings on law indicate can be ignored. It is not insignificant that the three possible analytical foci—rules/doctrine, dispute processing and sanctions—discussed above broadly parallel the three institutional clusters—professionalism (lawyers), adjudication (courts) and enforcement (police)—typically associated with contemporary Western law (and discussed in turn in Chapters 6 to 8). Whatever the range of sociological study, its concepts and concerns are shaped by present experience and by the questions that seem relevant to the researcher in the light of that experience. Most of these questions in the sociology of law reflect experience of the particular kind of state law that in contemporary Western societies has apparent autonomy as an independent legal system. In the next chapter it will be necessary to consider some of the ways in which the idea of this autonomy—so antipathetic to the conception of law in society expressed in the theories of Sumner, Savigny and Ehrlich—is asserted in the deliberate use of law to foster social change. In subsequent chapters we shall need to consider the reasons for the apparent autonomy of Western law as a social phenomenon and the major consequences that follow from it.

2 Law as an Instrument of Social Change

During the twentieth century, legislative policies in Western societies have become much more ambitious than early writers such as Savigny, Sumner or Ehrlich could have imagined. Each of them in different ways clearly saw the potential, and some of the problems, of legislation as a modern source of law. Nevertheless, they could hardly have known that in the mid and late twentieth century attempts would be made to use the law of the state to restructure, plan or encourage economic enterprise on a massive scale, to promote peaceful revolution in social relations (for example, through anti-discrimination law) and to shape attitudes and beliefs in a manner far more ambitious than could have been attempted in early periods of social development.

The modern idea of law as an instrument of wide-scale social and economic planning could hardly have been seriously entertained when the state was less powerful, had less technological facilities available to it for surveillance and control, and was less able to rely on vast networks of communication controlled by mass media.

The question of the relation of law to social change is clearly a central issue in the theory already considered, but in contemporary Western societies (and in many other present day societies) this question has acquired a new form. The theory discussed in the previous chapter stresses the roots of law in everyday experience of social life. Yet this way of thinking about law conflicts with 'common sense' views of law in contemporary Western societies. Law has now come to be recognised as an agency of power; an instrument of government. Insofar as government is centralised in the state, law appears exclusively as the law of the state.[1] In the lawyer's view and in the wider public view it has come to be seen as separate from the society it regulates. It has become possible to talk about law *acting upon* society, rather than law as an aspect of society. Thus law has come to be seen as an independent agency of social control and social direction. It appears autonomous within society. A modern legal system is understood as a distinct set of mechanisms of

1 With the growth of transnational government (as, for example, in the European Community), this includes what has been termed the 'international state' (e. g. Cain 1983d), superimposed over the nation state.

government employing rationally developed doctrine created, interpreted and applied by specialised state agencies.

Modern Law and Modern State

Consequently, the question of the relationship of law and social change has tended to become one of how far law can independently influence social change. Whether law can reshape the mores of society becomes an issue because the connection between modern law and whatever mores may exist in the society it seeks to regulate is far from clear or simple. Western law has become primarily legislation created by governing elites or professional specialists. Even where, as is typically the case with Western law, it is created by democratically elected assemblies, the legislation is often not the result of any specific popular mandate. Much of this legislation is not understood even in outline by most members of society. Many people are unaware even of the existence of much of it.[2]

The problem that has, therefore, been posed in much modern writing on law and social change, in the light of twentieth-century experience of Western law, is whether and in what way law has become (or can be) somehow freed from its social and cultural roots to the extent that it can be deliberately used as an instrument to change patterns of social life. Whether it should be so used is a policy issue for legislators and others to decide in the light of what can be established about law's capabilities and limitations. The whole climate of thought in which Savigny and Sumner wrote made their answers to this question almost a foregone conclusion. As long as law is seen as an aspect of society—a certain side of social life as a whole—there can be no possibility of it 'standing apart' in some way and 'acting upon' society.

But when law is seen as no more than an instrument of state power, as it has almost invariably been seen in contemporary Western societies, it is thought of as independent of other aspects of social regulation. It is no longer considered to derive its effectiveness from its congruence with popular mores but from the concentration of political power which the state represents. Links between law and morality seem to loosen and eventually largely to disappear in popular consciousness. Thus, in Ehrlich's writings, the relationship between the norms for decision applied by state agencies and the patterns of thought and behaviour actually existing in the wider society is uncertain and problematic. To legislators and ordinary citizens alike law appears increasingly as a purely technical regulation, much of it lacking any clear moral element. Its separation in consciousness from the mores of the social groups it

2 See further ch 5.

regulates eventually leads to much of it virtually ceasing to exist at all in the consciousness of many citizens. It thus becomes an alien realm of esoteric knowledge left only to lawyers.

As technical regulation, however, it appears to be available for *any* regulatory purpose. Its freeing from whatever community roots it may have possessed is paralleled by its liberation as a mechanism of purposeful government. Modern law is thus the instrument of the modern state.

Two aspects of the apparent autonomy of modern Western law need to be considered. The first is its capacity to function as an autonomous agency of social control not dependent on the support of morality or custom. This is merely an aspect of the apparent autonomy of the modern state from the society in which it exists (Mann 1984). In this context we need to think of the state as comprising the specifically political elements of organisation in a society. In modern societies these elements tend to become increasingly concentrated and centralised in specific institutions (for example, governmental bureaucracies) and processes. Thus the modern state represents a distinct concentration of political power. It holds the monopoly of legitimate force in society (Weber 1978: 56, 65). Nineteenth-century social theorists recognised that a particularly important historical development had occurred gradually in Western societies. They referred to this as the separation of 'state' and 'civil society'; that is, broadly speaking, the separation between, on the one hand, a 'public' realm of government, politics and collective interests, and, on the other, a 'private' realm of individual interests, social relationships reflecting these interests, and private transactions based on the concepts of private property and contract (Keane 1988). Only as this separation of public and private spheres of life came to be recognised as more pronounced while, at the same time, the reach of the state extended to control an ever-widening sector of social life, could law appear as inevitably standing apart from society in this way.

The second aspect of law's apparent autonomy in modern Western societies which needs to be considered is the extent to which legal institutions (and the legal systems made up of these institutions and the legal doctrine they create, interpret and apply) are autonomous of other aspects of the state. In what sense is the legal system autonomous of the political system?

This question is one which will be considered in Chapter 3 and subsequent chapters. In this chapter, however, we are concerned with the first-mentioned aspect of the apparent autonomy of modern Western law: its capacity, as a technical apparatus of government, to function as an independent agent of change in society. In the following discussion some of the literature specifically addressing the question of how far law or particular types of law can promote or shape social change in contemporary Western societies will be surveyed.

Social Change

It is clearly essential to try to pinpoint what is meant by social change in the relevant literature but this is not easy since the concept is often used in extremely loose fashion in discussions of law as though it were self-explanatory. Lawrence Friedman and Jack Ladinsky, however, in the context of a discussion of the social effects of law adopt a definition of social change as 'any nonrepetitive alteration in the established modes of behaviour in society' (Friedman and Ladinsky 1967: 50). The qualification 'nonrepetitive' is important here for the definition recognises that few societies, if any, are wholly static. Changes merely in economic well-being, technology or basic attitudes of members of society are understood as continuous and probably ubiquitous. Social change is held to occur only when social structure—patterns of social relations, established social norms and social roles—changes. Thus a change in the established pattern of social relations between racial or ethnic groups in a society would constitute social change, but a general increase or decrease in the amount of economic wealth in a society would not. Certainly the distinction between regulation of social change and economic management as objectives of legislation seems important, although undoubtedly each may have consequences for the other.

Other writers have preferred to use a broader concept of social change recognising within it 'different levels or orders of change' (Grossman and Grossman, eds, 1971: 4). Thus Joel and Mary Grossman discuss variation in social change not only in terms of rate, but also of magnitude and scope. Social change may be incremental, comprehensive or revolutionary in magnitude, and its scope can be understood in terms of three stages or levels. It may merely alter patterns of individual behaviour (for example, an increase or decrease in the number of abortions, or a change in the birth rate). More fundamentally, it may alter group norms or patterns of relations of individuals or groups to each other or to such common objects as the political, economic or social system (for example, the breakdown of barriers to employment of blacks in fields from which they were previously excluded by discrimination). Finally, it may alter the society's mores or basic values, a type of change which is 'the most difficult to describe and undoubtedly the most difficult to achieve' (1971: 6).

As long as it is recognised that these levels of change shade into each other and are interrelated in complex ways, the Grossman and Grossman conception seems a reasonable starting point. But it seems necessary to say more about the question of 'rate' of social change. That this varies considerably from one society to another is clear. It depends on such matters as technological progress, natural environment, the extent of development of political organisation and consciousness, the degree of cultural unity or diversity, and the extent and character of interaction with other societies. Undoubtedly, as the capacity to control and exploit the natural environment has increased, the pace of social change has similarly accelerated. Not only do modern societies change with great rapidity but their members are acutely conscious of the continual transformation of social life (Friedman 1990a: ch 4).

Yet most societies change over time in response to environmental change and internal and external pressures, whatever their level of social, political and economic development. Perhaps the conception of 'primitive' societies as changeless derives at least to some extent from the fact that only societies that possess writing are likely to be able to recognise and assess change in anything other than an impressionistic and unsystematic manner (see e.g. Goody 1977). In societies without writing, history and myth tend to be hard to separate. Writing makes possible a tally of change, a more accurate and extensive reflection on the experience of past generations, and planning for the future on the basis of systematic analysis of this collective experience.

Do similar considerations apply to conceptions of legal change? In modern societies the directive power of government and law is assumed. Law is seen as a political creation; it 'reveals the machinery inside the box—the political, human, instrumental elements' in its development (Friedman 1990a: 53). Is the emergence of *written* forms of law a prerequisite for the conception of law as in flux and capable of directing society as an instrument of government rather than a codification of established mores? Unwritten social norms of custom follow social development; indeed, change in these norms expresses social development. But, as has already been seen in the previous chapter, law once recorded in written rules tends to acquire an identity distinct from more nebulous community beliefs and mores (cf. Goodrich 1990: 116). As such it may gain the potential to influence custom and belief as an almost independent force if it has some special claim to authority derived from religion, myth or appeals to reason, nature or traditional wisdom. Thus it becomes available as a source of support for, or an instrument of, political power. Yet even the unwritten law of ancient or 'primitive' societies, revealed through the oracular pronouncements of wise men, priests or political leaders, could be employed for such purposes.

The deliberate use of law to foster or hinder change is, therefore, not an exclusively modern phenomenon. 'Major ages of social change and mobility almost always involve great use of law and litigation' (Nisbet 1975: 173). But it cannot be denied that, in many modern societies, law's capabilities in this respect have been seen as vastly greater than they appeared to be in earlier eras. The putting of law into written form might be considered historically one of the first steps towards developing its potential as a precision instrument of government. But numerous other elements—the accumulation of state power available for enforcement, the professionalisation of interpretation and application of legal doctrine, the institutionalisation of elaborate adjudicative processes, and the development of efficient legislative institutions—have been prerequisites for establishing the most ambitious modern assumptions about the capabilities of legislation: that, given the necessary will and skill behind it and a careful selection of the most appropriate strategies, law can do anything and everything to mould societies in accordance with legislators' wishes.

The Impact of Social Change on Law

In the law and social change literature most analysis has been concerned with one direction of influence: the effects of legal change on social change. That legal development reflects wider social development often seems too obvious to require discussion. For example, technological change is one important direct cause of legal change: the development of the internal combustion engine, the motor car and later of air transport produced vast areas of new or reshaped legal doctrine to regulate these new features of life with their attendant possibilities, risks and dangers. Yet, as current problems in adapting Western law to cope with the revolutionary consequences of computer technology and the information revolution demonstrate, this process of adjustment is often difficult and delayed. In fact, as Ehrlich suggested and as some recent writers have again stressed, the way in which social developments are reflected in modern legislation or legal practices is just as problematic as the reverse direction of influence (cf. Teubner 1989).

In addition, law can adapt to change in ways that may not be readily apparent on the face of legal doctrine. The Austrian Marxist jurist Karl Renner tried to show this in a classic study of the relationship between legal concepts of property and contract and patterns of social change in the development of capitalism in Western societies (Renner 1949). Renner's argument is that law can adapt to changed social circumstances without necessarily changing its form or structure. Legal concepts can remain in the same form while fundamentally changing their social functions.

For example, the legal form of property which originally encompassed the owner's patrimonial property of 'house and home and everything around it' (Renner 1949: 84) is used in the development of capitalist society to embody legal title to those assets that make possible the accumulation of capital. Capital itself exists as property in the form of a title to profit, interest or rent. But it also constitutes power; a power of command which its owner holds over other individuals. This is the very basis of capitalist social relations. Yet all this, remarks Renner, is invisible to the law which operates only with the basic concepts of property, ownership and contract and their doctrinal elaborations and which ignores the change that has occurred in the social context these legal forms enclose. 'Fundamentally the norms which make up the law have remained absolutely constant, and yet an enormous revolution has occurred without any change of norms' (1949: 88–9).

But much other social research on law has directly reflected the concerns of legislators and the ambitions of social reformers confident of their ability to influence the content of new law. It is this factor above all that has led to a traditional emphasis in the sociology of law on questions of legal effectiveness (on the capacity of law to bring about change) rather than on questions of the genesis of legislation or of judge-made law, which involve an exploration of the factors shaping law. And it is in the exploration of these questions of effectiveness that the sociology of law raises, in its most extreme form, the hypothesis of law's autonomy, actual or potential, from the cultural constraints and social bases that some of the nineteenth-century theorists stressed.

The Limits of Effective Legal Action

Despite the climate of opinion emphasising law's capacity to mould society, which has dominated much twentieth-century legal thought, some of those who have devoted careful study to the characteristics of modern law as an instrument of government have tended to see this capacity as severely limited. Of course, political preferences about what law should and should not do no doubt often colour perceptions of what it is practically possible for it to do. Conversely, 'the ethical limits of law often turn on empirical considerations. Thus it is important that social scientists and legal scholars study law's empirical limits' (Danelski 1974: 24). One writer concludes a study of the 'limits of law' by remarking 'that laws are often ineffective, doomed to stultification almost at birth, doomed by the over-ambitions of the legislator and the under-provision of the necessary requirements for an effective law, such as adequate preliminary survey, communication, acceptance, and enforcement machinery' (Allott 1980: 287).

It is not, however, true, as he suggests, that in determining the limits of law, scholars are hampered by 'the absence of appropriate in-depth field studies of the effectiveness of laws' (1980: 287). There are numerous such studies. The problem is to know how to interpret their findings; to generalise from a vast number of particular instances; to find appropriate methods for isolating the effects of law from other causal factors in change; and to draw general conclusions about law when the factors determining effectiveness (however it is measured) may vary greatly from one type of law to another.

Modern studies of 'the limits of effective legal action' can be traced back to a seminal article with that title published early in this century by the American jurist Roscoe Pound (Pound 1917). Pound attempts to lay down principles suggested by a consideration of basic characteristics of modern law. First, as a practical matter, law can, as he puts it, deal only with the outside, and not the inside of people and things. For many reasons, including problems of proof, law cannot attempt to control attitudes and beliefs but only observable behaviour. For Pound this is a practical basis of the distinction between law and morals—since the latter as a system of social control intrudes into areas of life and belief where the law dare not enter. Secondly, law as an instrument of government relies on some external agency to put its machinery in motion. Legal precepts do not enforce themselves. Law that cannot be enforced, or invoked by citizens, can hardly shape behaviour. Thirdly, there are interests and demands that it might be desirable for the law to recognise but that by their nature cannot be safeguarded or satisfied through law.

This last point refers to limitations apparently arising from the idea, which Ehrlich suggested, that law as a special form of control is characterised by a relative clarity of its precepts. If, as in modern law, these precepts are to be enforced by state agencies and to provide authority for the actions of numerous officials at all levels of the state, a high degree of clarity is essential. So there are limitations on law which arise from the difficulty of ascertaining the facts on which law is to operate (Pound 1917: 161–2). The caution of the common law in allowing redress for some mental and nervous injuries and for injury to feelings has been largely the result of the problem of fact-finding. Lévy-Bruhl writes that the aim of legal proof has been to put an end to disputes. What is acceptable as legal proof is, however, different from scientific proof. Truth as an object which the legal process seeks has to be pragmatically balanced against the need for speedy decision-making. A judge or jury cannot indefinitely defer a resolution of the matter. A decision must be handed down on the basis of the facts available. The judge cannot, like the scientist, continually make provisional judgments, ready to reopen the matter when new data comes to light. So legal proof can never equal scientific proof (Lévy-Bruhl 1964: 150–2). It follows that the imperatives of decision-making make courts reluctant to deal with certain matters in which evidence is likely to be particularly problematic, or so controversial that it cannot be handled by judges with apparent objectivity.

Pound's early essay also notes limitations arising because some morally important rights or duties defy legal enforcement. His examples refer to the legal responsibilities attached to individuals and modern welfare agencies with regard to care of family and children, and he sees the development of social welfare law in this form as incapable of substituting for or enforcing natural ties and moral duties of family life. Other important interests may be infringed in ways too subtle for the law to control. A 'right of privacy' is recognised as such in law, for example in the United States, but not in Britain (Wacks 1989: ch 2). Undoubtedly privacy is an interest of great importance yet its definition, in a manner that makes it a concept usable in the law, is a matter of great difficulty and controversy. The difficulty involved in tracing injuries to privacy to their source 'compels some sacrifice of the interests of the retiring and the sensitive' (Pound 1917: 163). Furthermore, Pound notes, echoing Ehrlich, that in many areas of social life the sanctions of state law appear useless, disrupting rather than repairing social relations.

In recent years these kinds of doubts about the intrusion of law into fields that it is ill-fitted to regulate have been strongly echoed in literature from a number of Western countries discussing, often critically, the 'juridification' or 'legalisation' of such social spheres as industrial relations, family life, commercial activity and the organisation of business enterprises (see e.g. Teubner, ed, 1986; Teubner, ed, 1987). Significantly, however, emphases have shifted somewhat from Pound's concern with legal ineffectiveness. For some contemporary writers the primary problem is law's powerful pathological effects - bureaucratising social relations and moral environments, and misinterpreting and so creating disruption in contexts previously regulated by extra-legal norms. Contrary to Pound's image of law as sometimes powerless, it may be, according to these more recent writers, all too 'effective'—but law's effect may be to create uncertainty, chaos, distrust or hostility rather than to regulate appropriately. What is necessary is to find an appropriate relationship between law and other normative orders to prevent this (Teubner 1987).

One other limitation Pound mentions is particularly important in the light of more recent writings. Law often depends on interested parties not professionally involved with the legal system to set its machinery in motion. It requires people who are motivated for some reason to invoke legal rules and procedures; that is, to call upon law in support of their interests. Even in criminal law where state agencies normally institute prosecution of offenders and where the prosecution is in the name of the Crown or the state, law enforcement depends heavily on public reporting of crime to enforcement agencies such as police. Much other law depends for its invocation on a civil (i.e. non-criminal) legal action[3] brought by an aggrieved individual, corporate body or group of individuals seeking redress, typically through such remedies as damages (compensatory or

3 The term 'civil law' has several meanings. Its use here in contrast to 'criminal law' should be distinguished from the use of the term to refer to the law of continental systems based in Roman law principles as opposed to English common law.

punitive money payment), injunction (order to carry out or desist from a particular course of action) or declaration (of applicable rights and duties). If law is to be effective it must be in the interests of those upon whom the law depends for its invocation or enforcement to set the legal machinery in motion. Law must provide incentives to ensure its own use. In many cases this will mean ensuring the availability of adequate and suitable remedies in the law for those whom it is designed to aid or protect; remedies sufficiently attractive to motivate the victim of illegal practices to seek the aid of the legal system.

Making People Good Through Law?

The need for adequate incentives to encourage invocation and enforcement of law may seem obvious, yet as Pound notes and later legal experience confirms, it is a consideration sometimes left out of account. There are laws that provide inadequate means of enforcement in the case of criminal law or only limited incentives for citizens to invoke provisions of civil law. Sometimes these are examples of what has been called 'educative legislation' whose significance seems primarily to be to set up or promote ideals through governmental action rather than to provide means by which a litigant can enforce rights. The approach of the first British Race Relations Act of 1965 stressed conciliation rather than redress. Not until the enactment of the 1976 Act was it possible for individuals claiming racial discrimination to take a case directly to court or to an industrial tribunal on their own initiative, with the possibility of a wide range of remedies. In 1967, shortly before a second Race Relations Act was enacted, the then Race Relations Board summed up the purpose of anti-discrimination legislation in five points. First, it would represent an unequivocal declaration of public policy against discrimination. Secondly, it would support those who wanted not to discriminate but found social pressure compelling them to do so. Thirdly, it would give protection and redress to minority groups. Fourthly, it would provide for the peaceful and orderly adjustment of grievances and the release of tensions. Fifthly, it would reduce prejudice by discouraging the behaviour in which prejudice finds expression (quoted in Lester and Bindman 1972: 85). Several of these purposes go well beyond the use of law to redress grievances or to control behaviour, and the last of them points unequivocally to the educative function of law: to change ideas by influencing behaviour.

Nothing in Pound's original discussion suggested that such legislation could never succeed. The point was simply that, in their zeal to promote ideals, legislators sometimes omit to identify social interests with individual advantage and so make it possible for the law to rely upon individual initiative for enforcement of its precepts (Pound 1917: 165–6). Many writers have pointed to the problems of law enforcement in relation to what have been called 'crimes without victims' (Schur 1965) or, at least, crimes where no one may recognise himself or herself as a victim. These include certain drugs offences and sexual offences in which consent is no defence and where the aim of the law seems to be to enforce particular moral principles in private life irrespective of whether the offender's acts can be shown to cause harm to others, or even to the offender.

In addition, there may be laws created solely or primarily to put certain symbols or ideals into the statute book. In the drafting and enactment of this legislation there may be no realistic consideration of the possibilities of effective enforcement of the law. Symbolic legislation can be distinguished from educative legislation on the grounds that there is no serious legislative intention of producing significant social change by means of the former. Rather the object is likely to be that of placating opposed interests of various sections of society while avoiding change. On the other hand, since legislative intention is a notoriously complex matter to determine conclusively,[4] these two categories of law cannot always be clearly separated. Symbolic legislation will be considered further in Chapter 4.

Can law change beliefs as well as behaviour? Can it act on the 'inside' of people as well as on the 'outside'? In a study published in 1952, two years before the landmark decision of the United States Supreme Court in *Brown v Board of Education of Topeka*[5] which outlawed racial segregation in the American state school system, Morroe Berger wrote: 'While it is true that the province of law is "external" behaviour, it is also true that in an urban, secular society an increasing number of relations fall within this province' and 'law can influence "external acts" which affect or constitute the conditions for the exercise of the private inclinations and tastes that are said to be beyond the realm of law' (Berger 1952: 172). On the other hand, it has been claimed that legislation appearing to control 'external' behaviour may have the effect of making the practices and attitudes at which the law is really aimed more covert and harder to detect (Dror 1959). What is perhaps most significant about this area of literature is the extreme diversity of views, reflecting different assumptions about law and observations of different areas and aspects of it in operation. To some writers, 'legislation and education are not incompatible, legislation is a powerful form of education' (Lester and Bindman 1972: 86). The American lawyer Lawrence Friedman wrote of a California Supreme Court decision upsetting the legal foundation of educational finance in the state that many *coups d'état* in small countries

4 See further p. 72, below.
5 347 US 483 (1954). Implementation decision 349 US 294 (1955).

had 'achieved less social change than this quiet *coup d'état* in a court' (Friedman 1973: 27). On the other hand, an eminent authority on industrial relations law in contemporary Western societies writes of the 'magic belief' in the efficacy of law in shaping human conduct and social relations as a *superstition* of political importance, but a superstition none the less (Kahn-Freund 1969: 311). And Ehrlich, polemical as ever, proclaims: 'We shall have to get used to the idea that certain things simply cannot be done by means of a statute' (1936: 375). As always the danger is of generalising too widely about law from particular legal experience.

There are, however, clear examples in legal history of grotesque and costly failures in the attempt to use law to alter deep-rooted patterns of social behaviour. The best known is the attempt in the United States in the 1920s and early 1930s to prohibit the manufacture, transportation and sale of alcoholic liquor for beverage purposes. An Amendment (the Eighteenth) to the United States Constitution and the provision of draconian legal sanctions did not make the law effective for its declared purpose. Sanctions provided under 1929 legislation included a $10,000 fine or five years' imprisonment, or both, for each offence; taxation and seizure of illicit liquor; forfeiture of vehicles used in transportation and the padlocking of buildings used for manufacture of illicit liquor. The owner of such a building had no redress even if he or she was not a party to the breach of the law and had no knowledge of it. More than 750,000 people were arrested for violation of the prohibition laws between 1920 and their repeal in 1932. Fines and penalties totalling in excess of $75,000,000 were imposed and more than $205,000,000 worth of property was seized (Warburton 1933: 505–6). The number of convictions in federal courts for liquor offences rose from about 35,000 a year after 1922 to 61,383 in 1932. In 1930, 282,122 illicit distilleries and related apparatuses and some 40 million gallons of distilled spirits, malt liquor, wine, cider, mash and pomace were seized. Yet the law had little effect on alcohol consumption especially among business and professional classes. In one commentator's view, ineffective enforcement disgusted America with prohibition but it was when the scale of enforcement activity under the Hoover administration 'began to put respectable citizens in jail' that the revolt of repeal was set in motion (Sinclair 1962: 212).

There is now substantial agreement about the main factors that made this experiment in social control through law a total failure. Enforcement by police was half-hearted at best and law enforcement agencies lacked co-ordination and adequate resources to prevail over the organised interests controlling a highly profitable illicit liquor trade. Neither Congress nor the individual states set up adequate enforcement machinery and Congress refused to allocate the large sums continually requested for this purpose. Yet perhaps even more important were the social forces ranged against the law. It grew from religious origins in the American temperance movement and was inevitably associated with bitter moral conflicts, and with conflicts of life style. One commentator sees it as an attempt by 'the rural and village populations of the country to retain their waning influence and to impose their ways of life upon the urban dwellers' since the maintenance of clubs, saloons, bars and an extensive liquor trade was substantially an urban phenomenon (Warburton 1933: 504).

Enactment of the law could be seen as an important victory for certain sections of American society over others by which the victors were able to have their values and beliefs enshrined in law (Gusfield 1963). In these and other respects prohibition law aggravated conflicts in society, moralised openly, and eventually appeared sectarian and arbitrary despite the apparently wide support the law received when first enacted. During the early 1970s laws penalising possession of marijuana were referred to as the 'new prohibition' to suggest that legal policy in this area was equally misguided in attempting (ineffectually) to penalise conduct not generally proved harmful but viewed moralistically by the law while being then widely accepted among large sectors of the American population (Kaplan 1971).

Legislative Strategies for Promoting Social Change

Even the grotesque and exotic case of prohibition provides some general lessons. How the law is put into effect is clearly as important as its content. The nature of the enforcement agencies used, the degree of commitment of enforcement agents to implementation of the law, their morale and—a closely related factor—the amount of resources available to ensure compliance, are all shown to be extremely significant factors. In addition, the particular strategy of coercion or persuasion employed in regulation is clearly of great importance. For example, the disastrous experience of liquor prohibition in the United States helped to convince politicians in Britain during the 1920s that direct legal prohibition of widespread forms of gambling should be replaced with a variety of more flexible administrative and fiscal controls on these activities (Dixon 1991: 202-3, 215-8). More generally, in a widely cited article the sociologist Yehezkel Dror (1959) distinguishes between direct and indirect uses of law in promoting change. Echoing earlier writers he asserts that the direct use of law—the attempt to change behaviour and perhaps also attitudes by imposing on individual legal subjects legal duties requiring such change—is fraught with problems. But law, Dror argues, can and does play an important indirect role in fostering social change in many ways.

First, it shapes various social institutions which, in turn, have a direct influence on the rate or character of social change. Thus laws structuring a national education system and providing for a national curriculum for schools[6] influence the scope and character of educational institutions which themselves may directly influence social change. Patent laws protecting inventors' rights may encourage invention and promote change in technological institutions which in turn may influence social change. Negatively, legal restrictions on freedom of association or discussion, on disclosure of the information necessary for realistic assessment of present conditions and policies, or on contact with other societies, may prevent or delay the spread of new ideas favouring social change.

Secondly, law often provides the institutional framework for an agency specifically set up to exert influence for change. In the twentieth century, legislation in Western societies has frequently been used to set up boards, commissions and agencies of various kinds charged with promoting particular policy goals. For example, in Britain, the National Enterprise Board was created by the Industry Act 1975, its main statutory object being to develop and assist the United Kingdom economy by providing large-scale investment in industrial undertakings through loans or guarantees or provision of funds in return for shares in the company's capital. In 1980, with a new set of social and economic priorities adopted in government, its functions were abruptly switched from promotion of public ownership and industrial democracy in economic undertakings to promotion of private ownership of industry through disposal of securities and other properties held by it.[7]

A third legal strategy which Dror mentions is the creation of legal duties to establish situations in which change is fostered. Examples would be the numerous specific duties placed on local authorities with regard to public services of many kinds. Finally Dror adds, polemically, that the preservation by law of the structure of a free market economy is 'one of the more important mechanisms of social change in many countries'. It will be necessary to leave until later chapters a consideration of some aspects of this claim.

An examination of the legislation of advanced Western states shows extensive use of all of these mechanisms of indirect promotion of change, plus many variations and refinements of legal strategy. The political values and policies of particular governments undoubtedly influence the choice of strategy but not, it seems, acceptance of the modern view of law as a powerful instrument of policy and its widespread use in attempting to control or influence social change. Legislation reaching the statute book in Britain in the 1970s showed enthusiastic use of special boards,

6 In Britain, the Education Reform Act 1988 now makes such provision.
7 Industry Act 1980, s.1(i).

commissions and agencies set up in the legislation to promote its policies. In more recent years there has been a political reaction against the proliferation of special governmental or quasi-governmental agencies yet they clearly remain major instruments of legislative policy (e. g. De Smith 1989: ch 12; and see Chapter 8).

Recent statute law shows continuing ambitious legislative efforts to promote change through the creation of new legal duties for existing administrative authorities[8]; the extension of legal powers of government ministers[9]; legislative provision for the making of special grants, loans or fiscal concessions[10]; alteration of the powers of existing governmental or quasi-governmental agencies and the setting up of new institutional structures to induce change in the practice of established ones. Legislation is used to influence the character of established institutions considered pivotal in the achievement of social change objectives.[11] Finally, British legislative practice also shows many examples of the direct use of law to influence significant social change through the imposition of legal duties on individuals. The most obvious examples are probably in the field of anti-discrimination law. The Sex Discrimination Act 1975 and the Race Relations Act 1976 enacted extensive institutional frameworks for individual redress and for investigation of complaints and discriminatory practices. More commonly, however, in recent years, legislation has been employed to promote change by removing or relaxing duties previously attaching to individuals in certain social or economic relationships.[12] All of these varied legislative strategies assume that law can achieve powerful effects in restructuring social relations.

8 During the 1980s, for example, legislation in Britain required local government authorities and health service authorities to promote in various ways the privatisation of public services. See e.g. Local Government, Planning and Land Act 1980 (requirement of private tendering for certain local authority works); Health Services Act 1980 (raising funds in National Health Service from private sources; treatment of private patients in NHS hospitals); London Regional Transport Act 1984 (provision for transfer of services to private companies).

9 Cf. Food Safety Act 1990 (advisory bodies to assist Minister in making regulations under statutory powers).

10 See e.g. Education Act 1980 (assisted places at independent schools).

11 See e.g. Education (No 2) Act 1986 (redefined powers of school governors; increased influence of local business communities in school government); Education Reform Act 1988 (delegation of powers of government of schools); Employment Act 1982 (restriction of closed shop practices; union funds liable for illegal strikes); Trade Union Act 1984 (requirement of secret ballots before strike action); Local Government Finance Acts 1982 and 1987 (local authority financial controls); Rates Act 1984 (central government power to limit local authority rates; local authorities' duties to consult representatives of industrial and commercial ratepayers with regard to expenditure proposals and financing of expenditure).

12 See e.g. Housing Act 1988 (deregulation of private rented housing arrangements).

Some Prerequisites for Effective Legislation

Various writers have tried to specify the conditions under which law can effectively influence behaviour and perhaps attitudes. The sociologist William M. Evan, writing in the light of American experience with race relations law, has listed seven such conditions (Evan 1965) which provide a convenient framework for discussion. First, the source of the new law must be authoritative and prestigious. In Western representative democracies, legislation, Evan argues, satisfies this condition better than do other types of regulation. The democratic mandate of the legislature provides a legitimacy for action by it to bring about substantial change. Next in prestige he ranks executive orders, the decisions of administrative agencies, and finally court decisions. It needs to be added, however, that as regards courts what is lacking is not necessarily prestige in general but legitimacy as policy-formulating agencies, a matter discussed more fully in Chapter 7. Undoubtedly the United States Supreme Court attracted immense controversy when during the 1950s and 1960s it consciously adopted an activist 'legislative' role in its interpretations of the United States Constitution. On the other hand, the special prestige of courts may, in some circumstances, be harnessed to promote change. For example, it has been claimed that the legitimacy of courts depends primarily on the perceived fairness of their decision-making procedures (Tyler 1990), and that where the application of these procedures produces decisions furthering policies unpopular with mass publics (for example, affirmation of the rights of extremist political groups) the prestige of the deciding court may aid acceptance of these policies, at least among leaders of public opinion (Gibson 1989).

Secondly, Evan proposes, the rationale of the new law must be expressed in terms of its compatibility and continuity with established cultural and legal principles. As the matter has also been put, law can be a powerful force for change 'when the change derives from a principle deeply embedded in our heritage' (Pennock and Chapman, eds, 1974: 2). The point seems to nod a brief acknowledgment to Savigny. Law must appear compatible with cultural assumptions and with the most general accepted patterns of legal development. Anti-discrimination law can be portrayed as a direct application of fundamental principles of citizenship and equality under the law which are considered to be deeply rooted in Anglo-American law and culture. But changes that smack too much of legal or social revolution are likely to be resisted.

Thirdly, as Evan puts it, pragmatic models for compliance must be identified. It must be possible to make clear both the nature and the significance of the new patterns of behaviour required by the law by pointing to groups, societies or communities in which these patterns exist. What seems to lie behind this is the insistence that law must not appear utopian but practical in its aims. There tends to be resistance to ideas that appear wholly untried.

Fourthly, Evan refers to a conscious use of the element of time in legislative action (cf. Allott 1980: 167). He suggests that the shorter the transition time the easier the adaptation to the change required by law. Reduction of delay minimises the chances for growth of organised or unorganised resistance to change. The time schedule for change is undoubtedly an important consideration in the framing of legislation yet Evan's remarks seem a schematic and somewhat unenlightening answer to a complex question. Modern legislation often specifies that the legislative provisions are not to come into force until some time after the enactment of the statute (for example, the Equal Pay Act 1970) or provides for them to be activated by ministerial order or given effect later through specification of detailed regulations (for example, the Consumer Credit Act 1974). The assumption is often that legislation requiring reorganisation of complex industrial or commercial practices will work better and less disruptively if the organisations concerned are given time to plan for change.

While this may mean time to invent avoidance techniques, the appropriate timing strategy probably depends on the extent and complexity of change that the law seeks to bring about, the nature of the practices and institutions at which the law is aimed, and the legislators' value judgments as to the relative importance of securing rapid change, on the one hand, and minimising disruption, on the other. The conspicuous programming of legal change as of any governmental action in stages over time is a means of providing reassurance that change is firmly controlled and that legal policy is governed by caution and forethought. It is also a way of allowing the law-making process to benefit from the experience (of enforcement agencies, of the regulated population and of those whose interests the law is intended to promote) gathered in implementation of the legislative programme. A vital element in securing the unanimity of the nine justices of the United States Supreme Court in support of the pathbreaking school desegregation decision in *Brown v Board of Education of Topeka* was the insertion in the court's judgment of the ambiguous qualification that desegregation be implemented 'with all deliberate speed' (e.g. White 1982: 168). Undoubtedly, however, in this case the effect of the qualification was to provide a degree of legitimacy for delaying tactics by authorities within the states.

Prohibition offers a clear enough illustration of the importance of Evan's fifth condition: that enforcement agents must be committed to the behaviour required by the law even if not to the values implicit in it. Any evidence of hypocrisy or corruption from this source is likely to undermine the law (see also Dixon 1991: ch 7). The point raises one aspect of a complex problem. In general it is important to ask what kinds of pressures tend to operate on and within the law enforcement agencies to promote or deter effective enforcement by them. This requires consideration of the nature of the agencies themselves, their institutional form and the particular political, social and economic environment within which they operate. These matters will be discussed in Chapter 8.

Evan's sixth point suggests a number of important issues. Positive sanctions, he suggests, are as important as negative ones. In other words, while legal sanctions are typically thought of as various forms of punishment, or provisions for redress of injury through compensation, positive incentives for compliance with law may also be used where the law seeks actively to promote social change. In modern legislation, provisions for grants, subsidies and tax and other fiscal concessions are important examples of such sanctions. As Grossman and Grossman suggest: 'Laws ... which seek positive societal changes of major proportions must rely as much on education and persuasion as on negative sanctions. For the carrot and stick approach to be successful, the latter must be visible and occasionally used' (1971: 70).

More generally, other writers have stressed that the kind of sanctions used in the law may have a vital bearing on its capacity to influence attitudes. William K. Muir argues that legal coercion may force a change of behaviour but where 'there is no sense of choice, a man acting in external conformity with the law may not be driven to change attitudes that are at odds with the law. A precondition of positive attitude change is a sense of volition' (Muir 1967: 49). If an individual is induced, not compelled, to act in a certain way 'he will search for information to support his commitment' (1967: 51) so as to remove the tensions involved in deciding to do one thing while feeling predisposed to do the opposite. Muir calls this the process of 'conversion', which may give rise to acceptance of the attitudes informing the law.

Where someone is undecided about appropriate conduct, legal coercion may, by removing choice and overcoming opposing social pressures, make up the individual's mind ('liberation') but is likely to do so in a way that only superficially disguises the original ambivalence without removing it. In other circumstances where people are coerced by law, they may keep their original inconsistent attitude and exaggerate the coercive effects of the law which force a change in their conduct, or they may accentuate their antagonistic attitude and condemn the law which forces them to act in a manner inconsistent with it. Muir sees these and other possible responses as adaptive reactions by which people can integrate attitudes and conduct in a way that minimises psychological tensions and inconsistencies.

Probably the best way to see legal strategies in this context is as part of a long-term process of negotiation of attitudes and perceptions of interests in which political and legal action constitute only one element in a complex network of influences on social change (cf. Paulus 1974: ch 3: Carson 1974). It has been claimed that studies of the consequences of desegregation in, for example, 'armed forces units, housing projects, and employment situations, indicate that change required by law *has* lessened prejudice' (Greenberg 1959: 26: and see Smith 1977: 311–2). But the problem with any such statement is not only that of finding a reliable relevant measure of attitude change but also that of isolating the effects of legal change from many other social developments (Grossman and Grossman, eds, 1971: 9), a point we must return to later.

Evan's final point is the one Pound stressed half a century earlier. Effective protection must be provided for the rights of those who would suffer as a result of evasion or violation of the law (cf. Lustgarten 1986: 73-6). They must be given the incentive to use the legislation. Significantly, consumer protection laws in the United States have attempted to encourage consumers to make use of the law by providing for minimum damages recoverable in litigation (for example $100 or $200 even if actual damages are less), punitive damages, double or treble damages or recovery of lawyers' fees (Nader and Shugart 1980: 58). In England, studies of the effects of 1960s race relations legislation found 'evidence of a certain reluctance to make a complaint [of discrimination] among a substantial proportion of Asians and West Indians' together with the fact that only a minority of immigrants interviewed had even heard of the Race Relations Board, the body then entrusted with handling complaints of discrimination. These findings have been associated with difficulties of proving racial discrimination and obtaining effective redress under the race relations legislation then in force (Smith 1977: 315, 316, 317). No doubt they also reflect more general attitudes among particular minority groups to the potential benefits and disadvantages of political and legal action involving relations with other social or cultural groups or institutions of the wider society (cf. Doo 1973; Chan and Hagan 1982).

In fact, of course, many of these factors are intimately linked. For example, there is a close connection between the problem of incentives to ensure invocation of the law, the kind of sanctioning strategy adopted and the role of enforcement agencies (see Chapter 8). Modern law does use a wide variety of incentives to secure its effectiveness. Robert Summers (1971) argues that most legal strategies involve one or more of five methods. First, law is used to facilitate private arrangements, such as contracts or wills, which require reliance on the law in order to secure the benefits of the arrangements. Here, because of the voluntary nature of the arrangements, rights and duties are largely fixed by the parties themselves and not by officials of the legal system, who merely remain in readiness to enforce these voluntarily adopted rights and duties if required to by the parties. Secondly, law is used to remedy grievances by fixing private rights and providing remedies for their infringement in civil courts. Here, unlike the situation in private arrangements, duties are imposed by officials but the decision whether or not to enforce the duty generally remains one for private parties. Thirdly, law is used directly to control behaviour through threat or use of punishment, as in criminal law. Here both imposition of legal duties and enforcement of the duties is usually dependent on the action of state officials. Fourthly, 'public benefit conferral' methods distribute public goods and services to defined categories of 'distributees', for example in provision of health, education and welfare services, and raise finance to do so through taxation. Here implementation of law is dependent on specialised bureaucracies. Fifthly, law is used to set standards for specific classes of 'regulatees' (for example, public utilities, business organisations) and to regulate their behaviour through licensing or some other regulatory device. Again, such law usually depends on specialised agencies to supervise its operation. In modern legal systems these five basic methods of using law to influence behaviour are combined in complex ways. It is clear, therefore, that the importance of specialised enforcement agencies, of particular techniques of enforcement, and of public knowledge of and support for the law, may vary considerably depending not only on the aims of the law but on its form.

Limitations of 'Law and Social Change' Studies

Evan's schematic listing of factors influencing the effectiveness of legal strategies for social change points up the character of much writing in this field. What is offered is not a theory explaining in systematic manner the relationship between legal change and social change but, in essence, practical guidance for the legislator derived from legal experience and empirical studies of the effects of law. The listing of factors provides a peg on which to hang the results of many diverse studies of the social consequences of particular laws. It offers relatively few insights into the nature of 'society', the entity upon which law is intended to act. Indeed much of the literature proceeds on the basis of important implicit assumptions about the nature of 'society'. As in the impact studies referred to in the previous chapter and to which the researches under consideration here are closely related, society is viewed through a legal prism in terms of legislators' concerns and lawyers' professional outlook. Thus for Grossman and Grossman (1971: 2), law is 'a desirable and necessary, if not a highly efficient means of inducing change' and 'wherever possible, its institutions and procedures are preferable to others of which we are aware'.

Yet such commonly espoused views are often unconnected with any explicit and rigorously developed theory of what kind of social institution law is. Without theory which attempts to explain the character of law as a social phenomenon and the position that it occupies in the overall structure of social life, discussions of the conditions under which law can influence other aspects of society can hardly progress beyond the listing of factors, often with no convincing means of analysing the way they interrelate and their relative importance. This is not, of course, to say that such discussions, within their limitations, are unenlightening. The literature discussed in this chapter helps us to begin to understand what Summers calls the 'technique element' in law, the range of legal mechanisms and strategies through which attempts are made deliberately to influence social change (Summers 1971). It is important, however, to recognise what is left out of consideration.

Much of the law and social change literature expresses aspirations about law that are characteristic of a liberal progressive era and are now seen in a different light in a less optimistic age. The stress on law's capacity to promote change tends to divert attention from the extent to which it prevents change. What is important—and, again, requires theoretical analysis—is to understand when and why stability or change seems particularly to be demanded from law, why these demands may operate differently in different areas of law, in different legal systems, at different times; why change does occur and why there is not more of it; why law reform movements sometimes succeed and sometimes do not (cf. Handler 1978); why particular struggles for or against change focus on the legal system at particular times and in relation to particular kinds of issues. Contrary to the implication in Grossman and Grossman's statement quoted above, change often occurs without explicit recognition by or use of the legal system and may be more orderly and easily assimilated because of this—because legal continuity is preserved despite social change. Continuities in legal concepts of property despite revolutionary transformations in the form and use of property in social relations offer particularly clear historical examples of this (Renner 1949).

Another problem of many studies of law and social change arises from the tendency to 'reify' law; that is, to treat legal institutions and even legal doctrine as social forces in themselves without regard to the interests that they represent. Thus, when we ask whether law can promote social change, we are really considering whether the actions of those members of the population who for one reason or another have been able to get their demands or interests recognised by law will be successful in overcoming resistance to the pursuance through law of their claims. Law is not, therefore, an actor in itself but only the instrument of the human actors whose interests it represents. Thus a full consideration of the effects of particular laws cannot be separated from an analysis of the forces that shaped those laws. Nevertheless it is central to the argument of subsequent chapters of this book that in contemporary Western societies certain *general* sociological characteristics and effects of legal doctrine can be identified and that legal institutions can be analysed in terms of their own distinctive characteristics to explain much about law's general social effects.

An understanding of law's social effects and of the social factors that shape it requires legal theory—theory which attempts to explain systematically the nature of law. However, because law is *an aspect of society*, a part of a larger social field, this theory must, itself, be informed by—and a part of—social theory. Social theory seeks to explain systematically the structure of societies and the conditions of social order and stability, and of social change. Undoubtedly it seems natural to many observers of legal processes to see law as set apart from 'society' as a discrete mechanism acting upon social life. Current conceptions of legislation presuppose such a view. Yet 'law ... is only one component of a large set of policy instruments and usually cannot [be] ... and is not used by itself. Therefore, focusing of exclusive attention on law as a tool of directed social change is a case of tunnel vision, which lacks the minimum perspective necessary for making sense from the observed phenomena' (Dror 1970: 554). A failure on the part of legislators in many Western societies in recent decades to recognise this may have contributed powerfully to current disillusionment with the proliferation in these societies of costly and seemingly ineffective bureaucracies, and more generally with the concept of 'the directive state' and of social planning. The failure to see law as merely one aspect of a complex social whole affected by many social forces, and to see law as shaped by these forces probably to a far greater extent than it can shape them, leads to inevitable disillusionment when the legal instrument fails to achieve what the legal reformer intended.

A Note on Autopoiesis Theory

This kind of disillusionment with law's capabilities as an instrument of change easily links with a more general disquiet about the very idea of considering law in purely instrumental terms. Instrumentalist views of law that tend to treat it almost entirely as a means of implementing policy typify much law and social change literature. They have been fiercely attacked in recent years on at least three major fronts. First, harking back to the problems identified in some of the earliest writing on the limits of effective legal action, law's inefficiency and limited capabilities when considered as an agent of change have been emphasised. Sometimes this seems to go as far as suggesting that law cannot steer society at all in any effective way (apparently ignoring the fact that law is continually used for this purpose in all contemporary societies, whatever their political complexion: see Cotterrell 1988; Thompson 1984b). Secondly, legal instrumentalism has been attacked for ignoring the serious problems of 'juridification' or 'legalisation' of social life; for encouraging, indeed, the intrusion of legal regulation into areas of life which might be better governed by means other than those of state law (see e. g. Teubner, ed, 1986; Teubner, ed, 1987). Sometimes the image is one of 'legal pollution' (Teubner 1987: 3), as though law were not steering society but smothering it, or somehow destroying its life forces (cf. Habermas 1986). Thirdly, the very idea that law should be thought of as an instrument of government has been considered inadequate and harmful, ignoring the problem of law's integrity as a specific mode of reasoning, discourse or system of communication. Here, the threat is seen as being not so much to the life forces of society, as to law itself. Legal instrumentalism threatens to undermine or trivialise law's intellectual integrity, its values (such as those associated with the ideal of the rule of law)[13] and its autonomy from politics (Teubner 1987: 25–7).

These attitudes have undoubtedly provided a significant momentum for the recent application to legal studies of what has come to be known as autopoiesis theory (Teubner, ed, 1988), though it would be wrong to see them as having directly given rise to this development. Whereas the theories to be considered in subsequent chapters are primarily social theories which locate law in a broader picture of the character of social relations and structures, autopoiesis theory appears significantly different. Viewed as a contribution to the sociology of law it seems, very specifically, a theory of the relationship of law and social change, but one which offers not an empirical portrayal of the character of law within society but a highly abstract, even *a priori*, conception of law as a system confronted by its environment. Autopoiesis theory, applied to legal analysis primarily by the German theorists Niklas Luhmann and Gunther Teubner, does not, indeed, derive from sociology or any kind of social theory[14], but from biological theory of living systems, and its application in the analysis of social phenomena remains controversial. Its central claim is that law is to be considered an essentially self-referential system of communication. Thus, legal communication or discourse is distinctive. It does not depend, for example, on the criteria of efficiency present in economic discourse or of truth as understood in scientific discourse. Though neither truth nor efficiency is irrelevant to legal discourse, law understands

13 See further ch 5.

14 Luhmann's ideas draw to some extent on Talcott Parsons' sociological systems theory, to be considered in Chapter 3. Luhmann's primary indebtedness to Parsons seems to be for the general idea that the differentiation of sub-systems in modern societies is a fundamental response to the increasing complexity of social life in the modern world.

these in its own particular ways. Legal communications are essentially in terms of 'right' and 'wrong' developed as specifically legal categories; that is, in terms of legality or illegality. All legal communication centres around and ultimately produces a binary output: yes/no decisions as to whether something is legal or illegal, right or wrong within the terms of law's own discourse. Around this characteristic form of legal communications, a whole apparatus of distinctive concepts and modes of reasoning develops (Luhmann 1988b: 340–1).

The legal system as a system of communication in this specific sense is, in Luhmann's often repeated formula, cognitively open but normatively closed (Luhmann 1985: 283; 1986: 113–4). In part, what this means is that law as a communication system is open to cognitive input in the sense that it can, and does, routinely recognise and respond to economic, scientific, political or other events or phenomena. But it can only 'observe' its environment in relation to its *own* categories of evaluation and interpretation. The system is normatively closed in the sense that it can, and does, operate only with its own imperatives as a system of communication, centred specifically on the differentiation of right and wrong, legality and illegality. It adopts always its own normative criteria which in themselves owe nothing to its environment. To this extent it neither receives input from external sources, nor directly provides output to them. Law's responses are not to an environment that in some way impacts directly on it, but to an environment that law itself constructs intellectually in its own terms and understands in terms of its own communicative criteria. Equally, insofar as law has a product this can be considered to be strictly only decisions about legality, not, for example, infusions of efficiency or revelations of truth.

It will be necessary to return to this important line of modern theory in later chapters. For the moment it is enough to note the direct relevance of the general thrust of autopoiesis theory for the considerations of relationships between legal and social change introduced in this chapter. The essential point seems to be that law as a system cannot operate to provide direct outputs to steer economic life or any other part of social life in any simple manner because direct communications are possible only *within* communication systems and not between them. The fundamental sociological idea underpinning legal autopoiesis theory seems to be that modern societies are characterised by increasing complexity which leads to, or is responded to by, the differentiation of distinct communication systems within social life. Thus, economic calculation—in terms of efficiency—is ultimately quite different from legal discourse, or scientific discourse. These different forms of communication can be thought of as inhabiting their own systems, which are self-referential in the sense of being maintained not by inputs from their environment but through the specific discursive criteria that they endlessly reproduce. Hence, for adherents of autopoiesis theory it is no surprise that law seems relatively unsuccessful when it is employed to steer an economy in some direct fashion, or when it is entrusted with the realisation of intricate policy programmes. An economic system, for example, can 'observe' legal decisions as part of *its* environment, but it too will respond in terms of its *own* self-referential system criteria.

In practical terms, this kind of theoretical view of law leads to suggestions that efforts to use law to engineer social development in direct ways should be largely discarded. Instead, law should produce regulatory signals to which various spheres, or sub-systems within social life, can respond in terms of their own criteria of understanding and evaluation. In other words, law should encourage and help to frame self-regulation of the various social spheres that make up complex modern societies; for example, industrial relations, corporate structures, trade practice, or family life and social welfare (cf. Teubner, ed, 1987). The primary theoretical problem then becomes one of examining the most effective means of influence that can be achieved from law's primary product—its decisions on right and wrong, legality or illegality, after it has been clearly recognised that the problem of the relationship of legal and social change can no longer be considered in terms of inputs and outputs of control between law and society (Teubner 1986).

In what sense is this a *sociological* theory, or indeed a contribution to the sociology of law? It plainly inhabits an extremely high level of abstraction and, as has been noted, it depends on biological analogies rather than a direct development of social theory. Autopoiesis theory is highly suggestive in offering a rigorous means of conceptualising a radical autonomy of law and a particular image of the character of legal discourse in conditions of great social complexity. It challenges researchers to examine theoretically the complex ways in which legal change can relate to—or, indeed, seem to lack clear relation to—change in various spheres of social life that the law 'observes'. And the theory has, indeed, already been used in Britain to illuminate the way legal discourse confronts, and often seems to misinterpret or distort, the discourses of child welfare presented to courts in child abuse, child custody and juvenile crime cases (King and Piper 1990).

Ultimately, however, it seems to this writer to offer—as Teubner, its most eloquent advocate, has admitted—'a strictly heuristic device' (Teubner 1988b: 2), at the present time. If treated as more than this—as a framework for empirical explanation of the situation of law in society—it may be, in one way, opposed to the most productive tendencies of sociology of law, for it does threaten to reify law, treating it as a system with a life of its own irrespective of the social forces and social interests that are represented and pursued through legal institutions and processes. Autopoiesis theory encourages us to examine 'how the law thinks'

(Teubner 1989), emphasising that its communication system has an existence and capacity for self-renewal independent of the motives and interests of those who work with, seek to influence, produce or avoid, or are objects of legal communications. But sociology of law should, in my view, be concerned always with how *people* think and act, within complex patterns of freedom and constraint. It should understand legal doctrine and discourse always in terms of the interests and motivations of such people. And it certainly has the resources to examine the powerful constraints within which they think and act. It can do this, for example, by building on existing literature on the character of organisations and institutions (such as courts, regulatory agencies, professions, or police: see Chapters 6 to 8, below) and on the nature of ideology (see especially Chapter 4). On this basis it may be possible, as later chapters will suggest, to provide convincing explanations of many specific kinds of regulatory failures without conceptualising law's confrontations with its environment in the stark and seemingly permanently pessimistic terms of autopoiesis theory (cf. Rottleuthner 1989).

If we avoid reifying law and focus on the elites that shape the content of legal doctrine and legal communications important questions then arise. For example, what influences the actions of legislative elites? What conditions are of major significance in determining whether, when and how law is used to promote or resist change? Is the law created best considered as an expression of general social needs, of the self-interest of those holding the reins of power, or of social or economic forces that constrain the legislators' decisions as much as they constrain those of ordinary citizens? In terms of the practical concerns of law and social change studies and legal impact studies these are important questions. They have direct significance for the immediate aspirations of law reformers as well as those who seek to resist particular changes in the law; for those who seek more rational social policy no less than those who distrust all social planning.

Study of the effects of 'law' on 'society' cannot therefore be isolated from theoretical analysis of the nature of law in society. The autonomy of law, so apparent in contemporary Western societies, is of a different character from the simple instrumental independence often assumed in law and social change studies. A full analysis of law must take account of both its reality as an agency of government, emphasised by many of the studies discussed in this chapter, and its dependence on social and cultural conditions beyond its control. The autonomy of law arises from the character of the society in which law exists. The nature and limits of that autonomy cannot be understood except by analysing law as an aspect of society—in other words, in terms of a social theory of law.

Consequently, in the chapters that follow, some insights of social theory will be considered insofar as they are directly relevant to analysis of patterns of legal change and to any attempt to understand the nature of law in contemporary Western societies. But a warning is in order. No theory provides a magic key to understanding (though the temptation to treat theory as dogma or ideology is often strong). Scientific method was characterised in the introduction to this book as the continuous attempt to create knowledge that transcends partial perspectives. Theories merely make explicit the logical and empirical implications of particular perspectives on law and society. Yet by doing so they provide a necessary step to further advance, towards the transcending of the particular perspective they reflect. For this reason the development of legal theory as a special form of social theory is an inevitably unfinished yet always necessary task.

3 Law as an Integrative Mechanism

Any study that attempts to relate law to social change or to assess the 'impact' of law on 'society' presupposes—even if it does not make explicit—a particular view of the nature of law and a particular view of the nature of society. 'Each sociologist carries in his head one or more "models" of society and man which greatly influence what he looks for, what he sees, and what he does with his observations by way of fitting them along with other facts, into a larger scheme of explanation. In this respect the sociologist is no different from any other scientist' (quoted in Chambliss 1973: 2). Only when such models are made explicit can the assumptions they contain be examined. The significance of empirical findings can be looked at carefully in the light of such an examination. Only in such a way can knowledge of law in society progress.

Lawyers also tend to have definite views, reinforced and refined through a long tradition of legal philosophy, about law's contribution to the society in which it exists. Law promotes justice. But justice has many meanings and it often remains undefined. Law is often seen as promoting social welfare—again, in many definitions—or, in utilitarian terms, as balancing conflicting individual claims and interests. In an important body of speculative theory from the seventeenth-century writings of the philosopher Thomas Hobbes to the present, law appears as the embodiment and guarantee of a 'social contract'—a notional agreement of members of a society living together, under which elements of individual freedom are mutually relinquished in the interests of collective peace and good order. In fact Hobbes' 'problem of order'—the problem of explaining the conditions under which individuals are prepared to accept constraints on their freedom in order to live as members of a cohesive society—is fundamental to the concerns of this chapter. The 'problem of order' is the problem of explaining what gives politically organised societies (such as those of modern nation states)—or, for that matter, systems of social relations within or extending beyond such societies—sufficient cohesion to make it possible to think of them as entities. Only if this can be done are the concepts of social order and social change meaningful in sociological analysis of law.

The concern of this chapter is with ways in which modern Western societies have been theoretically portrayed as cohesive entities and, specifically, with ways in which law has been seen in this theory as expressing this cohesion and playing a significant part in guaranteeing it.

Function and Purpose in Law

In many jurisprudential writings the social objectives to which law is seen to be directed are often expressed *ex cathedra* as morally necessary purposes. These writings tend to confuse what law does with what it is thought it ought to do. They tend to confuse the concepts of *function* and *purpose.* So critics complain of a 'naive instrumentalism' (Summers 1977) of much writing on law which, it is claimed, assumes that all laws have specific purposes against which their effectiveness can be measured. In fact, their purposes may be seen differently at different times and they may exist for reasons quite different from those contained in explicit legislative or judicial justifications. Further, many laws may have no discernible purpose (Timasheff 1939: 339), existing perhaps only, for example, because of tradition, legislative inertia, or the need to compromise radically different purposes of interest groups. The purpose of the Statute of Frauds is historically located in the motivations of the English legislators who enacted it in 1677. The *function* of the Statute, in sociological terms, is, however, a very different matter, not dependent on the will of its creators but on its present contribution to the maintenance of existing social and economic institutions. So the function of the law may have no relation at all to the original purpose for which the Statute was passed. Social or legal institutions may, therefore, have significant functions—perhaps quite different from those generally recognised even by people directly concerned with their maintenance—which derive from their position as elements of a wider social system, such as a cohesive society.[1] Their functions can be understood as their contribution to stability or change in this wider system. The concept of 'system' itself presupposes a degree of integration of elements within a larger whole.

Functional analysis in this sense is not directly concerned with the historical causes or origins of social phenomena. This is implicit in what has already been said about the distinction between purpose and function. The historical origins of the English doctrine of estates or of the jury system are totally different objects of inquiry from their present social, economic or political functions. On the other hand, functions themselves can be seen to change over time. A monarchy which once provided

1 Here the term 'system' is taken in a broad sense (implying patterned interactions and relationships that constitute social life), rather than, for example, in the specific sense adopted in autopoiesis theory where, as noted at the end of the previous chapter, it refers to the highly abstract notion of a system of communication.

political and military leadership may come to fulfil purely symbolic or ideological functions. Elements once functional may become 'dysfunctional'—detrimental to the cohesive functioning of a social system—and vice versa. Systems change their character historically, but it is assumed that they can be analysed—as systems—in terms of the functional relationships of their component elements at a particular time. Analysis of tensions in functional relationships can provide a basis for explanations of social change.

When an attempt is made to analyse the relations of the 'part' (for example, a legal system) to the 'whole' (for example, the society in which it exists) the analysis can proceed in one of two directions. It can develop a theoretical analysis of a particular politically organised society, such as that of Britain or the United States, or perhaps of societies in general—elaborating the conditions that make it possible for a society to exist as a cohesive entity and finally relating law to these specified functional requirements. Otherwise it can start by looking at the detail of law itself in particular legal systems or phases of legal history and trying to extrapolate, from a study of legal doctrine and legal institutions, insights into law's functions in society and into the nature of that society itself. Each kind of inquiry needs the other. The method of functional analysis implies the need for a continual shuttling between detailed study of relationships between particular narrowly defined social phenomena and the broadest overall view of the manner in which and the extent to which large-scale patterns of social arrangements are integrated into the complex unity of a society.

The description of society as 'a complex unity' and of the 'integration' of elements within it suggests that functional analysis is more than a sociological method. It has often been claimed to imply or entail also a particular outlook on society: the idea that contemporary Western societies, as examples of comparatively stable societies, are best understood as relatively cohesive, integrated systems or structures; that, despite friction, tensions, failures of co-ordination or co-operation within them which may often pose serious problems, they are in essence founded on consensus, not conflict and repression as, for example, the Marxist analysts to be considered in the next chapter claim. Thus in the pages that follow four authors—Pound, Durkheim, Llewellyn and Parsons—are taken as illustrative of various kinds of functional analysis of law. At the same time, despite important differences in approach, each of them offers a conception of law as an integrative mechanism; a means of dealing with the tensions and frictions that threaten the basically cohesive nature of society. A primary concern of the discussion that follows will be to elaborate major implications of this view of law and to examine how far it is dictated by the basic premises of functional analysis.

A Law-centred Conception of Social Cohesion: Pound

The theoretical writings of the American legal scholar Roscoe Pound, developed throughout the first half of the twentieth century, provide a convenient starting place. In them, the functions of law—and the mode of their fulfilment—are deduced primarily from a rationalisation of legal rules and principles, especially from Anglo-American common law. Pound tried systematically to interpret legal doctrine and institutions in functional terms; to replace the lawyer's conception of the logical unity of the law with a conception of its functional unity.

In Pound's analysis the modern lawyer's and legislator's concern is 'social engineering'. Law secures social cohesion and orderly social change by balancing conflicting interests—individual (the private interests of individual citizens), social (arising from the common conditions of social life) and public (specifically the interests of the state). These interests are made visible to lawmakers in the claims brought before courts and lobbied within legislatures (in his early writings Pound advocated social scientific research to identify interests but later rejected this as impracticable). New claims and new situations of conflict of interests (particularly of social interests) are the raw materials that courts and legislatures must work on to transform the turmoil of social change into the order of social engineering through legal regulation. Legal doctrine—established rules, principles, precedents—records the interests that have been successfully pressed upon the law for recognition and protection, as well as those that have been rejected. It records the extent of recognition and the ways in which particular kinds of interest have been balanced when they come into conflict. In a massive survey and distillation of Anglo-American legal doctrine Pound provides an inventory of interests, a kind of handbook of the law's established policy concerns and precedents for conflict resolution.

Orderly social engineering through law requires that interests be balanced in a rational and consistent manner. For Pound, legal policy depends on the application of known values. But the values law applies in its integration of conflicting claims are specifically legal, derived from the particular experience of the legal system and society in which they arise. They cannot be universal or timeless. They are specific to a particular society and its law at a particular moment in its history. Pound calls these legal values the 'jural postulates' of the time and place. Just as the scheme of established interests is drawn from legal doctrine, so the jural postulates are distilled from the value implications of the overall scheme of interests already recognised by the law.

In Pound's work, the assumption that the basic condition of Anglo-American society is one of harmony and fundamental consensus is clear enough. But this remains an unexplained assumption since there is, for all Pound's often proclaimed sociological sympathies, no systematic sociology in his legal theory. The inward-looking character of the theory is apparent. All its components ultimately derive from legal doctrine. New elements are seen as entering the legal system with the doctrinal recognition of new interests. Otherwise changes in the situations in which interest claims are made promote changes in the extent to which interests are protected by law or in the manner in which they are balanced against others. The theory offers no explanation of such changes nor any guidance in interpreting them. Legal values change but only slowly as new doctrine gradually alters the scheme of interests and hence, even more gradually, the jural postulates which can be deduced from it. The legal system—and in particular the body of legal doctrine—thus appears as a great inertia system continually limiting and sifting pressures and demands for change and, itself, turning gradually—almost imperceptibly—like a great ship perpetually buffeted by small waves. In Pound's theory the relationship between legal values and social values is not made clear. It can be assumed that social values influence and are influenced by the kinds of claims being pressed upon the law. But it seems that the jural postulates derive their content from incremental, professionally managed change in the legal processes they largely control, not from anything happening in the wider society. Law as a functional system is imbued with specifically professional values. Yet it often appears that for Pound—although he is never explicit in making the claim—these professional values of the law are the values of society, the values on which social cohesion is built.

Pound's theory is also pre-eminently a theory of the common law (Cotterrell 1989: ch 6). The jural postulates are the values of judge-made law. What considerations control legislative innovation? Pound offers no answer. But law is seen as a neutral mechanism holding the balance between all individual, social and public claims. It must represent a general consensus. Adapting Pound's terminology, it must correspond to a pre-eminent general social interest in the orderly resolution of conflicts and an individual interest of each citizen in having access to a forum for assertion and adjudication of his claims. The theory presupposes a modern representative democracy. Pound's discussion of the function of law in various historical phases and different kinds of societies makes clear that what he sees as the use of law to express a social consensus may be a very recent phenomenon. In earlier phases of legal history, he claims, law does not exist to balance interests but merely to keep the peace or to preserve a given status quo or to provide maximum freedom for enterprise for those fortunate enough to be able to take advantage of it (Pound 1954: 33–42). Pound clearly recognises that social order and the use of law to guarantee it can be less a matter of value consensus and 'balancing' than of repression and coercion. But these, it appears, are matters of history and conditions only of less fortunate societies. Furthermore, Pound's failure to distinguish purpose and function in his discussions is such that it is never very clear whether his description of the balancing processes of modern Western law (in the courts, in the legislature) is a representation—hard to reconcile with experience—of what actually goes on, or a prescription of the way the legal system *should* function if it is to contribute properly to the cohesion of society.

Pound's work provides a warning against attempting to theorise about law's social effects and functions without serious sociological analysis, for his conclusions about law's functions in society are derived not from an examination of social conditions and the manner in which they may be affected by law, but from the official pronouncements of courts and legislators. Thus, they do not penetrate the rhetoric of the law to examine evidence of what law can and does achieve. Yet his theory does highlight several central concerns of major sociological theories of law as a mechanism of social cohesion: the relation of law to ultimate social values, the conception of law as a neutral agent of conflict management, and (in the uneasy and vague relations of Pound's individual and social interests) the problem of the relationship between individual autonomy and social cohesion. Further, it suggests that analysis of these matters may indicate important characteristics distinguishing modern Western industrialised societies from some other, particularly earlier, forms of society.

Law and Solidarity in Modern Society: Durkheim

If law is to be portrayed as a mechanism of social integration, a theory that explains both the nature of this integration and the conditions under which it can exist seems essential. In this respect the ideas on law and society of the French sociologist Emile Durkheim—whose late nineteenth and early twentieth-century writings form one of the major foundations of present day sociology—provide a means of grounding in social theory the assumptions about social cohesion implicit in Pound's work.

For Durkheim, as for Pound, analysis of legal doctrine provides a route towards an understanding of social cohesion. Society is, for Durkheim, a moral phenomenon. It is 'nothing more than the moral milieu that surrounds the individual' (Durkheim 1960: 367). Social cohesion depends on moral commitment to the collective welfare. Law is the visible 'index' of this invisible moral milieu, the different forms of law expressing different kinds of cohesion. Thus, *penal* or *repressive* law (which Durkheim identifies as aimed at punishment of the wrongdoer) expresses and guarantees what he calls mechanical solidarity—cohesion based on shared values and outlook among average members of the same society. In societies in which mechanical solidarity predominates, law and religion work side by side and are often undifferentiated, protecting and expressing the shared beliefs and ways of thought (*conscience collective*) that unite society and suppressing deviance from the common values. If a purely mechanically solidary society could exist there would be no place in it for individuality, for private rights or individual justice (cf. Miller 1976: 257–72). The individual would be wholly merged in society. What Durkheim calls *restitutive* or *co-operative* law (typified by contract law in its modern Western forms) is concerned not primarily with punishment but with compensation or the restoration of the status quo between parties in conflict. It reflects and guarantees a different kind of social cohesion which Durkheim terms organic solidarity. This solidarity is not based on uniformity of values and outlook among members of a society, but on functional interdependence of differentiated groups in society and specialised occupational or social roles of individual members (Durkheim 1984).

Many social theorists of the nineteenth century sought to characterise the features of what they termed 'modern society' and which was epitomised by the Western industrialised societies of their time. For Durkheim these societies are characterised by a preponderance of organic rather than mechanical solidarity, though all societies combine both types in some measure. In these 'modern' societies the division of labour—the differentiation of occupational roles and functions among members of a society which progresses as a result of population growth and increase in social interaction through travel and trade—is particularly highly developed. Consequently cohesion can no longer be based primarily on identity and uniformity. Different occupational groups, social classes, professions and so on, adopt different outlooks. Different experience and different roles and social positions foster different attitudes, social values and forms of knowledge. Presumably, in Durkheim's understanding, the process is one way. The division of labour can only become more complex, more intense, more specialised. It follows that the role of uniform social values in securing social cohesion through their direct expression and elaboration in law and morality can only become more problematic. In place of one morality and one social outlook there are many. Modern societies are pluralistic. Yet they are also characterised by centralised political power (the modern state) and by legal systems laying down a society-wide code of behaviour.

Durkheim's primary contribution to the analysis of law as an integrative mechanism in society lies in his attempt to reconcile the apparent absence of universal shared values as the basis of cohesion in modern societies with the belief that society is a cohesive system of moral regulation and that law is, in contemporary secular societies, the primary expression and support of this moral system. Durkheim argues against the view (for example, of Comte and Marx) that the consequence of intensification of the division of labour must be increased fragmentation of societies and social conflict (cf. Durkheim 1984: 301). But neither are these societies naturally balanced and integrated by the unfettered interplay of self-interested individual wills. Durkheim writes that a 'contract is not sufficient by itself, but is only possible because of the regulation of contracts which is of social origin' (1984: 162). Today self-interest makes me your friend; tomorrow it may make me your enemy. The fulfilment of individual self-interest through contractual agreements depends on the existence of stable legal and moral principles governing the conditions under which bargains can be made and enforced (1984: 301–2). Without a pre-existing moral milieu expressed in the law, Durkheim claims, social relations could have no permanence or predictability. Social solidarity would be impossible.

The image of modern societies which we can construct from Durkheim's writings is one in which social cohesion is always problematic, yet possible. The all-embracing shared social values of earlier societies no longer exist. Criminal law—the basic though not exclusive form of penal law—still expresses and protects the residue of the *conscience collective*. But this is reduced, more and more, to a single principle: respect for the human dignity of the individual. Thus punishment of crime remains, as in earlier times or other societies, a public condemnation of the wrongdoer for breaking the common social code. In modern conditions, however, this condemnation is informed by a strongly individualistic morality which is the only generally shared system of beliefs available to ensure a moral unity of society (cf. Durkheim 1969: 66).[2]

No other shared values guarantee social solidarity and it might be said that individualism, as such, emphasises the separateness of society's members rather than their moral cohesion. Durkheim argues that the regulatory problems of modern societies require forms of law (primarily restitutive) that can provide a suitable framework for the natural development of the division of labour. In his own time administrative regulation was beginning to assume the complex forms familiar in Western societies in the late twentieth century. But the demands put upon such regulation are great. Commercial failures and industrial relations

2 Although Durkheim never makes the point, his analysis of criminal law can be used to ground an explanation of the distinction in popular consciousness between 'real crime' (protecting individuals as such) and regulatory offences concerned, for example, with the protection of public health or public resources (cf. Seagle 1941: ch 16; and see Chapter 8).

breakdowns are characteristic of what Durkheim calls an anomic division of labour (Durkheim 1984: 291ff.). These breakdowns reveal *anomie,* a lack of the normative regulation necessary to ensure social integration. They are often caused, Durkheim explains, by failures of communication, lack of appreciation by those involved of the conditions of functional interdependence, class prejudice, insensitive or inappropriate law, and irrationality arising from frustration. Conversely, arbitrary allocation of advantages and disadvantages, especially through inherited wealth and reservation of occupations for those of particular classes or races, is characteristic of what Durkheim calls a forced division of labour: a situation of *over*-regulation which stifles spontaneous development (1984: 310ff.).

For Durkheim law and morality are inseparable. Without moral commitment to support it law is not part of society but mere words written on official paper—barren and socially irrelevant (Durkheim 1982: 233). In modern society the state is too distant from the innumerable continuously changing relationships it seeks to regulate. Moral commitment and attitudes develop from these relationships. Yet law is created in the often ignorant isolation of high-level decision-making of the state. The enduring problem of regulation in the modern state—less a Leviathan than an often helpless, clumsy and inadequate regulator—is to bridge this gap between the local moral conditions of organic solidarity and the uniform society-wide system of state-created law. The problem is, of course, one that was seen in Chapter 1 to be central to Ehrlich's sociology of law. Yet in Durkheim's work, the relationship between state law and living law is presented in the context of a comprehensive theory of social order and cohesion.

The problem of the 'gap' between state and citizen, between centralised social co-ordination and spontaneous co-operation, between political domination and community solidarity, between technical legal regulation and moral commitment remains unsolved in Durkheim's writing. Indeed it remains a central problem of the sociology of law today. It is no small tribute to Durkheim's perceptiveness that his writings here, as elsewhere, address issues of continuing central relevance. He discusses the importance of intermediate groups standing between the individual and the state, the delegation of law-making functions to professional or occupational groups or other functionally identifiable elements of society, the need to remove impediments to occupational mobility and to replace the lost absolutes of religion which in past times made social solidarity less problematic. What is missing above all, however, is an adequate analysis of power relations in society, a problem which dogs social integration theory and, as will be seen in the next chapter, has given rise to different theoretical approaches.

Universal Functions of Law?: Llewellyn

It appears that to analyse the functions of law in contemporary societies it is necessary to develop a fully elaborated theory of the nature of such societies, or at least assume one. But could this problem be avoided by demonstrating that law has certain universal functions to perform in any society, ancient or modern, simple or complex; that it has a functional 'essence' not dependent on particular, perhaps controversial, characterisations of particular types of society?

Some of the consequences of such an inquiry are illustrated in the 'law-jobs' conception of the American legal scholar Karl Llewellyn. If all questions of the relevance for law of particular state forms, political systems and cultural conditions are to be set aside on the assumption that law may have functions that exist independently of these conditions, then the 'pure' regulatory needs of a society may not be fundamentally different from those of any stable group existing within the society. In an insight clearly related to Ehrlich's conception of numerous associations within a society, each having its own system of legal regulation, Llewellyn suggests that the 'law'—the framework of normative regulation—of any group (not merely a society, but also a family, a partnership, even a group of children at play) has constant basic functions (Llewellyn 1940). Llewellyn's aim in discarding (temporarily) the lawyer's concept of law as state law is not, as with Ehrlich, merely a polemical one. His idea is that by broadening the concept of law in this way for a specific analytical purpose we may be able to understand better the functions of law—in the usual sense of state law—and to compare radically different forms of law in functional terms.

On this basis four law-jobs, or basic functions of law, can be identified. Llewellyn considers the disposition of 'trouble-cases'—orderly resolution of disputes as they arise—to be pre-eminent. The second function of law is what he calls preventive channelling and reorientation of conduct and expectations to avoid conflict. Appropriate forms of social relations (for example, property relations) need specification and protection to minimise future friction. The third law-job is the allocation of authority in the group and fourth is what Llewellyn calls 'net drive'—the organisation and harmonisation of activity within the group to provide direction and incentive to its members. The law-jobs are claimed to be deductions from and rationalisations of observable patterns of behaviour in stable groups of any kind.

Llewellyn does not explain the relation between the law-jobs, other than to point out that the first—dispute resolution—continually throws up material for fulfilment of the others. Is the pre-eminence of trouble-case disposition theoretically necessary or merely an empirical inference influenced by the centrality of the judge in the common law system? As with Pound, common law bias may well enter the picture.

Law's relation with social stability and change and social values is also somewhat ambiguous. The law-jobs are said to have 'bare bones' and 'questing' aspects, which simply means that they may be fulfilled to a minimum for group survival or elevated to a proud craft. In this, 'juristic method'—that is, the techniques developed in a particular group or society to fulfil the law-jobs—is central. The fourth law-job, however, appears to relate law to development or fulfilment of specific group goals or maintenance of values. Significantly one commentator interprets Llewellyn's 'net drive' as 'goal attainment', a group being two or more persons associated for achievement of common goals (Hartzler 1976: 78). Another, however, sees this function merely as the need to adapt group life to its environment and considers that only with the (perhaps desirable but not sociologically necessary) 'questing' aspect added to the law-jobs are they actively concerned with promoting basic values of society through law (Hoebel 1954: 275, 281). Consequently, because of Llewellyn's perhaps deliberate ambiguity, law's relation to social values is problematic, just as it is consciously and explicitly shown to be in Durkheim's analysis of social solidarity.

Law appears neither conservative nor progressive in Llewellyn's functional conception. It is simply the regulatory aspect of group life. The dynamo of legal life is the group, but no particular aspect of group life—or of society—has precedence over any other in determining change or stability. Law merely reacts to system needs. The very high level of abstraction of the law-jobs conception is the price paid for its universality; its applicability as a general framework for functional analysis of law in all times and places. How the jobs are fulfilled is not theoretically in issue—this is a matter for empirical study and, as with Pound, professionalism is assumed to have a key role—but Llewellyn makes clear that in any group or society the law-jobs must be fulfilled. Law, therefore, has a functionally defined place in *every* society. Whatever the political or economic conditions, it constitutes, according to this view, an irreducible minimum of regulation. Law's functions can be specified theoretically before considering the way they are fulfilled in the political, economic and social conditions of particular societies.

Social System and Social Structure: Parsons

Llewellyn's analysis is wholly in tune with the major tradition of functional analysis in sociology, with its tendency to abstract classification and its consistent search for irreducible functional relations. But it is in the monumental work of the American Talcott Parsons that this approach is taken to its most ambitious level, in a systems-analysis of societies that represents one of the most important twentieth-century contributions to sociological theory. Its importance for the sociological study of law is that Parsons' analysis makes possible a clear specification of law's location within this comprehensive picture of relationships between functional elements in social systems.

Functional Requisites of Social Systems

For Parsons a society is only one kind of social system ('group' in Llewellyn's sense). Others may be wider in territorial scope (for example, the Roman Catholic Church), or more restricted (for example, a local or business community). All social systems have similar 'system needs' or functional requisites which must be met if they are to survive. But Llewellyn's universal law-jobs (apart perhaps from the ambiguous 'net drive') correspond to only *one* of the four functional requisites of social systems that Parsons identifies. This particular functional requisite is internal *integration* of the system—maintaining appropriate social and emotional relations between members of the system; in Durkheim's sense, creating and maintaining solidarity. Like Durkheim and Llewellyn, Parsons recognises this system need as the one that law most directly serves in a society. Yet there are three other equally important problems to be solved in all kinds of social system. They are *goal attainment*—keeping the system moving steadily towards its goals whatever they may be; *pattern maintenance* (or latency, as Parsons sometimes calls it)—creating, maintaining and restoring the energies, motives and values of system members so that the overall pattern of activity and energy in the system is continually reproduced; and *adaptation* of the system to the broad conditions of its environment including its physical environment.

As with Llewellyn's law-jobs conception, Parsons' four functional requisites of social systems provide only an abstract analytical scheme. In itself the four-way analytical division of functions says nothing about the way particular societies are organised. There is no theoretical necessity for particular specialised agencies, institutions or sub-systems to exist to fulfil each of the functional requisites. Nevertheless Parsons claims that contemporary Western industrialised societies are, for reasons we shall examine, characterised by a particularly high degree of separation of these four functions within analytically distinct *sub-systems* of society. Thus the 'polity' or political system corresponds with the goal attainment function; the 'economy' as a sub-system of society corresponds with the function of adaptation. The other sub-systems are less clearly defined. Parsons calls the integrative sub-system, concerned with citizenship and social solidarity and with which law has a special connection, the 'societal community'. Further, the family as a social institution plays a major part in pattern maintenance, for example through the inculcation of social values in the young. In general, pattern maintenance is the special task of the numerous processes of influence and education (usually termed socialisation processes in the literature of functional analysis) by which the attitudes and outlook of individuals are shaped to conform to established social values and expectations.

Normative Structure

Societies can thus be analysed in terms of the way the functional requisites are met. But they can also be analysed in terms of their *normative structure*. In Parsons' analysis this structure consists of four hierarchically ordered elements: values, norms, collectivities and roles. A society's *values* are 'conceptions of the desirable society ... held in common by its members' (Parsons 1960b: 8). Insofar as they are seen to be embodied in social institutions they become part of the regulatory structure of the society as a social system. More generally they legitimise the system—that is, they provide ultimate justification for it in the eyes of members of the society. The existence of shared values as the basis of social cohesion in modern Western societies—the central problem with which Durkheim wrestled—is simply accepted as a postulate in Parsons' theory. Societal *norms* (of which law in the lawyer's sense constitutes the most important category) are the application of these fundamental values to the special conditions of functionally differentiated groups or sub-systems within the society. So they are specific with regard to the kinds of situations they regulate whereas values make no such situation reference. At a still more concrete level particular *collectivities* define patterns of required action in a *specific* situation (for example, within the state bureaucracy or a particular business firm, school, hospital or family) and individual *roles* are the normative expectations attaching to actions of particular individuals as members of collectivities.

Although these appear wholly static elements of structure they are essential to Parsons' explanations of social change. Values exert control over the content of norms, norms control collectivities, collectivities determine roles. Control 'flows' down the hierarchy of normative structure from values through norms, through collectivities, to roles; and the 'downward flow of normative content serves to stabilize the system and to limit the forms and processes of change within broad limits' (Mayhew 1971: 189). But the lower levels of the hierarchy have to reflect changing social experience more directly than the higher levels. At the base of the structural hierarchy, roles must accurately reflect the pressure of day-to-day life in the community, at home, at work. Thus individual roles (for example, particular jobs and their conditions) change rapidly, collectivities (for example, the structure of a particular business firm or industry) less so, norms (for example, industrial relations laws) even less and values (for example, fundamental conceptions of social justice) least of all. Thus in Parsons' conception, *conditioning*, moving upwards through the hierarchy, creates pressures for change to respond to demands and tensions, while *control*, moving down it, promotes stability. Social order and change are the result of continuous 'negotiation' and neutralisation of these opposite pressures through constant adjustments of normative content occurring at various levels in the hierarchy of values, norms, collectivities and roles.

The Autonomy of Law in Western Society

To understand the place of law in Parsons' theory it is necessary to realise the link between the normative structure of values, norms, collectivities and roles and the functional requisites of adaptation, integration, goal attainment and pattern maintenance. In modern Western societies (unlike many other and earlier societies) not only are functional sub-systems (economy, polity, etc.) highly differentiated but so also are the elements of normative structure. Law, as indicated above, is particularly associated with the integrative function and with a specific level of normative structure—that of societal norms. To the extent that the separation of functional tasks and elements of normative structure takes place in certain societies, so law becomes separated from other aspects of society. Thus the autonomous legal system characteristic of Western societies is the result of functional specialisation together with the emergence of societal norms as a *distinct* element of normative structure.

Also, this process of functional and normative differentiation in modern Western societies is such that the four levels of normative structure closely correspond with the four functional sub-systems. So norms are identified as the structural component of the 'societal community', roles are the corresponding element in the 'economy', collectivities in the 'polity', and values in the pattern maintenance sub-system. It follows that in the hierarchy of control and conditioning determined by the normative structure, conditioning pressures for change are felt most strongly in the economy, are next reflected in the polity in administrative planning and organisation, less so in the societal community at the level of legal norms and least of all in the pattern maintenance system at the level of societal values. Thus roles may change rapidly but values only very slowly. It follows also that law ultimately reflects and depends on the society's shared values, but at the same time in Western societies it normatively controls the *forms* of both economic and political action. The 'rule of law' prevails.

Finally, the clear separation of elements of normative structure in these societies explains the characteristic form of Western law. It is typically *general* in application rather than particularistic (norms and collectivities are distinct). By contrast, in systems of regulation in some other kinds of society law is relatively undifferentiated from administration and direct political planning and control. Western law is *secular* and strongly shaped by *formal* requirements as well as by particular substantive aims (though law derives from values it exists at a distinct level apart from them; its function is not to enforce a shared morality but to foster organic solidarity in Durkheim's sense). By contrast, in religious legal systems law is often merged with societal values derived from religious doctrine. Further, since Western law is located analytically in a different sub-system from the polity, it is seen as analytically and functionally separate from—though closely interrelated with—politics. There is in Western societies 'a relative independence of the judiciary from both executive and legislative organs of the state' (Parsons 1960a: 144).

Why has this differentiation of social elements occurred to such an extent in these societies? Parsons' argument seems merely a special application at the most general and abstract level of Durkheim's ideas on the consequences of intensification of the division of labour (that is, functional specialisation) in modern society. In complex Western societies functional specialisation has been both a prerequisite of and a consequence of high levels of economic, social and political development. Following Durkheim's conception of organic solidarity, greater functional differentiation has to be accompanied by greater *interdependence* between the various sectors of the social system fulfilling these functions. For example, although characteristically in Western societies the economy and the political system are seen as separate functional spheres, their relationship is necessarily one of close functional interdependence. Law is seen as having played and as still playing a vital part in securing this sub-system differentiation. Economy and polity are kept functionally separate and at the same time intimately interdependent primarily through the existence of the relatively distinct societal community—the system of social solidarity based on the bond of equal citizenship of members of the community. Consequently the legal foundation of this societal community, what Parsons calls a 'general legal system'—cutting across all traditional special statuses and providing a universal system of rights and obligations independent of kin or locality allegiances—is 'the most important single hallmark of modern society' (Parsons 1964: 353).

The strength of Parsons' analysis is in showing that what appears in Western societies as the substantial *autonomy* of law and the legal system is a finely balanced and inevitably precarious condition rooted in complex sociological factors touching most important aspects of social life. Law too closely merged with values (for example, religious principles) or reduced to particularistic political administration and direction cannot maintain the substantially autonomous societal community, hence cannot maintain law's own autonomy within the social structure, and the fine balance of political and economic life. Law's function is not so much social integration as *system* integration, the holding together of an increasingly complex social system based on ties of interdependence between elements in that society. Hence, in recognising the complex differentiations—functional and structural—in modern societies, Parsons goes well beyond Durkheim. Nevertheless, some recent systems theory, building to an extent on Parsons' insights (Luhmann 1982: ch 3), has so strongly emphasised system differentiation as a response to complexity that it has even discarded altogether the idea of integration between or by means of sub-systems within society. Instead, as noted in Chapter 2, autopoiesis theory has adopted the radical position that differentiated systems such as those of law, economy or science, considered as systems of communication, merely observe, as more or less autonomous spheres of interpretation, evaluation and decision, the social environment in which they exist (e.g. Teubner, ed, 1988).

The most problematic element in Parsons' theory is the conception of societal values. How far shared values secure social cohesion in modern Western societies was the problem Durkheim could not solve and insofar as the problem dogs his writings it provides their critical thrust and keeps complacency at bay. Parsons' later writings can be interpreted as similarly recognising that value consensus, like all other elements of social order, is a problem to be solved rather than a fact to be assumed (Mayhew 1971). It is arguable, however, that his theoretical approach lacks the resources to explain adequately either the nature of shared beliefs as a basis of social order or the manner in which they are formed. Law flourishes, Parsons merely remarks, in societies where fundamental societal values are not in issue and (presumably because of this) enforcement problems are not too acute (Parsons 1962: 71). The existence of shared values tends to be offered in his writings as an adequate explanation of complex social conditions. These values provided the core of motivation for industrialisation in the West; today they underpin social order. This is reminiscent of Savigny's reliance on culture as an explanation of law, rather than as something to be explained. Understanding the nature and origin of the values that underlie law surely is a central problem for sociological analysis of law. By contrast, the soft core of complacency in Parsons' theory is that the creation and maintenance of consensus in contemporary Western societies tends to appear as a mechanical process of system adjustment and so hardly features as a pressing problem for analysis.

The Legal Profession and its Functions

The writings considered so far in this chapter develop, in very abstract form, an image of modern Western societies as relatively functionally cohesive and integrated. However, we can begin to penetrate behind these abstractions by looking at specific aspects of social organisation using the concepts and approach of functional theory. In one limited area of social organisation—that of the professions—their implications are particularly sharply clarified.

Professions, including the legal profession, occupy a specially important place in the picture of modern society typically presented by the theories of social integration considered in this chapter. For Durkheim professions are carriers of occupational morality—an essential regulatory structure which can bridge the gap between state-created laws and the actual conditions of social life. Thus, for him, a viable system of normative regulation to guarantee and express organic solidarity requires the extension of systems of professional ethics to cover all other spheres of life including, particularly, business life. For Pound and Llewellyn, too, the legal profession has a special role in social integration, fostering legal values and juristic method.

In Parsons' view, professions 'occupy a position of importance in our society … unique in history' (Parsons 1939: 34). The activities of the legal profession are 'one of the very important mechanisms by which a relative balance of stability is maintained in a dynamic and precariously balanced society' (Parsons 1954b: 385). Why should professionalism be of such central importance in these conceptions of society as a functionally integrated system? The essential reason is that, as David Miller has pointed out in another context, the self-image of professions—their proclaimed ideal of public service and professional responsibility—matches the conception of modern society organised in terms of organic solidarity or, in Parsons' terms, functional differentiation and reintegration. Professionalism stresses 'functional specialisation, expertise and selection by merit' (Miller 1976: 305).

In functional analysis the professional ideal of public service, even if it may become tarnished, is no sham. It is the price paid for professional autonomy, for the fact that the profession is entrusted with independent guardianship of an important part of the society's cultural tradition and allowed effectively to monopolise this knowledge as the basis of special expertise. Further, unlike the narrow conception of individual or group interest that characterises market relations and so business life, the public service orientation of the professional outlook is, in the view of both Durkheim and Parsons, appropriate to a society of increasingly complex functional differentiation and interdependence. The outlook that the professions at least claim to hold appears as the *necessary outlook of all citizens* in a society dependent for its cohesion and harmony on the most highly developed forms of organic solidarity. In this sense highly motivated professionals, imbued with specific values of public service maintained by the occupational morality of their organised profession, are central figures in promoting and supporting the cohesion of society, not only through the functions they perform but through the morality that their outlook represents. The theory implies an awesome responsibility of professions, to say the least.

In Parsons' analysis, the *legal* profession has the task of integrating the legal system to maintain the latter's authority and autonomy in fulfilling its functions outlined in the previous section. Among the profession's problems are those of maintaining the internal consistency of the system of legal doctrine, relating the law through interpretation to particular client situations, and balancing the goals of legislation as set by the state with particular client problems and situations and with the need for doctrinal consistency. It seems reasonable to suppose that treating the legal system as a social system and arranging its system problems in terms of the adaptation (A)—goal attainment (G)—integration (I)—pattern maintenance (L) scheme, they would appear more or less as in Figure 1 below.

FIGURE 1 **Functional Imperatives of a Legal System**

I		L
Integration of legal doctrine, practice and procedures in internally coherent doctrinal and institutional system	Maintenance of legal tradition and established values of legal profession and legal system	
Organisation of legal doctrine, practice and procedures to fulfil legislative goals	Satisfaction of client needs	
G		A

Within the legal profession, viewed in this way, there is today a significant and perhaps increasing differentiation of sub-system functions. Relatively autonomous university legal education, the development of numerous special forms of legal practice (for example, in law centres and in specialised fields of business and administration) and the proliferation of special tribunals and forms of administrative adjudication and regulation are developments having particular relevance to the L, A and G functions respectively. The problem for the legal system, as for any social system, is to maintain its integration (I) in the face of these tendencies to differentiation.

The analysis of professions provides a convenient illustration of one of the major weaknesses of functional analysis. In essence its method is to relate one set of observed social phenomena to another and explain each in terms of their mutual relations. But this is an approach that by its nature tends to concentrate on what appear as the positive effects of social phenomena—the way they appear 'from the outside' taken in conjunction with other phenomena—rather than on the complex and often contradictory processes at work *within* these observed social situations. Thus in sociological functional analysis the legal profession tends to be analysed in terms of the way it, like other professions, justifies itself within the wider society, not in terms of the complex internal processes and historical struggles that have shaped its present social position in various Western societies. Similarly Parsons' analysis of the functions of law takes at face value popular conceptions of Western law and never betrays any realisation of the complex and important transformations in the character of legal doctrine (for example, as regards the relation of rules and discretion and the concept of the 'rule of law' to be discussed in Chapter 5) that are familiar, if often puzzling, to the contemporary Western lawyer (cf. Parsons 1977: 148). None of this is to deny the insights a functional approach can offer, but merely to note that certain important matters tend to escape attention almost completely.

The Legal System as a Sub-System of Society

Parsons (1954b) admits that functional analysis of law may tend towards justification of established practices and that other methods may be necessary to bring into central focus the less praiseworthy aspects. But the claim made is that by showing what is 'normal' or predictable in terms of overall requirements of society conceived as a social system, the 'dysfunctional' becomes identifiable and can be analysed sociologically in value neutral terms, as well as criticised on other evaluative bases. The problem is in being sure that system needs are indeed as the theory claims them to be.

What is 'dysfunctional' is to be revealed by analysing actual empirical conditions in terms of the theoretically specified relationships between system functions. Parsons did not provide such an analysis of law's relations with other parts of the social system of society but an attempt by the American sociologist Harry Bredemeier to do so using Parsons' analytical framework (Bredemeier 1962) shows that functional analysis can certainly identify tension points in legal systems.

It must be noted that Bredemeier modifies Parsons' concepts in three ways. First, the legal system is treated as the integrative sub-system of society. Although for Bredemeier's purposes the identification is heuristically useful, it is an oversimplification which treats law as identical with societal norms in general. Secondly, the adaptive sub-system of modern society is treated as wider than the economy and refers to all problems of scientific or technological adaptation to the environment. Thirdly, Bredemeier seems to adopt Llewellyn's view that dispute resolution is the central element in law's integrative function so his analysis of law focuses on courts. On this basis the interaction between the legal system and the other sub-systems of society can be conceptualised as in Figure 2.

FIGURE 2 **The Legal System's Relations with Other Sub-systems of Society**

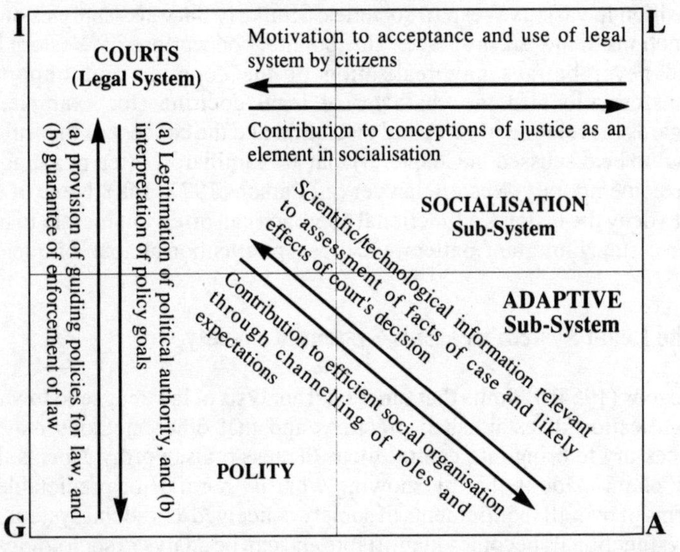

There is thus a system of 'exchanges' by which the interdependence of the four sub-systems is guaranteed. Law and the *political sub-system* (polity) are linked by the state's need for legitimacy based on the ideal of the rule of law and the need for legal elaboration of policy goals so that they can be interpreted and implemented in specific contexts. They are also linked by the legal system's need for policy guidance and a machinery of enforcement. Law contributes to *socialisation* of basic societal values by elaborating and applying conceptions of justice in the decision of cases. In turn it relies on citizens' socialisation to general acceptance of law and their willingness to call upon it. Law contributes to efficient social and economic organisation (Llewellyn's 'preventive channelling') in the *adaptive sub-system* and relies on inputs of general and special knowledge of the conditions and environment of social life without which rules or judicial decisions make no sense as guides to conduct and frameworks for future social relations.

In all these exchanges, as Bredemeier recognises, serious problems can and do arise. Legal decisions are often made with wholly inadequate knowledge of background social conditions and of the likely social effects of new rules or principles. In some courts, particularly in the United States, serious attempts have been made to use social scientific knowledge or social and economic statistics in deciding cases, but with controversial results (see Chapter 7). In Britain, resistance to explicit policy analysis in the courts tends to promote decision-making in a vacuum with legal rules taken in isolation from any serious assessment of their social significance. In addition, functional imbalance between legal and political systems may produce enforcement problems for law, judicial timidity in the face of government pressure, overt political interference and influence in the legal system, or judicial 'wrecking' of legislative policy. Further problems exist in the relationship between the legal and pattern maintenance (socialisation) systems. The tension between 'doing justice' and maintaining stability and predictability in the law seems endemic in the judicial role and is usually resolved in favour of stability and predictability when the choice has to be made. The development of concepts of equity, the use of legal fictions and the invocation of ideas of natural law have at various times been means of reducing this tension but its existence makes law's contribution to socialisation of basic values of justice problematic. Partly as a result, public acceptance of legal processes and involvement with them has typically been reluctant.

Law and Equal Opportunity: An Empirical Test of Parsonian Theory

Parsons' work represents one of the most unrelievedly abstract bodies of theory in sociology. It has, however, been used as a basis for detailed empirical research on law. One of the most instructive attempts to apply Parsons' ideas in research on legal institutions is a study carried out in the early 1960s by Leon Mayhew of the working and effects of the Massachusetts Commission Against Discrimination—a body charged with responsibility for implementing Massachusetts laws prohibiting racial discrimination in housing provision and employment (Mayhew 1968). Mayhew sought to assess how far the values reflected in the law had permeated community life, what factors of resistance to law had proved significant, what strategies the Commission had adopted and what factors determined its selection of strategies.

Mayhew's study uses Parsons' conception of the mechanisms of social change to avoid adopting either a negative view (such as Sumner's) of law's capacity to induce change or a view that assumes law can achieve any kind of change that might be sought. As discussed above, according to Parsons social change can be understood as the continuous 'negotiation' of opposite pressures ('control' and 'conditioning') for stability and change reflected in a society's normative structure of values, norms, collectivities and roles. In considering how law can influence race relations, the question to be asked is under what conditions can law institutionalise—that is, embody in established social practices and expectations—social values supporting racial harmony. What is the nature of the process of 'negotiation' of tensions between conditioning forces existing in everyday life—in the housing and job markets, for example—and controlling forces deriving from fundamental social values interpreted by a legislating elite and giving rise to anti-discrimination law?

Mayhew found that the law met 'a number of deeply entrenched structural obstacles' (1968: 258), and the activities of the Commission could be regarded as a compromise response to the opposite pressures from advocates of the legislative ideals and those with vested interests in maintaining existing patterns of discrimination. During the first 16 years of its existence the Commission played an integrative role in the community, Mayhew concludes, by creating an equilibrium between these opposing pressures. The conditions opposed to the legislative ideals—hostile beliefs and prejudices, difficulties of discovering infringements of the law, opposed private and group interests—'were attacked with sufficient vigour to meet the most pressing demands of the community, but not so militantly as to endanger the precarious foundation of the equal treatment standard' (1968: 259).

What seems to be implied in this idea of a 'precarious foundation' of the law is the governmental problem of maintaining the universal acceptance of fundamental societal values as uncontroversial, despite the fact that those values must be interpreted to give rise to particular laws which will inevitably engage in 'confrontation' with conditioning forces arising from the situations in which individuals live their lives. Presumably if confrontation and controversy were to reach the highest level of the normative hierarchy—fundamental societal values—the whole stability and cohesion of the society would be threatened. This would be the ultimate failure of government. Yet a legislature must, if it is to create laws that are to be successful in implementation and socially accepted, continually associate these values with its new laws; in this way it 'draws on' societal values almost as though they were a kind of credit bank.

Mayhew notes that the equilibrium the Massachusetts Commission was able to maintain for many years was not ultimately stable. Eventually civil rights groups became impatient with the Commission's methods. It deliberately avoided use of some of its legal powers for fear of provoking determined opposition, preferred to deal without publicity with individual complaints of discrimination rather than positively to promote equal opportunity through campaigns or inquiries, and involved business representatives on its committees in its efforts to maintain goodwill and take account of business views. It sought compromise and consensus and avoided confrontation wherever possible.

In a sense, the Massachusetts Commission, as Mayhew describes it, embodied in its policy the political implications and assumptions of the social integration theory considered in this chapter. It is tempting to push the analogy as far as saying that the failure of the equilibrium policy of the Commission at the end of the 1960s is a symbol of the untenability after that time, in the view of many, of the assumption that law and society can be analysed in terms of a relatively harmonious balancing and compromising of interests within a 'neutral' social and legal system. Mayhew's *Law and Equal Opportunity* is dedicated to Parsons and proclaims its reliance on his concepts throughout. In a later paper on law and social change, however, Mayhew is much more concerned to ask what is missing in the Parsonian scheme to explain why race relations laws, as well as other legal reforms designed to give new rights to disadvantaged social groups, have not achieved what reformers hoped for and have often seemed only to encourage resentment of the legal system among these groups (Mayhew 1971). Mayhew concludes that the legal system is much more *isolated* from other elements of normative structure in society than Parsons' ideas suggest. Accordingly it is much harder for law to control collectivities and roles than the theory supposes. What tends to happen, then, is that explicit legal commitments are made through the incorporation of particular interpretations of societal values in new legislation. When these commitments are not realised in changes at the level of collectivities and roles, the legitimacy of the legal order itself can be put in issue. Those impatient for better race relations, for example, may come to see the professed ideals of the law as a sham, merely a device to mislead the relatively powerless into believing that the injustices they suffer are a matter of real concern to the relatively powerful.

Functionalism as Social Theory

Functionalism—the complex of methods of analysis and orientations in social theory that are typically associated with functional analysis in sociology—posits no single motor or agent of change in social systems. In theory all elements in such a system may contribute to stability or change and the relative significance of different elements in doing so may vary in different systems and at different times. So functional analysis has been claimed as a fully sociological method of analysis of social phenomena because it does not reduce them to any consistent 'external' (that is, external to the disciplinary scope of academic sociology) element such as economic conditions or psychological factors. But a consequence of the approach is that historical analysis of conditions shaping social phenomena—for example, why pressures for change or particular social tensions and conflicts arise at particular times and why legal doctrine and institutions in particular societies have come to present particular characteristics—is less than central to research. These characteristics tend to be rationalised in functional terms without reference to the complex history of human actions—often of competing interest groups or classes—that influence the shape of social institutions. The functionalist logic of 'system' and 'structure' is sometimes hard to reconcile with the untidy data of history and the complexities of human motivations.

This last point leads to the frequently made claim that functional analysis tends to leave human beings out of the sociological picture, treating systems and normative structures as having a kind of independent existence when, in fact, social relations and the normative structures and meanings that govern them are created by individuals in a continuous process of interaction. Far from being stable monolithic elements of societies, they may be more appropriately seen as in a continuous flux reflecting the innumerable different (and changing) outlooks, expectations, understandings and beliefs of the individuals who make up a society. Finally, the concept of power as control which a person has *over another* often tends to find little place in sociological functionalism. Relationships between sub-systems are seen as relations of exchange. Power, if considered at all, tends to be viewed as a resource for fulfilment of system functions, not as a potentially divisive element which may work against the realisation of a genuine social solidarity.

These orientations appear to be built into the functionalist perspective. The presupposition that societies can be thought of as systems promotes the assumption that their natural condition is one of stability and that, from this essential nature, system needs or imperatives can be theoretically derived. Even if these assumptions are accepted, the functional approach tends to offer little guidance in considering why system needs are met one way rather than another in particular societies.

Yet, as a general approach to the study of social phenomena, functional analysis is a basic, probably indispensable, tool of sociological interpretation of law. Because of this the characteristics of functionalism discussed above appear in social analyses inspired by very varied political ideals. Indeed, as will be seen in the next chapter, these characteristics are present in some forms of Marxist theory. It is, therefore, not the case, as some critics have charged, that functionalism necessarily glorifies the existing social order although, as has been suggested, it tends to emphasise the forces promoting stability. Further, the attempt, characteristic of (non-Marxist) sociological functionalism, to analyse law in terms of the integrative problems of social systems raises many questions which are important. In this book a functional approach will be used in Chapter 7 specifically to analyse certain aspects of the work of courts. But functional analysis must be undertaken with a clear awareness of its constraints. Almost inevitably, it seems to make assumptions about the way social systems—including legal systems (cf. Rottleuthner 1989: 273-6)—function in terms of postulated needs, or essential characteristics or conditions of existence, which imply the way such systems *should* function. The analysis cannot be value neutral—totally uninfluenced by the analyst's own values.

One approach to these difficulties in sociological analysis of law has been to try to divorce functional analysis from broad concepts of 'system' and to develop so-called 'middle-range' theory which eschews the kind of immense ambitions demonstrated by Parsonian theory and merely tries to analyse the relationship between particular closely defined social phenomena. The danger is that of a somewhat programmatic listing of legal functions (cf. Podgorecki 1974: 274). Another approach is to accept that specifications of legal functions make sense only if particular guiding values for law are accepted by the researcher. In this view sociological analysis of law cannot pretend to be neutral with regard to these values. The *moral* principles of law are seen as encapsulated in the ideal of 'legality' which implies minimum procedural conditions for justice including particularly those encompassed by the concepts of 'natural justice' or 'due process of law'. In the perspective of writers such as Philip Selznick and Jerome Skolnick, sociological research on law must recognise the principle of legality as the central organising concept of this research as well as the explicit ideal of legal practice. Selznick used the concept in studying industrial relations (Selznick 1969) and Skolnick has done so in analysing police work (Skolnick 1975). In this approach, the dichotomy of 'purpose' and 'function' from which the discussion in this chapter began, appears to have almost disappeared. The 'official values' of Western law become also the criteria of functional need.

The Integrative Functions of Law

The literature discussed in this chapter does suggest some solutions to the primary theoretical question that the material in the first two chapters posed: how is it possible for law to act as an apparently autonomous agency in society at the same time as it depends upon and reflects particular social and cultural conditions? This literature sees law as having the specific task of integrating the diverse elements of collective life. In Western societies law's autonomy derives from this specific function. Thus, for Parsons, law gradually emerges as a distinct element of normative structure as a consequence of, and an element in, a vast historical process of sub-system differentiation in Western societies, centred on the relations of economy and polity. Law's special functions are also defined in terms of these conditions and the requirements for their maintenance and extension. At the same time law depends upon shared societal values. By contrast, Durkheim does not develop a concept of law clearly distinguished from morality or societal values. For him, however, law's autonomy emerges in a conception of organic solidarity in which shared values are inherently problematic but a uniform legal order is necessarily assumed. From being a mere reflection and expression of shared beliefs and values, law becomes a moral agency to substitute for them. It has the specific task of co-ordinating and structuring diverse moral milieux into an overall social unity.

From another viewpoint, the theory discussed here elaborates the implications of Ehrlich's conception of law as the inner ordering of social associations. In some functional theory (in Pound's work and in Parsons' major writings) law is taken to mean state law or lawyers' law (but cf. Parsons 1977: 149); elsewhere (certainly for Llewellyn, but Durkheim is often ambiguous) a wider view of law is taken. This distinction, however, is immaterial for present purposes because even when law is taken to mean the regulatory framework of the state it is considered to be the law of an integrated association in Ehrlich's sense, a 'group' in Llewellyn's sense, or a 'social system' in Parsons', and law's functions are elaborated through an examination of the problems of integration of such an entity.

It is the way these problems are perceived in this theory that is most open to question. Integration is conceived here in two ways. Parsons' analyses are primarily concerned with what can be called system integration—the integration of sub-systems within a social system. Here it can be accepted that law has important and complex functions, although their specification runs into the problems of functionalist logic discussed in the previous section. Durkheim, however, understands integration primarily as solidarity—spontaneous social cohesion arising from shared beliefs or attitudes or mutual co-operation. Does the law of the state contribute to social solidarity? It seems often to assume importance when solidarity is patently absent. 'In the midst of strangers, law reaches its highest level' (Black 1976: 41). Much literature considered so far in this book has tended to suggest that social relations exhibit most harmony when lawyers' law intrudes least. The demonstration of this has, however, generally relied on evidence of relatively small-scale systems of social relations (for example, a business community or local community) in which strong ties of common interest or shared attitude and belief exist.

It is difficult to draw clear conclusions from empirical evidence about the relationship between size (however measured) of a social system and its political organisation (cf. Dahl and Tufte 1974). It seems reasonable, however, to hypothesise that, *ceteris paribus*, the more extensive or dispersed the association or group the greater will be the problem of creating social solidarity because of the social and geographical distances between members arising from group size and complexity. As such groups increase in size and complexity of social organisation it would seem that organisational questions of leadership, power and authority as well as the problem of maintenance of shared outlooks and beliefs of members must become pressing (Taylor 1982). This is not, however, to suggest that problems of power and potential conflict do not exist in smaller social units. Indeed some writers have suggested that conflict may be potentially much more dangerous and disruptive in smaller social systems, whereas the larger the system the more conflict can be accepted with equanimity as a normal, and sometimes constructive element in social development.

In small systems it may well be essential to suppress all conflict (and all diversity) in the stifling conformity of mechanical solidarity (Coser 1956: 67–85; Newton 1982: 203–4). In larger systems it may be that power struggles and conflict cannot easily be suppressed but can be ordered and to some extent controlled by more complex and subtle methods including those associated in modern societies with law. However, there is no reason to assume that law itself is not a part of these power struggles. Unless the observer is convinced that all aspects of law and its institutions can be properly understood in terms of the elaboration—according to functional imperatives of the society as a social system—of shared basic values, then the questions of who *controls* the processes of law-making, interpretation and enforcement and in whose interests these processes are directed become theoretically important. Most analyses of contemporary Western law that claim its basis to be in shared values make little attempt to demonstrate empirically the existence of such a consensus among members of society.

Insofar as law regularises and formalises power relations in various ways it contributes to social stability. This stability may, in turn, give rise to or protect forms of social solidarity existing even in the most complex, diverse and disunified contemporary societies. Further, insofar as solidarity exists in complex societies it has to be translated into co-ordination. Social rules, as Durkheim argued, are necessary to provide this co-ordination, communicating the general or special responsibilities attaching to individuals and diverse groups or collectivities within a solidary society. Communication and co-operation are essential to social cohesion through organic solidarity.

Yet coercion seems an inherent and central feature of state law. In contemporary Western societies this law is recognised as the dominant category of social rules. The police power and military force of the state are explicitly linked to it. Through it state power permeates social relations. However, if law is seen as formalising and framing relations of coercion and dependence, its compatibility with solidary relations of co-operation and mutual interdependence is put in doubt. These considerations suggest a need to approach the question of the relation of law, shared beliefs and social solidarity from a different perspective. Contrary to Durkheim's conception of organic solidarity, solidarity does not necessarily arise from interdependence. To take an extreme example, in a slave society there may be considerable functional interdependence between slave and master (e. g. Cooper 1987: 233-4) yet little solidarity. It may be much more accurate to say that organic solidarity as a moral phenomenon arises from a positive recognition and acceptance by individuals and groups of their interdependence and of important mutual obligations based on it; in other words it depends on perceptions and beliefs about a social situation or social order. In this way solidarity based on interdependence is closely connected with beliefs of individuals about the nature of their society; beliefs that somehow neutralise the apparent incompatibility between the coercive character of law and the co-operative character of solidary social relations. What is important is to explain the conditions under which such beliefs may exist and the contribution that law itself may make to their propagation.

4 Law, Power and Ideology

In addressing questions about law's functions in contemporary Western societies the theory considered in the previous chapter makes important assumptions which need examination. This chapter will be concerned with three clusters of issues suggested by the limitations of functionalist theories of law as an integrative mechanism. First, how far is it correct to assume that the order or cohesion of complex Western societies is founded on consensus, that is, on values, beliefs or outlooks generally shared by members of these societies? Secondly, if it is correct to understand legal doctrine as, in some sense, elaborating or applying shared values, beliefs and outlooks, what serves to sustain these ideas or attitudes held in common and, specifically, what does law contribute to their maintenance or development? This question will require an examination of the concept of ideology as it relates to legal ideas. Thirdly, is law a 'neutral' agency of social integration, as the theorists considered in the previous chapter uniformly assume or assert, or does it operate consistently to promote the interests of particular groups or classes within society at the expense of those of others? How does law relate to the power structures of Western societies?

As will appear, these clusters of issues are closely related. The discussion which follows will begin by considering evidence bearing on the assumption of widespread consensus in Western societies. This will lead to a consideration of various analyses of law's ideological effects and of the relationship between law, ideology and power in contemporary Western societies.

The Consensus Constituency

The idea that members of a society share a common outlook may mean no more than that they are influenced by elements of common culture or experience which differentiate them—whatever their relative positions within the society—from members of some other societies. Theorists of consensus usually mean something more specific than this, however, for consensus is held to be a basis of cohesion supporting the established social order and not merely a background against which the struggle for social order takes place. Some writers stress shared commitment to ultimate values, such as equality, liberty or individual achievement. Others stress commitment to social norms, such as adherence to 'rules of the democratic game'. Still others stress commitment to beliefs about how society is actually organised (Mann 1970: 423–4). Whichever interpretation is taken, many writers have interpreted the relative stability of contemporary Western industrialised societies as attributable to and dependent upon a relatively high degree of consensus among citizens.

However, the problems of specifying the components of consensus at a high level of abstraction and of empirically testing claims about its nature are such that it is no easy task to connect the form and content of law in a particular society with the existence of a postulated consensus. Roman Tomasic (1980: 23) writes, 'where popular consensus exists regarding legislation, it does so only at the level of rhetorical or normative pronouncements', highly general statements which may give little guidance about specific attitudes, interests or actions related to the law. A conception of societal values such as Parsons' pitches them at such a high level of abstraction that not only are they generally insulated from the effects of changes in law or other elements of normative structure but their specific relationship with law is hard to confront in empirical study. Certainly there is evidence to suggest that laws can be accepted by individuals espousing values seemingly directly opposed to those that appear to inform the laws (e.g. Podgorecki 1985). More generally, empirical studies have found that individuals often espouse abstract political values seemingly directly opposed to the principles that they accept as guiding their everyday conduct (Mann 1970: 429, 432).

Studies of strongly moralistic law reform or law enforcement campaigns have suggested that the law that results may be not so much the expression of consensus values as of 'moral panics' (for example, about such phenomena as hooliganism or 'mugging') fanned by mass media or other influences on opinion (Cohen 1980; and see Dixon 1991: 48-53) or 'moral crusades' in which opposed social groups battle for status by trying to impose their beliefs on society as a whole. J.R. Gusfield suggests, as a result of his study of the 'moral crusade' of the American temperance movement, that it is when consensus is least attainable that the pressure to establish legal norms seems greatest (Gusfield 1963). Furious controversies in recent decades over the constitutional status of the death penalty in the United States have been interpreted in terms of the actions of 'moral elites' reflecting and expressing 'deeper social forces moving slowly, albeit erratically and far from implacably, in the same direction' (Bedau 1979: 51). No doubt similar interpretations could be offered of recent controversies over the legality of abortion (e. g. Lovenduski and Outshoorn, eds, 1986; Luker 1984).

In an attempt to test the existence of consensus on values, norms and beliefs in Britain and the United States, Michael Mann synthesised the findings of a wide variety of empirical studies to reach the following tentative conclusions. First, society-wide value consensus does not exist to any significant extent. Secondly, there is more consensus among the middle class than among the working class. Thirdly, the working class is more likely to support values antagonistic to the maintenance of the existing social order if those values are related to everyday experience (for example, about the position of rich and poor) than if they relate to 'an abstract political philosophy'. Fourthly, working-class individuals show less internal consistency in their values than middle-class individuals (Mann 1970). Whatever the utility of these broad class categorisations it can at least be said that the notion of any identifiable general societal consensus seems problematic (Held 1984: 306–10).

That there are 'dominant' ideas or values which consistently influence law and government more powerfully than others seems more plausible. In this perspective the consensus that determines the way law operates can be seen as the consensus of an elite—an influential minority—or a number of elites; what might be termed a specific consensus constituency. Thus Mann writes, 'only those actually sharing in societal power need develop consistent societal values' (1970: 435). When the Victorian jurist A.V. Dicey wrote of law in nineteenth-century England as being the expression of public opinion, he meant the opinion of 'the majority of those citizens who have at a given moment taken an effective part in public life' (Dicey 1905: 10) and he described what he saw as a process of consensus formation within such an elite. The sociologist Edward Shils suggests the concept of a 'central value system' of society formed by a consensus of elites which dominate the major institutions of society. In this view contemporary Western societies have a 'centre' and a 'periphery', not defined in spacial terms but in terms of values and beliefs. Membership in the society is defined sociologically by the location of individuals or groups in relation to the central value system and its institutional supports (Shils 1975: 3–16).

Despite the empirical complexity of questions about consensus and shared values, it is clear that the *assumption* of general societal consensus is often present in legal doctrine and used to justify it. One of the few relatively rigorously expounded social philosophies of law produced from within the ranks of the modern British judiciary has as its central claim that law has the task of enforcing the shared morality of society (Devlin 1965). Other judicial pronouncements and decisions relying on the idea of judges as custodians of public morality show that these are not isolated views.[1] General moral principles are often invoked, particularly

1 See e. g. *Shaw v Director of Public Prosecutions* [1962] AC 20; *Knuller (Publishing, Printing and Promotions) Ltd v Director of Public Prosecutions* [1973] AC 435. Cf. Ely 1980: 63–69 (expression of societal consensus as an explicit justification of US Supreme Court decisions).

in judicial reasoning, as part of the justification of new or established legal doctrine.

It is important to consider what significance such confident appeals to consensus values have in the light of evidence of the complexity of empirical patterns of acceptance of values and beliefs. Are these appeals deliberate attempts at ideological persuasion in an effort to *create* value consensus in support of the law, or expressions of a genuine but erroneous belief that law elaborates values universally shared within society? Undoubtedly, those who accept apparently dominant social values often do assume their universality and so equate the consensus constituency with the society as a whole. This kind of confusion is well illustrated by the story of a woman dining at the Savoy Hotel in London in 1945 who is said to have declared, on learning of the General Election results: 'But they've elected a Labour Government—and the country will never stand for that' (quoted in Bankowski and Mungham 1976: 43). What must be examined here, however, are the effects of invocation of value consensus in support of law, and the ways in which it is possible for law to rely upon and contribute to general ideals, beliefs and ways of thought within a society *despite* the empirical difficulties of specifying any general value consensus in the form suggested by much functionalist theory.

Symbolic Functions of Law

Acceptance of the idea that conflicting values and beliefs struggle for dominance in a society suggests a need to modify the notion that socialisation of values is a neutral, almost mechanical process dictated solely by the functional requisites of a social system. In a thoughtful and stimulating book, *The Symbols of Government*, published in 1935, and in other works, Thurman Arnold, an American lawyer and sometime judge, argued that law can be considered a mechanism of social integration based on the interpretation of societal values, despite the diversity of individuals' beliefs and aspirations. In Arnold's view the proclamation and maintenance of symbols—values, ideals, and ways of thinking about government and society—to which individuals can adhere, is a fundamental task of law by which it promotes social integration. The development and application of legal doctrine has the special function of creating an *illusion* of unity, coherence and system out of the reality of the irreconcilable diversity, contradiction and opposition of individual and group interests and desires. Thus, for Arnold, law is primarily a way of thinking about government, a reservoir of emotionally important social symbols—of freedom of contract, equality before the law, personal and political liberty, sanctity of property, 'law and order', equity and fairness, moral responsibility—many of them mutually inconsistent if applied in practice with the meaning that they possess as symbolic ideals (cf. Lévy-Bruhl 1961: 48–9).

According to Arnold's analysis it is through the art of law—its mystificatory brilliance—that abstract ideals are manipulated to disguise the impossibility of realising them in practice. Thus law proclaims symbols so vague or all-embracing that most members of society can accept and support them in some interpretation. Law holds up its mutually contradictory ideals like a beacon around which otherwise divided elements in society rally. 'And herein lies the greatness of the law. It preserves the appearance of unity while tolerating and enforcing ideals which run in all sorts of opposing directions.' It 'fulfils its functions best when it represents the maximum of competing symbols' (Arnold 1935: 247, 249).

An analysis of police powers in law and practice in Britain concluded, in language strikingly reminiscent of Arnold, that the combination of broad civil rights rhetoric and intricate, complex case law with its numerous exceptions, special cases and ambiguous categories is the strength of law in this field as symbol and instrument, allowing it 'to be all things to all men ... The rhetoric is rarely actually denied, it is simply whittled away by exceptions, provisos, qualifications' (McBarnet 1982: 414).[2] More generally, one of the often claimed strengths of English law has been that its fundamental principles have remained vague and flexible in interpretation. 'It is a constant source of wonder to foreigners that our law is built up to so great an extent on assumption: that in the most fundamental matters ... there are so few direct commands and prohibitions ... In all branches, the assumptions on which our law is built are so many and so vital that it is tempting to regard them as spontaneous outcrops of the national genius' (quoted in Bankowski and Mungham 1976: 33). What is missing from Arnold's analysis, however, is a consideration of the forces that determine why, how and by whom symbols are manipulated in the law. The analysis points to conflicting interests disguised by the consensus rhetoric of the law. Yet the analysis is still in functionalist terms of system needs.

The importance of social symbols has long been recognised. Some writers distinguish two types: referential symbols which refer directly to what they symbolise, for example a flag or national anthem symbolising a nation or national culture, and condensation symbols which 'condense

2 The Police and Criminal Evidence Act 1984 has now consolidated and reformed much of the relevant law but this development does not necessarily invalidate McBarnet's primary conclusions. Recent research on the effects of the Act on police practice has suggested that, in at least certain respects, it operates as 'presentational rules' which 'exist to give an acceptable appearance to the way that police work is carried out' (Dixon et al. 1990: 347).

into one symbolic event, sign, or act patriotic pride, remembrances of past glories or humiliations, promises of future greatness: some one or all of these' (Edelman 1964: 6). Legal and political analysts have stressed the vital symbolic elements of the British (Bagehot 1963) and United States (Corwin 1936; Lerner 1937) constitutions. Discussing the latter Max Lerner argues that, while an established constitution can be viewed unemotionally from one perspective as an instrument for promoting welfare, as a major political symbol it is a part of mass consciousness, looking towards the past, 'loaded with a terrible inertia' (Lerner 1937: 1294). In this sense a constitution like other elements of a legal order may be a condensation symbol, although the labels referential and condensation symbols are probably most useful in suggesting a continuum of symbolic functions rather than distinct categories.

As Lerner remarks, the making and breaking of symbols is a part of fundamental social change and 'one of the essential techniques of power groups is to manipulate the most effective symbols in such a way that they become instruments of mass persuasion' (1937: 1292). Murray Edelman writes that it is central to the potency of political symbols that they are 'remote, set apart, omnipresent as the ultimate threat or means of succour, yet not susceptible to effective influence through any act we as individuals can perform' (Edelman 1964: 6). Their potency is that they control, yet appear absolute and self-evident, immune from control themselves. The unifying symbols of government disguise the political struggles by which these symbols are established and the structures of power by which they are maintained, and which they in turn help to guarantee.

The idea that law has symbolic functions suggests that the effectiveness of a law does not necessarily depend on whether it can be invoked or enforced. Edelman writes, 'law [for example, about monopoly and economic concentration, antitrust policy, public utility regulation, banking controls, and curbs on management and labour] may be repealed in effect by administrative policy, budgetary starvation, or other little publicised means; but the laws as symbols must stand because they satisfy interests that are very strong indeed: interests that politicians fear will be expressed actively if a large number of voters are led to believe that their shield against a threat has been removed' (1964: 37).

In a famous study Vilhelm Aubert sought to discover the reasons for the apparent ineffectiveness of a 1948 Norwegian statute passed to regulate the conditions of work of women working as housemaids or domestic helps. The legislation limited working hours, prescribed minimum rates of overtime pay and laid down other conditions to protect the housemaids' position. Aubert found the law had not altered conditions of work to conform with the legislated norms and the contents of the legislation were not widely known among those it concerned. He identified two major causes of ineffectiveness. Little attempt was made by the legislature to make the law comprehensible to those it was apparently designed to influence or protect; and the enforcement machinery provided was remarkably weak. The Act made *repeated* violations of the law despite protest by the victim a condition for legal redress, limitations which Aubert argued were utterly unrealistic given employment conditions. He claimed that the explanation for the apparently naive approach of the legislation could be found in the parliamentary debates which preceded enactment of the housemaids' law. In the debates it was claimed, on the one hand, that the new law would be merely a codification of existing custom so that powerful enforcement procedures were unnecessary. On the other hand, there was a tendency to claim that the law was an important piece of social reform legislation attempting to change conditions for the better. Some speakers used both arguments but Conservatives tended to adopt the codification argument while the Left adopted the reform argument. 'The crucial point here,' writes Aubert, 'is the remarkable ease with which such apparently contradictory claims were suffused in one and the same legislative action, which in the end received unanimous support from all political groups' (Aubert 1966: 110). Rhetoric appeared more important than factual evidence relating to the operation of the law. It was possible for the legislation to satisfy conflicting group interests by setting up a reformist ideal but ensuring that the legislation would not be enforced and would not in fact alter established behaviour patterns.

Undoubtedly the concept of 'symbolic legislation' can be overused. There is a tendency to refer to any apparently ineffective legislation in these terms, so suggesting that the law is functional in some way even if not enforced. Here, the danger is of adopting what has been called a postulate of 'universal functionalism'—assuming every element in society to have a function in relation to the social system as a whole (Merton 1968). Further, the concept of symbolic legislation often tends to imply a deliberate legislative intention to mystify by creating law that will not be enforced. The danger of overuse is that of what Paul Rock (1974: 144) has called 'anthropomorphic conspiracy theory'—assuming that laws are merely instruments of a conspiracy of legislators, rather than being dependent in their creation and enforcement on complex processes reflecting the conflicts of diverse interests (Dixon 1991: 32). Law may be neutralised by opposed interests or become unworkable for reasons not foreseen. Legislators themselves may be bemused by symbolic or mythical representations of the problems or the offenders their legislation is intended to confront, with the result that the legislation misses its mark (Dixon 1991: 34–5).

More generally, as was noted in Chapter 2, it is often extremely difficult to ascertain the effects of particular laws. The mere lack of cases brought before courts or of police or administrative enforcement action is not, in itself, evidence that law is ineffective in practice in controlling behaviour (Carbonnier 1988: 130–1). Further, Carbonnier argues that even unenforced or ambiguous law (for example in relation to police powers) may create a climate of legal insecurity, of responsibility or 'bad conscience' which limits violation (1988: 137). On the other hand, in an important study of criminal law in operation in Scotland and England, Doreen McBarnet has argued that while law appears to hold out the symbol of individual liberty, the details of legal doctrine give the police most of the powers they claim they need. Limitations 'exist largely in the unrealised rhetoric' (McBarnet 1981b: 155).[3]

Rhetoric can, however, be influential. Who can doubt the great symbolic importance for race relations in the United States of the *Brown* case (see Chapter 2) and the string of unanimous Supreme Court decisions which followed it outlawing discriminatory practices? (White 1982: 169ff). As Richard Abel has written, symbolic legislation may be of liberating value; it can provide a focus around which forces for change can mobilise (Abel 1981b: 252). But such possibilities depend on clearly identifying the symbolic elements in law, and their effects and non-effects, and on theoretical analysis which links these elements with structures of power in society.

Marx: Repressive and Ideological Functions of Law

Dissatisfaction with consensus theory led to the development of 'conflict' analyses of law, stressing law's repressive aspects as an instrument of the power of certain groups or classes over others. They directed attention to important but previously widely neglected aspects of legal regulation. However, their general defect was that, as consensus theory failed to explain the forces operating to establish and maintain dominant ideas and beliefs about society, so conflict theory failed to account for the fact that law does not operate as a purely repressive mechanism in contemporary Western societies; on the contrary, it seems to command wide support and acceptance throughout these societies. Varieties of Marxist analysis of law have provided the most important attempts to overcome the limitations of both conflict and consensus theories. They seek to explain how law operates as an instrument of repression promoting the interests of certain classes at the expense of those of others in contemporary Western societies while, at the same time, contributing to shape a climate

3 Recent research suggests that the use by police of provisions in the Police and Criminal Evidence Act 1984 for obtaining the consent of citizens to certain police actions makes possible the avoidance of important legal constraints ostensibly imposed by the Act on police powers (Dixon et al. 1990; see also Dixon et al. 1989).

of thought in these societies that makes possible a reduction of direct repression through law to a minimum.

Marxism as a body of explanatory theory claims to attempt a total analysis of social phenomena which recognises no disciplinary boundaries. Marx's own mature writings are concerned primarily with the nature of capitalism as the social and economic order characteristic of Western industrialised societies. These writings contain no developed legal theory but merely scattered passages and ideas about law where these appeared relevant to Marx's project. Further, like most original and creative thinkers, Marx changed his views considerably over time. His early writings express a humanist philosophy in which law is seen as the essence of human liberty: 'A statute book is a people's bible of freedom,' Marx wrote in 1842 (Cain and Hunt, eds, 1979: 42). In his subsequent writings, which are the basis of the discussion here, legal doctrine and institutions appear very differently.

The later writings culminating in Marx's masterpiece, *Capital* (the first volume of which appeared in 1867 with two more after his death in 1883), gave rise to the theory of historical materialism. Its claim, in essence, is that human history can be explained in terms of changes in the conditions of economic production and the effects of those changes; that is, changes in the material basis of societies. The key to understanding all aspects of a society including its law is in its economic structure. Economic structure is constituted by *relations of production*; that is, the system of social relations on the basis of which economic (material) production is organised. In capitalism this is the system of free labour under which the wage earner sells his labour power to the employer in return for wages and his employer is free to take the profits of the employee's labour as his own. The economy in the full sense, however, consists of relations of production together with what Marx calls the *productive forces*—that is, the means of production (such as materials and machinery), labour resources and conditions of production including the level of technological development. Relations of production, therefore, exist in relation to material productive forces and at any given time they more or less correspond with the stage of development of the latter. For example, wage labour as a general system of productive relations only becomes possible with the development of a large pool of relatively mobile workers; modern factory production depends on a certain level of technological development.

On this economic base a *superstructure* arises, ultimately determined by the economic structure. The superstructure includes legal and political institutions and 'forms of social consciousness'—ideology. The development of productive forces determines the kinds of relations of production appropriate at a particular stage of the history of a society. Legal and political institutions are created to protect those relations and the social conditions that guarantee their continuance. Correspondingly, forms of consciousness develop that make the relations of production and their conditions of existence appear natural and obvious so that any other form of organisation of society is virtually inconceivable. The combination of the economic base of relations of production and the institutions and social practices that support the relations of production, Marx calls the *mode of production*.

Any particular society is likely to show characteristics associated with more than one mode of production, but the features of one (for example, the feudal mode or the capitalist mode) are likely to be dominant. A mode of production becomes unstable when the development of productive forces is such that established relations of production are no longer appropriate or workable. 'At a certain stage of their development, the material productive forces of society come in conflict with the existing relations of production, or—what is but a legal expression for the same thing—with the property relations within which they have been at work hitherto. From forms of development of the productive forces these relations turn into their fetters. Then begins an epoch of social revolution. With the change of the economic foundation the entire immense superstructure is more or less rapidly transformed' (Cain and Hunt, eds, 1979: 52). But although the material base of society changes in a manner that can be analysed 'with the precision of natural science', changes in the legal, political and ideological aspects of society have to be viewed differently because here human wills are at work. They are engaged in struggle, which can take various forms although its ultimate outcome is determined by what happens to the economic base. In the areas of law, politics, religion and philosophy—in institutional and ideological struggle—people become conscious of the conflict engendered in the economic base and 'fight it out' (Cain and Hunt, eds, 1979: 52).

These processes can be illustrated with some of Marx's ideas about the feudal and capitalist modes of production and the transition from the former to the latter. Under feudalism serfs own the means of production necessary to their own labour. They work with their own tools on their own land and the lord extorts a share of the serf's produce by force or threat of it or by guarantee of military protection. Military compulsion is the basis of the socio-economic system. But it produces a static system eventually incapable of adapting to fundamental changes in technology and resources. In more complex circumstances of production a labour process built around economic rather than military compulsion is far more efficient, but this requires a definite legal form and ideology. Freedom to monopolise the means of production is made possible by legal rules guaranteeing security of transactions and of property irrespective of the use to which property is put or the status of the property holder. In this way law provides the means of, and legitimises, separation of the mass of labourers from the means of production necessary to their livelihood. The dispossessed labourer is, therefore, forced in order to live to sell his own labour power to those who own the means of production. His labour power is the only commodity he has to sell in the market of 'free and equal' property owners.

This free labour system based on economic compulsion requires a new ideological basis which makes law under capitalism fundamentally different from that under feudalism. It requires the development of the legal concept of the universal legal subject—universal in the sense that, in general, individuals are to be treated as identical in legal status. The labourer is thus a legal subject, a free and equal possessor of himself (unlike the status-bound serf) who can hire his own faculties to the capitalist in a formally free contract. To the law the economic coercion determining the free contract between legal equals remains invisible.

It is now possible to specify the repressive and ideological functions of law in capitalist society as Marxist analysis usually portrays them. Law is rarely capable of being interpreted as the direct expression of the will of a dominant class (Collins 1982: ch 2). The main thrust of Marx's analyses is that the capitalist state is not the direct servant of the capitalist class. Rather, it is an institution that emerges to maintain the order and stability of the dominant mode of production in a society. Sometimes, as with the development of late nineteenth-century legal controls on the length of the working day, the state protects the capitalist social order (which relies on the replenishment of labour power) against the greed of particular capitalists. The modern state appears normally as an impartial referee maintaining a system that benefits some more than others. The class essence of the state is usually hidden but appears in time of crisis. Similarly, it is a vital ideological function of law to appear neutral, serving the interests of all, maintaining equality before the law.

The repressive mechanisms of law are, however, brought into play against any serious challenges to the conditions of existence of the dominant mode of production. Marx's own writings attempt to show how, historically, law's repressive apparatus played an important role (for example, through land enclosures, confiscations, forced conditions of work, control of population movements) in establishing a capitalist social order when the development of productive forces made feudal relations unsustainable. Early Marxist theorists stressed law's repressive, police functions and its importance as an agency of direct class power, controlled by or acting on behalf of the dominant class. But Marx's own writings suggest that in modern capitalism the ideological functions of law are at least as important and perhaps more important to the maintenance of the social order. Indeed, state power and ideology are mutually reinforcing. Thus it is vital to the ideological basis of capitalism that worker and capitalist alike are, as legal subjects, equal before the law.

The free contract between them gives the worker the wage which provides the resources necessary to replenish his labour power, and the capitalist the right to retain all profits derived from use of the worker's labour power. Legal freedom and legal equality are, for Marxists, the basis of economic coercion.

That working-class political power and welfare provision have grown considerably since Marx wrote is explicable in terms of his writings. Marx foresaw a tendency for the rate of profit in capitalist enterprise to fall as inherent in the logic of the system. Lower profit margins plus the consequently more serious threat of industrial disruption induce concessions as an alternative to repression. The winning of the franchise was a major victory of the working class. Yet Marx believed that increased working-class power could only make the social order ultimately more insecure. The prognosis for capitalism's future, in Marx's interpretation, is a growth of tension between relations and forces of production which, becoming gradually more serious, will pave the way for a revolutionary transformation of the economic structure of society leading to socialism and eventually communism.

Law, Class and Power

As a contribution to social science Marxist theory elaborates, like all social theory, the implications of a particular, partial perspective on social life. Its predictions of a post-capitalist future are now inevitably judged in the light of the dramatic collapse of European state socialist regimes formerly claiming to adhere to Marxist doctrines. Yet its analysis of the structure of capitalist societies remains provocative. For analysis of law the major problems that challenge Marxist theory are those of the relationship between law and class and of the nature of ideology. It will be necessary to look at each of these matters in turn in order to follow some of the implications of Marxist interpretations of law. In this section we shall consider aspects of the first of these areas and, more generally, the connection between law and power relations in society.

Many writers have treated the relationship between law and social stratification—the hierarchical ordering of individuals within a society—as self-evident. 'Laws grind the poor and rich men rule the law,' declared Oliver Goldsmith, the eighteenth-century poet. To a late nineteenth-century writer, 'The great lesson we learn [from seven centuries of legislation of English Parliaments] is that legislation with regard to labour has almost always been class-legislation. It is the effort of some dominant body to keep down a lower class, which had begun to show inconvenient aspirations' (Jevons quoted in Hayek 1982 I: 168). Similarly in the legal history of relations between landlord and tenant, creditor and debtor, organised business and consumers, 'the rules have been shaped largely by the views of one of the parties and their particular interests—especially where ... it was one of the groups concerned which almost exclusively supplied the judges' (Hayek 1982 I: 89). Much sociological 'conflict' theory has relied on similar identification: 'Acts are defined as criminal because it is in the interests of the ruling class so to define them' (Chambliss 1978: 194). And judicial pronouncements have sometimes made Marx's comment 'your jurisprudence is but the will of your class made into a law for all' (Marx and Engels 1888) extremely plausible.[4]

It is industrial (labour) law—what used to be called in England the law of master and servant—which is most often seen as the central site of class struggle. Indeed it is so almost by definition if a Marxist conception of class is adopted. For Marx, as has been seen, classes are defined in terms of their position with regard to the relations of production. Yet there are serious problems both with this concept of class and with the interpretation of law in class terms. The essence of the former problem is that the distinction between those who own the means of production and those who labour through means of production owned by others seems inadequate to provide a basis for theorising the relationship in contemporary Western societies between numerous social groups categorised in terms of an immense array of different occupations and social positions. Most—business executives, factory workers, independent professionals, state employees—'have no direct financial tie to the means of work, much less any legal claims upon the proceeds from property ... Yet if bookkeepers and coal miners, insurance agents and farm labourers, doctors in a clinic and crane operators in an open pit have this condition in common, certainly their class situations are not the same. To understand the variety of modern class positions we must go beyond the common fact of source of income and consider as well the amount of income' (Gerth and Mills 1954: 312; see e.g. Bottomore 1991).

Indeed the concept of class is now widely used in sociology to encompass occupational group and income level, or occupational group alone. For many purposes this is useful but it undermines the theoretical status of the concept in social theory as Marx sought to establish it (cf. Wright, ed, 1989). Indeed, if we seek to understand the relative access which different sections of society have to law—their capacity to shape its content and form and the mode of its application—a whole variety of empirical factors, such as social status, education levels, access to technical knowledge, associational ties, opportunity and personality

4 See e.g. Brown 1986 ch 2 (history of judicial attacks on trade unionism); Fennell 1986 (judicial responses to municipal socialism).

become relevant, as well as the complex determinants of racial, sexual, religious and other forms of discrimination and prejudice against individuals and social groups. Thus, at a superficial level, differences between 'haves' and 'have-nots' are easy to identify and to relate to the effects of law (Galanter 1974) because such vague general concepts embrace all or any of the differentiating factors which can determine the powerful from the relatively powerless in society. But the concept of class becomes overloaded when employed in theory to explain processes by which these varied factors operate.

The determinants of power and the ways in which law expresses and formalises power relations in society are, therefore, highly complex. Few Marxists today would claim, for example, that judicial law-making is in any sense a direct expression of class interest: 'to disbelieve in the process of legal reasoning entirely requires a great deal of cynicism' (Collins 1982: 66). Marxist legal theorists, influenced by the notion (particularly associated with the work of the philosopher Louis Althusser) that ideology is itself a distinct and independent terrain of political struggle, have recognised legal doctrine itself as an important part of this terrain (Poulantzas 1978: 92). Thus even where class relations can be seen as directly expressed in law, as in labour law, the law is claimed by one Marxist analyst to represent 'none other than the registered, codified and formalised *victories* of the working class' (Edelman 1979: 131. My emphasis). Law is not, then, merely an agent of dominant classes. It is, itself, a prize: the 'site and stake of class struggle' (Edelman 1979: 134). This kind of class analysis at least recognises the complexity of legal doctrine and its effects and that rigorous analysis of legal doctrine does not usually reveal the consistent favouring of interests of an easily identified social class. Further, many writers, Marxist and non-Marxist alike, have seen law that purportedly benefits the 'have-nots' more than the 'haves'—for example, social welfare law—as a device for incorporating the working class in the state by buying its allegiance (Barker 1990: 94–8). Provision of certain legal benefits is seen as defusing class antagonism while maintaining the class system. It is a way of 'regulating the poor' (Piven and Cloward 1972; and see Cranston 1985: 191–209), making explicit their dependence not only on the economic order but also on its political and legal structure and facilitating more sophisticated forms of surveillance and control of the recipients of social welfare benefits as the price of providing these benefits.

Clearly these arguments suggest that whatever the difficulties of finding adequate concepts to explain social stratification theoretically, the link between law and power relations in society must be a centrally important matter for sociological study of law. The concept of power is not entirely free from difficulty. It can be thought of as the probability of being able to carry out one's own will despite resistance (Weber 1978:

53) or the capacity to produce intended effects on the behaviour of others. It has been treated as a generalised medium of interaction (Parsons 1967: ch 10), a kind of catalyst of events (Luhmann 1979: 114), or a diffuse resource—'the multiplicity of force relations' by means of which strategies are pursued (Foucault 1979: 92–3; Foucault 1980: 142). Undoubtedly control of material benefits—economic power—is one of its major forms. In the context of politics it includes the power to shape not only policies but also the agenda of debate.

Pluralist political theories argue that power is widely distributed in Western societies so that some groups in society (or at least their leaders) are powerful or influential in some respects, others in other respects (Held 1987: ch 6). One person's power is, therefore, not necessarily at the expense of another's powerlessness. Law arises as the compromise of various conflicting interests, in a process of negotiation between sources of power. *Power elite* theorists, by contrast, argue that in Western societies certain stable elites—in business, the military, the permanent political establishment, for example—always hold the power to shape national policies (Held 1987: ch 5; Dunleavy and O'Leary 1987: ch 4). Important studies have sought to demonstrate empirically the nature of these elites and the links between them (Mills 1956: Miliband 1969), although highly convincing empirical studies of family, associational and attitudinal ties within and between elites can often be challenged as not *proving* actual political unity (Poulantzas 1972).

Whichever view is taken, law can be seen as both the *expression* of power relations and an important mechanism for *formalising* and *regularising* such relations. It protects and legitimises power, for example by guaranteeing economic power through the development of concepts of property and maintenance of rules to protect property. Further, it derives its own power partly from the political power that it expresses—whether of a permanent power elite or the results of a struggle between power centres—and partly from the benefits that regularisation and formalisation of power, in themselves, are seen to offer. Insofar as in complex large-scale modern societies the relatively powerful need elaborate rule systems to direct and co-ordinate the exercise of their power, they *depend* upon law and upon legal structures which, in order to organise and formalise power, impose important conditions on its use.

Thus, contrary to the assumption in much legal writing that the essential connection between law and power is that of control of power by law (e.g. Denning 1982: 307–31) and to the assumption in much critical writing that law is merely a weapon of power, law controls and expresses power at the same time, as two sides of the same process. And since, as has been seen, the nature and distribution of power are complex questions, legal doctrine and the workings of legal institutions necessarily show complex and often contradictory patterns. Nevertheless, what must be kept clearly in view is that, however difficult it may be to define 'haves' and 'have-nots' in ways that are theoretically acceptable, enough sound empirical evidence of the workings of law now exists for us to be able to say with total confidence that law in its practical effects is not 'neutral'; that the 'haves'—identified by almost any non-legal criterion—tend to 'come out ahead' (Galanter 1974) in their capacity to invoke law, to obtain legal advice and assistance, to benefit from prosecutorial or sentencing discretion, to avoid or ensure law enforcement, and to obtain considerate treatment at the hands of legal officials.[5] Law is a major (but by no means the sole) instrument for the organisation and extension of power relations in contemporary Western societies. Insofar as it protects the powerless it does so not by removing the sources of power exercised over them, but by directing this power, to some extent, into relatively predictable forms. In these societies law may well provide more protection by this means for the powerless than it does in many other societies. If this is so, it is because it formalises power relations more comprehensively and appears as a more valuable and reliable agency of stability than it does elsewhere. This is not merely because of the coercive power of the state on which law can rely but also because of its intimate connections with prevailing currents of thought and belief—or ideology—influencing 'haves' and 'have-nots' alike. It is these connections which we must now examine.

Law and Ideology

Sociological study of law is centrally concerned with the influence of ideas on action; with the sociological significance of the cognitive and evaluative ideas expressed in legal doctrine or presupposed by it. Sociology of law cannot, however, treat these ideas as given. It must seek to understand their origins in social practices and conditions, despite the fact that many such ideas about law and society seem self-evident, 'common sense,' so obvious that the question of their origin may seem unreal because to not accept them seems unthinkable. It is precisely because of this common-sense quality, which makes many ideas associated with law largely unquestioned in legal practice and in everyday life, that a scientific study of law must be concerned with them. It follows from the conception of science used in this book that its hallmark is perpetual constructive inquiry and scepticism of 'absolute truths'. By contrast, in social life, systems or currents of generally accepted ideas about society and its character, about rights and responsibilities, law, morality, religion and politics and numerous other matters, provide certainty and security,

5 Empirical studies bearing on these matters are discussed in chs 6, 7 and 8.

the basis of beliefs, and guides for conduct. Thus, these systems of ideas, which can be termed ideologies or currents of ideology, by their nature tend towards apparent comprehensiveness. Unlike scientific thought, which must never escape the recognition that its insights are always partial, limited, fated to be forever incomplete and subject to revision,[6] ideology tends to assume that its perspective at least in relation to a particular area of experience is total and complete; that its vision is correct and not subject to change. Thus, ideologies are often seen, by those who accept them, not as constructed like scientific theories but as having been revealed or discovered as eternal truths.

Ideology is a concept both broader in scope and more specific than those of 'societal consensus' and 'social symbols' used earlier. The existence of a pervasive or controlling ideological system in a society does not guarantee consensus but merely limits dissension within certain bounds. This is because it provides the framework of thought within which individuals and social groups interpret the nature of the conflicts in which they are involved and recognise and understand the interests that they seek to promote. Similarly, ideology provides the context in which social symbols are interpreted. It fixes their meaning and significance. The symbols of law and government do not exist in isolation but as part of wide currents of understanding about the nature of society and individual life. The manipulation of social or political symbols relies on existing ideology and at the same time contributes to sustaining or directing it. At the same time Arnold's very important insight that socially significant symbols can exist in mutual contradiction has to be preserved. Thus, ideology tends to disguise its inconsistencies in vague, infinitely fluid concepts. Emotion may substitute the perfect coherence and completeness that cannot be obtained through rigorous and systematic analysis of experience. In ideological thought, social experience tends to be perceived and interpreted selectively in order to preserve and generalise values taken as immutable. One simply believes absolutely in certain truths. No contrary evidence can shake them.

Legal ideology can be thought of, then, not as legal doctrine itself but as 'forms of social consciousness'—systems of values and cognitive assumptions—reflected in and expressed through legal doctrine. The task of an analysis of legal ideology is to explain its nature, sources and effects in particular societies. Marxist theory shows, broadly, three approaches to explanation of the social sources and functions of legal doctrine and ideas in capitalist society. For some writers, adopting what

6 Cf. Wolff 1979: 500: 'Science is the most obviously self-critical and self-questioning of intellectual activities, systematically searching for negative cases and for explanations, hypotheses and interpretations precisely other than the ones that to the best of one's knowledge are true or certain. Science (at least "empirical" science) is that knowledge which is valid only "until further notice".'

can be called an *economic derivation* approach, the form of law is a reflection of essential characteristics of the economic structure. Its character is explained by the logic of the economic order. Law is autonomous of economy only in a strictly limited sense. For other theorists, adopting what can be termed a *structuralist* approach, law and the dominant forms of ideology in a society are explicable as relatively autonomous of the economic base. A social formation—that is, a politically organised society at a certain historical moment (cf. Althusser 1969: 251)—is thought of as a structure made up of relatively independent 'levels'—the economic, the ideological and the political. All of these levels are, however, unified by the dominant mode of production—for example, capitalist or feudal—and their character is determined by the functional requirements for maintaining this mode of production, the nature of which is, itself, ultimately determined by the economic structure. For yet other writers, adopting a *class instrumentalist* approach, law and dominant ideology can be understood as developed and promoted at the behest of a dominant class whose interests the law ultimately serves and whose values and beliefs the dominant ideology reflects. For this approach, empirical studies of control of the mass media by powerful interests and of relationships between occupants of strategic positions of power and influence in society are of major importance.

The structuralist and class instrumentalist approaches tend to suffer from opposite problems. For the former, represented particularly in the work of French theorists such as Louis Althusser, Nicos Poulantzas and Bernard Edelman, functions and effects of law and ideology tend to be specified theoretically in advance of empirical analysis. As with the functionalist theory discussed in the previous chapter, there is a tendency to assume that the needs of the social system—or rather, the mode of production—will be met, and that law and ideology *necessarily* operate to ensure this result. On the other hand, the assumption of law and ideology as 'relatively autonomous' of the economic base does make possible a conception of them as areas of political struggle, and justifies—as in Edelman's work (Edelman 1979)—sophisticated analysis of the complexities of law's doctrinal development. But the 'relative autonomy' formulation often merely ignores the difficult problem of specifying the exact nature of the relationship between law and economic structure.

By contrast, the chief problem with class instrumentalist theories tends to be their empiricism. They rely on the difficult task of providing adequate empirical demonstration of class cohesion and of general processes by which classes dominate the creation and application of law and development of ideology (Collins 1982). The thesis of class instrumentality is of such awesome generality, the empirical patterns of causality to be considered are so complex, and the concepts employed—especially that of 'class' itself—are often so ambiguous or difficult to use in empirical research that, despite the persuasiveness of much that these theories suggest, they may be inadequate frameworks for the empirical studies needed to fulfil them (cf. Hunt 1991: 123ff).

Pashukanis

The most sophisticated development of the economic derivation approach is in the writings of the Soviet jurist Evgeny Pashukanis, which offer a subtle development in legal theory of Marx's ideas. In *Capital* Marx explains what he calls the fetishism of commodities. One of the most important characteristics of capitalism is that creative human processes are seen in terms of commodities. Everything can be bought and sold and so is understood in terms of its commodity value. The commodity form dominates life. Social relations themselves become, paradoxically, relations between things. What this means is that individuals relate to each other primarily as property owners, that is, in terms of the commodities they hold (including their labour power) or around which their dealings are organised. It has already been explained that in Marx's understanding of capitalism this taken for granted feature of social life is of primary ideological importance since capitalism depends on the freedom of market transactions. These transactions include, most fundamentally, those embodied in relations of production in which labour power itself is a commodity sold in the market. The ideological basis of capitalism makes it 'obvious' why the capitalist can retain all the profit (surplus value) from another man's labour: it is because he has bought, in a freely made contract, the labourer's labour power and so holds it and its fruits as his own.

Pashukanis elaborates these ideas by arguing that the essence of law in capitalist society is to be found in its distinctive form, that of the rights and duties of individual legal subjects equal before the law. This form of law is the direct juridical analogy and necessary fulfilment of commodity form (Pashukanis 1978). The central foundation of the law is the concept of the universal legal subject. Whatever the real economic and social differences between individuals, capitalist law tends towards the idea that all are equal in its eyes. Special determinants of legal status based on property, religion, nobility, race, sex or other qualifications tend gradually to disappear with the development of the law. The application of law may greatly discriminate between classes and groups, but on its face—in legal doctrine and legal ideology—capitalist law tends to treat all as equals, so disguising the structures of real inequality which it maintains. This irony has even survived popularisation, such is law's ideological strength. 'The majestic equality of the law … forbids rich and poor alike to sleep under bridges, to beg in the streets, and to steal bread,' declared the nineteenth-century novelist Anatole France. And an English judge is reputed to have authored the famous observation that the law courts of England are open to everyone, like the doors of the Ritz Hotel.

Legal subjects are recognised by law as free and equal insofar as they can be seen as property owners. They own, at least, their faculties, their power to work. This commodity - labour power, if no other, they can bring to market. Thus legal relations are fundamentally the relations of commodity owners in the market. Law is born with the market, reaches its highest and most abstract form in capitalism where all social relations are dominated by commodity form, and, Pashukanis argues, will eventually disappear in a socialist society which dispenses with market mechanisms of the economy, and the ideology that reflects and supports them. In those areas of capitalist law that serve primarily repressive functions the legal forms of freedom and equality, entailing bargaining and negotiation of rights and duties, are superimposed—as particularly in the criminal trial—over the exercise of state power. Similarly, public law represents the 'legal face' of the state; the extremely uneasy and contradictory superimposition on coercive state power of the legal form of a balancing of rights and duties as between state and citizen, or between state agencies.

Pashukanis' analysis, while making the general assumption of Marxist theory that law can be understood only as state law, nevertheless stresses the origins of law in social relations. Further it offers a rigorous explanation of the relationship between economic structure and legal form. Its major defect, however, is that in reducing legal form to commodity form it stresses only one of perhaps several determinants of legal form, and so underestimates the diversity of legal doctrine and the possibility of adaptations and variations in the forms of Western law. The identification of law with commodity relations makes it difficult to analyse adequately those areas of law, in capitalist and non-capitalist societies, that are distant from market relations in any meaningful sense. Although Pashukanis points to very important connections between legal form and economic structure, his legal theory does not provide an adequate means of analysing the complexities and contradictions of legal doctrine.

Legal Individualism

Whatever the problems of Pashukanis' attempt to identify the specific character of legal doctrine in Western societies, it highlights effectively a feature of these societies and their law which has been treated as central by virtually all major social theorists. 'Our [English] law,' wrote the comparative lawyer H.C. Gutteridge, 'has not hesitated to place the seal of its approval upon a theory of the extent of individual rights which can only be described as the consecration of the spirit of unrestricted egoism'

(Gutteridge 1933: 22). It is the *individualism* of Western law and society which has appeared as its hallmark. Legal individualism will serve, in this context of discussion, as a major example of legal ideology; of one vital current of ideology which has been developed in and through Western legal doctrine in complex and pervasive ways.

The idea is expressed in the jurist Sir Henry Maine's celebrated late nineteenth-century thesis that the history of progressive societies had hitherto been one of movement from social relations based on status to relations of contract (Maine 1861); in the German sociologist Ferdinand Tönnies' conception of modern societies as based on impersonal, instrumental, limited and temporary social relations of *Gesellschaft* (association) rather than on the intimate, universalistic, and permanent ones of *Gemeinschaft* (community) (Tönnies 1957); and in Weber's notion of the 'community of strangers' created by the market whose natural relationship is through specific and limited (purposive) contracts, rather than all-embracing, 'fraternal' bonds of comradeship or kinship (Weber 1978: 668ff; 1954: 100ff). Ehrlich writes, 'the ideal of justice of individualism is the individual and his property, the individual who has an untrammeled power of disposition over his property, who recognizes no superior but the state, and is not bound by anything but the contracts he has entered into' (1936: 235).

Individualism in Western societies is a complex amalgam of various ideological components. Many writers, Marxist and non-Marxist, have agreed, however, that law has had a major part to play in developing these ideological conditions and is a major form of their expression. Echoing Weber, the American sociologist Robert Nisbet writes, 'The historic passage of Europe from *Gemeinschaft* to *Gesellschaft* could never have taken place had it not been for instruments of law first fashioned in the imperial despotism that was Rome under the caesars' (Nisbet 1975: 172). The individualism embodied in modern law stresses above all that individuals are the makers of their own destiny; standing alone they bear responsibility for the acts or omissions attributed to them. When someone suffers harm or loss, the responsibility is his or her own, or that of another individual or specific individuals, or the result of accident. As ideology, individualism suggests an absolute view of social and individual life. Thus, in its purest form, it takes no account of social or cultural factors that may remove the possibility of choice from individual actors, or severely limit the choices available to them, or determine the way these choices are interpreted.

Contract and Agreement

Western law has expressed this general idea of society as made up of free, isolated, individually responsible individuals in many forms (cf. Ehrlich

1936: 236) though never with complete consistency. The full elaboration of a general theory of contract in legal doctrine, as an explicit component and basis of the law, did not occur until the nineteenth century, the English development reflecting the influence of continental jurists (Atiyah 1979: ch 14; Cornish and Clark 1989: 200–26; Baker 1990: 400). Yet the ideology of contract as the voluntary bargain of free individuals had been socially and politically significant in England long before (Nenner 1977). Further, the idea of freedom of contract could be seen as already declining as far as its reflection in the detail of legal doctrine was concerned, at the same time as it was increasingly recognised explicitly as a general theoretical foundation of doctrine by judges and jurists (cf. Atiyah 1979: 681ff).

This merely illustrates that ideology develops in many contexts and by various processes, and that its explicit 'official' elaboration may sometimes be a response to challenges to it (often in the form of elaborated opposing ideologies). It has been seen that the literature on symbolic functions of law suggests that the articulation of highly abstract legal principles may be ideologically important in itself. It may disguise the actual results of judicial decisions or the contradictory practical effects of doctrinal detail or institutional arrangements. When relatively unchallenged, however, ideology is assumed or implied rather than systematically expounded. After all, as noted earlier, it tends to appear self-evident, as 'common sense'.

Furthermore, like all other aspects of a society, ideology adapts to or acts upon processes of social change. For example, the legal ideology of contract assumes the contract to be the product of agreement, yet, necessarily, legal doctrine must formalise the recognition of agreement to some extent. The presumption of free agreement in English law led early to the doctrine of *caveat emptor* (let the buyer beware) (Hamilton 1931). Law increasingly presumed the capacity of bargaining parties to look after their own interests as trade expanded (Morrow 1940). Developing assumptions about contract contrasted strongly with the extensive legal regulation of trade and industry in Western Europe in the Middle Ages. Yet the assumption of free bargaining is appropriate to economic and social conditions only in limited circumstances. With the development of large corporations facilitating accumulations of capital and so economic power undreamt of in simple commodity production, the assumption of freely negotiated bargains has been confronted ever more dramatically with the consequence of contracts made between parties of vastly unequal power.

This situation is reflected, above all, in the use of adhesion (or standard form) contracts, in which one party presents the other with standard contractual terms to be accepted or rejected *in toto*. Contractual planning thus becomes, in these circumstances, the prerogative of one party having economic or other power to impose its terms on the other. In one aspect the development of adhesion contracts is merely an expression of commercial necessity and convenience (Goode 1982: 39); standard terms are important to the calculation of risk or its exclusion when numerous or large-scale transactions are involved (Kessler 1943). But the freedom of contract doctrine caused much uncertainty in the nineteenth and early twentieth centuries in dealing with the increasing problem of unfair consumer bargains. The individualism of the basic structure of contract law reflected, in the words of an American lawyer, 'the ethics of free enterprise capitalism and the ideals of justice of a mobile society of small enterprisers, individual merchants and independent craftsmen' (Kessler 1943: 640).

Thus, judges who saw that the social and economic conditions upon which legal ideology had been superimposed were changing, and who understood that ideology in terms of the conditions of free enterprise capitalism, sought doctrinal devices to avoid its effects in the very different conditions of *monopoly capitalism* (Kessler 1943: 640). In England clauses excluding liability to the consumer 'were construed *contra proferentum* and given the narrowest effect consistent with the words used' (Baker 1990: 406). Standard contract terms have been an instrument of economic power for many centuries (Prausnitz 1937). However, the inadequacies of individualistic contract analysis have been highlighted clearly by the dominance in important consumer markets of modern monopolistic business enterprises of great size and power, by the greater 'negotiating distance' between contracting parties in the modern consumer society, and by the increased scale of risk arising from modern consumer products such as automobiles or high technology services such as air transport. The recent proliferation in modern Western societies of contracts involving central or local government, or state agencies, among the parties has further shown the problems of analysis of what is to a large extent in these contexts an instrument of a power relationship inseparable from other aspects of public administration (Turpin 1989). In England as elsewhere, since the nineteenth century, many important controls on contractual terms and their effects have been introduced to take account of problems posed in the conflict of doctrine and experience by the individualist outlook of the law while, nevertheless, preserving that outlook (for example, by the use of fictional 'implied terms') in the basic form and principles of contractual transactions.

The Employment Contract and the Marriage Contract

The adventures of individualism contrast interestingly in different fields of law. Not until 1875 was the employment contract seen in English law as the bargain of legal equals. Until the Conspiracy and Protection of Property Act of that year it was a criminal offence for employees, but not employers, to act in breach of the contract of employment. Indeed, in this field 'the era in which practically unrestricted liberty of contract did exist ... was a relatively short interval [at the end of the nineteenth century] between two periods of regimentation' (Dodd 1943: 643). Yet the rhetoric of freedom of contract was of great importance, justifying, for example, in the mid nineteenth century the (now abolished) doctrine of common employment protecting employers from liability for injuries caused to employees by the negligence of fellow employees (Cornish and Clark 1989: 496–9). 'This was a risk which [the victim] must be taken to have agreed to run when he entered into the defendants' service, and for the consequences of which, therefore, they are not responsible.'[7] In modern employment law the contract of employment appears as a motif of individualism overlaid with the legal accretions of generations of conflict between organised groups. The recognition and definition in law of these groups as the bearers of specific rights and responsibilities creates tensions and inconsistencies in individualist ideology but is dictated as a political problem by the realities of industrial life.

Family law provides a different picture again. 'Marriage is but a civil contract,' declared John Selden, the seventeenth-century legal historian. But this is a position that, in modern Western societies, has come close to recognition only in very recent times with the development of laws providing for relatively simple formalities for marriage and divorce (Phillips 1988; Glendon 1981: 32ff; Stone 1990). The law of marriage appears as the latecomer to 'contractualisation' among areas of Western legal doctrine, reaching this stage at a time when most other areas of law show major modifications to or discarding of individualist doctrine. An explanation is hinted at by Weber when he refers to 'the idea which has become powerful through the very rationalisation of life in the contractual society ... that the formal integrity of the family is a source of certain vaguely specified irrational values or is the supporting supra-individual bond for needful and weak individuals' (Weber 1978: 691). More simply, in an individualist society, the family appears as an island of

7 *Hutchinson v York Newcastle Rly* (1850)5 Exch 343 at 351 per Alderson B. One of the most explicit statements of this view is by another judge, Baron Bramwell, in evidence to the Select Committee on Employers' Liability for Injuries to their Servants: 'Why does he not leave the employment if he knows that it is dangerous? To my mind, it is a sad thing to hear men come into court, as I have heard them, and excuse themselves for not having done that on the ground that their bread depended upon it, or something of that sort. I should like to see a more independent feeling on the part of workmen, so that they would say, "I will have nothing to do with a man who employs dangerous things or dangerous persons."' Select Committee Report No. 285. (1877) p.63, Q.1157.

Gemeinschaft values (cf. O'Donovan 1985: 11–2); tending to become the sole remaining communal nucleus in a society of isolated individuals.

Marriage is still far from being transformed in law from what Weber calls a 'status contract' (altering social status and 'total legal position') to a limited, instrumental 'purposive contract'. Can it be said that insofar as Western law retains its individualist *Gesellschaft* character, its jurisdiction tends to stop outside the *Gemeinschaft* realm of family life—the maintenance of which is implicitly recognised in individualist ideology as the essential foundation of individualism in all other spheres of social relations? Hence Pound's idea of the incompatibility between law and the intimacy of family relations (see Chapter 2). Perhaps, also, this ideological consideration may partially[8] explain resistance within the legal system itself to intrusion in the family realm, even where (as in cases of domestic violence) such intrusion may be welcome and very necessary (cf. Bourlet 1990). It may also help to explain the tendency to discard individualist assumptions of responsibility in the law, in favour of treatment, supervision and control strategies, as the state intervenes more extensively (for example, through social welfare agencies and juvenile justice systems) in the field of family life.

Law in Corporate Society

The Variety of Legal Persons

The foregoing discussion has illustrated some ways in which legal individualism, one important current of legal ideology, has confronted the changing social and economic conditions of contemporary Western societies and retained its hegemony—its dominance as a mode of understanding and interpreting social relations. We must now consider how elements of legal ideology associated with legal individualism still provide, through certain adaptations, an underpinning for forms of power—especially economic power—that are distinctive features of contemporary societies.

The concept of the legal person or legal subject defines who or what the law will recognise as a being capable of having rights and duties. As Pashukanis clearly recognised, this concept is the foundation, in a sense, of all legal ideology. It allows legal doctrine to spin intricate webs of interpretation of social relations, since the law defines persons in ways that empower or disable, distinguish and classify individuals for its special regulatory purposes. For example, children, slaves, mentally

8 The well-documented patriarchal biases in law and its enforcement (see e.g. O'Donovan 1985) may, however, be even more important elements of explanation.

disordered individuals, prisoners or married women may be partially, or wholly, invisible to the law in particular societies and eras; not recognised as persons at all, or treated as possessing only limited legal capacities to contract, to own property, or to bring legal actions (e.g. Cornish and Clark 1989: 398–402; O'Donovan 1985: 30ff; Stone 1982). In this way, throughout history, law has not merely defined social relations but *defined the nature of the beings involved in them*. Alongside law, religion and various forms of ideology similarly serve to define personality. As Althusser (1971: 160ff) puts the matter, individual subjects are 'hailed' in ideology and recognise themselves in it, as if looking in a mirror.

Marxist theory tends to assume, however, as Althusser's analogy of the mirror suggests, that the locus of the person or subject is necessarily a human being (Hirst 1979: 98ff). However, it is clear that the most important legal persons in capitalist enterprise in contemporary Western societies are *not* human individuals but *corporations*. Since a business corporation is recognised as a person in law it is capable of acquiring legal rights and assuming legal responsibilities: for example, by making contracts, owning property, committing crimes. This is a particularly important modern instance of the more general point that legal history shows law recognising in various times and places not just human individuals as persons but numerous other kinds of legal persons —for example, animals, funds, idols, temples,[9] gods, and many varieties of corporate organisations. Thus historically, legal doctrine has struggled, in parallel with religion and philosophy, to define individuality and humanity and the relationships between collective and individual life. Further, it has done so in ways that necessarily reflect the interests and concerns of those with power to influence or control legal institutions.

What is apparent is the dominance of a particular conception of the relationship between the individual and society in modern Western law, and what is of particular sociological interest is the way in which individualism in legal doctrine has confronted the increasingly apparent domination of Western societies by large corporate structures. The unit of decision is increasingly the group, not the individual; large occupational organisations such as business corporations and trade unions are increasingly the focus of personal and group needs (Bell 1973: 301ff; Black 1989: 45). Non-Marxist theorists of 'post-industrial society' have tended to see this development as an aspect of a general historical tendency in Western societies towards rationalisation and bureaucratisation. The major regulatory problem of 'post-industrial society' is seen as control of the power of large organisations of many

9 For a recent illustration see *Bumper Development Corporation* v *Commissioner of Police for the Metropolis* [1991] 4 All ER 638 (CA) (Indian Hindu temple, recognised as a legal person in Indian law, entitled to sue, through its representative, in an English court for recovery of stolen property).

kinds, not only business enterprises. Thus the American lawyer Christopher Stone (1980) has argued for a new legal focus on the problem of 'giant corporate bureaucracies' claiming that, in some respects, business corporations may be easier to regulate by law than some of the numerous other bureaucratic organisations of contemporary society, since the profit-orientation of the former provides a lever on which the law can act by facilitating or limiting conditions of profitability. By contrast many other analyses stress economic concentration in large business enterprises as the essence of power in contemporary capitalism. Hence, in this view, law, reflecting and expressing the major power structures of the society in which it exists, is hardly likely to curtail corporate power effectively (Black 1989: 55) but rather to make its exercise more orderly and efficient.

Individualism and the Corporation

In certain respects the corporate organisation of Western societies has challenged fundamental assumptions of legal individualism. Notions of individual responsibility are confronted, for example, with the prevalence of insurance against risk, so that the individual is able effectively to devolve liability on to a risk-bearing collectivity such as an insurance company. Whatever the law may say about individual responsibility, in practice in many areas of law in which compensation for harm done is in issue actual liability is a matter to be resolved between large associations (or concentrations of capital) with which the individuals involved have allied themselves and under whose shelter they enter into social relationships (cf. Black 1989: ch 3). The variety of forms of collective organisation has inevitably demanded special legal regimes of control in which the notion of universal, equally treated legal subjects can hardly be seen as an adequate basis for legal analysis.

On the other hand, the doctrinal question of how far organisations or groups can be recognised in law as persons and how far such persons can be assimilated to individual human persons is of obvious ideological significance, since it implies broad ideas about the legal legitimacy, rights and duties of organisations. It is unsurprising, for example, that the nature of corporate legal personality has been a long-debated, yet still unclear, matter in modern Western legal philosophy (Hallis 1930) and that the historical form of the debate reflects major social and political changes. Thus, historical arguments about the nature of corporate personality were important for writers, such as the highly influential legal historian Otto von Gierke in late-nineteenth-century Germany, resisting the increasingly *gesellschaftlich* character of Western societies (Zweigert and Kötz 1987: 148), while in another context, for example that of early-twentieth-century Britain and the United States, they reflected the increasing social and economic significance of large business corporations (Horwitz 1985) and also, particularly, the development of modern trade unions (e.g. Geldart 1911: Witmer 1941).

In a 1612 case, an eminent English judge declared that corporations 'cannot commit treason, nor be outlawed, nor excommunicated, for they have no souls.'[10] In 1839 the United States Supreme Court held a corporation, not being a 'citizen', should not be given a citizen's constitutional rights.[11] But, as economic enterprise increasingly focused on organisations rather than entrepreneurs, business corporations came to be treated more like human beings. In the late nineteenth century, for example, after the United States Supreme Court had held that the Fourteenth Amendment to the Constitution guaranteeing 'due process' applied to corporations as persons, courts used it to protect them from economic regulation by the states (Hurst 1970). In England the term 'person' is defined in law as including a body corporate.[12] Conceptual misgivings in early modern law as to whether a corporation itself could bear liability for wrongdoing 'have virtually disappeared' (Stone 1980: 7). It seems clear that economic considerations have determined that whatever doctrinal problems may have existed in different Western societies they have had to be resolved as best they might to recognise and facilitate the needs of corporate economic actors. The logic of legal concepts has not stood in the way of this development (Friedmann 1967: 522–3). A commentator on American legal development writes, 'I find nothing in the history of corporation law that inhibited development of big corporations, much that expedited it. I have found a steady line of growth from the earliest public corporations to today's multinational giants' (Werner 1981: 1662). Neither is corporate personality necessary for legal regulation of corporate organisation. In different Western legal systems numerous different doctrinal devices (for example, trusts) have evolved to facilitate collective rights in property and collective organisation of action (e.g. Friedmann 1967: ch 34; Friedmann 1972: ch 9).

Thus the ideological significance of law is to some extent separable from its technical effects, as discussion of symbolic functions of law earlier in this chapter suggested. Yet ideology provides the climate of expectation and belief in which the technical aid of law is sought. Thus Thurman Arnold, noting that 'great organisations can be treated as individuals', argues that by means of legal recognition of corporate personality the '*laissez faire* religion, based on a conception of a society composed of competing individuals, was transferred automatically to industrial organisations with nationwide power and dictatorial forms of

10 *Sutton's Hospital Case* (1612) 77 ER 937 at 973, per Coke CJ.

11 *Bank of Augusta v Earle* (1839) 13 Pet 519 at 587.

12 Interpretation Act 1978, Sch 1.

government' (Arnold 1937: 185,189). Legal individualism as ideology has been carried along in legal doctrine to inform the regulation of social conditions in which much has changed—the law, its meaning, its effects, and the environment in which it operates—but not, perhaps, the ideology itself.

Corporate Liability and Corporate Power

Problems of the regulation of business corporations illustrate many aspects of the relationship between ideology and power. The corporation is a person yet, in certain ways, is more favoured morally than the human individual (Hagan 1982). It has been argued that 'much of the deterrent effect of heavy fines on individual business people comes from the social stigma of a criminal conviction. But individuals within a corporation may feel shielded from any stigma that attaches to the corporate entity; then, too, a corporation's conviction may not produce the same degree of moral revulsion among the populace' (Nader and Shugart 1980: 71). The corporation, although a person in law, remains a nebulous moral entity because in reality it can act only through human agents.

While adverse publicity attaching to a corporation because of its unlawful activities can have important consequences for the corporation's operations (Braithwaite 1989: ch 9), it may be very difficult to attach liability to the corporation unless specific human agents of misfortune acting in its name can be identified. 'Corporate penalties often impose losses in circumstances when no one appears blameworthy, least of all the investors, employees, consumers, and dependent communities, who will bear the brunt of the burden' (Stone 1980: 27). But conversely the identification of particular human agents of the corporation who should bear the entire blame for harm done in the context of corporate activities may be difficult or may lead to lenient penalties imposed on individuals seen by the courts as representatives of a collective enterprise (Stone 1980: 32–3). Further, the recognition of corporations as persons solves certain problems of individualist ideology but creates others, especially that of the balance of legal rights between the individual owners of the corporation's capital (shareholders) and the corporate entity itself represented through its management. Given the importance of the individualist strand in legal ideology it is unsurprising that this matter has remained a consistent theme of twentieth-century debate about corporation law, more central in many respects than questions about the control of corporation power to protect general social interests (Werner 1981).

Earlier discussion of the relationship between law and power should suggest the need to reformulate the long debated question of how far law can effectively control corporate power. What is important is to analyse the kinds and sources of power acting upon and through law. Insofar as large business corporations dominate Western economies, the state depends upon their welfare in a basic sense. As Ehrlich puts it, 'the state cannot destroy the economic conditions of its own existence. The state is conditioned upon the production of economic goods within society in sufficient quantities to supply it with nourishment' (1936: 374), to furnish the resources to finance state activity. He goes on to note that, in the short term, the state can build its own power 'by committing depredations upon the national economic system … for the ruin which will come after the lapse of decades or centuries need not worry the persons that are in power at the present time' (1936: 374). This suggests both dependence upon and extensive power to influence the economic structure.

The concept of the 'state' often lacks precision in literature about law. It is probably best understood in the context of contemporary Western societies as the organised concentration of political power in a society (see also Chapter 2). Taken in this sense the concept is wider than that of government and embraces the whole range of institutions, agencies and processes by means of which political power is exercised within a defined territory. It follows that government, in the sense of a governing regime, is only one element within this complex structure of administration and control.

Marxist theories analyse the nature of the state in various ways. For some, influenced to some extent by Pashukanis' ideas on law, the form and functions of the state are derived from the logic of capital relations, specifically from the need to contain contradictions inherent in the mechanisms of capital accumulation and so maintain these mechanisms (Jessop 1982: ch 3). For others the state is seen as an agency of co-ordination and regulatory power on behalf of the huge, increasingly monopolistic business corporations of contemporary capitalism. Thus 'state monopoly capitalism is usually treated as a distinct stage of capitalism characterised by the fusion of monopoly forces with the bourgeois state to form a single mechanism of economic exploitation and political domination' (Jessop 1982: 32). Since, in Marxist analysis, economic relations ultimately determine state action, the state can be, at most, 'relatively autonomous' of the economic base. Its necessary function in relation to the economy is pre-given by theory. The problem here, however, as will be seen when other aspects of economic determinism are considered, is not the assertion of powerful influence on state activity from specifically economic considerations, which most non-Marxists today would accept as obvious, but the difficulty of explaining the effects of this influence theoretically without either dogmatism or incoherence.

Many forces influence government policies and state activity, including pressures for and assumptions or beliefs about public order and security, economic and social welfare, external defence, individual and collective interests, as well as the institutional interests of state bureaucracies themselves—all of these mediated by ideology. The state relies upon economic resources. Increasingly, however, corporate power requires the security that state law offers. Business fears unwanted legal intervention and control—'more red tape to contend with, another restriction on ... merchandising, another brake on business and therefore on the economy' (Eaton 1980: 278)—yet depends upon legal structures. Historically law's primary contribution to the business corporation has been, according to one influential writer, to fix its internal authority structures and facilitate the raising of capital (Hurst 1970). However, increasing size and complexity of business organisations and their transactions, together with attendant economic risks, make corporations increasingly dependent on state co-ordination and protection. Furthermore, the growth in corporate size seems to be accompanied by efforts by 'big business' to direct the law specifically against 'small business' which, perhaps with certain advantages of flexibility arising from limited size, poses threats to the stable, monopolistically structured economic environment on which huge corporations depend. The power relations involved here may perhaps best be seen as a combination—reflected in the content of law—of conflict and co-operation between the state (composed of not necessarily united, but in some respects competing, governmental agencies or bureaucracies) and other corporate power structures.

If the matter is seen in this way various predictions are possible. Marxism's conception of the state asserts that class and economic relations will in one way or another determine the nature of state activity. But competing modern theories of 'corporatism' argue that in modern corporate society the state can direct society by co-opting within itself and co-ordinating the centres of corporate power existing in society (Held 1987: 214–20). Both views may suffer from a certain dogmatism. The advantage of conceptualising relationships between corporate power centres in terms of both conflict and co-operation is to avoid assuming that patterns of domination and subjection in these relationships must be pre-given by theory.

In any event it is important to note the character of the main participants in such relationships. The bureaucratisation of social life, stressed particularly by theorists of 'post-industrial society', is paralleled by a development identified in modern Marxist analysis. This is that capital (rather than capitalist entrepreneurs as such) has increasingly become an actor on the social stage. It seems more and more to dwarf the individuals associated with it and to find its vehicle in large corporate structures. Capital is increasingly owned by organisations in bureaucratically administered funds (such as insurance and pension funds). The customers who are the source of these funds hold 'titles to interest, right to money sums in certain circumstances, etc., not capital' (Hirst 1979: 135). Corporations own the shares of other corporations in complex chains in which the agency of individual human beings seems dwarfed by the structures of capital holding. The twentieth-century discussion of a collapse of shareholder power over the management of corporations (e.g. Berle and Means 1933; cf. Werner 1981)—the divorce of ownership of capital from control of capital—seems to suggest a recognition that the corporation is to be seen as the modern holder and embodiment, in itself, of capital—that capital is the actor whose instrument is the corporation. As Bernard Edelman (1979: 57) remarks in a different context: 'Capital assumes the mask of the subject, it is animated, it speaks and it signs contracts.' Thus if the relationships that determine the shape of contemporary law are largely relationships between huge corporate bureaucracies, these bureaucracies represent (and derive their power and vitality from) seemingly autonomous concentrations of capital, the intricacies of ownership of which are increasingly difficult to unravel.

State and Individual

Corporate society does not mark a return, even of a limited character, to *Gemeinschaft* relationships of fraternity and community. Although various writers have noted legal trends that suggest a reversal of the historical progression from status to contract relationships which Maine identified (e.g. Kahn-Freund 1967), it has usually been stressed that the new statuses of corporate society—for example, with regard to employment rights, social welfare entitlements or trading franchises—are qualitatively different from those of *Gemeinschaft* law (Rehbinder 1971). The bureaucratised collective organisation of contemporary Western societies is strongly hierarchical, suggesting powerful controls over the individual rather than the expression of relationships like those of community or kinship which founded *Gemeinschaft* statuses. The individual is dwarfed by the power of organisations, including particularly the power of the modern state.

Many of the most perceptive social theorists recognised early that a thoroughgoing individualism in law and ideology, despite its proclamation of liberty, paved the way directly for the massive concentration of state power characteristic of modern Western societies (Nisbet 1975: 199–200). The development of this power was, thus, not an aberration from individualism but its authoritarian face. De Tocqueville's mid-nineteenth-century classic *Democracy in America* saw the guarantee of democracy in numerous voluntary associations interposed between the solitary individual and the state. Durkheim saw the destruction of such autonomous legally recognised organisations in France after the French Revolution as helping to create what he viewed as the longstanding isolation of the state from individual citizens in his country and the accompanying threat of autocracy. Numerous other writers have echoed similar themes. With the triumph of individualism autonomous organisations based on solidarity, such as communities, become largely invisible to the law (lacking personality) and so insignificant for many purposes as between the individual and the state. 'Ownership, contract and the state' become 'the only connecting links that remain between the individual and society' (Ehrlich 1936: 235; cf. Gurvitch 1947: 222). Attempts around the turn of the century by jurists such as Ehrlich and Durkheim's follower Léon Duguit to argue that law derives from sources in collective life independent of the state; or by others such as Gierke in Germany, Hauriou and Renard in France and Romano in Italy to claim the autonomous legal existence of numerous groups or institutions within society; or by anarchist and syndicalist political writers to organise resistance to the state through intermediate social institutions, can all be seen as attempts to theorise the possibility of countering these tendencies towards concentration of state power.

Western law, the law of the centralised state, could hardly be expected to counter them. The problem has been formulated legally in two main ways. First, it has been expressed in terms of the distinction between public law and private law which establishes the separation of state and civil society in legal doctrine itself. Thus, private law is seen as the regulation of social relationships in which the state has no direct interest except to maintain orderly processes for the resolution of disputes. Public law is seen as the legal framework of relationships between state agencies and between state and citizen. Consequently, while private law in modern Western societies can, to a considerable extent, take the form of legal relations between formally equal legal persons, public law as the reflection and expression of the changing and developing forms of state power can only maintain elements of private law form, as Pashukanis argued, in limited and imperfect ways. The doctrinal separation of public and private law makes it possible to avoid recognising in ideology the two faces of law—as expression of apparent equality and as expression of actual power—in a manner that would reveal the contradictions of legal individualism. The two faces are presented as two different kinds of law. Thus recently fashionable government policies of 'deregulation' in the 'private' sphere in the United States, Britain and elsewhere have co-existed with an increasing concentration of state power: 'what is currently emerging in the name of the free market is a kind of "strong statism" masquerading as the minimalist state' (Lewis and Harden 1983: 228; Cotterrell 1988; Norrie and Adelman 1989).

Secondly, the problem of state power has been expressed as a problem of checks and balances *within* the state, in the doctrine of separation of powers. In Montesquieu's original formulation the doctrine held that particular branches of the state apparatus—judicial, legislative and administrative—should not trespass on each other's specific functions and that each, retaining its functional independence, would act as a check on the power of the others. In Britain it serves only to justify the independence of the judiciary—a matter to be discussed in detail in Chapter 7—and, although the effects of the doctrine are not insignificant, a modern critic has argued that a rigid separation of powers may constrain the efficient use of state power rather than limit that power as such. 'Liberty is not threatened by legislative activity of the administration but by a structure of society that makes the rise of contending political forces impossible or difficult. A pluralistic social structure and a flexible multi-party system are far more important to liberty than the monopolisation of legislation by the legislature and the reduction of the administrative power into a law enforcing agency' (Neumann 1949: lxiv). Again, the primary importance of the doctrine is symbolic.

Yet, as will appear in the next chapter, the state's need for legitimacy gives rise to legal limitations on the *manner* in which its power is exercised which are far from insignificant. Further, quite apart from formal legal separation of governmental powers, competition, dissension or simply poor co-ordination between different parts of the state structure (for example, between central and local government, or between judiciary, legislature and executive) may impose important limitations on governmental activity or on its effects.[13] However, competition for power between various parts of the state apparatus may promote a general expansion of the scope of state intervention in social life, so that state organs 'increase their prerogative at the expense of society rather than directly of one another' (Poggi 1978: 136).

Much modern literature stresses in one way or another that not only has state power in contemporary Western societies greatly increased but it is expressed in relatively new forms which undermine in the most fundamental manner the individualism that originally aided it. The modern state exercises surveillance and control through welfare agencies which can penetrate the previously 'private' sphere of home and family (Donzelot 1980), and through technologies of 'treatment' (for example, of criminal offenders) which undermine individualist conceptions of responsibility. It has been seen as increasingly 'absorbing' civil society (e.g. Mathiesen 1980; Santos 1982). The French writer Michel Foucault asserts that 'the new methods of power ... rest not on right but on technique, not on law but on normalisation, not on punishment but on

13 See further ch 9.

control ... exercised at specific levels and in particular forms that go beyond the state and its apparatuses' (quoted in Poulantzas 1978: 77). Non-Marxists such as Foucault tend to see these forms of control as pervasive and somehow undirected; the development of what Weber's sociology emphasised as the routinisation and bureaucratisation of modern life. For Marxists they indicate the complexity of the problems facing the state in maintaining the increasingly fragile yet ever more complex and massive structures of capitalism. These are matters which will be considered further in the last chapter of this book.

The Problem of Economic Determinism

Throughout much of this chapter the Marxist framework of concepts has provided a structure and a starting point for analysis. Yet it has been necessary continually to modify or extend these concepts since they do not offer the self-contained structure of explanation that Marxism as an *ideology* has claimed to provide. As has been seen, the concept of class, which is central to Marxist theory, appears problematic as a basis for social theory in relation to contemporary Western societies. Again, the relationship between state and economy remains complex and multifaceted so that broad general theory of the kind attempted in Marxism—though it inspires illuminating detailed studies—can appear dogmatic and limiting. The plausibility of Marxist claims about the economic determination of legal ideology remains the major question to be confronted here if we are to take stock of Marxism's specific theoretical contribution to understanding of law.

Marx's contribution to social theory starts from the vitally important insight that moral, political, legal or other ideas cannot be assumed to be causal factors in history, but that, because most people do indeed generally assume them so to be, the material conditions which give rise to these ideas often remain unexamined. Hence ideas, and institutions that embody them, are 'reified'—treated as though they were independent actors on the stage of social life. Perhaps, of all systems of ideas, legal doctrine and legal ideology are most often reified in this way, in the idea of the 'rule of law' and a 'government of laws and not of men' (cf. D'Entrèves 1967: 69ff). But if Marxism stopped here it would assert merely what has become the uncontroversial basis of the sociological study of law; the need to understand law in terms of its sources and effects in society. Marxism adds the thesis that law and ideology are determined by specific economic or material structures. In so doing it creates two related and extremely difficult theoretical problems: first, what is the nature of the consistent determining element ('materiality') and, second, what are the mechanisms of this determination?

Marxism was born from the need to confront idealist philosophy; to oppose theories claiming that ideas are the determining forces in history. Marx's strategy was to turn this philosophy (specifically Hegel's) 'on its head'; to claim that what it saw as determined by ideas was actually the determinant of them. Thus materialism in opposition to idealism maintained the same analytical separation of ideas and 'material reality' and made the same claim that they could be conceptualised in a way that showed one of these determining the other. It followed, further, that the determining material reality had to be conceptualised as a theoretical unity which Marx eventually specified as the economic structure of forces and relations of production. Marxism has been dogged ever since by the need to work with concepts that specify ideas and material reality as analytically separate, with each of the opposites in some way theoretically unified so that one of them can be seen as ultimately determining the other.

Thus, currents of ideas, or at least the dominant ideas in a society, tend to be seen in Marxist writings as a unity, as 'ideology'. Yet the complex and often contradictory patterns of legal doctrine, the varying tendencies of development in different areas of law, and the different doctrinal approaches of various Western legal systems to similar areas of legal problems, should make one hesitate to assert that legal ideology—let alone an overarching 'dominant ideology' encompassing much besides legal ideas—constitutes a unity. It seems more realistic to think of it as a complex of many elements or currents of ideology originating in diverse sources.

Certainly, insofar as law is recognised as a means of influencing ideas and beliefs—insofar as its ideological importance is recognised by judges, legislators and others professionally or politically concerned with its uses—attempts are consistently made to assert and demonstrate the unity of legal doctrine (cf. Cotterrell 1986) and the consistency of its ideological foundations. Law claims authoritativeness, not the tentativeness of science. Thus, there is a strong tendency in modern legal reasoning to see legal doctrine as a 'gapless' system covering all cases, or capable of being elaborated through its own internal canons of reasoning to provide a legal viewpoint on any new situation (Weber 1978: 657-8). Similarly, at the most abstract level of legal practice, legal philosophers ceaselessly attempt to rationalise, from the contingencies of doctrinal development, systems of consistent legal values. At the most concrete level, for example in the practice of magistrates' courts in Britain, the presentation of legal doctrine in the courtroom has been portrayed as suggesting timeless, unchallengeable and comprehensive 'absolute truth' (Carlen 1976b). All of this is consistent with the character of ideological thought as described earlier; to portray as unified and complete that which is not and cannot be. A scientific approach to the study of legal ideology must recognise the complexity and contradictions of the latter and avoid oversimplifying the patterns of legal doctrine. At the same time it must analyse the means by which ideological thought glosses over its own internal inconsistencies.

Equally, while the concept of ideology makes possible a systematic analysis of the social sources and effects of currents of ideas, the variety of these sources and effects has to be clearly recognised. Just as ideology does not form a unity, neither do the material interests, social conditions and experiences, psychological characteristics and other matters that might be considered to influence the development of ideas. Yet Marxism is forced by the logic of economic determinism to maintain both kinds of unity as central concepts in theory.

These problems have, of course, been recognised in various ways in Marxist writing itself. Most significant is the attempt to discard or radically revise the base–superstructure metaphor. In this context the location of law is particularly important. Is law a part of base or of superstructure? Orthodox Marxist theory would argue the latter, as has been seen. John Plamenatz (1963: 281) and others have argued, however, that law defining rights of property is a necessary expression and definition of the relations of production without which they cannot exist. Thus law is a part of the economic base. It would seem that the economic base cannot be defined in a way that excludes superstructural elements since law cannot be separated from wider ideological and political elements of the superstructure.

Attempts have been made to argue that relations of production can be established initially through lawless power which only later becomes formalised by law (Cohen 1978: ch 8) or on the basis of conventional rules which only later become legal (Collins 1982: ch 4) but neither defence is free from difficulty (Collins 1982: 84; Hunt 1991: 121–3). Similarly, on the basis of his important historical studies, E.P. Thompson concluded 'that law did not keep politely to a "level" ... it was imbricated within the mode of production and productive relations themselves (as property-rights, definitions of agrarian practice) and it was similarly present in the philosophy of Locke; it intruded brusquely within alien categories, reappearing bewigged and gowned in the guise of ideology; it danced a cotillion with religion, moralising over the theatre of Tyburn; it was an arm of politics and politics was one of its arms; it was an academic discipline, subjected to the rigour of its own autonomous logic; it contributed to the definition of the self-identity both of rulers and of ruled; above all, it afforded an arena for class struggle, within which alternative notions of law were fought out' (Thompson 1978: 288). As other Marxists have recognised, the problem in such a formulation is that the concept of economic determination threatens to lapse into incoherence (Sugarman 1981: 96). To argue that 'an advance in our understanding of the relative autonomy of law is unlikely to occur at a high level of abstraction' (Sugarman 1981: 97) is in effect to admit the inadequacy of the conceptual framework of Marxism.

Althusserian structuralism offers the idea of the different levels of the social formation acting on each other to produce through their action a 'structural causality' of social developments. It suggests an *ultimate* and *indirect* determination by the economic level only as a result of the complex actions of elements of ideological, political and economic structure on each other (Althusser 1969: ch 3). But this disguises the problems rather than solves them, introducing new sophisticated concepts to shore up the inadequate framework of economic determinism bequeathed by the classic texts of Marx and Engels. Thomas Mathiesen, who applies some of Althusser's ideas to legal analysis argues that the 'precedence of materiality' and the 'feedback effect' of the law on what he calls 'material structures' 'cannot be separated, but constitute an interwoven whole' and he admits doubt as to whether 'one can ever prove—in a strict sense—the materialist conception of law. Like other generalized conceptions of society, the materialist conception remains in the final analysis a political and theoretical interpretation of the world, a paradigm, a way of grasping the world conceptually' (Mathiesen 1980: 72, 155).

The issue here is not proof, for social theory cannot prove or be proved, but can merely elaborate a perspective on society. The issue is the rigour of the concepts used. On this basis Marxist theory is best seen as a politically important polemic against idealism, constantly warning against the reification of ideas and focusing attention on the vital importance of economic considerations which are often disguised in idealist rhetoric. In this respect it remains of great and enduring value. Thus, for example, while Parsonian and Durkheimian theory treats norms and values as fundamental to the integration of societies Marxist theory demands always that we ask where these controlling ideas come from and whose interests they favour. It challenges the notion of law's neutrality and stresses through the concept of ideology—not an invention of Marxism but one to which Marxist writing has particularly contributed—that currents of ideas and beliefs are instruments of power. What is necessary now, however, is for sociological analysis of law to transcend the terms of the idealism–materialism polemic. It seems particularly important to recognise both the complexity of interaction and the close relationship between law and economic structure; and to analyse the diverse sources of ideology and its varied social effects. Marxist writing illuminates many aspects of these matters. Yet neither the sources nor the effects of ideology can be *definitively* specified by theory in advance of analysis of particular legal ideas and legal institutions in particular societies.

5 The Acceptance and Legitimacy of Law

Despite great differences in approach and emphasis, sociological functional theory as discussed in Chapter 3 and the Marxist theory discussed in Chapter 4 raise some similar problems. Reduced to their simplest form these problems amount to whether general theory can take full account of the numerous complex determinations of the actions and outlooks of human beings as individuals.

Functionalism, as has been seen, is criticised for 'leaving human beings out of the picture', for making assumptions about 'system needs', about the normal conditions or functional requisites of social systems, and typically deducing both the 'normal' patterns of actions of individual system-members and the mechanisms for guaranteeing these patterns from system analyses. As was seen in Chapter 2, autopoiesis theory goes even further, treating social systems (including legal systems) as 'self-referential' systems of communication, capable of maintaining themselves and reacting to their environments in ways that relate only indeterminately to the motivations, intentions or values of individuals (e.g. Luhmann 1985: 281ff; Teubner 1989). Again, within Marxist theory, the relationship between the scope of autonomous social and political action and the structural constraints imposed by economic determination is a permanent problem. How can a theory of society—adequate to serve the needs of legal theory—be developed without oversimplifying the complexities of individual life; without reducing individuals to mere units in or agents of systems, actors whose socially significant actions are determined by structures that exist quite independently of them; or to class caricatures having no significance for social analysis except in terms of their positions in the economic structure of society?

Clearly it is necessary to refocus on the individual, without losing the important insights about social systems and power structures that are offered by the theory considered earlier in this book. For example, as has been seen in the previous chapter, general theory can suggest both the social origins and the mechanisms of promulgation of currents of widely held ideas, such as those associated with or reflected in legal doctrine. But these general explanations cannot, themselves, show the reasons why individual citizens accept or reject law, nor why individuals or groups choose either to call upon the law or to ignore it as far as possible. As the German social theorist Jürgen Habermas has argued, systems theory which sees societies as objective structures cannot alone analyse the conditions of 'crisis' in a political or legal system. Crises involve not only objective structural problems affecting the functioning of the system but also the subjective feeling of impairment of freedom of action in certain circumstances on the part of those who experience the system (Habermas 1976). A general consideration of law's ideological effects is not enough to explain the motivations of individual actors. So this chapter will be concerned with various ways in which attempts have been made to discover and interpret the motivations and attitudes that bear upon citizens' acceptance of law and the manner and extent to which law plays a part in their everyday experience.

The Experience of Law: Positivist Approaches and KOL Studies

Many empirical studies of knowledge of law and attitudes to law have been positivist in orientation. That is, they have treated levels and degrees of public knowledge and opinion about law as social facts to be discovered and recorded, rather than as, for example, merely indicators of continuous and complex processes of adjustment of behaviour and attitudes arising in interaction between citizens, and between citizens and officials. Attitudes tend to be seen as measurable data, which can be compared with the content or policy of legal provisions. This approach, typical of what has come to be called the KOL (knowledge and opinion about law) literature, is understandable given the positivistic orientation of much social science and legal scholarship, the reformist policy concerns of many of those involved in research in this area, and the assumptions about the nature of law that have become dominant in contemporary Western societies.

Thus we have noted the *emergence* of modern state law from various normative systems (Chapter 1), its asserted official and technical *dominance* over other normative orders (Chapter 2), the idea of the functional *autonomy* of modern Western state law within society—law as a distinct normative order with specific functions as such (Chapter 3) and, finally, modern tendencies towards state *absorption* of all forms of normative regulation in contemporary Western societies. In Chapter 4, the concept of the 'absorbent state' gathering within itself or co-opting other regulatory systems through corporatist strategies or using new means of surveillance and control to reach all levels of social life including previously relatively self-regulating domains such as the family, was noted. Furthermore, the steadily enlarging regulatory and directive functions of the state have been seen to be explicable in various ways: for example, in terms of increasing societal complexity, differentiation or corporate concentration; or in terms of economic and related structural problems of capitalism.

What this seems to show is that as law itself has been seen, positivistically, more and more as a mere technical device of regulation, this development has been accompanied by a progressive divorce of law from the consciousness of citizens, a divorce which increasingly appears as a problem for the state not only of efficient social control but also, to some extent, of political legitimacy. Law—in the sense of a state-monopolised, comprehensive, society-wide, dominant normative order—has provided the foundation and the instrument of the modern power of the state in Western societies. In this sense, modern Western states have typically depended upon an appeal to the ideology of the 'rule of law'—the conception of government as bounded by known legal rules and exercising its power over the citizen solely through the medium of such rules, which it is considered to have the authority to create through publicly recognised formal procedures. In this way law has been central to the Western state as both instrument of power and legitimation of power. The legitimacy and efficiency problems of the modern state involve two questions specifically related to law. First, is the form of law that underpins the 'rule of law' legitimation of Western political power still appropriate to meet the problems of regulation that face the state today? Secondly, are new modes of exercise of state power which have developed in response to these regulatory problems threatening to the bases of public acceptance of the political order; that is, to its legitimacy?

In this situation studies of knowledge and opinion about law are of great significance for those who view law positivistically as an autonomous agency acting upon society. KOL studies are often indistinguishable in aim and philosophy from studies of the impact or effectiveness of laws. They may be an aid in determining how law can be made more effective as an agency of social control; how it can secure popular support; how it can be most effective in 'social engineering' (Bankowski and Mungham 1976: 20ff). They can reveal attitudes that spell danger for the authority and prestige of law and hence for its effectiveness (Podgorecki 1985). Early work, such as that of Cohen, Robson and Bates (1958) in the United States on the relationships between family law and attitudes within the family, was much concerned to map the 'general sense of justice' within the community, a perhaps somewhat over-ambitious approach given the range of variables involved. But more limited studies have tried to ascertain attitudes of particular social groups to certain types of conduct or offences and much work has revealed considerable variations in legal knowledge and attitudes to law as between different socio-economic groups, different areas of law, men and women, different age groups and ethnic groups, and urban and rural populations. The literature removes any lingering legitimacy of a general concept of 'public opinion'. As Grossman and Grossman note, 'There is no such thing as *the* public; to understand legal culture, one must carefully define *a* relevant public; for various issues this will be a different group of people' (Grossman and Grossman, eds, 1971: 32).

Further, as the Danish researcher Berl Kutchinsky remarks in a survey of KOL literature, 'public knowledge concerning legal topics is considerably poorer than presumed by the legal authorities and by many scholars' (Kutchinsky 1973: 105). Even among groups for whose benefit laws are passed, such as the housemaids in Aubert's famous Norwegian study (see Chapter 4), legal knowledge may be very limited. Podgorecki notes the existence of reasonable knowledge of 'the nature of basic rights and obligations and broad categories of what is allowed and forbidden'—which we might consider an underpinning for the general effects of legal ideology—but only limited knowledge of technical and procedural precepts concerned with 'available methods for the realisation of the objectives enshrined in legal principles' (Podgorecki 1973: 71). Recent ethnographic studies paint similar pictures of legal awareness (Merry 1990). But levels of knowledge of law often vary greatly with general education levels, socio-economic group, and occupation.

The numerous apparently conflicting findings in the KOL studies point to the difficulty of framing inquiries and to the range of variables involved, and severely limit permissible generalisation. Nevertheless, statistical findings of low levels of legal knowledge and of very considerable variations in attitude to laws and the legal system are far from insignificant. Western law has long relied on the maxim that ignorance of the law is no excuse, although it may mitigate punishment. As John Selden noted in the seventeenth century (in his *Table Talk* 1689), it is 'not that all men know the law, but because 'tis an excuse every man will plead, and no man can tell how to refute him.' The *ignorantia iuris* maxim strains legal legitimacy, however, when law is so far removed from popular consciousness that little or nothing of its content enters that consciousness. The French legal sociologist Carbonnier writes that 'there is an obvious misunderstanding of reality to require of a man that he should know intuitively what four years of university and 10 years of practice are not always sufficient to teach' (Carbonnier 1988: 170). He adds that the *ignorantia iuris* maxim made sense when law was the embodiment of custom, less so when most law is of recent origin. Sociologically, however, the maxim is of fundamental significance since it encapsulates the modern situation of law which can retain its ideological dominance only by proclaiming that none can ignore it—at the same time as its remoteness and technicality guarantee that, as the KOL studies show, most people do. The general effect of the maxim, Poulantzas claims, is to make everyone dependent on the functionaries of the state for knowledge and aid (Poulantzas 1978: 90). In addition, while individual citizens' lack of access to legal knowledge has no bearing on the power of the state or of other people or organisations to enforce law against them, it makes the citizen powerless to invoke law. Thus differential legal knowledge is an aspect and support of the power differentials existing in society.

Legal Socialisation

In considering Parsonian systems theory in Chapter 3 it was seen that questions about acceptance of values and norms upon which the maintenance of a social system is considered to depend are framed as problems of *socialisation*; that is, of the mechanisms by which the social system reproduces the appropriate motivations and attitudes of system members. Effective socialisation is thus seen as a functional requisite of the social system; a task of fostering and shaping attitudes and outlooks of individuals which is to be accomplished for the system's well-being. More generally the concept of socialisation is used to refer to the development of particular kinds of values or attitudes which are seen as functionally appropriate or necessary to a given legal, political, economic or other system. Thus, various writers have developed the idea of legal socialisation and sought to specify mechanisms or processes by which commitment to law is developed in the individual.

The American social psychologist June Tapp has drawn on the work of major cognitive development theorists such as Jean Piaget and Lawrence Kohlberg to suggest stages of development of the individual's orientation to legal rules from childhood. Kohlberg specifies six stages of moral development linked to maturation of cognitive capacities and developing social experience of the individual. Joined with Tapp's data on legal attitudes these suggest a sequence of levels and stages in orientation of the individual to law (Tapp and Kohlberg 1971). The first (pre-conventional) level includes the stage of conformity merely to avoid punishment and the further 'hedonistic stage' of conformity to obtain reward. The second (conventional) level involves conformity to rules because they are rules. Its initial stage is conformity to please others followed by the stage of conformity to 'do one's duty' or express respect for authority. The third (post-conventional) level is that of supporting moral principles as such, apart from any demands of authority. In its 'social contract' stage this involves upholding constitutionalism and the processes that guard social stability and orderly processes of change. Its ultimate stage (though most people do not reach this final position) is one of obeying only when law reflects proper ethics. Law is thus seen as an element in the wider socialisation processes that shape the adult's outlook. At the same time socialisation into the legal order is seen as dependent on wider processes of cognitive and moral development. Particular programmes of legal education for citizens are proposed as practical applications of these theoretical perspectives to heighten individual involvement in, as well as an aware and knowledgeable commitment to, the legal order (Tapp and Levine 1974).

The literature on legal socialisation, like the closely related but much more extensive literature on political socialisation developed by sociologists and political scientists, reflects both a consciousness of the isolation of state institutions from everyday popular experience and a profound uncertainty about the effects of this isolation. The hypothesis of definite stages of development of attitudes to law links individual cognitive and moral development to social conditions determining general levels of moral development within a society and within sections of it (Danelski 1974). The stage approach has been criticised not only on the grounds of the apparent rigidity of the developmental sequence (Kurtines and Greif 1974) but also more generally as embodying value judgments about moral progress which reflect particular Western values (Irvine 1979).

Kohlberg's depiction of moral development has also been influentially criticised from a feminist standpoint as an abstraction of male, rather than female, experience and circumstances. Men as they develop may tend to speak of fairness and rights, reciprocity and equality, stressing values of autonomy. It has been argued, however, that a different 'female' voice of morality, emphasising relationships, caring and connection, co-operation, responsibility and avoidance of hurt, reflects a different path of moral development unrecognised in the uniformity of the stage approach, although the developed moral outlook of most individuals may combine elements of both moral 'voices' (Gilligan 1982). These criticisms of the stage approach are important. Nevertheless it offers an interesting attempt to provide a framework for understanding complex processes of individual development in a manner that is relevant to general theory of social systems.

Deterrence and Compliance with Law

It is important to recognise that actual conformity to the requirements of legal rules requires neither acceptance of the law as binding, legitimate, authoritative or worthy of respect nor even knowledge of the relevant legal provisions. Use of the threat or application of legal sanctions as a means of deterrence presupposes some degree of *general* knowledge of the workings of the relevant law on the part of those whose behaviour is to be controlled by it. But this may be limited to the notion that certain acts constitute crimes of some sort and are subject to some kind of legal punishment (Gibbs 1978: 112).

Given these strictly limited links between the quality of legal knowledge and the possible deterrent effects of law, it has been possible to develop an extensive literature on deterrence and compliance with law that largely ignores many of the complex issues about knowledge and opinion concerning law which have already been suggested. There are, however, considerable difficulties in assessing deterrent effects of law, as criminology has shown. Classical criminology assumed the rationality of the potential criminal: a calculation of gains from criminal activity balanced against an assessment of likely detriment from sanctions imposed for breach of law would determine conduct. Contemporary criminological research, stressing the range of crimes committed on impulse, the absence of calculation by offenders of legal consequences of their action, and the range of motivations for or against criminal behaviour which may often be of far greater significance than those controllable by the law, has made the general idea of deterrence through legal sanctions extremely problematic. Nevertheless legal sanctions obviously provide a potential influence on conduct in some circumstances, even if it is difficult to specify what the circumstances are and what kinds of sanctions are most likely to be effective. Proof of deterrent effect of law is a cherished aspiration for those who seek a justification of law as an effective technology of social control; and perhaps particularly for those who seek a justification not complicated by moral and political problems of the relationship between legal order and social solidarity.

Unfortunately the complexity of questions of causation as well as the political importance of findings—for example on the heavily researched question of the relationship between capital punishment and homicide rates—have made virtually all research in this area highly controversial. Numerous studies over many years have found no evidence of any special deterrent effects of capital punishment, and rare empirical claims of such effects have been subjected to a barrage of criticism on methodological grounds (see e.g. Beyleveld 1982). On the deterrent effects of legal sanctions in general it is impossible to offer confident conclusions from the results of numerous often inconsistent studies using a wide variety of methods and varying considerably in analytical sophistication. Recent literature has, however, plausibly distinguished as variables the *severity* of sanctions and the *certainty* with which sanctions are imposed, treating the latter as more relevant to deterrence than the former. In a 1969 study of homicide, assault, rape, burglary, larceny, robbery and car theft, Charles Tittle found that reduced homicide rates correlated with greater certainty of punishment and, to a lesser extent, with greater severity of punishment. But in relation to the other offences crime rates seemed to be affected only by the degree of certainty and not by the level of severity of punishment (Tittle 1969). Perhaps inevitably, these findings have not gone unchallenged (Chiricos and Waldo 1970), but the certainty/severity distinction seems clearly significant (Antunes and Hunt 1973; Tittle and Rowe 1974; Paternoster 1989).

The literature raises the possibility that the deterrent effects of law may vary considerably from one kind of offence to another. Thus it has been suggested that in relation to parking or other minor traffic offences, legal sanctions do have an important demonstrable effect on conduct, both certainty and severity of sanctions being relevant factors (Chambliss 1966; 1967). Even here, however, studies of the use of law to deter drinking and driving suggest that enforcement drives in relation to this kind of law may have only short-term deterrent effects in the absence of continuous publicity and enforcement activity (Ross 1984). But the risks of detection and of prosecution may be important variables in deterring 'rationally calculated' offending such as tax evasion (Klepper and Nagin 1989). Overall, the literature implies the conclusion that as the technology of law enforcement becomes more extensive, social control as a merely technical matter can be pursued with increasing efficiency by increasing the certainty of sanction imposition, through ever more extensive surveillance and simplification or routinisation of sanctioning processes (for example, automatic fines or other penalties) and without escalating the severity of sanctions to anything approaching 'terror levels'. Thus, given the resources of the contemporary state, it may be that this technical problem of social control can be addressed without confronting more intractable problems of popular acceptance of law and of legal and political legitimacy. Whether the matter *should* be dealt with in this way is another question entirely.

In the absence of this kind of strategy, the relatively low actual probability of legal sanctions being imposed on many offenders makes it plausible to argue that the importance of sanctioning action is not so much deterrence as public affirmation of the importance of the rule that has been broken. Sanctioning is thus a contribution to maintaining the integrity of the rule system in the minds of the normally law-abiding, rather than a strategy for keeping the potential law breaker in check (cf. Garland 1990: 58–61).

Apart from such considerations, these studies of the deterrent effects of legal sanctions seem to have major inherent limitations. In particular they suffer from 'the researcher's inability to discern those social-psychological processes by which the presumed effects of punishment are realised' (Waldo and Chiricos 1972: 524), processes which may vary considerably with situation and personality. In this respect they are subject to limitations similar to those of much KOL and legal socialisation literature. KOL studies frequently fail to ask about the processes by which attitudes about law are formed in the minds of individual citizens and about the connections between levels of legal knowledge and the motivations of the individual; legal socialisation studies seek to discover *general* processes of moral and cognitive development which, again, cannot stress individuality. Equally, most deterrence studies conflate the effects of numerous factors acting upon the situation of the individual citizen (Paternoster 1989: 8-9). Because of this they are unlikely to give more than relatively vague and general indications of likely patterns of compliance with or deviance from law.

Microsociological Approaches: Phenomenology, Ethnomethodology and Social Interaction

The problem of taking account of individual motivations in sociological analysis emphasises the limitations of positivism referred to in the introduction to this book. Understanding these motivations is not a matter of reducing sociological explanations to psychological ones but of recognising that social phenomena—laws, political institutions, social norms, economic systems—do not merely act *externally* on individuals but are themselves also the result of and the embodiment of social interaction.[1]

For example, to the lawyer, laws seem to exist in a very concrete form as the tools of professional practice; they are objectively verifiable as 'valid' law because they can be identified according to certain formal tests which define what constitutes legislation or judge-made law—that is, binding judicial precedent. From another viewpoint, however, laws and legal practices like other social phenomena exist only as shared ideas or understandings of individuals—judges, police, lawyers, citizens. If none of these adjusted their personal or professional expectations in a way that implies 'recognition' of the law—that is, the attribution of a particular meaning and significance to particular statements made or documents created or actions taken in particular circumstances—it would be impossible to say that the laws 'existed' with any sociological relevance. Thus law, like other social phenomena, exists in the sense that it is embodied as a set of expectations or understandings about behaviour.

Legal systems are, therefore, not only structures recognisable objectively in positivistic terms as autonomous social phenomena—'social facts' in Durkheim's sense. They exist in the subjective experience of individual actors. They are made up of the myriad everyday interactions

1 By social interaction in this general sense is meant the actions of individuals in relation to other individuals, and the patterns of expectations, understandings and recognisable routines of behaviour that result from and influence these actions.

of lawyers and officials—police, bailiffs, administrators, judges, clerks—amongst themselves and with citizens who experience (and also contribute to shape the character of) the legal system in interactions with these officials. From this point of view the positivist identification of law as something 'acting upon' society or existing autonomously cannot be maintained. Law is the label given to a certain aspect of society, a certain field of human interaction. To understand law is to understand the processes of interaction associated with the idea of 'law'.

Since all social phenomena can be thought of as constructed in the interaction of individual actors, there has been in sociology over recent decades a strong emphasis on the need for a 'microsociology' looking at small-scale situations of interaction (for example, the organisation of interaction in a courtroom, the formation of a queue or a pattern of deference in a small group, the structure of children's conversation, the way a specific local dispute is solved). The assumption has been that the building bricks of 'society' are to be found in the way such small-scale structures of social life are established and patterned, and particularly in the way that shared meanings or understandings come to be accepted or imposed in these situations.

A great variety of approaches in sociology with such labels as symbolic interactionism, phenomenological sociology and ethnomethodology has explored ideas such as these about the nature of social life. In criminology, the so-called 'interactionist approach' has emphasised that criminality or deviance may be best thought of not positivistically as an objective condition, quality or characteristic of the criminal or other deviant, but as a situation constructed in social interaction (e.g. Becker 1963), or a process of adaptation of individuals to circumstances in which they find themselves, or a set of rules or practices by which the individual copes with or makes sense of the situations or relationships with which he or she is faced. 'Labelling theory', a variant of this approach, similarly sees deviance not as an objective situation but as a label imposed by some members of society on the behaviour or attitudes of others. Phenomenological approaches in sociology tend to stress the idea that 'social reality' consists in the shared meanings or understandings attached by actors to social situations, that is, to situations involving relationships or dealings with other actors. Thus, for some writers, the appropriate way to understand the apparently solid and stable major political, social, and economic institutions of contemporary Western societies is as structures of habitual, generally accepted thought and action built upon innumerable subjective experiences of individual actors. The actions of individuals in everyday life tend to become habituated and fall into established patterns. The reciprocal observation and acceptance of these patterns by other actors affected by them and the consequent orientation by these actors of their own thoughts and actions in patterns that take account of them is the basis of the establishment of social institutions (Berger and Luckmann 1967: 70ff). Institutions make it unnecessary to think out afresh our reactions to situations. The situations become standardised. Their meaning and the appropriate way to act in relation to them become taken for granted.

This has an obvious direct relevance to legal analysis. From a phenomenological viewpoint, social rules and their meanings are created in interaction. Thus even if to the lawyer law seems fixed as a positive code or collection of rules, in reality—so it is claimed—it operates through the negotiation of meanings in interaction between individuals: between judge and counsel in court, between police and suspect, probation officer and delinquent, lawyer and client. These negotiations fix numerous informal rules about appropriate behaviour and expectations, which determine the 'real' effects and meaning of the formal rules in the law books.

While some writers adopting a phenomenological stance of this kind see the possibility of developing social theory on the basis of a microsociology of social interactions, a more radical school of thought labelling itself 'ethnomethodology' has largely rejected the generalising and theorising ambitions of sociology. One writer suggests 'an alternative to viewing the task of sociology as being to address the big social problems (whether in revolutionary or revisionist terms) is to propose and pursue a programme of research that is motivated not by policy concerns, but by a willingness to regard social order as a puzzle, to treat the familiar and the obvious as "anthropologically strange", and to accept that quick and easy solutions are unlikely to be forthcoming' (Atkinson 1981: 104). The concern of ethnomethodology is with the Hobbesian question: How is social order possible? But the claim made is that no general theoretical answer is possible. What is necessary is to understand, through specific small-scale studies of particular situations, the rules developed by individuals in everyday life to create the possibility of order. This involves, amongst other matters, understanding the means by which an individual defines or recognises a certain situation—for example, a coroner's definition of 'suicide' (Atkinson 1978; 1971), a police or probation officer's categorisation of a youth as 'delinquent', or a police identification of a 'suspicious character' (Sacks 1972)—and so decides on an appropriate response to it. As the quotation above suggests, ethnomethodology is concerned with examining what determines 'common sense' in various situations. It seeks to understand the taken-for-granted rules that define those situations and so to connect the general problem of social order in sociology with the motivations and outlook of the individual.

In recent years a further approach to the study of law, as shaped and experienced in social interaction, has flourished, having developed from quite different intellectual traditions from those just mentioned. It has involved trying to study empirically how the experience of coping with disputes and grievances, and sometimes bringing these before legal institutions, shapes or expresses the legal consciousness of ordinary citizens. Some of those who have been most active in this work have been anthropologists and the fieldwork involved is often detailed descriptive ethnography of the kind that has typified modern sophistic anthropological studies of social interaction. Thus, the studies attempt to analyse the complex, multifacetted and often contradictory or ambiguous characteristics of the legal consciousness and experience of ordinary citizens. Typically, they use detailed observations of settings of social interaction (such as courts, lawyers' offices, welfare agencies and local communities) and interviews to reveal individuals' subjective experience of courts, their ways of thinking about and asserting rights (e.g. Merry 1990), their assumptions about how grievances or disputes can be and are resolved or contained in their social environment (e.g. Greenhouse 1986), and the understandings created, shaped or transformed by their contacts with lawyers (e.g. Sarat and Felstiner 1989), court officials (e.g. Yngvesson 1988) or other state agencies (e.g. Sarat 1990a). Unlike the ethnomethodological studies, these writings seem generally relatively unconcerned to focus on the processes by which order and stability are maintained in understandings of the social world, and more interested in identifying the complex and variable content of those understandings. Their often rich, multitextured descriptions of the ambiguities and contingencies of experienced reality suggest that they represent a promising contemporary approach to empirical research on law in society.

Instrumental Acceptance of Law: Max Weber

Is it possible to reconcile a determined emphasis on the actions and motivations of individuals with a quest for general theoretical perspectives on law and society? In other words, is it possible to develop a kind of half-way position which keeps the virtues of 'understanding' approaches in sociology emphasising the variety of individual experiences and subjectivity and yet which, at the same time, makes it possible to recognise and explain theoretically law as the positive, objective system of doctrine and regulation familiar to the lawyer?

The most important attempt to develop an analysis of law on this basis—and one of the most important bodies of writing in sociology of law—is contained in the work of the German sociologist Max Weber, today one of the most revered and important figures among classic social theorists. Weber's major analyses of law are contained in his huge and intricate masterpiece *Economy and Society*, in effect a summation of his entire sociology, begun in 1910 and unfinished at his death in 1920. He sought to combine a positivist conception of law, in harmony with the general view of the German jurists of his day, with an insistence on the notion that sociology's concern is with understanding social action—that is, action subjectively meaningful to the actor and oriented to or taking account of the behaviour of others (Weber 1978: 4ff). In his stress on the need to understand the subjective meaning which social action has for those engaged in it and his claim that this kind of understanding—and not the recording or prediction of behaviour—constitutes the objective of sociology, Weber provided much of the methodological foundation on which later phenomenological approaches in sociology were built. Yet his contribution to the sociological analysis of law is so substantial and detailed that it stands alone and addresses issues and aspects of law hardly touched upon in much later work.

A Method of Analysis of Social Action

Weber adopts two strategies—the use of 'ideal types' and the development of particular concepts of rationality—in an attempt to reconcile a positivist orientation to law with the social action approach to analysis. Since social reality is infinitely varied it cannot, in Weber's view, be the subject of general scientific laws or 'a closed system of concepts' encompassing or classifying it in some definitive manner (cf. Weber 1978: lxiii). Thus if we are to extrapolate from individual cases, occurrences, instances of action, and motivations we cannot do so by a method of generalisation. History consists of an endless stream of unique occurrences. We can pick certain chains of causation by various means from this stream in order to consider particular events but we cannot imprison the infinity of historical data (which provides the data of sociology) within general theories that explain it. Any such theories must, at best, offer explanations of a few elements from this infinity. We can, however, understand particular occurrences or instances of social action in relation to deliberately constructed models or 'ideal types' of social action. These are not generalised from experience but constructed on the assumption of particular kinds of consistent motivations of action. The most important ideal types Weber uses are based on assumptions of *rational* motivations of conduct. Rationality is, thus, the major key which sociological observers can use to understand the social action of those they wish to study. The ideal type provides a model of rationality which can aid in understanding the meaning or motivation underlying actually observed social action (Weber 1949). It provides a yardstick against which empirical reality can be compared.

This is not, however, to assume that all action is rational. Weber uses four basic ideal types of action (1978: 24–6), two of which embody different kinds of rationality: *value-rational* action is motivated by the actor's aim of expressing certain values (for example, moral precepts to which he or she adheres) in action, while *purpose-rational* action is motivated by the actor's aim of achieving chosen goals (for example, the acquisition of some desired benefit). But other action may be guided by *emotion* or *tradition.* These four categories are ideal types insofar as it is not assumed that they exist in pure form in experience; they are merely models of possible motivations of action. Thus, nowhere in Weber's sociology is there any claim that the concepts he uses describe or generalise from actual conditions of social life. Weber continually stresses the infinite complexity and variety of actual motivations and situations. Ideal types merely provide tools to aid in understanding such unique instances.

In practice the use of ideal types makes it possible for Weber to analyse such phenomena as law, political authority and economic activity in general terms while continually stressing the variety of social action encompassed within them. Central to all his work is one particular ideal type—that of capitalism—because Weber's primary project is to explain the nature of the forms of economic action associated with Western capitalism, the reasons for their development in the West and the consequences of that development for social and political life, and the corresponding reasons for a lack of comparable capitalist development, up to the time he wrote, outside the Western world. Thus Weber constructs an ideal type of capitalism in order to pursue this inquiry and to provide a framework for interpretation of historical data on the development of Western economies and societies. The essence of capitalism is, as we should assume from the tenets of Weberian sociology, a particular kind of social action—purpose-rational economic action oriented to profit in the market. In capitalism economic rationality becomes freed from subordination to ultimate (for example, religious) values, as also from emotional or purely traditional considerations.

Weber devoted much of his relatively brief but brilliant career of scholarship to the demonstration, through intricate historical analyses, of the processes by which the economic rationality of capitalism established itself and came to dominate in the West, but not in the East during the same period of history. Although he never denied, and indeed often strongly emphasised, the importance of material interests as basic motivations of action, his work has often been interpreted as 'a debate with the ghost of Marx' because of the great emphasis that it puts upon the significance of currents of ideas as influences on the development of economic, political and social institutions, and hence the contrast between its orientation and that of Marxist materialism (e.g. Weber 1930: 90-2).

Thus many of Weber's analyses are concerned with the influence of religious ideas on secular activity. For example, he sees the role of the Protestant sects in creating the climate of thought and belief in which capitalist economic action could become dominant as crucial to the unique historical development of capitalism in the West (Weber 1930). Similarly his political sociology—as will be seen in more detail shortly—is centrally concerned with the variety and significance of different kinds of belief about the basis of political authority. Finally, law as a system of ideas—as doctrine—occupies a unique place of importance in Weber's analyses as compared with those of other social theorists. Weber was originally trained in law. He never doubted its central social significance and though his writings range with encyclopedic erudition through a bewildering array of subjects he regarded his sociology of law as 'the most complete' part of his work (Lachmann 1970: 63).

Law as a Framework for Social Action

Two general concerns regarding law emerge, in Weber's work, from this background. First, given his central concern with the analysis of Western capitalism understood as a social phenomenon based on specific forms of economic calculation and action, it is unsurprising that the relationship between law and economy should be as pervasive a theme of his sociology of law as it is in Marx's legal theory. But capitalism is understood by Weber in very different terms from those of Marx—not primarily as exploitative relations of production but essentially as rational entrepreneurial activity oriented to market exchanges. Thus Weber's emphasis in analysing law is on its significance in facilitating the forms of rational planning and calculation that underpin capitalist enterprise and hardly at all, as with Marx, on law's repressive or mystificatory functions. Secondly, however, Weber's concern as a sociologist is to understand the social order of modern Western societies and not merely their economic basis. Thus the development of the specific forms of rational calculation that constitute capitalist economic activity is seen as representing only one strand of a far more general process of rationalisation of social life in these societies. It is hard to pin down the exact nature of this pervasive rationalisation. It shows itself, according to Weber, in extremely diverse forms which extend from the relatively fixed harmonic and compositional conventions of Western classical music as compared with oriental forms (Weber 1958) to the 'routinisation' of life through development of impersonal rule-governed bureaucratic administration. The latter characteristic is present not only in government but in numerous fields of social organisation including eventually—with increasing size and concentration of production units—the economy.

It is clear that, in Weber's view, law has a central importance both for the economic foundations of capitalism—that is, in facilitating the forms of social action on which capitalism depends—and in fostering and expressing the more general processes of rationalisation of life in capitalist society. Law is accepted in modern Western societies, not because it expresses dearly held values, nor because of the overriding sanctioning power of the state, nor through tradition, nor the charisma of political leaders. It is accepted, simply, because it provides a commonsensical and comprehensive framework of predictable rules which make it possible for individuals to pursue purpose-rational social action; that is, to fulfil their perceived self-interest in a rational manner. In earlier and other societies the basis of acceptance of law may well have been different and, Weber suggests, almost necessarily was. But in the distinctive 'modern society' of Western capitalism law provides the basis for its own acceptance through its own logical form: as a set of rules within which individuals can orient their own conduct in a purpose-rational manner, a manner that becomes pervasive not only within economic life but well beyond it too.

It follows that, in Weber's view, law is accepted for primarily instrumental reasons. The relationship between law and economy is thus relatively straightforward. Law can often hamper economic activity through the imposition of rigid rules and fixed bureaucratic procedures. But it basically provides the predictable guarantees of enforcement or support of economic transactions that make rational economic calculation possible in sophisticated forms. Thus, by guaranteeing future performance of obligations, law facilitates numerous transactions and arrangements beyond face-to-face exchange. It allows the creation of corporate entities involving structures of rights and obligations that will survive the individuals presently concerned with them. It makes possible the assignment in commercial transactions of present or future obligations expressed or recorded in documentary form (Goode 1982: 66ff). And it facilitates long-term property arrangements embodied in trusts which may benefit persons unborn or even uncontemplated when the arrangements are set up. While capitalist enterprise promoted modern forms of Western law—because of demands put upon legislatures and courts for the development of doctrine relevant to burgeoning commerce—law, for Weber, underpins capitalist calculation in an obvious and fundamental way.

Legality and Legitimacy

This claim and Weber's related arguments about the general basis of the legitimacy of law in modern Western societies can only be understood if his conception of the form of contemporary Western law is made clear. Weber's major analyses of law are concerned with distinguishing different forms of legal thought and then considering their social, economic and political relevance. As ever, the method of analysis depends on specification of ideal types.

Types of Legal Thought

According to Weber law can be irrational or rational and it can be formal or substantive in orientation. Law is rational to the extent that its operation is guided by general rules rather than by subjective reaction to the individual case (empirical law finding) or by irrational formal means such as oracles and ordeals. *Substantively rational* law is guided by general rules determined by an ideological system other than the law itself, for example, a system of morality, a religion, or a political ideology. *Formally rational* law is guided by general rules in such a manner that 'in both substantive and procedural matters, only unambiguous general characteristics of the facts of the case are taken into account'. In *logically formal* law, which Weber treats as the chief kind of formally rational law, 'the legally relevant characteristics of the facts are disclosed through the logical analysis of meaning and ... accordingly, definitely fixed legal concepts in the form of highly abstract rules are formulated and applied' (Weber 1978: 657; 1954: 63).

What is essential to note is that in Weber's view it is this last type of law which is typical of modern Western societies and which has been vital to capitalist development. It is only this logically formal kind of legal thought which lends itself to the highest degree of *systematisation*—a process appearing only 'in late stages of legal modes of thought'. As understood in modern law, systematisation involves 'an integration of all analytically derived legal propositions in such a way that they constitute a logically clear, internally consistent, and, at least in theory, gapless system of rules under which, it is implied, all conceivable fact situations must be capable of being logically subsumed lest their order lack an effective guarantee' (1978: 656; 1954: 62).

Like all ideal types, Weber's categories of legal thought do not exist in pure form in reality. Nevertheless, the dominance of formal rationality in modern Western law is the key to the significance of this law for economic calculation and also for the political legitimacy of Western societies. Only when law is based on its own internal logical processes, rather than existing to express systems of religious, moral or political doctrine in the form of rules or judgments about conduct, can it provide an adequate and intelligible doctrinal support for purpose-rational economic activity. This is so despite the fact that legal and economic rationality are not the same and that economic actors' expectations may often be frustrated by legal doctrine developed to satisfy demands for legal formality (Weber 1978: 885; 1954: 307).

A serious problem seems to exist for Weber's thesis, however. In England, legal doctrinal development was dominated by a pragmatically oriented legal profession concerned with case-by-case problem solving, rather than, as on the Continent, by jurists in the universities stressing the need for doctrinal systematisation. Largely because of this, formal legal rationality did not dominate English law in the heyday of capitalist development. Judges belatedly and pragmatically provided devices to aid commercial development and even the case law development of the English common law gave rise to a certain amount of systematisation. But Weber admits: 'It may indeed be said that England achieved capitalistic supremacy among the nations not because but rather in spite of its judicial system' (1978: 814; 1954: 231).

Much has been made of the 'England problem' in Weber's sociology of law. Does the historical success of capitalist development in England despite the 'irrationality' of English law undermine the thesis of law's contribution to the establishment and growth of capitalism? Weber's discussion of the England problem illustrates a number of important aspects of his method. First, historical occurrences are analysed as having no single cause but as being the consequence of many. Thus a particular legal development could not be regarded as *essential* to a particular economic one. Similar problems might be solved by alternative means in different contexts (cf. Teubner 1984: 296). On this view what may be fundamental for capitalist development is not formal rational law as such but predictable legal procedures and reliable guarantees of rights (Ewing 1987). Secondly, the ideal types of legal thought provide only a starting point for considering the complexity of social effects and social origins of legal doctrine. Weber's analysis of aspects of English legal history shows the combination of irrational and rational elements and formal and substantive characteristics that was produced in the law. The complex effects of these legal patterns on social and economic life may not easily be captured through any simple linking of concepts of formal legal rationality and capitalistic economic rationality. What can perhaps be most usefully concluded, if Weber's framework of explanation is accepted, is that in England the processes of rationalisation of life that accompanied the growth of capitalism were focused on law in a different or perhaps more peripheral manner than in the comparable continental developments.

Legal Domination

Weber sees political legitimacy in Western societies as being based primarily on what he terms *legal domination*, that is, the acceptance of governmental actions as legitimate insofar as they derive their authority from a legal order made up of an abstract and comprehensive system of rules. Such a legal order is accepted on the ground that it provides the common sense framework within which the individual purposes of citizens can be fulfilled. Legal domination is an ideal type in Weber's discussion of forms of authority and is considered alongside two other possible types of legitimate domination. These are *charismatic domination* (acceptance of authority on an emotional basis—for example, allegiance to a particular revered leader) and *traditional domination* (acceptance of authority merely because it is regarded as long established) (Weber 1978: ch 3). All three types of legitimate domination may be present in any actual empirical situation. But legal domination, like formal legal rationality upon which it depends, is clearly seen by Weber as characteristic of modern Western societies.

Weber's conception of modern law as providing a morally and politically 'neutral' framework for purpose-rational action is compatible with views of law in modern Western society expressed by many subsequent writers. It is reflected in the ideas of so-called 'exchange theorists' who see acceptance of the social order as being grounded in the capacity of members of a society to engage in ordered exchange—not merely of economic or material benefits but of social benefits in the widest sense. In a more specifically economic focus it is reflected in Friedrich Hayek's conception of the free society as a 'catallaxy'—the social order brought about by the mutual adjustment of many individual economies in a market (Hayek 1982 II: 108–9). In Hayek's conception law itself has no purpose except to provide the abstract rules within which numerous individual purposes of individual citizens can be pursued. The idea remains popular today among neo-libertarian thinkers.

Yet Weber's deeply ambivalent attitude to legal domination and the rule-governed order of economy, politics and society which goes with it is very different from the enthusiasm of true believers in the libertarian catallaxy. Legal domination involves acceptance of rules because they *are* rules; not for their moral worth or political virtue. Thus the price of a thoroughly rational social order is a 'disenchantment' of the world in which routine replaces vision, in which what Weber calls an 'iron cage' (Weber 1930: 181) envelops individuals who increasingly 'need "order" and nothing but order, who become nervous and cowardly if for one moment this order wavers, and helpless if they are torn away from their total incorporation in it' (Weber quoted in Mayer 1956: 127–8). In Weber's vision, as in Marx's, there is no dramatic divide between the liberal world of entrepreneurial capitalism and the bureaucratised world of organised or monopoly capitalism. The latter is the outgrowth of the former. It is the consequence of the massive expansion of 'neutral' rules, practices and procedures, accepted largely without question because of their assumed technical indispensability within a web of regulation ever more comprehensive and intimidating. This huge regulatory system dwarfs citizens who see no way—and no moral or political reason—to dispute its legitimate domination of their lives. Weber's analysis suggests no possibility of reversing this development—of retaining the framework of neutral rules but making it less intrusive in life as neo-libertarians wish. The only possibility of change is through replacement of the domination of rules with *another* form of legitimate domination. But traditional authority seems increasingly out of place in modern society. What remains is the possibility of charismatic domination: the rise of the demagogue, the appeal of a particular leader or regime to popular emotions, the irrational 'outburst' of political leadership and loyalty which for a time—until routinisation sets in again—sweeps society into new paths.

Weber's analysis makes clear that such charismatic 'disruptions' are both unpredictable (the irrational element for which a place is preserved in his sociology of rationality) and temporary. The concept of legal domination entails an autonomy of Western law even more complete than that which, for example, Parsonian systems theory describes. In a Durkheimian or Parsonian perspective, as was seen in Chapter 3, law still remains tied to societal values—though the nature of the tie may be hard to specify. But Weber is quite explicit: under legal domination law is *self-justifying*. It requires no appeal to moral or political values for its legitimacy. Its own systematic logical structures provide its legitimacy. Law is accepted solely as a rational system of rules. The religious, traditional or ethical natural law principles that grounded it in earlier eras are lost as law is 'unmasked' as merely technical rules of ever increasing intricacy: 'the product or the technical means of a compromise between conflicting interests' (1978: 875; 1954: 298). Thus, the autonomy of law takes on a sinister aspect. Law frees itself from the sources that could challenge its legitimacy. Its technical imperatives replace moral judgment. It provides the bars of the 'iron cage' in which life is turned into a routine of instrumental action; in which organisation means bureaucracy; in which values seem to cease to matter very much.

These ideas about modern law and about Western societies have been highly influential. Indeed, most contemporary writers on the sociological basis of political legitimacy in contemporary Western societies start from Weber's ideas. Various avenues of challenge to them can, however, be suggested. First, the assumption that law is accepted by citizens as a framework of purpose-rational action seems to involve the kind of lawyers' assumptions that were challenged in Chapter 1. There it was recognised that frequently state law does not enter into calculations of conduct. In the areas of economic action for which, in Weber's view, law has particular significance, the relationship between law and business dealings is complex and sometimes even extremely tenuous. As was noted in Chapter 4, the tension between state (and state law) and economy may be as important a characteristic of contemporary Western societies as the congruence between them. Here Weber makes assumptions about the social importance of state law for everyday conduct that are typical of legal positivism and have been criticised earlier in this book. Viewed in this light Weber's 'England problem' may not be a problem at all. In the context of capitalist development, the pragmatism of common law practice coupled with basic legal guarantees of order may have been ample compensation for a lack of formal rationality of doctrine (cf. Ewing 1987).

A second point is that even if law has provided a common-sense framework for purpose-rational action, it is not necessarily the case that contemporary Western law can or will retain the form that Weber sees as essential to this role. It is necessary to consider changes in the character of Western law which raise doubts on this score. In particular, an examination of characteristics of law and lawyers' practice associated with the concept of the 'rule of law' is essential. Thirdly, changes in the nature of the Western state may necessitate a different kind of legitimation from that provided by law alone. Here recent theories of the state and political legitimacy are relevant in assessing the adequacy of Weber's concepts as a basis for explaining contemporary political conditions. Finally, even if legal domination can be understood without reference to any particular values underlying legitimacy, except the value of rational order, this may be possible only because law is assumed to uphold other values which citizens accept and, under certain conditions, this assumption may be challenged. The following sections will discuss in turn the second, third and fourth of these points, the first having been considered earlier.

The Meaning of the Rule of Law

For Anglo-American lawyers the ideas associated with Weber's concept of legal domination are reflected most familiarly in the notion of the 'rule of law'. The English jurist A. V. Dicey formulated in the late nineteenth century the most celebrated conception of the rule of law as involving three elements: first, the absolute supremacy of law over arbitrary power including wide discretionary powers of government; secondly, that every citizen is subject to the ordinary law of the nation administered in the ordinary courts; and thirdly, that rights are based not upon abstract constitutional statements but upon the actual decisions of courts (Dicey 1959). The third of these is a generalised defence of common law methods and the second a defence of what Dicey saw as English practice as compared with continental special legal procedures to deal with claims arising out of the activities or jurisdictions of agencies of the state (the field of administrative law). The first, however, suggests an essence of the rule of law as understood in a more general Western sense.[2] In this conception law is reified as the 'ruler' of society. Government, no less than citizens, is seen as subject to law. The state can change law freely as it requires, through recognised processes, but the actions of all state servants and agencies are to be subject to law. Weber's analysis of legal domination, as has been seen, provides an explanation of the sociological significance of the rule of law in this sense as the 'common-sense' basis of rational social order and as the essential foundation of a highly developed capitalist economy.

The doctrine of the rule of law demands that law consist of known, predictable rules. Thus, it presupposes a positivistic view of law on the part of legal officials and citizens. But while lawyers tend to think of the doctrine as a professional invention it is, as Weber's historical analyses demonstrate, the result of economic and political necessities. It serves the need for security of economic transactions and the general conditions of individual liberty which accompany that need. But it also serves the technical and ideological needs of the state and more generally of the efficient structuring of power relations. Public bureaucracies follow legal rules, it has been argued, because of the economic structure within which they operate, because of their internal organisational needs for resources, legitimacy and order, and because of the socialisation of officials to rule-following attitudes and behaviour (Sajo 1981). The comprehensive framework of rational rules not only facilitates dispute resolution but, much more importantly in complex modern societies, helps to prevent friction and dispute by setting out more or less clear guidelines for permissible action: what Llewellyn (1940) calls preventive channelling of conduct and expectations—efficient co-ordination and administration to avoid disruption of the intricate patterns of social life.

However, a consideration of the ideas discussed earlier in this chapter, about the creation of rules and 'shared meanings' in social interaction, should suggest that the rule of law as such—that is, the authority of a

2 The German concept of *Rechtsstaat*, as typically understood in the period when Weber wrote, may be easier to relate directly to the analysis of legal domination than is Dicey's particular concept of the rule of law. Böckenförde defines the *Rechtsstaat* in this sense as entailing, first, that the state is neither divinely ordained nor supreme but merely a 'body politic' existing for the benefit of each and every individual; secondly, that the functions of the state are to safeguard individual liberty and facilitate individual self-fulfilment; and thirdly, that the state and its activities are organised 'in accordance with reason', implying recognition of civil rights, equality before the law, guarantee of private property, independence of the judiciary, constitutional government, and clear and definite laws in legislative form (Böckenförde 1991: 49-50).

comprehensive logically coherent set of positivistically defined official rules—cannot achieve this co-ordination. Rather, it depends on the continual reformulation of rules and practices in experience. Thus, whatever the importance of the rule of law as ideology, as a legitimation of government, it can be doubted whether a comprehensive system of legal rules binding state agencies and citizens alike has ever been a primary basis of social order. In the nineteenth-century heyday of the doctrine it applied only to relatively limited spheres of social life. In England, for example, Dicey ignored the problem of vicarious liability in relation to Crown servants. Because of the immunity of the Crown from liability it could not be held responsible for the acts of its officials, a matter only rectified gradually and not necessarily satisfactorily long after Dicey's time (Harlow 1982: 21ff). Dicey wrote (thinking of the personal liability of officials and citizens): 'In England the idea of legal equality, or of the universal subjection of all classes to one law administered by the ordinary courts, has been pushed to its utmost limit' (Dicey 1959: 193). But Weber, followed by many more recent observers, stressed the fundamental difference in the quality of justice dispensed to different social classes by the higher English courts and the lowly justices' (magistrates') courts (Weber 1978: 814; 1954: 230). While the upper classes and rising middle classes could make use of the relatively rational legal processes of the former, the lower classes met 'the law' only in caricature form in the processes of the latter, which Weber scathingly termed 'Khadi justice'—decision-making based on subjective reaction to the individual case rather than on the careful application of known legal rules and procedures (1978: 976–8). For Weber, this two-tier system amounted to a systematic denial of justice to the poor.

That the professional expertise necessary to ensure that legal procedures are governed by the highest legal standards is more likely to be found at higher levels of the judicial system, and that those litigants with greatest resources of knowledge, wealth and influence are most likely to be able to make use of those higher levels, seems obvious. In this way the rule of law is available to the 'haves' to a far greater extent than to the 'have-nots'. Many studies of magistrates' justice have shown the inability of unrepresented defendants (the overwhelming majority of defendants) in criminal cases to put over their cases effectively. Doreen McBarnet (1981a) has shown how procedures in magistrates' courts contribute to this situation. Defendants who are unfamiliar with the court procedures are continually prevented by procedural objections (for example, that the evidence they wish to cite is inadmissible, or that they are seeking to make a statement at a time when they should restrict themselves to questioning a witness) as they try to explain the situation as they see it. McBarnet's main point is not that the rule of law does not exist at this lowest level of the judicial system today, but that it operates in such a different way from that in the higher courts as to make a mockery of the idea of one system of law administered to all classes by the courts. Further, the pervasive assumption that these cases are *trivial* supports, first, a relaxation of formal legal procedure governing fair trial (due process of law) to the extent that the defendant's liberty is thought not seriously to be threatened; secondly, a general absence of public interest in the system; and, thirdly, the idea that professional legal expertise and advocacy is generally unnecessary in these cases (McBarnet 1981a).

Most defendants in English magistrates' courts plead guilty (see Chapter 7). Of contested cases, again a substantial majority results in verdicts of guilty (Vennard 1982). The impression is one of 'conveyor belt justice'; of the speedy processing of cases within crowded court schedules.[3] McBarnet remarks: 'the decision to plead guilty is itself partly a product of people's expectation that they have little chance of being found not guilty if they opt for trial by magistrates' (McBarnet 1981a: 181). Insofar as such courts deal with more 'middle-class cases' (for example, traffic offences or matrimonial matters) there has been a tendency to use tariff systems or routine administrative procedures to speed up processes, standardise practice and—to a considerable extent—to remove such cases from the courtroom altogether. Similar points about the class differentials inscribed in the rule of law seem to be implied by much writing that has emphasised the poor quality of tribunals in England concerned with the assessment of welfare entitlements of the poor, and the lack of adequate supervision of these tribunals by higher courts (Smith 1975). These criticisms must be read in the light of changes in welfare law and administration in the 1980s which, at least ostensibly, reduced the scope of decision-making discretion in this area—as well as the scope of welfare rights. The introduction of the Social Fund system at the end of the decade, however, heralded a return to significant discretion in welfare administration (see e.g. Mesher 1990; Alcock 1989; Cranston 1985: 165–91).

These illustrations support the view that the rule of law is more important as legitimating ideology than as a practice of equality before the law (Black 1989: 57). Anglo-American lawyers tend to be ambivalent about the doctrine, often forcefully championing it when advocating clear rules to limit or control administrative discretion seen as threatening the liberty of the citizen, but at the same time recognising the existence of so many exceptions to the doctrine in practice as to cast doubt on whether it continues to describe a recognisable characteristic of Western law. Wide areas of discretionary power in many areas of the legal system constitute the clearest exceptions. The following will serve as a few illustrations from many: the numerous discretions available to the judge

3 A comparable situation in New York courts is graphically depicted in McConville and Mirsky 1987.

in a criminal trial (Pattenden 1990); leeways in judicial fact-finding and interpretation of legal doctrine which, it has been claimed, made possible a flexible judicial policy allowing the covert extension of police powers in England (McBarnet 1981b); the jury system 'which is certainly inconsistent with the meticulous observance of rules of law for, as is well known, the jury often makes its own law' (Seagle 1941: 221; Baldwin and McConville 1979a), although in theory decision on the law is for the judge and decision on the facts for the jury; the immunity of large areas of governmental activity from effective judicial scrutiny (Hunt 1991: 119–20); the deliberate abrogation of the rule of law by governments and state agencies in times of emergency (the concept of emergency being itself one open to flexible official interpretation) (Jeffery and Hennessy 1983); the acceptance by courts in England and elsewhere of illegally obtained evidence in criminal cases (Pattenden 1990: 264–88; Dawson 1982); operational factors that encourage police to treat maintaining order as an overriding objective even at the expense of legality (see Chapter 8); and the existence of wide prosecutorial and pre-trial discretion in criminal cases (Vorenberg 1981; Galligan 1987; Carbonnier 1988: 132–3).

The Transformations of Modern Law: Discretionary, Mechanical and Particularised Regulation

The claim frequently made in current literature of sociological analysis of law is not that the Weberian picture of modern Western law as a rational, coherent and comprehensive rule system was wrong at the time he presented it, nor more particularly in relation to the nineteenth-century society and legal order that provided its perspective, but that Western law has been steadily transformed to create a kind of regulation no longer describable in the terms Weber uses. For some writers this change has been registered simply as a decline in the rule of law and a rise of administrative autocracy (Hewart 1929; Keeton 1952); for others it has appeared as a 'crisis of law and legal ideology' (Kamenka and Tay 1975); for yet others it has seemed to suggest that law itself may be on the way to its demise to be replaced by scientific-technical administration and control (cf. Fitzpatrick 1983).

What has happened to provoke such claims? Lawyers, particularly in those countries where the Diceyan concept of the rule of law has been influential, have devoted considerable and ever-increasing attention to specification of major qualitative differences between the forms and structures of contemporary law and those characteristics of law that Dicey's concept envisaged. We can refer to the most noticeable and pervasive of the 'new' forms and structures briefly within three categories which will be termed here 'discretionary regulation', 'mechanical regulation' and 'particularised regulation'.

Discretionary Regulation

Discretionary regulation is characterised by the use of 'indeterminate prescriptions': 'open-ended standards and general clauses in legislation, administration, and adjudication' (Unger 1976: 194). While the rule of law requires that official action should be controlled by clear rules which make possible a definite specification of the citizen's rights, freedoms and obligations, discretionary regulation emphasises flexibility and the primacy in official action of policy implementation rather than formal rule application. Discretionary regulation is thus often associated with the dominance of substantive legal rationality, in Weber's sense, over formal legal rationality: that is, the subjugation of the internal logic of legal analysis to the fulfilment through law of particular political aims, requirements of social utility, or moral values.

The infusion of substantive rationality into Western law is not, in itself, a new development. Pound wrote that 'almost all of the problems of jurisprudence come down to a fundamental one of rule or discretion ... both are necessary elements in the administration of justice ... there has been a continual movement in legal history back and forth between wide discretion and strict detailed rule, between justice without law, as it were, and justice according to law' (Pound 1954: 54). For Weber, substantive and formal legal rationality are ideal types and, therefore, 'pure' distillations of legal forms which appear in historical reality in complex combination. Most if not all doctrinally sophisticated legal systems have known a form of 'equity'—that is, a system of discretionary justice softening the effect of application of rigid legal rules (Newman 1973).

Weber's claim, however, was that in the late nineteenth-century *Rechtsstaat*—the state founding its legitimacy on the guarantee of legal security for its citizens—substantive rationality had clearly been *subordinated* in the law to formal rationality with the result that law could claim a powerful 'value neutral' basis of authority in no way dependent on acceptance by citizens of specific political or moral values. Weber himself saw the rise of modern political currents challenging this stability though he did not consider they would succeed in dislodging the bases of legal legitimacy (Weber 1978: 868-73, 882-95). Many more recent writers, however, have argued that modern law shows a major qualitative change towards substantive rationality in preference to formal rationality; towards the acceptance of ever-increasing discretionary regulation guided by general policy considerations. There remains much disagreement about the wider consequences of this, although the major response of lawyers has been to argue for the reassertion of the rule of law by removal of discretionary powers or, more realistically, by construction of adequate supervision and control of discretion (e.g. Davis 1969; cf. Galligan 1986: 167ff), particularly through judicial review of administrative action and more generally the development of an effective body of administrative law doctrine.

The growth of discretionary regulation has been observed in a proliferation of twentieth-century statutory provisions creating wide areas of official discretion particularly in fields of regulation associated with the welfare state, such as housing, town and country planning, personal social services, health and education provision (e.g. Adler and Asquith, eds, 1981). Discretionary powers in the criminal justice system became more extensive as 'treatment' of the offender and management of deterrence tended to supplant retribution as an expressed aim of the system and hence administrative decision-making became important at the expense of legal assessments of guilt (McClintock 1981). Whether sentencing in the criminal justice process is more or less consistent today than in the past is a matter for debate but two British commentators have noted that 'sentencers currently have an almost unlimited discretion in dealing with cases involving serious criminal violations' (Baldwin and McConville 1979b: 218; cf. Pattenden 1990: 13–4) and an American judge has written that 'the almost wholly unchecked and sweeping powers we give to judges in the fashioning of sentences are terrifying and intolerable for a society that professes devotion to the rule of law' (quoted in Baldwin and McConville 1979b: 218).

Discretionary regulation has seemed to increase in scope as the legal system has more extensively intervened in organisation of the lives of the poor and the working class.[4] Administration of social security law often tends to foster the idea of 'requesting assistance' rather than asserting rights, and claimants and their advisers often have difficulty finding out whether or not certain benefits are allowed (Greenberg 1980: 395, 396). Consequently, social welfare agencies exercise control through their ability to fix entitlements and to delay or expedite action on claims. Sometimes, modes of exercise of discretion or interpretations of welfare rules can facilitate the most intrusive moral controls on claimants' private lives (Cranston 1985: 197–8). As one American welfare rights worker put it: 'People just don't know what's going to get that cheque taken away from them, and they're near scared of their shadow because of it' (quoted in Greenberg 1980: 413). Thus, to the welfare claimant, law is likely to appear as 'a thoroughly politicised patronage system' (Sarat 1990a: 356). In earlier eras, as the historian Douglas Hay's researches have shown, this kind of control through discretion was focused on the

4 Although this term is hopelessly inexact, like most of those employing the concept of 'class', no other seems available.

criminal law as the primary area of law directly bearing on the 'have-nots' of society. The ferocious eighteenth-century English criminal law with its fixed and brutal penalties was mitigated by the frequently exercised discretion to pardon the offender: a discretion which allowed no rights to be asserted but encouraged begging for 'gracious favours' of mercy in affirmation of the majesty of the law (Hay 1975).

Mechanical Regulation

By the term 'mechanical regulation' is meant here regulation that seeks to accelerate or simplify the disposition of cases by removing some of the legal complexities of proof of responsibility, or by standardising penalties or turning judicial procedures to a greater or lesser extent into routine bureaucratic procedures. Thus, the development of so-called strict liability—liability not dependent on proof of usual categories of fault—in criminal law and the law of tort (civil wrongs) provides an illustration of such regulation which has been important in, for example, health and safety legislation governing working conditions and the quality of food and drugs, and certain road traffic offences. Although strict liability may have ancient origins in legal history (Wigmore 1894; cf. Moore 1978: ch 3), it became generally accepted in modern legislation only as business and industry found means—for example, through insurance—of absorbing the burden of liability and as the benefits of maintaining consumer confidence, industrial peace or exclusion of further government intervention came to seem to business and industry to outweigh the costs involved.

The modern development of 'tariff systems' of fixed penalties and simple means of processing cases, most notably in relation to minor traffic offences, is primarily a response to the overloading of court systems and to the demand for uniform treatment of a vast number of similar cases dealt with in the lower courts. Again, in the perspective of legal history this is no innovation because early law—often faced with serious problems of lack of resources for establishing proof, maintaining legal authority in the face of litigants' disputes, and enforcement—similarly shows reliance on tariff systems of penalties and mechanical modes of proof (for example, trial by ordeal, or wager of law) designed to simplify process and avoid legal dispute (Pound 1954: 33). Although strict liability and tariff liability involve diverse legal considerations, their sociological basis and their contemporary effects on the basis of acceptance and legitimacy of the legal system are similar in kind if not identical. Neither challenges the basic principle of the rule of law since both developments involve general application of known rules. But they do have possible adverse consequences for the maintenance of legitimacy through legal domination. This is because they cast doubt on the individual's capacity to apply rules of law to govern purpose-rational decisions on conduct: that is, they challenge the basis of law's self-sufficient legitimacy claims. The more extensively procedures and rule applications are 'mechanised' the less possibility there is for taking account in them of the individual's purposes and intentions and of the particular circumstances of his or her acts. Thus, the less possibility there is for measuring the rationality of individual citizens' conduct against that of the law—just as citizens, according to Weber's legal domination concept, measure the rationality of the law against their own conduct and that of other citizens.

Particularised Regulation

Particularised regulation refers here to regulation directed to particular persons or relatively limited groups of persons, or to particular narrowly defined cases, thus tending away from the assumption of generality of the law which the rule of law doctrine—emphasising known general rules and the equality of subjects before the law—implies. The development of particularised regulation has been noted in diverse fields: in the apparent decline of general contract law and the rise of legal controls over numerous specific kinds of contract (Gilmore 1974; Atiyah 1979; cf. Weber 1978: 880-1); in ambitious legal intervention in management of the national economy over past decades, with laws expressing government policy in considerable detail and in a directive manner (Thompson 1984a; De Smith 1989: 215–7); and in a perceived proliferation of new status relationships, in which the idea of equality before the law has been modified by numerous particular legal statuses arising from the individual's circumstances—for example, as employee, trade union member, consumer, welfare recipient, tenant or business franchisee (Glendon 1981; Kahn-Freund 1967; Gibson and Baldwin, eds, 1985: 331; Nader and Shugart 1980: 65).

While many legislative provisions and consequent regulations give wide, loosely defined powers to state agencies and officials, others specify legal consequences in minute detail. Thus the Shops Act 1950 forbids the sale in England and Wales on Sundays of anything except perishable goods. Schedule 5 of the Act contains a detailed list of goods which can be sold. Fish and chips cannot be sold but chicken and chips and take-away Chinese foods can be because they were not considered when the Act was passed. The sale of 'cooked or partly cooked tripe' is specifically authorised. Jewish traders can open their shops on Sunday if they are registered synagogue attenders and keep their shops shut on Saturdays. The Act contains special provisions relating to newsagents and tobacconists, confectioners, premises for the sale of refreshments, meat traders and hairdressers. Like much other modern legislation it combines this kind of detailed particularised provision with general discretionary powers conferred on administrative authorities. Often legislation confers wide discretionary powers on particular officials or agencies to create particularised regulation as subordinate or delegated legislation. Thus, the Food Safety Act 1990 gives very broad powers of this kind to Ministers who, before making regulations on food safety, are required to consult with representatives of interests likely to be affected by regulation. The statute's approach may be partly determined by a situation in which the production and marketing of an immense variety of foodstuffs necessitates many specific, intricate and contrasting regulatory regimes, and where rapid changes in scientific knowledge and technology are likely to demand continually evolving regulatory frameworks (Scott 1990: 789).

Thus the concept of the generality of legal rules is attacked on two fronts by modern developments. Discretionary regulation threatens to dissolve away rules altogether in favour of administrative freedom to implement policy, while particularised regulation threatens to reduce rules to specific directives, like the contents of a detailed manual of bureaucratic or technical practice.[5]

Sociological Explanations of Changes in the Form of Western Law

These changes can be viewed sociologically in two broad perspectives. In a long view of legal history they can be seen as one phase in a continuous cycle of movement between rule and discretion (Pound 1954) or formalism and informalism (Abel 1979). From a different viewpoint they can be seen specifically in relation to their effects on the late-nineteenth-century model of Western law on which legal domination and the *Rechtsstaat* are apparently founded. In this latter perspective various writers have noted a transition from law to bureaucratic administration and seen in this a 'crisis of law and legal ideology' (Kamenka and Tay 1975); the gradual demise of legal autonomy as law, policy and administration become merged (Nonet and Selznick 1978); the decline of private law and the increasing dominance of public law (Friedmann 1972: ch 16); the blurring of the distinction between private and public law and between private and public spheres of life (Friedman 1985: ch 5; Unger 1976: 200ff); or the elevation of the 'contingency and complexity' of law to a situation in which an indefinite range of regulatory issues float

5 See e. g. Consumer Products (Safety) (Amendment) Regulations 1987 (SI 1987/1920) Sch. 1. specifying, with startling precision, that in a particular chemical compound used in cosmetics manufacture: 'The ratio of the number of aluminium atoms to that of zirconium atoms must be between two and ten'.

temporarily and provisionally within law's scope, to be dealt with differently at different times with 'a multitude of detail' (Luhmann 1985: 161-2).

Most commentators link the causes of these changes with the increasingly difficult problems of management and administration of contemporary Western societies. They are thus aspects and expressions of the change in the nature of state power discussed in the previous chapter. Problems of functional co-ordination (from a functionalist point of view), crisis management in the capitalist economy and its superstructure (from a Marxist viewpoint) and competition and co-ordination between centres of corporate power (from a corporatist viewpoint) are all seen as provoking official demands for forms of regulation both more precise in effect and more flexible in use than those encompassed by the rule of law, if the state is to maintain the existing social, economic and political order. The point was not lost on Ehrlich three-quarters of a century ago. Remarking on the 'enormous difficulty' of regulating and directing great multitudes of people he notes: 'It is most difficult perhaps when it is to be done on the basis of universal abstract rules' (1936: 376).

Some radical analyses claim that these developments in regulation illustrate the gradual replacement of law as a normative structure of rules by scientific or technological mechanisms of social order and control. One simple version of this argument can be put in the following terms. Most evolutionary theories of law, whatever the specific concepts used, distinguish a 'pre-modern' *Gemeinschaft* law, based in community values, from a modern *Gesellschaft* law in which the link with shared morality has become indirect and tenuous, and law has developed as a technical device of government more or less detached from community sentiment. As this has occurred, law has become increasingly dependent on science, in various ways, to provide certain foundations of objectivity which, in a sense, replace the foundation of community moral consensus. Indeed positivist science has provided continuous justification for numerous actions of government. In modern times the views of scientific advisers are used to justify government policy. Law has increasingly appealed to scientific expertise to provide objective proof of facts (for example, forensic scientists' evidence in criminal trials), to assess mental states (for example, by means of psychiatrists' testimony) or to determine appropriate legal sanctions (by courts' reliance, for example, on reports assessing the likely consequences of particular court orders on an offender; or by adoption of 'treatment' rather than punishment strategies in sentencing). It can be suggested that this position is itself a transitional one in a movement from community-based normative regulation to technological administrative control. As the technological resources of control, surveillance and information-handling available to the state increase together with its perceived regulatory problems, law becomes increasingly subordinated to administrative 'scientific' control. 'Legal autonomy', and with it the rule of law, thus appears—according to this view—as a relatively brief phase in the evolution of social control.

According to a quite different schema, associated with the recent work of the German theorists Niklas Luhmann and Gunther Teubner, the increasing complexity of modern societies, reflected in the proliferation of forms of regulation, can only be managed by a correspondingly intense *differentiation* of various sub-systems (for example, legal, economic, political and scientific) within these societies. Law, treated as a system of communication by means of which decisions on right or wrong (legality or illegality) are produced, can avoid overload only by remaining functionally distinct from other social sub-systems such as that of science, preoccupied with issues of truth or falsity, or from politics and economics with their specific concerns with power and efficiency (e.g. Teubner 1987; and see Chapter 2).

Indeed, Luhmann's view—clearly related, in this respect, to Parsons'—seems to be that the increasing complexity of modern societies has been paralleled by this vital functional differentiation. Thus, for law, viewed in this way, 'autonomy is not a desired goal but a fateful necessity' (Luhmann 1986: 112). The practical consequence is that, given the functional differentiation of legal, economic, political, and other spheres of modern life, attempts to extend law's reach through ever more ambitious planning, administration, policy setting and other tasks, are undesirable (since they deny the functional differentiation or specialisation essential to cope with modern social complexity). But, equally, these attempts are also pointless (since law as a communication system is fundamentally incapable of substituting for or adopting the outlook of any other sub-system of modern society). Modern law, according to Luhmann and Teubner, may certainly be highly varied, and even indeterminate in its forms. Equally, it may have 'far-reaching interdependencies with the political system' (Teubner 1984: 295). But none of this means that it has lost its autonomy or merged with politics or administration. Its essential character as a communication system is rather one of ever-increasing technicality and complexity (mirroring the society for which it provides decisions) and immunity from any meaningful evaluation except in terms of this specifically legal technicality. In a sense, legal formality validates itself in these conditions (Luhmann 1988a: 23). Legal decisions are valid only because founded on legal rules; but legal rules are given significance only because they are the basis of legal decisions (Teubner 1984: 295). Justice, moral worth, scientific truth or even economic efficiency are revealed, in this view, as wholly inappropriate criteria for judging the content of modern law. This law has become no more than a highly specialised technical sub-system (specialising only in decisions on legality) within the immense complexity of contemporary society.

Legal Legitimacy After the Rule of Law?

Arguments about the nature and consequences of regulatory change in contemporary Western societies must take into account not only the technical problems and capabilities of regulation—which inspire hypotheses about the replacement of law or, in Luhmann's case, the narrowing of its scope—but also the ideological problems of legitimation. Can Western societies manage to maintain the legitimacy of political power structures *without* the rule of law or, at least, despite substantial modifications of the *Gesellschaft* form of law?

On one view it is misleading to talk about the replacement of *Gesellschaft* law by other forms of regulation. A fundamental substratum of such law remains, and perhaps must continue to remain, in order to provide the underpinning of legitimacy that contemporary state power requires. From this viewpoint, talk of a possible crisis of legitimacy may be premature (Nelken 1982). By contrast, some optimistic analyses of contemporary legal developments argue that, contrary to the bleak vision of technological control suggested in the previous section, they raise the possibility of 'responsive' law in place of 'autonomous' law; law which is less remote from everyday experience because explicitly policy oriented and, at the same time, more 'responsive' to pressures and demands from citizens. In essence, the possibility is seen to exist because law must retain legitimacy in terms of the acceptability to citizens of its explicit policies if it can no longer retain legitimacy merely as a rational rule system (Nonet and Selznick 1978).

Modern systems theorists put the matter differently. In Teubner's view, the 'responsiveness' of law is not a matter of its relationship with the aspirations of individual citizens. It is rather a matter of the responsiveness or sensitivity of the legal sub-system of society to the conditions of autonomy of society's other sub-systems (such as economy or polity). Hence, modern law should not engage in wholesale efforts to control directly an increasingly complex social reality in all its aspects. Law should be aimed at providing a sophisticated, carefully modulated 'external stimulation' of the 'internal self-regulating processes' of society's various sub-systems of activity (Teubner 1984).

Wider-ranging arguments about the basis of political legitimacy have been developed in the work of another German social theorist Jürgen Habermas. Habermas' subtle and complex theories, extending well beyond the concerns of legal analysis, cannot be adequately summarised here but certain relevant themes can be extracted from them. For example, Habermas has challenged the view that legitimacy in contemporary Western societies depends upon legal domination in Weber's sense (Habermas 1976). At the same time he has sought to develop a critical analysis of these societies to replace what he sees as the outdated critical conceptualisations of Marxism. Today state and society increasingly interpenetrate. The economy is no longer autonomously regulated by the market but depends upon extensive state direction and control. The old form of political legitimation based on the ideology of fair exchange expressed in classical political economy (and in the purpose-rational foundation of legal domination) has become increasingly obsolete. Modern forms of legitimation are 'technocratic'—they emphasise the capability of governing elites to manage successfully the economy and sustain economic growth (cf. Gamble 1988). This technocratic emphasis indicates the centrality of scientific-technical innovation in the contemporary social order. The central resource in Marxist analysis, labour power, has become less central. So has direct class conflict which has tended to become subordinated to managerial-administrative considerations.

Whereas for Weber a crisis of legal domination could not be predictable but merely occurs with a 'charismatic outburst' upsetting the established order, for Habermas crisis can occur on several levels as a result of failure of elites to 'manage' effectively. Economic crises rarely occur in pure form for the same reason that class conflict does not—because economic questions come to be seen as administrative-managerial matters. Thus the first significant level of crisis is that of 'rationality crisis'—an inability of the state to cope with these matters. This can worsen to a 'legitimation crisis' involving the possibility of mass withdrawal of political loyalty. The final level is that of 'motivation crisis' in which the commitment of the population to the normative order of advanced capitalism is reduced or threatened. Habermas' concepts do not provide the basis for predicting specific crises but they recognise that legitimacy is not an all-or-nothing matter; that there are levels of commitment and gradations in the seriousness of challenges to that commitment. His theories also recognise explicitly that legitimacy is both a matter for system analysis and a matter of the subjective reactions of individual citizens.

Indeed, much of Habermas' recent work has been concerned with the analysis of the conditions of human interaction and of the forms of communication that give rise to normative orders. But, increasingly, he seems to have emphasised those tendencies in modern societies by which the administrative, 'steering' activities of the modern state—and the proliferation of law and regulation that accompanies these activities—threaten the production of moral meaning in everyday life (e.g. Habermas

1986). In part, Habermas' positions are a response to Luhmann's. Like Luhmann he sees the complexity of modern societies as giving rise to a differentiation of sub-systems such as those of law, science or economy, each possessing its own kind of communicative logic to cope with a certain aspect of social life. How are individuals to relate to such dominating system-structures, which control life with their judgments and demands? Is there any scope left for the spontaneous creation of consensus among individuals about 'truth', 'moral worth', 'justice' or other such ideas and ideals? Luhmann has come to the conclusion that modern societies can *only* be analysed in system terms. Legitimacy, therefore, is a matter of the successful interaction of sub-systems of communication; the individual seems to have no say in the matter. But Habermas has continued to insist that a place must be found for the ongoing creation of 'meaning' by individuals in their lives, even in contemporary societies where the scope for this seems to be continually reduced by the twin developments of increasing complexity and greater system differentiation. 'The point is to protect areas of life that are functionally dependent on social integration through values, norms and consensus formation; and to protect them from falling prey to the system imperatives of economic and administrative subsystems that grow with a dynamic of their own' (Habermas 1986: 22). Ultimately, however, it is not clear whether his arguments about the necessity and possibility of communicative rationality can be related to specific empirical claims about the character of contemporary societies or whether they remain at the level of philosophical speculation about the conditions necessary for a more emancipated social existence.

Ideology, Personal Values and Support for Law

Theories such as that of Habermas, together with those of many Marxist and Marxist-influenced thinkers, are designed in part to demonstrate that Weber's pessimistic image of the 'iron cage' of routinisation and bureaucracy nullifying the pursuit of political and moral ideals is unwarranted. They seek to challenge the idea that law itself embodies, in a world dominated by purpose-rational considerations, the ultimate general criterion of appropriate conduct and attitude. But to be effective this challenge involves specifying criteria of acceptability or legitimacy against which law can *itself* be judged. In earlier ages of Western law, systems of natural law—that is, ethical rules and principles derived from religious doctrine or secular philosophical speculation—provided such criteria. Weber considered that, because of the processes of rationalisation and secularisation in Western societies, natural law had disappeared forever as a significant influence on the authority of positive law by the time he wrote (1978: 865–76; 1954: ch 10). In Roman Catholic countries, at least, natural law theory is still the concern of jurists, yet Weber was surely correct to doubt the possibility of a challenge to positive law on the basis of consistent, generally accepted, competing norm systems in Western societies. The dominance of positive law over all other normative systems that could compete with it as a general normative basis of society-wide order seems too complete to allow this possibility.

All that has been discussed earlier about empirical evidence of consensus suggests that alongside positive law in contemporary Western societies there may exist *numerous* more or less coherent, more or less comprehensive, value systems of individuals and groups; but not competing or compatible general normative systems representing a *society-wide* consensus. The cynical but realistic claim embodied in the concept of legal domination is that these diverse value orientations effectively cancel each other out so as to prevent any consistent challenge to law and to leave the fulfilment of a diversity of individual interests as the sole common focus of allegiance to it. The satisfaction of these interests may indeed be threatened by management failure on the part of a governing elite. But if this is so there is no reason to assume that citizens' demands upon law for interest satisfaction will not be 'rationally' scaled down to levels that the existing system can accommodate,[6] in the absence of a competing set of norms to provide a foundation for critical evaluation of the performance of government (cf. Luhmann 1985: 201). The assumption of legitimation or motivation crises as likely to arise from such circumstances is not necessarily warranted.

Does Acceptance Depend on Ignorance?

Those writers who see acceptance of law, even in contemporary Western societies, as contingent rather than inevitable tend to stress the way in which the citizen's experiences in relation to law may affect this acceptance. It might be said that law's ideals must always appear attainable, yet law must appear always an idealised form of social relations, not a replication of actually existing ones. Roberto Unger writes, 'The deepest root of all historical change is manifest or latent conflict between the view of the ideal and the experience of actuality'

6 The scaling down of legal demands or expectations may result from experience of litigation. In an important recent study of litigants before American lower courts, Sally Merry (1990: 135) found that, despite their often being frustrated by failure to obtain legal satisfaction, these litigants 'do not consider that the court is illegitimate but that the court considers them and their problems unworthy of help. The experience is a challenge less to the legitimacy of the legal system than to their sense of entitlement'. See also Conley and O'Barr 1990: 165.

(1976: 153). An important American study by Austin Sarat found that knowledge of law and support for the legal system were inversely related. The more people knew about the law the more dissatisfied they were with it (Sarat 1975). Sometimes, for example, the shock of discovering that matters the litigant considers of great importance are viewed quite differently within the legal system—for example, as trivial, as not raising real legal issues, or as not meriting official time and action—can be powerfully disillusioning (Merry 1990: 134). The way lawyers represent law to their clients may also contribute to disillusionment (Sarat and Felstiner 1989). Correspondingly some analysts of democratic political institutions have argued that the relative stability of these institutions may depend on apathy or ignorance among substantial sections of the population (e.g. Lipset 1960). Sarat comments on his research findings: 'So long as people have an idealised and unrealistic conception of the way the legal system operates, a conception conveyed by the mass media and other popular sources, support for it is likely to remain at least relatively widespread; where this conception is tempered by information, as it is for many people in my sample, support, at least as reflected in feelings of satisfaction, is likely to erode' (1975: 20–1). This is consistent with the theory—discussed in Chapter 4—of legal symbols which are seen to depend on a vagueness that hides their mutual incompatibility or unrealisability in practice. Thus the legitimacy of law may be affected by the nature and extent of citizens' direct experience of its effects.

Two types of difficulty arise with this potentially fruitful line of analysis. First, certain sections of society (especially the relatively economically powerful) have long had contact with the legal system as users of it. Others have traditionally had little contact with it except when it has been used to punish them. And there is evidence that while sporadic contact with legal institutions correlates with relatively cynical attitudes towards them, more extensive contact with lawyers tends to correlate with more favourable attitudes to law (Tomasic 1985: 92–5). Must we draw important distinctions, in considering the general sociological bases of legal legitimacy, between attitudes of different kinds or classes of people affected by law (cf. Barker 1990: ch 6)? Insofar as, for reasons discussed in Chapter 4, the legal system consistently serves the interests of the relatively powerful in facilitating the exercise of their power, it would seem superficially that acceptance of law by individuals or groups is likely to vary directly with their relative power. This is not necessarily so, however, since a judgment as to whether law is satisfactorily securing interests depends on the relevant individuals' or social groups' subjective conception of what their interests are; of what expectations are appropriate or reasonable. Such a conception depends on a variety of cognitive and evaluative assumptions. Ideology is important in determining this structure of assumptions. Thus, a legal system might lose support from the 'haves' when, despite the protection and guarantee of power that it gives them, it is perceived as being 'too soft' on the 'have-nots' or when it is perceived as serving values inconsistent with those regarded as of particular importance to the 'haves'. Conversely, a legal system will retain considerable support from the 'have-nots' when the social order that it guarantees is seen by them as 'natural' and as providing security and 'order' which are perceived more clearly as benefits than any potential changes in favour of a redistribution of social advantages. In this context the balance between the individual's subjective conceptions of 'order' and 'justice' as social and legal values is of great significance. The meaning that individuals give to these two values, which may vary very considerably in content, and—in particular—the relative importance attached to these values when they are seen to conflict, might be considered the key factors in determining whether and when individuals accept the legitimacy of law or particular laws (Cotterrell 1983b).[7]

Interpretation of Legal Experience

The second difficulty is with the concept of 'experience' of law or 'actuality' against which legal ideals or doctrine can be measured. In Chapter 4 it was seen that one important contribution of theories of ideology is to emphasise that experience is mediated by the particular pre-existing structures of ideas available to the individual to interpret it. It was further suggested that these ideas are themselves shaped in part by law. If so, in what way can 'experience' challenge perceptions of law? Experience is already shaped by sets of cognitive and evaluative concepts to which law contributes. Thus, presumably, the values of order and justice as understood by many individuals are themselves powerfully shaped by law. Further, ideology, as explained in the previous chapter, tends to seek self-sufficiency and to claim comprehensiveness as knowledge. Thus ideological thought tends to interpret all empirical data

7 Recent empirical research in the United States has emphasised that citizens tend to accord legitimacy to legal processes if they experience legal procedures as fair and even if the outcome of these processes is unfavourable to their interests (e.g. Tyler 1990). But this finding, taken alone, is less illuminating than might be wished. On the one hand, it merely seems to confirm the general significance of ideas associated with the ideal of the rule of law as a basis of legitimacy (predictability, individual security, formal rationality). But, on the other, it may suggest an *indeterminate* range of combinations of the values of order and justice referred to in the text, for a judgment of the fairness of procedures entails some view of what the procedures are or should be for, of what criteria are most significant as components of fairness in the light of those purposes, and of what alternative modes of redress or satisfaction of claims could serve as models against which legal fairness could be judged.

in conformity with pre-established values and treats this data as fully confirming accepted understandings of reality. Where such interpretations are difficult to sustain, ideological thought ignores inconsistent data. What this suggests is that insofar as law contributes to currents of ideology it helps to provide the conditions for its own acceptance as 'common sense'. Empiricist explanations of the effects of 'experience' on individuals tend to ignore these considerations.

The problem can be at least partially overcome by recognising, as we sought to do at the end of the previous chapter, that currents of ideas are, despite these stabilising and self-perpetuating tendencies, created and modified through many interacting conditions and circumstances. While ideas interpret experience, experience gives life and relevance to ideas (cf. Merry 1990: ch 7). The difficulty we have in theorising this two-way relationship adequately is the legacy of the materialism-idealism dichotomy in social theory, discussed at the end of the previous chapter.

Further, it is important to specify exactly what *kind* of legal experience may bear significantly on the way individuals think about law. A general awareness of legal institutions and practices as part of the background of social life is unlikely, in itself, to set up the tensions between 'experience' and 'ideals' referred to earlier. But detailed knowledge of, for example, legal doctrine as interpreted and applied by courts and other legal institutions and as contrasted with the broad legal ideals or symbols associated in public consciousness with the law might create such tensions even for persons without an immediate personal interest at stake. Thus many of the strongest and most persistent critics of law are lawyers committed to such ideals. One of the strengths of law's legitimacy is that few people acquire this kind of detailed knowledge of legal doctrine and practice and most of those who do have specific personal or professional commitments to the legal system. Doreen McBarnet has noted that, in particular, case law, originating in the everyday business of the courts, has 'a surprisingly low profile in public affairs' owing, no doubt, to its complexity and detail and the 'convoluted and archaic style in which it is presented' (McBarnet 1982: 412). This may suggest that developed judge-made common law may have a more powerful mechanism of self-legitimation than the more 'visible' legal principles of some code-based systems of law or of some modern legislation.

More significant, perhaps, given the changes in the form of Western law with which this chapter has been concerned, is that relevant experience of law may arise from the law's impact on the individual's personal conditions of life. Consider this in two contexts: first, that of legitimacy based on legal domination or the rule of law and, secondly, that of legitimacy based on the state's efficient management of economic and related social conditions. In the former, since law is required only as a backdrop against which individuals are free to act in pursuance of their own purposes, experience of law for most people is remote and the opportunity for assessing the exact nature of the contribution law makes to facilitation of purpose-rational action may be limited. Law is not expected to fulfil individuals' needs directly and, in general, it does not intrude into their lives. What is required, however, is that law be seen as being concerned to make possible for *all* citizens a framework of rational rules within which purposive action may take place. Hence the rule of law requires that when individuals do encounter law they encounter it as a predictable set of rules and procedures around which they can organise their own rational actions (cf. Tyler 1990).

The ideology of the rule of law thus not only encourages attention to clarity, formality and predictability in legal doctrine and its application but also the creation of new rights in law or the extension of existing ones to extend the freedom of all classes of citizens to pursue purpose-rational action. On this reasoning there is much to be said for the view expressed by many writers, including even such a radical critic as the English scholar E. P. Thompson (1975: 258–69), that the legitimacy of the rule of law provides a significant political weapon for the 'have-nots' of Western capitalist societies since it necessarily provides them with the protection of known or knowable rules, limits arbitrary discretion, and forces many valuable legal concessions from the powerful. The protection of law for political action aimed at radical social change seems, however, to be bought at the cost of abandoning radical criticism of the basis of legitimacy of the legal order itself.

Experience of Law in the Welfare State

If, however, legitimacy based solely on the rule of law is being superseded by legitimacy based on the state's claim to be able to 'manage' economy and society, one aspect of this change is the intrusion of law (in the form of, for example, social security law, consumer law, family law, planning law and labour law) into the lives of individual citizens far more extensively than in the past. If much of the distributive activity of the welfare state is based on discretion as much as rule and on control as much as benefit, it nevertheless represents, in effect, a promise of aid to the poorer sections of the population in return for political allegiance. It directly involves the reach of law—as an affair of entitlements and not merely repression—into the lives of far wider classes of ordinary citizens than in earlier eras. This situation greatly extends both the range of individuals and the range of circumstances in relation to which the 'promise', the ideals or symbols of law can be confronted with 'experience' of law (Sarat 1990a). Thus, for some writers, the crisis of the escalating costs and cut-backs of the welfare state raises the ultimate possibility of a serious legitimation crisis of Western political systems. Again, however, everything would seem to depend on the complex balance of personal values of order and justice in the individual's response to experience of law.

Whether or not it is appropriate to talk of legitimation crisis, the sociological analyses discussed in this chapter clearly point—whatever their disagreements—to a serious dilemma for contemporary Western states. Law intrudes increasingly into citizens' lives. But this is not, of course, a return to the pre-modern situation in which law, as customary rules, was an aspect of community life. Law remains remote in its technical complexity at the same time as its increasingly detailed regulations relate it more and more concretely to particular narrowly defined situations and relationships. The potential for inefficiency and tension in the combination of regulatory *intimacy* and regulatory *isolation* in state activity is considerable.[8]

On the other hand, discretionary regulation provides an often effective means of facilitating regulation of minute administrative detail. In addition it denies the advantage to the 'have-nots' of formalisation of power through rules. Discretionary regulation, insofar as it avoids the need for definite specification of rights, prevents to some extent the kind of 'experiential' challenge to legal doctrine discussed earlier. Further it can obscure contradictions in legal policy or its implementation (e.g. Scott 1990).

If, however, this kind of regulation cannot invoke legitimacy through the rule of law and relies instead on its legitimacy as an instrument of efficient governmental management, it depends on continued popular belief in this efficiency. As the capacity of government to deliver economic success and other aspects of this efficient management comes increasingly into question, there have been signs of renewed emphasis on rule rather than discretion in some regulatory areas. Aspects of social welfare law reform in Britain showed this tendency for a time in the 1980s before a move back to significant discretionary arrangements (e.g. Cranston 1985: 184–91; Alcock 1989; Mesher 1990). Equally similar tendencies are apparent in the resurgence of 'justice models' of punishment (von Hirsch 1976), emphasising the offender's just deserts rather than appropriate treatment of his case as an instance of social or psychological problems.

Thus while technical problems of regulation seem to point the state in one direction (towards particularised and discretionary regulation), legitimation problems seem to point it in another (towards a renewed emphasis on clearly defined rules). There is, however, no reason to believe that this latter impetus can return the modern state to the optimum condition of Weberian legal domination. Weber's sociology ultimately

8 See further ch 9.

tends to treat 'rationality' as a shaping force in history, reified as an actor on the world stage, finally fulfilling itself in its dominance over modern Western society. But what is 'rational' varies as between different individuals, societies, cultures and periods (e.g. Hollis and Lukes, eds, 1982). As Parsonian and later systems theories, on the one hand, and Marxist analyses, on the other, show, albeit in very different ways, the characteristics of the *Rechtsstaat* arise at a particular juncture in history and as the result of specific sociological conditions. They cannot be appropriately treated as either the permanent achievement of professional development of Western law or the final destiny of rationalisation processes in Western society. They mark merely a particular moment in the development of particular social systems.

6 Professional Guardianship of Law

In the preceding chapters law has generally been treated as synonymous with legal doctrine and the concern of the discussion has been primarily to explore various theoretical analyses of the sociological significance of legal ideas in Western societies and of some conditions that have contributed to the formation of particular modes of legal thought in these societies. Whatever specific concept of law is adopted, however, three clusters of institutions tend to be particularly associated with it, not only in contemporary complex societies but also in much earlier or simpler ones. Long before law is considered, as in its modern forms, a matter for deliberate creation by legislation, the need for institutionalised means of resolving or containing disputes is apparent. Again, long before law becomes a matter of established doctrine, the need may be felt, by those likely to be affected by or wanting to make use of certain established governmental practices or policies for their own purposes, to call upon people with special knowledge of such matters for advice and aid. They seek help from experts in preparing a 'case' or working out a strategy for invoking these practices or policies in support of their own interests, or at least to protect themselves as far as possible from the likely exercise of governmental power. Again, as the exercise of power in societies becomes formalised by means of institutions of government and as regulation extends itself beyond taken-for-granted customary practice, the need for institutionalised means of enforcement of this regulation emerges. Thus three institutional clusters, in particular, emerge, focused respectively on the resolution of disputes, the guardianship of legal knowledge and expertise, and the enforcement of regulation.

In a well-known study Richard Schwartz and James Miller systematically compared levels of legal development in 51 societies varying widely in size and complexity (Schwartz and Miller 1964). The three institutional criteria of development ('mediation', 'counsel' and 'police') that they used directly correspond with the institutional clusters just described. Schwartz and Miller found that mediation existed alone in some societies, that where police existed mediation was almost invariably also present and that where specialised counsel existed in a society so did police and mediation. Thus, an evolutionary scheme was suggested by the evidence. The use of third party agents for dispute resolution might be regarded as the primary legal development, followed by the development of institutions for enforcement of regulation. 'Counsel' emerge last, and this is unsurprising because the development of a class of specialist advisers and experts who know their way around legal processes and can interpret these processes to ordinary people affected by them becomes essential only as legal procedures themselves develop in sophisticated forms and as the workings of legal institutions need to be interpreted in the form of doctrine.

Although the emergence of a specialist class of legal advisers thus appears a less basic legal development than that of dispute or enforcement institutions, it is an appropriate starting point for considering the relationship between the institutional structures of law and the characteristics of contemporary Western legal ideas that have been discussed in relation to social theory in previous chapters. This is because the progress of what is seen as the professionalisation of legal practice is intimately connected with the development of those distinctive features of modern Western law that previous chapters have sought to highlight. Accordingly this chapter will consider some sociologically significant aspects of the organisation of legal practice. Our concern, however, is not to describe legal professions nor to sketch their history. It is to consider those aspects of empirical and theoretical analysis of legal practice that make it possible to develop, illustrate or criticise in a concrete manner the sociological ideas about law set out in previous chapters. In Chapters 7 and 8 the other two institutional clusters referred to earlier—dispute processing and enforcement—will be discussed in turn, again with a similar purpose in view.

What is a Legal Profession?

It was Weber's writings which, in the early literature of the sociology of law, most clearly and elaborately argued the crucial importance of particular forms of professional guardianship of law in helping to determine the nature of legal systems and their distinctive modes of legal thought and procedure, and hence their wider effects on social action and ideas (e.g. Weber 1978: 784ff). In this, Weber reiterated the claim which most lawyers make about the significance of their profession for the law and the society in which it exists. He supported it, however, with detailed and wide-ranging historical study and theoretical analysis. In particular he claimed that the distinction between professional organisation of law in England and on the Continent explained much about contrasts in legal ideas which influenced wider currents of social life. Weber saw English law in the formative era of capitalism as dominated by a practising profession organised around relatively autonomous professional associations such as the Inns of Court and closely attuned to pragmatic accommodation to client demands. The centralisation of political authority from an early period in English history made possible the gradual establishment of a relatively unified court system and hence a clear organisational focus of legal work. A relatively independent and unified legal profession could aid, receive aid from, and at times compete with or challenge developing state power and the classes that sought to control it. By contrast, continental law was typified historically by the survival of numerous local and customary laws and a corresponding diversity of legal practice (Zweigert and Kötz 1987: 79, 140). In Germany it was the university jurists rather than the practising lawyers who forged an eventual doctrinal unity of private law on the basis of highly abstract principles finally consummated in the great Civil Code of 1900. In France systematisation received its impetus from state direction of lawyers' energies (Zweigert and Kötz 1987: 82ff). What Weber saw as the sociologically important contrast between the empirical law-finding of the English common law and the formally rational law of the code systems (see Chapter 5) could not be attributed to any simple cause but he stressed differences in the forms of legal professionalism as a vital contributory factor.

Weber's work suggests the need to consider the relationship between the organisation of legal work and the rationalising, bureaucratising tendencies of 'modern society'. It points to the need to analyse professional knowledge, lawyers' values and attitudes and the way these are formed in the environment of practice and profession. It requires us to ask how legal professionalisation is related to the development of legal ideology. As has been seen in Chapter 3, functionalist integration theory stresses the importance of professionalisation for its ostensible orientation to public service and thus its implicit recognition of the functional interdependence on which social solidarity depends. It emphasises the 'bargain' struck between professions and society, the terms of which are codified in professional ethics and the establishment of professional monopolies of specialised knowledge and practice. It assesses professions in terms of their responsibilities and privileges determined by the system-logic of a functionally differentiated and reintegrated social system of which they are a part. Finally, Marxist perspectives stress the class basis of professions as servants of either capitalist structure or capitalist classes. They highlight the need to examine the structure of the legal profession and its economic basis; to understand how lawyers and their work fit into the system of capitalist social relations (cf. Abel 1988: 21–30).

All of these approaches suggest that the analysis of 'professions' is important, yet sociologists have gradually reached the view that the concept of profession as a distinct kind of occupation is extremely problematic. It is possible to identify at least seven approaches (which can be considered, to some extent, stages) in sociological thinking on this matter. First, Parsons' early analyses (e.g. Parsons 1939) stressed the way in which professional conduct, like other occupational behaviour and roles in general, was governed by normative expectations, which could themselves be seen as determined by the position that a profession was required to fill in the social order. Thus, as has been seen in Chapter 3, Parsons, like Durkheim before him, uses the case of professions to stress that social action is governed not merely by the free play of individuals' interests but by particular values and norms which are socially determined. Functionalist analysis of professions elaborated the functional basis of this normative regulation and so stressed the distinctiveness of professions from other occupations in terms of their special bargain with society based on monopoly of special expertise and self-regulation (e.g. Goode 1957).

A second approach, deriving largely from the work of Everett Hughes, refuses to see professions as a distinct category of occupations (Hughes 1958). In Hughes' terms, all occupations have a 'licence' to carry on certain activities for profit. If members of an occupation have a sense of community they are likely also to seek a 'mandate' to define the terms under which this is to be done. The extent of such a mandate successfully claimed can be considered the extent of professionalisation. The establishment and extent of a mandate thus depends on the outcome of the interaction between occupation members and those with whom they deal in exercising their 'licence'.

The idea of profession as a status which various occupations achieve led to a third approach which sought to specify 'traits' of professionalism, the criteria that make it possible to recognise an occupation as having attained professional status. The problem of the approach was that often the identified traits—for example, professional association, canons of ethics, public service ideal, special training and test of competence, skill based on theoretical knowledge (Millerson 1964)—could not be theoretically related to each other (Johnson 1972: 23ff) and hence appeared as an arbitrary list lacking explanatory power, or they remained ambiguous.

A fourth approach was to compromise between the identification of traits and the construction of an analytically coherent concept. Thus various writers sought to specify a strictly limited number of distinguishing characteristics of profession which could be related in an analytical scheme (Goode 1969; Freidson 1970: 71–84). Eliot Freidson in an important 1970 study of medical practice went further in identifying autonomous control of occupational work and conditions as the defining characteristic of profession, such control depending on political power which could itself be achieved in a variety of ways represented in some of the previously identified 'traits' of profession (Freidson 1970: ch 4).

This last approach seems to lead into a fifth, represented especially in writings of Terence Johnson (1972) and M. S. Larson (1977) and adapted to research on the organisation of legal practice especially in the recent work of Richard Abel (e.g. Abel 1988; 1989a; 1989b). Here emphasis is on the means by which the market for services in capitalist societies can be controlled. Professional organisation is a means by which a particular occupational group seeks to control supply of its services in the market for its own benefit. Other methods—control by consumers of services, control by the state—are possible so professionalism represents a historically specific form of mediation of supply. Far from entering into an altruistic public service bargain with society, professions are seen as cornering a market in scarce resources and establishing a supply monopoly through organisation and political influence. In recent writings this view has inspired the clear recognition not only that professionalisation is, as a means of supply control, a historically specific phenomenon but that the concept of profession as developed in most of the relevant sociological literature may refer only to a specifically *Anglo-American* phenomenon (Freidson 1986; Freidson 1983). This point, which stresses the very considerable differences in the organisation and outlook of continental European equivalents of what are thought of as the established professions in the Anglo-American world, is of the utmost importance, particularly when such matters as a legal profession's autonomy, outlook and relationship with the state are under consideration. Thus Dietrich Rueschemeyer has shown fundamental differences between American and West German legal professions in each of these areas (Rueschemeyer 1973; see also Blankenburg and Schultz 1988). At the same time this claim casts doubt on easy explanations of the relationship between professionalisation (as understood in the Anglo-American context) and capitalist society in a generic sense. Thus profession becomes 'a historical construction in a limited number of societies' and not necessarily one generally applicable to comparable occupations even within the limited context of contemporary Western societies (Freidson 1983: 20).

At least two responses (our sixth and seventh approaches) to this position seem possible. One is to discard the category of profession altogether (Cain 1983a) or at least treat it as insignificant. The object then becomes explicitly that of studying the specific practices of particular occupational groups. The way is opened up for considering, for example, the organisation of legal practice (of varied kinds) comparatively. And this can be done not just by treating the organisation of legal work as a response to the varying conditions of the market for legal services in different countries, but also in terms of the relations of legal work and its organisation to the various structures, mechanisms and patterns of development of the modern state in different nations (e.g. Rueschemeyer 1989; Halliday 1989).

Finally, some writers have advocated a different response building on the distinction recognised early (H. S. Becker 1970) in the literature between a sociological and a 'folk' (or popular, commonsense) concept of profession, recognising that, whatever the sociological difficulties of the concept of profession, it is widely used or in various ways implied by members of occupations in interaction with fellow members and outsiders. In this context an occupational group develops certain self-perceptions and convinces outsiders to accept its self-image. Hence it 'accomplishes profession' in interaction. The way it does this and the way ideas of profession are manipulated are important. In this context folk concepts of profession are sociologically significant as objects of study for researchers adopting interactionist or ethnomethodological approaches (see Chapter 5) even if such common sense concepts lack theoretical coherence (Dingwall 1976).

Folk concepts of profession provide a useful starting point for discussion as long as it is recognised that they are not necessarily any more than a particular occupational group's self-rationalisations. What is important is to examine the empirical evidence tending to support or contradict such rationalisations and to identify the conditions under which they are accepted by outsiders as well as the social consequences of that acceptance. Thus in the following pages it will be necessary to consider three major assumptions about lawyers and legal work: first, the idea that the legal profession forms a *community*, an identifiable unified body of functionaries linked by common values and interest; secondly, the idea of *service orientation* before profit which is often held to distinguish professions from business; and thirdly, the idea of special expertise and *specialised knowledge* which is often held to provide the basis of legal professionalism. 'For lawyers, the most important truth about the Law is that it is a profession ... and so ... must be thought of as ignoring commercial standards of success—as possessing special duties to serve the State's justice—and as an applied science requiring special training. And if it is thus set apart as a profession, it must have traditions and tenets of its own, which are to be mastered and lived up to' (Dean John H. Wigmore quoted in Rueschemeyer 1973: 110).

Professional Unity and the Stratification of Legal Work

The idea that lawyers make up a professional community is realistic only in a strictly limited sense. Although much early literature on the professions assumed that community of interest and outlook was one of their clearest hallmarks (Goode 1957)—the correlate in 'internal' structure of the 'external' condition of professional independence or autonomy—this is plainly untenable as a general proposition. First, in certain jurisdictions major divisions in legal work are formally recognised and entrenched, and can give rise to intra-professional competition, jealousies, and isolation. Thus the historical functional differentiation between attorneys, concerned with general representation of clients in their legal affairs, and advocates, concerned to speak on behalf of clients before tribunals or courts, survives in modified form in the rigid professional division between solicitors and barristers in England and Wales, each branch of the profession having its separate professional associations, qualifications, training and prerogatives and jealous of its particular privileges.[1] In continental civil law jurisdictions, one commentator notes, 'a choice among a variety of distinct professional careers faces the young law graduate. He can embark on a career as a judge, a public prosecutor, a government lawyer, an advocate or a notary. He must make this decision early and then live with it. Although it is theoretically possible to move from one of these professions to another, such moves are comparatively rare' (Merryman 1985: 101).

Equally if not more important than formal, officially recognised occupational divisions is the professional stratification that exists whether or not a legal profession is formally divided into branches (see Abel 1988: 290–2). The 'single, unified legal profession' of the United States (Merryman 1985: 102) in fact consists of several distinct strata of large firms, smaller group practices and sole practitioners between which there is negligible social and professional contact (Abel 1989a: 202–11), quite apart from the distinct position of the much smaller (but significantly increasing) number of lawyers working in government or business employment (Spangler 1986). David Podmore identified 14 distinct types of solicitors' firms in England and Wales varying widely in the nature and environment of practice (Podmore 1980: 23–4). In the United States, huge 'law factories' (Mills 1951: 121–9) sometimes have well over 200 lawyers and branches in several cities and abroad; are bureaucratically organised with specialist departments, formalised internal career structure and training system; and serve large business enterprises in litigation or expert legal planning often with vast sums at stake (Galanter and Palay 1991; Nelson 1988). They typify what Marc Galanter (1983) has called 'mega-lawyering', a practice far removed from the image of the sole practitioner upon which many elements of the Anglo-American folk concept of a legal profession are based. In the middle range of private practice in the United States are medium-sized firms 'rooted in the local affairs of their business communities, dividing their time between local politics and the practice of local litigations'; and at the

1 Cf. the old distinction between *avocat* and *avoué* in France: Zweigert and Kötz 1987: 130ff.

base of the profession is the individual practitioner, 'the genuine entrepreneur of the law who handles the legal affairs of individuals and small businesses' (Mills 1951: 127–8). But sole practitioners, once the mainstay of the profession, are now a species in rapid decline (Abel 1989a: 179).

As detailed studies have shown, the distance between the work environment, career pattern and outlook of the high prestige corporation lawyer and the sole practitioner in a large American urban centre is so great as to make it difficult to see any significant bonds of common experience and interest between them within a single professional community (Heinz and Laumann 1982). Erwin Smigel's classic study of Wall Street law firms showed them as the elite of the profession, recruiting their staff from top students of the most prestigious national university law schools and typically excluding members of minority groups (Smigel 1969). Jerome Carlin's contrasting study of Chicago sole practitioners presented them as existing at the margins of their profession, economically insecure, carrying out relatively mundane work rarely requiring even a faint reflection of the conspicuous professional expertise of elite legal practice, and jealous of the prestige of doctors—seen as a 'real' profession with high recognised social value and better financial rewards. They continually had to balance professional ethics against the need to make a living, often sacrificing the former to the latter, and saw themselves as unrepresented within the professional bar associations dominated by members of large or medium-sized firms (Carlin 1962).

It is neither necessary nor wise to try to generalise from particular studies of particular categories of lawyers. The point is to recognise the extreme diversity of lawyers' work, outlook and environment even in a formally unified legal profession such as that of the United States. Rueschemeyer (1973: 48) writes that such conditions create a 'highly fragmented' image of the profession on the part of lawyers. Different kinds of lawyers are subject to the influence of different kinds of client groups. This 'reduces identification with the profession as a group and severely limits the efficiency of that self-control which the profession is supposed to exercise according to the theoretical model of professional autonomy. It particularly impedes the moral commitment of the profession to obligations that transcend the lawyer–client relationship' (1973: 24). What tends to exist is a generalised commitment to 'the legal profession' in a highly abstract sense, coupled with acceptance of certain kinds of lawyer elites as desirable models (1973: 111). At the same time there are distinct benefits to be gained by lawyers from their representation, through professional associations and in other ways, as a united professional group (cf. Abel 1989a: 208-10). The image of 'profession' confers status and the embodiment of the image in formal professional organisations makes it possible for at least certain sections of the occupational group to speak with a louder public voice to protect and, if possible, extend the group's licence and mandate.

Interestingly, Rueschemeyer's study of German lawyers shows that despite much clearer formal divisions of function within the legal profession, as compared with that in the United States, there may be more professional solidarity (see also Blankenburg and Schultz 1988: 140–1). This seems to be primarily because of a different cultural environment of legal work which has complex historical causes. German lawyers, as Rueschemeyer describes them, have much less client identification, especially tending to keep a distinction between specifically professional values and those of business clients. Further, in Germany modern legal practice developed under the very direct tutelage of the state (cf. Rueschemeyer 1989), hence a 'civil service outlook'—alien to the folk concept of profession in the Anglo-American context—is natural within important sections of the German profession.[2] Associated with this, however, in the view of many commentators, has been a specific idea of responsibility in public service, a conservatism which stresses state or public interests, a detachment from emotional or specifically political controversial issues, and a tendency to view law as, in some sense, 'absolute truth' (Rueschemeyer 1973: 87). It would be unwise to make too much of national cultural generalisations of this kind but what is suggested is a professional self-confidence and detachment based in a conception of public interest which justifies legal expertise and differentiates its practice from particular everyday client concerns. Thus, while professional unity, its elements and its limitations constitute a necessary focus in considering the effect of 'lawyers' as a group on law and society, the determinants of the degree of unity depend on a variety of empirical conditions in different societies.

Official Values of Legal Practice

Within such a diversity of practice, what, if any, common foci can be identified? Can a unity of sorts be found in certain relatively consistent values which lawyers adopt and promote in relation to law and legal practice? The rhetoric of 'profession' in law stresses that legal work is organised in terms of a service ideal which puts obligations to the client and to the legal system (hence to public service) before personal profit and that it is governed by a strict code of professional ethics. Can such

2 Although the proportion of private legal practitioners in Germany is increasing significantly as cutbacks in public funding reduce the number of available civil service legal positions, about 50 per cent of lawyers enter salaried positions in government, the judiciary, or business: Blankenburg and Schultz 1988:130.

official values account for what empirical studies of legal practice reveal?

Professional ethics are fundamental to the public image and self-image of a legal profession. Various studies have shown, however, that in the United States, adherence to common professional ethics varies considerably in different strata of the legal profession (Carlin 1966; Reichstein 1965; Carlin 1962). For many of the low status Chicago individual practitioners whom Jerome Carlin studied, adherence to professional ethics governing such matters as solicitation, buying or trading of special favours from officials, or acting in the best interests of clients was a luxury which economic necessity required them to forego (Carlin 1962: ch 4). Wide variations in kinds of legal work and occupational environment appear more important in determining the lawyer's working values than generalised professional prescriptions. Carlin's later study of lawyers' ethics in New York found only a limited acceptance by lawyers of the canons of professional ethics, only those norms preventing fraud, bribery or interference with the administration of justice and those condemning taking advantage of clients being widely accepted (Carlin 1966). Later research has revealed similar patterns of ambivalence towards professional ethics, and has also shown widespread ignorance among lawyers of many ethical rules (Abel 1989a: 143–4).

It has been suggested that this situation reflects the extreme client identification of the American bar in comparison with European legal professions and Rueschemeyer (1973: 139, 144) claims that there is much less divergence from professional ethics within the German legal profession (see also Blankenburg and Schultz 1988: 139–40). The idea of self-regulation must, however, be considered in the light of evidence of the apparently highly inadequate or selective enforcement of professional norms of conduct by legal professional associations (Abel 1989a: 143ff; Abel 1988: 133-6, 252-4; Rosenthal 1974: 117–28) as well as in the light of the ambiguity and uncertainty of professional attitudes on some of the most crucial ethical canons, such as those governing the balance between duty to client and duty to court and legal system. Thus a study of codes of professional ethics alone will not reveal values of legal practice that necessarily influence law or legal ideology in an obviously significant way. In fact such codes may best be seen not so much as a hallmark of lawyering as, on the one hand, a part of the deliberately constructed public image of particular occupational groups whose work centres on law and, on the other, a means of self-regulation of work within particular occupational groups of lawyers to control competition within the group and from outside.

The idea of a 'service ideal' uniting lawyers—a crucial element in the functionalist analysis of professions—must, like that of professional ethics, be considered in the context of differing work situations of lawyers. The image of lawyers as serving an impersonal legal order and hence, in a certain sense, an official 'public interest' which contrasts with the profit interest of the businessman is not wholly false but apt to be misleading. Lawyers' commitment to 'law' and the 'legal order' as abstract foci of their work is far from insignificant for law's ideological functions, as will be discussed shortly. Despite much professional rhetoric, however, the folk idea of a professional service ideal should be interpreted only to suggest that there are certain potential or actual tensions between, on the one hand, the conditions under which lawyers' occupational prerogatives can be maintained and, on the other, the wholehearted adoption of a business approach to the selling of legal work in the market like any other commodity.

Insofar as profitable legal work involves selling advice and aid in negotiation of the law, it depends on a considerable degree of freedom being available to lawyers to choose those to whom they will sell their expertise and to determine the conditions under which this will be done. Salaried lawyers in business or government are not necessarily prevented from creating favourable conditions for the exploitation of their expertise (Spangler 1986: 89–92, 120–2; Murray et al. 1983). Ideally, however, profitable enterprise in legal practice, as in other forms of business, depends on a minimum of interference from external sources such as government as long as satisfactory market conditions can be secured. For a professional group, as for a business elite, this freedom can be acquired through direct political influence but it normally requires legitimation. The freedom of business from state control is today defended in terms of economic theories and assumptions about the conditions of business efficiency and wealth creation. Legitimation of professional freedom in politically and socially sensitive areas such as the provision of medical and legal services depends upon the belief that the doctor or lawyer 'like all professional men always puts his client's interests before his own' (Council of the Law Society quoted in Podmore 1980: 71) or, at least, that professions can be trusted to use their special expertise for the public good and to exercise effective self-regulation to prevent abuses arising from unrestrained pursuit of profit.

In this context the way lawyers promote themselves and their services is crucially significant. Touting for business is contrary to professional ethics because unrestrained public competition destroys the image of a professional community of lawyers and reveals legal practice as a business like any other (Fennell 1982: 146ff). In recent years there have been tendencies, especially in common law jurisdictions, towards very significant relaxations of what were formerly strict professional controls on advertising by lawyers. The fear of serious competition from other occupational groups, or between fragments of legal professions, seems to underlie this development. But many American lawyers have been slow to take advantage of liberalised advertising rules (Abel 1989a: 119–21) and, in Britain at least, lawyer advertising remains, for the time being, relatively low-key (Paterson et al. 1988; Abel 1988: 189–93). No doubt this is at least partly because of a sense that to adopt the most aggressive methods of business promotion would directly undermine certain elements of professional dignity and status (cf. Blacksell et al. 1991: 87).

Traditionally, lawyers have obtained business through the development of contacts outside the immediate work environment. Involvement in community and political organisations might appear imperative in order to become known and attract business (Podmore 1980: 72ff). A lawyers' practice manual endorsed by the American Bar Association noted: 'The corporation president with whom you work on the orphan's milk fund drive may soon need a lawyer. If you impressed him favourably ... he may decide you are just the man to handle the important transaction his corporation is going to undertake' (quoted in Podmore 1980: 74). Thus the expression of the service ideal in public service of various kinds has been promoted by and helped to meet lawyers' business needs, both in the situation of the occupational group as a whole and that of individual practitioners. Nevertheless, economic pressures on legal practitioners, together with counterproductive effects on the image of their profession arising, for example, from apparent collective price fixing (Abel 1988: 193–6), encourage demands from some lawyers for a further loosening of professional rules limiting direct competition.

The service ideal demands the continual reaffirmation of an image of moral rectitude. This, however, is hard to translate into concrete terms given the inherent moral ambiguity of the lawyer's roles (e.g. Kirchheimer 1961: 242ff; Fried 1976). Consequently the ideal of moral rectitude is asserted specifically in firm action taken by professional bodies against clearly defined wrongs likely to scandalise the professional image; for example, the determined and usually very severe disciplinary action taken against financial improprieties by solicitors involving clients' money (cf. Kirk 1976: 97–105; Abel 1988: 257–8). By contrast, effective collective policing by the profession itself (for example, through its professional associations) of other kinds of behaviour inconsistent with fulfilment of the service ideal—for example, negligent preparation of or action in relation to a client's case—may be seen by the profession as setting up intolerable constraints on practitioners' freedom to determine the conditions under which they can maintain a successful business.

As discussed earlier, these conditions may vary greatly in different strata of the profession. Thus, rigid and energetic enforcement of professional norms, although demanded by the service ideal image, may have the effect of revealing the diversity of business conditions of legal work and the lack of unity of outlook of the occupational group of lawyers as a whole and of opening deep controversy within the occupational group about the relationships between business necessity and professional image. Even worse for the folk image of 'profession', such enforcement may eventually be seen, not only by those in the lower strata of the profession who are most likely to be found in breach of professional norms and to be on the receiving end of disciplinary action (Abel 1989a: 144–5; Podmore 1980: 26; Reichstein 1965; Carlin 1962), but also by the public at large, as action taken by certain sections of the profession against others as part of the competitive struggle for business, status and power between different categories of legal practitioners.

In general, therefore, the official values of professional ethics are more important as symbols or rhetoric than as actual controls which define the character of legal work. Yet the rhetoric is, as has been seen, grounded in definite requirements of the occupational group of lawyers. Hence the professional need to be seen to be maintaining professional norms interacts continuously with the business needs of legal practice which support those norms and pull against them at the same time.

Client Interests and 'Public Interest'

Rueschemeyer distinguishes the outlook of German lawyers with their more generalised commitment to law and the values of good public administration, from that of American lawyers lacking a comparably strong orientation to common professional values and being characterised by strong identification with the interests and values of the client groups they serve. Thus the significance of the business community as a reference group for lawyers' values and outlook is seen as far greater in the United States than in Germany (Rueschemeyer 1973: 112). The image of the lawyer as a 'hired gun' is a familiar one. The 'great bulk of the profession, fortified by the ideology that all, even [sic] great corporations, deserve quality representation and that adversary confrontation will ensure just results, eschews moral screening of client interests' (Galanter 1983: 159; see also Fried 1976). In England, the primary identification of lawyers seems to be with property interests in general, and less specifically with business interests than in the case of the American profession. The highly uneven geographical distribution of solicitors in England has been explained in terms of the level of economic activity in the areas concerned (Blacksell et al. 1991: ch 2) and similar factors no doubt explain the distribution of lawyers in many jurisdictions (Abel 1989b: 120–1; Rueschemeyer 1989: 291–2). The demand for lawyers in the United States has been found to correlate with levels of wealth rather than with the extent of government regulation (Pashigian 1982: 4). In England, the central importance of conveyancing (transfer of interests in land) for the economic viability of many solicitors' practices (Blacksell et al. 1991: 80, 85–92) highlights the traditional identification of the profession with individual property owners' interests (Offer 1981).

The kinds of interests with which the lawyer identifies are clearly vital in determining the nature of lawyers' influence on law as doctrine and on the working legal system. These interests will depend on the structural position of lawyers as an occupational group in a particular society and upon the structural position of particular kinds of lawyer and legal practice within that occupational group. On the one hand it has been frequently argued that lawyers, like other occupational groups that have achieved the status of professions, are in a position to manipulate or exert control over clients through their monopoly of expertise and consequent ability to redefine client problems in professional terms and hence remove them from client supervision (e.g. Christie 1977; Carlin and Howard 1965). On the other hand, lawyers are often seen, particularly from a Marxist standpoint, as the servants of particular classes (especially the middle classes from which Western legal professions are also typically recruited) and hence reflect and express the interests of those classes directly (Cain 1983a).

These views are not necessarily incompatible. Maureen Cain, adopting Marx's term (Marx and Engels 1974: 65), argues that the lawyer is a 'conceptive ideologist': a translator rather than a controller; not dominating the client but translating the client's objectives into the terms of legal discourse and devising the means of achieving them within the framework of law (Cain 1983a; and see Sarat and Felstiner 1988). If this role can be attributed to the solicitors Cain studied and whom she sees as serving middle-class clients it fits still more obviously elite lawyers serving powerful business organisations. Their role is to innovate and find ways within the legal system to protect their clients' interests. Today this is clearly a role that takes account of the uncertainties or leeways of legal doctrine—the complex interactions of rule and discretion—discussed in the previous chapter. Thus the elite legal adviser's role is far from being merely to 'state the law'. The expertise required is one that can use creatively both the certainties and uncertainties of law in strategies that are to the client's advantage (cf. Galanter 1983: 161). In general, insofar as the business world requires lawyers it needs strategists and troubleshooters not jurists; experts who can obtain maximum freedom and maximum benefits for the enterprise from government and who can use the threat but rarely the reality of litigation creatively as a precision tool for furtherance of corporate interest. This situation reflects both the increasing significance of legal expertise in a climate of extensive government regulation of business (Pashigian 1982; Spangler 1986: ch 3) and differences, noted earlier in this book, between businessmen's and lawyers' typical views of business transactions (Macaulay 1963; and see Chapter 1).

In other situations, however, client interests—as the client defines them—may not be treated as the sole or even primary determinant of professional strategy. Where, as in Germany, the development of the modern legal profession was, to a considerable extent, directly promoted by the state, the choice of professional loyalties to private clients may ultimately be subordinated to overall conceptions of public responsibility focused on state interests (Rueschemeyer 1973; 1989). In the Anglo-American environment, however, a relative independence of legal professions from the state has left them free to adhere to the interests of their most economically valuable clients. Yet lawyers deal with the relatively powerless and economically weak members of society as well as the wealthy and powerful. Cain's analysis underemphasises the extent to which lawyers are entrusted with the rights of 'have-nots' as well as of the relatively prosperous. In such cases, many empirical studies suggest, they may reinterpret client interests in ways that the client cannot fully evaluate; for example, in the conduct of the adversary process of trial (e.g. Blumberg 1967), in plea bargains in criminal trials and other forms of negotiation between lawyers or between lawyers and judge (McConville and Mirsky 1987: 770–4), or between lawyers and insurance companies in the settlement of personal injury claims (Genn 1987).

As the American lawyer Marc Galanter (1983: 159) argues: 'Loyalty is often deflected from the onetime client to the forum or opposite party with whom the lawyer has continuing relations'. The result may be a decision to take no action in the case, to settle it more quickly and on easier terms than might be thought to be in the client's best interests, to minimise the time and thought expended on action, or to avoid action that might antagonise parties who may on other occasions provide valuable business (Macaulay 1979; and see McConville and Mirsky 1987: 751ff, 840–4). Thus, even in legal aid work in criminal trials, lawyers' loyalties may for economic reasons (quite apart from specific legal obligations) be significantly shaped by the official relationships constituting the judicial system which pays their fees (cf. Carlen 1976a; 1976b: ch 3; Blumberg 1967). These loyalties may be influenced by a felt need to make some effort to accommodate the interests of police or court officials who can direct work towards the lawyer (Bankowski and Mungham 1976: 54–60; Carlen 1976b: 46–8), rather than being exclusively centred on the single case 'client' in a position of dependence. In other cases, such as personal injury actions, purely economic considerations may sometimes encourage the rapid settling of cases, even at the expense of clients' interests, so that the lawyer can obtain fees and move on to other business (Genn 1987: 107–8).

Private practice lawyers are, therefore, likely either to be influenced significantly by the interests of state agencies or officials capable of affecting the flow of profitable legal work, or to espouse the interests of client groups sufficiently knowledgeable about the context of legal work (for example in business fields) and sufficiently powerful economically to provide adequate financial rewards for legal service.

Strong client identification brings to light further ambiguities of the service ideal when individual clients (in the case of giant corporations) can exert major influence on general public welfare. Is the lawyers' primary obligation in such a situation to the client or to 'the public'? More specifically, is the corporate client properly identified as the management of the corporation, its board of directors, its existing shareholders or its potential shareholders? In the United States the matter has been a major item of controversy since the 1970s in connection with the scope of lawyer-client privilege, that is, the privilege of maintaining the confidentiality of lawyer-client dealings and communications (Pashigian 1982). Again the relationship between the business foundations of legal practice and the rhetoric of profession remains ambiguous.

Insofar, however, as lawyers' primary identification will necessarily be with those interests (of official agencies or of economically powerful client groups) that provide the economic foundation of their work, they can be thought of as occupying two primary roles: first, as 'ideologists' in Cain's sense—elaborating concepts as devices to incorporate the changing interests of their valued client groups (for example, business firms or substantial property owners) within established normative structures of order in society—and, secondly, as technicians of social control watching over and facilitating the routine legal mechanisms by which the established social order is maintained (and so sections of society other than those represented in favoured client groups tend to be kept in their positions of relative powerlessness). As has been seen, different strata of the legal profession may be primarily concerned with each of these aspects of legal work. However, as will appear, some lawyers may to some extent escape the constraints of both roles by adopting a particular radical interpretation of them.

Professional Knowledge

The discussion in the previous sections should suggest that lawyers' work is not to be thought of merely as the expert assimilation and application of legal doctrine—the rules, principles and concepts of law to be found in the law books. Newcomers to legal practice are frequently surprised to discover how little of the corpus of doctrine they learned as law students is actually regularly used in practice. Carlin's Chicago sole practitioners generally found themselves doing low level work requiring little if any special expertise ('a fairly routine, clerical-bookkeeping job'); work that could be done by other occupational groups and often was (Carlin 1962: 207). Bankowski and Mungham, studying solicitors in Wales, found that the 'good case' in the eyes of their respondents was 'never simply the case that had held some special legal interest (unlike the medical profession, where the good case is almost always seen as the clinically interesting one), or even one that was financially profitable in its own terms. Instead the good case was the one that might conceivably lead to a bonanza'—for example, getting work from a rich family (Bankowski and Mungham 1976: 63). Respondents also remarked on the limited intellectual demands of criminal advocacy in magistrates' courts—an important source of work: 'It's a matter of acclimatisation, not skill ... Anybody can tackle criminal advocacy; just learn the mumbo-jumbo, that's all' (quoted in Bankowski and Mungham 1976: 63). Rueschemeyer (1973: 23) argues that for legal practice 'organisational "know-how", economic experience, wisdom about personal relations, connections and "inside" knowledge are often as important for the lawyer's work as knowledge of the law'. Carlin's study of New York lawyers found that more than half of his sample assisted their business clients in getting finance and seeking investment opportunities and took a direct interest in general corporate affairs. No strict line was maintained between specifically legal and other advice and services (Carlin 1966).

The point is not, of course, to deny that many areas of legal practice depend upon expert knowledge of legal doctrine, nor that for certain elite strata of a legal profession the ability to arrange client affairs depends upon extremely high levels of virtuosity in interpretation and application of this doctrine. It is, however, to recognise as many recent writers on professions have done, that the folk concept of specialised, esoteric professional knowledge as being at the heart of professional status hides a complex reality. For example, the legal information employed in a barrister's practice might be best thought of not as a body of esoteric knowledge but as a continually modified compendium of data and experience related to cases at hand (Morison and Leith 1992: ch 4). The importance of expert knowledge of doctrinal detail varies in different kinds of legal practice. Arguably it is most centrally significant in the practice of those elite strata of the legal profession that dominate professional organisations and contribute most to shaping the way the profession presents its public image. Otherwise legal practice encompasses a great diversity of legal and non-legal skills and services.

The claim to professional autonomy is, however, often based on the idea that the special knowledge and expertise of the profession is *unique* and *wholly distinct* from other forms of knowledge; hence that the special practice of the profession can be clearly distinguished from the practice of other occupations (e.g. Abbott 1988: 52-7; Freidson 1986). Legal doctrine and the techniques of its interpretation are held to constitute this special knowledge. The maintenance of the professional claim that legal doctrine constitutes a self-contained body of knowledge capable of being interpreted in terms of its own distinctive techniques *and without reference to any other discipline or occupational practice* has been a central concern of Western lawyers in their strategies of 'achieving profession'.

To a considerable extent, establishment of the Western idea of the autonomy of law from other aspects of society has paralleled the struggle by lawyers in Western societies to achieve the full 'mandate' associated with the idea of an autonomous legal profession.[3] The two developments have necessarily reinforced each other. In this way the quest for professionalisation has contributed powerfully to the distinctive characteristics of Western law discussed in previous chapters. In addition, it is vital to recognise the manner in which the characteristics of legal professionalisation have contributed to the effectiveness of legal ideology in modern Western societies. Legal ideology can be thought of as becoming a part of popular consciousness partly through the practical activities of lawyers solving everyday client problems; that is, through activities in which, as has been seen above, knowledge of legal doctrine is continually blended with 'non-legal' knowledge. At the same time, the lawyer's professional identification, dependent on the claim of special professional knowledge, makes it likely that the integrity and self-sufficiency of legal doctrine (and so of legal ideology) will often be proclaimed in legal practice.[4] In this way, as 'conceptive ideologists' lawyers help to diffuse legal ideas as ideology in the varied circumstances and relationships encountered in practice at the same time as they contribute to the reshaping of legal doctrine to take account of the claims and aspirations of those client groups upon whose patronage they depend.

Professional Knowledge and the Changing Forms of Western Law

These considerations, apart from any others, should indicate major reasons why, typically, lawyers tenaciously defend the rule of law and

3 This theme is explored in a variety of ways in Cotterrell 1989.

4 That this is certainly not always the case is suggested by a recent study of lawyer-client interactions in divorce cases in California and Massachusetts. The study found that lawyers often talked to clients in ways that suggested the ambiguity, irrelevance or incompleteness of legal doctrine (Sarat and Felstiner 1989). But insofar as lawyers seek to maintain a specific image of professionalism and its status grounded in expert knowledge it would seem that this approach to the field of practice cannot be carried very far.

fiercely attack the growth of administrative discretion and other legal developments discussed in Chapter 5. As Weber clearly saw, it is the *formally rational* elements of modern law which provide some basis for thinking of legal doctrine as a self-contained system, hence as self-contained professional knowledge. It is this which lawyers presuppose when they demand 'certainty' in the law so as to be able to provide proper advice and aid to their clients. The intrusion of substantive rationality as a dominating characteristic of legal thought—in explicit policy considerations, ethical evaluations, considerations of social welfare, etc.—makes experts in policy formation (social and economic analysts, administrators) in certain respects equal or even superior to the lawyer as relevant experts in legal development and application. The claim that legal professional expertise is unique and exclusive becomes increasingly untenable in such circumstances.

In retrospect it can be seen that common law practice, combining the image of law as accumulated custom with the assertion that only the lawyer could probe the arcane traditional wisdom of this custom embodied in the practice of courts, provided the greatest security for the autonomy of legal work. With the triumph of legal positivism lawyers accepted that legislation, the content of which was beyond their direct control, was fated to become the primary source of new legal doctrine. They pinned their professional faith on positivist normative legal theory's capacity to maintain the viability of legal professional knowledge as a 'science of law' (Cotterrell 1989: ch 3). But, inevitably as it seems now, once the idea of law as a mere instrument of government had been accepted, modern government would use rules and administrative devices of all kinds in ever more complex combination[5] paying little attention to the lawyer's professional need to identify a distinctive form of legal knowledge encompassed by a formally rational system of rules.

In those Western countries where the legal profession saw itself as shaped, sponsored and given legitimacy primarily by the state, such developments would tend to lead particularly to a closer identification of legal and administrative mentality (Rueschemeyer 1973; 1989). In the Anglo-American world, however, they have often been seen within the legal profession as a crisis of law and the legal system (e.g. Hewart 1929; Keeton 1952; Kamenka and Tay 1975). Today the legal expert needs to understand particularly: administrative processes and activities (so as to predict and influence the ways in which official discretions are exercised); indexing systems of government regulations; and the policy and practice of governmental (including judicial) agencies in the fields with which he or she is concerned.

5 See the discussion of discretionary, particularised and mechanical regulation in ch 5.

The problems of maintaining the professional claim to unique special knowledge help to explain lawyers' traditional 'all or nothing approach' to regulation of administrative processes, opting either for fully formal trial-type hearings or no procedural safeguards at all (Davis 1969: 228); that is, requiring that proceedings be fully legal in the lawyer's sense of bounded by legal rules, or else wholly external to law. The growth of discretionary regulation may however require fine combinations of formality and informality, in which considerable flexibility can be maintained within workable and predictable forms of procedure (cf. Galligan 1986: ch 4). Related difficulties of defining the legal sphere arise in areas such as health and safety regulation where the distinction between legal rules and scientific or technical standards may be extremely difficult to draw (cf. Livock 1979: 189; and see Chapter 8, below). Yet the interpretation of scientific standards requires expert knowledge different from that which the lawyer claims.

Lawyers, however, typically assume that the ability to assimilate specialised forms of non-legal knowledge essential to the case in hand (for example, about accounting and other business practices, medical reports regarding injuries, or scientific knowledge relevant to patent claims) is a normal part of legal practice. This knowledge can be subordinated to legal professional knowledge. It offers no challenge to the latter, merely playing a supporting role in the application of legal doctrine. Social scientific knowledge offers an interesting special case, however. Given lawyers' professional approach to the use of other forms of knowledge, the explanation that their 'scepticism verging on hostility' to social science is based on ignorance (Collins 1978: 572) seems inadequate. So, for similar reasons, does the suggestion (Fahr 1961) that this scepticism is based on the impenetrability of 'jargon' in economics, sociology or psychology (since all fields of expert knowledge, including those that lawyers use, have their special concepts); or that it is based on the 'uncertainty' of social scientific knowledge (Collins 1978: 573) since the certainty frequently demanded of social science by lawyers (for example, 'the rigour of the most advanced of the physical sciences'; cf. Cohen et al. 1958: v) is one that law itself may never attain (cf. D'Amato 1983).

Resistance may arise primarily from the fact that social scientific knowledge has the potential, in some circumstances, to challenge legal professional knowledge in a way that none of the other knowledge sources relating to particular cases or circumstances can (Cotterrell 1986). Social scientific and legal knowledge compete in the interpretation of social relationships: the latter presupposes a world that is malleable through human agency and normatively controlled by man-made rules; the positivistic tendencies in the social or human sciences presuppose a human world governed by its own scientifically discoverable principles of behaviour. While, for example, the lawyer is concerned to assess responsibility for acts, the psychiatrist can label mental states in 'scientific' terms of 'health' or 'illness' which cut across the legal-moral assessment of blame; and the social scientist may assert social causes of behaviour which cast doubt on the concepts of individual responsibility generally presupposed in legal practice. The English M'Naghten Rules (1843) designed to provide a legal test of insanity survive (although their importance has been much reduced by legislation and they have been significantly modified in United States and Commonwealth jurisdictions) despite being seriously out of touch with psychiatric knowledge (Finkel 1988). They form a part of lawyers' knowledge and a professional apparatus by means of which to control reality.

Understandably, lawyers resist accepting that legal solutions to problems may depend on a foundation of non-legal knowledge; that is, knowledge outside lawyers' control through their recognised professional expertise. Attempts are made to present modern law as necessarily having its own autonomous ways of thinking (cf. Teubner 1989). The practice of the medical profession, by contrast, is recognised as dependent on the advance of science in a variety of fields beyond the specific sphere of medical practice. Doctors, however, have a virtual monopoly of curing physical illness. Lawyers are necessarily less professionally secure: they do not monopolise dispute processing, nor—to use Llewellyn's phrase—the preventive channelling of conduct to avoid friction, nor the assignment and maintenance of political legitimacy. Within the social, economic and political order their role is more pervasive than that of doctors but also more diffuse. And the power of lawyers' professional knowledge is guaranteed ultimately not by its integrity, autonomy, unity or systematic character, but by its specific relation to the coercive and allocative power of the state.

With the development of forms of regulation and administration that undermine the assumption of autonomy of professionally guarded legal doctrine, influential sections of Western legal professions have tended to seek replacements for or supplements to the traditional concept of professional legal knowledge. In particular, economic analysis of law has been seen as offering a theoretical basis for legal doctrine, policy and practice (e.g. Ogus and Veljanovski, eds, 1984). The lawyer has increasingly found it necessary to make alliances with the social researcher by using in court the testimony of experts or social scientific or statistical evidence collected specially for the case or available in the scientific literature. In the United States, where this development has probably been taken furthest, economic evidence is said to be 'relatively intensively used ... Exclusive use of sociological evidence is rare; more frequently it is used in conjunction with psychological evidence'; thus 'social psychological evidence exhibits the most extensive range of input to court cases' beginning with the use of sociological research to expose the detrimental effects of racial segregation on personality and later to prove discrimination (Collins 1978: 563–4).[6] The popularity among legal scholars in the United States, and to some extent in Britain, of economic analysis of law as an alternative to traditional modes of demonstrating the coherence of doctrine may reflect not only the high scientific status of economics among the social sciences but also its relatively (among the social sciences) individualistic orientation and its stress on rationality of action, both of which mirror dominant assumptions of Western legal thought, particularly in the individualist, client-oriented, case-by-case approach of Anglo-American legal practice.

The Effects of Lawyers on the Law

If it were to be assumed that common-sense concepts of class are theoretically useful (an assumption challenged in Chapter 4) and that an individual's class situation determines his or her outlook, it would be plausible to say that since lawyers are recruited almost exclusively from the middle classes (Abel 1988: 74–6, 170–2; 1989a: 87–90; 1989b: 113–5), they necessarily infuse middle-class values into the law. Certainly lawyers have had considerable involvement in political life in Western countries (especially as members of legislatures) and, although this involvement seems to be declining (Rueschemeyer 1989: 309–10), it suggests that lawyers have often been in a position to exert much direct influence on legislation as well as in other aspects of legal development. Nevertheless, matters are more complex than this. Discussion in this chapter has emphasised the complexities and ambiguities of legal professionalisation (which suggest that the organisation of legal work itself may strongly promote particular attitudes of lawyers to the law). More generally, aspects of the discussion of ideology in Chapter 4 are relevant here. Ideologies and perceptions of interest are interdependent, and both of these are shaped in and, at the same time, influence a complex variety of circumstances. Legal practice, therefore, is conducted within a certain ideological climate which shapes this practice in important ways while being, itself, influenced and, in part, sustained by it. The social background of lawyers is, however, undoubtedly relevant to many aspects of their practice. For example, that women and members of ethnic minority groups form only a small proportion of the legal profession and are generally found in its low status strata (Abel 1988: 76–85, 172–6; 1989a: 85–7, 90–108; 1989b: 115–9) is highly significant in reinforcing homogeneity of professional outlook and values and isolating the profession from the concerns of major social groups.

6 See further ch 7.

Lawyers' Conservatism

Nevertheless, the characteristics of professional organisation of legal work and the nature of that work itself may be as significant as the social origins of lawyers in shaping dominant values of legal practice. Thus, for example, one writer has suggested that the general conservatism that almost all commentators see as a dominant characteristic of lawyers derives from three sources related specifically to legal practice. First, lawyers are preoccupied with application of a *continuing* set of rules and principles—a stable, monolithic doctrinal structure of order. Secondly, there is the lawyer's 'more immediate and selfish interest in preserving his intellectual capital—the knowledge of the system in which he was trained' and, thirdly, 'there is the tendency of lawyers, and especially of the leading and most able lawyers, to be closely identified in interest with the establishment of the time—the men in power or the men who have prospered' (Sawer 1965: 125). De Tocqueville (1945: 275, 278) wrote of lawyers as 'attached to public order beyond every other consideration',[7] as having 'nothing to gain by innovation'. Morris Finer, himself an eminent British lawyer, remarked that the '*status quo* is part of [the lawyer's] mental capital. Every legal reform robs him of an asset he has worked hard to acquire' (quoted in Podmore 1980: 39).

To write of conservatism in this context may be, however, to use too crude and unenlightening a concept. Throughout modern history there have been 'rebel' or 'radical' lawyers (Kirchheimer 1961: 246ff). Lawyers, after all, are not merely concerned with order, but with a particular kind of order: that which can be embodied in the legal doctrine that provides the basis of their professional claim to special expertise. The lawyer's professional commitment to the integrity of doctrine may easily be extended to a professional rejection and condemnation of those forms of order (for example, government by arbitrary terror or unfettered administrative discretion) that are not seen as encompassed by rational, systematic legal doctrine.

Furthermore, certain characteristics of legal doctrine which are adopted as the basis of lawyers' values may assume such importance in elaborated and extended forms that they become the basis of radical legal practice. Thus the concept of the rule of law (with its derivative principles of equal protection under the law and due process of law or natural justice in trial or quasi-judicial proceedings), together with the individualistic orientation of Western law, sometimes become the foundation of forceful advocacy of human rights or civil rights and demands for new forms of representation to bring the claims of the poor and of disadvantaged minorities before the law.

7 Cf. Weber's strikingly similar phrase quoted on p. 155, above describing the condition of mind associated with legal domination and pervasive bureaucratisation.

Finally, if lawyers in general have a strong interest in the protection of their 'mental capital', they are also sufficiently close to legal doctrine to recognise its contingent character, its *lacunae* and ambiguities, and to put into perspective (and so identify means of reforming) what appear to others as its awesome complexities.

Individualism and Independence

Rueschemeyer has compared value orientations of the American and German bars in terms of the different degrees of identification with client interests and values in the two professions and the different value orientations of the most influential strata of clients served by these legal professions. On this basis he identifies important differences in attitudes to economic success, conflict, respect for law, achievement and equality (Rueschemeyer 1973: 84ff), all of which must have an important bearing on the way in which lawyers approach legal work.

We should, therefore, expect that the effect of lawyers on the law will vary significantly in different Western societies. In those (especially Anglo-American) legal systems where strong identification with client interests and a pragmatic case-by-case approach is characteristic of legal practice and where for historical reasons the profession enjoys substantial independence from state control, legal individualism is likely to be powerfully reinforced in professional practice. For example, the conception of the lawyer's essential role as being to fight for his or her client, so that justice is seen as safeguarded primarily by a battle of lawyers committed to their clients' interests, reinforces the 'naturalness' of the adversary system of trial in common law jurisdictions and emphasises contrasts with continental inquisitorial approaches. In the latter, judges may take a much more active role in the examination of witnesses, rather than passively observing the confrontation of lawyers (Merryman 1985: ch 16). As various pressures—for example, increasing cost of administration of justice, increasing congestion in the courts—have reduced the importance of criminal *trial* and led to a less ambivalent recognition that the lawyer's 'fight' in these circumstances takes place only within close limits set by the administrative demands of the criminal justice system (see Chapter 7), emphasis has centred, particularly in the United States, on securing the 'right to counsel'. Justice in the criminal process is coming to be seen, no less than in the past, as dependent on having a lawyer to take one's side: but not so much to fight battles in open court as expertly to negotiate plea bargains and other behind-the-scenes arrangements (McDonald, ed, 1983).

At the same time, the conditions of independent and strongly client-oriented practice may particularly encourage considerable diversity in lawyers' values and attitudes to the content of legal doctrine. Thus the profession may include highly conservative lawyers and committed reformers or radicals, although, for reasons discussed earlier, protection of the interests of property owners will generally provide a *leitmotiv* of legal practice. This fragmentation of professional outlook, together with the diversity of forms of practice discussed earlier, creates at least some scope for powerful pressures for legal change to come from *within* legal professions.

Identification with client interests may even create pressures that undermine legal individualism, when it appears that client interests can only be safeguarded as part of wider collective interests. Thus, in the United States, class actions—legal actions brought on behalf of classes of claimants, rather than individuals—have been important weapons in 'public interest' law practice on behalf of minority groups and the poor. Further, the attempt, by means of neighbourhood law firms and law centres, to extend the rule of law to benefit potential client groups not served by orthodox legal practice has challenged numerous assumptions underlying this practice.

These developments reflect important changes in the basis of professional legal practice. Legal professional autonomy has become more problematic with the change in the character of legal doctrine noted in this and the previous chapter and with the consequent emergence of other occupational groups competing with lawyers in administrative, social control, policy-implementing and rights-safeguarding roles. This has encouraged a looser professional identification among some lawyers and a willingness to dispense with professional prerogatives: for example, to ally with community workers in law centres in a common programme. At the same time it has highlighted the politicisation of law, so that with the breakdown of legal autonomy and the increasing identification of law with policy and administration legal practice is seen much more clearly as involving recognition, among lawyers themselves, of the ambiguity of the values symbolised in legal doctrine; a development closely related to the challenges to legal legitimacy discussed in Chapter 5.

Lawyers and Legal Ideology

We can conclude that lawyers are of vital importance in producing in contemporary Western societies the ideological effects of law discussed in Chapters 4 and 5. First, they are interpreters and mediators, in the numerous social situations that the state seeks to regulate, of legal doctrine created by state agencies. In this sense they carry legal ideology into numerous fields of social life served by often strongly contrasting forms of legal practice. Secondly, at the same time they are interpreters and mediators in the reverse direction. They carry before state agencies (for example through litigation, demands for legal reform, and technical and consultancy work for public administrative agencies of all kinds) contradictions thrown up by confrontations between legal doctrine and particular social circumstances. Thirdly, insofar as they remain committed to a firm assertion of a status of independent professionalism, they tend to seek to affirm in all these activities the integrity of legal doctrine as professional knowledge. Hence they tend to promote through highly developed techniques of legal argument and doctrinal reasoning the idea of law as a rational, integrated system of knowledge. Thus the contradictions that they bring before state agencies for solution are not usually posed as a challenge to the very idea of legal doctrine as a coherent system of thought but as technical problems of interpretation or elaboration within doctrine.

Finally, other contradictions which cannot be portrayed as merely technical but which are endemic and fundamental in legal ideology—contradictions between the perceived symbols, values, ideals of the law and the impossibility of their full realisation in practice—are partly contained by a kind of selectivity in legal professional practice. As has been seen, the interests of certain client groups are interpreted differently in professional practice from those of others. The demands of the 'haves' will (for reasons inherent in the structure of professional practice) usually be heard more clearly than those of the 'have-nots'. Thus, for example, the ideal of equality before the law as a symbol is preserved because inequalities of access to lawyers and in services available from lawyers are inequalities based not in legal doctrine itself but in numerous 'extra-legal factors'. The conditions of professional guardianship of doctrine explain some but by no means all of these factors. But, as has also been seen, lawyers can be and often are agents of change as well as stability. To consider other aspects of the effects of law we must look at its other major institutional settings.

7 Judges, Courts, Disputes

From many standpoints adjudication and courts seem obviously central institutions of legal systems. Whether they are held to be present in all legal systems will depend on how the relevant concepts are defined but in Western societies what is frequently termed 'the judicial process' seems reasonably identifiable as a distinct set of institutional practices.

It is in Anglo-American legal thought that the centrality of the judge in the legal system is perhaps most strongly emphasised. Despite Ehrlich's proclamation that the centre of all legal life is not the courtroom, for many other writers judges are—in Blackstone's words—'the depositories of the law, the living oracles' (Dawson 1968). At the turn of the century the eminent American Supreme Court judge Oliver Wendell Holmes defined law, polemically, as the prophesies of what courts will decide (Holmes 1897). Holmes' pronouncement helped to set a fashion through much of the first half of the twentieth century in American 'realist' legal thought, which stressed in its most uncompromising forms that law was to be understood in terms of judicial practice rather than rules. The worship of judicial oracles is perhaps taken to its ultimate extreme in the view expressed most forcefully by the American legal scholar John Chipman Gray that even statutes enacted by legislatures are not law but only a source of law since their meaning and legal effect are determined only when they have been considered in cases before the courts. Judicial decisions constitute the law itself (Gray 1921: 125).

Such views as these are plainly influenced by the special character of particular judicial systems. The United States entrusts to the nine judges of its prestigious Supreme Court the responsibility for interpreting the legal meaning of the Constitution, one of the most important repositories of political symbols and ideals in the Western world. The formal separation of legal powers as between executive, legislature and judiciary in the United States Constitution, bolstered by strong political traditions together with the traditions of English common law and of a strongly independent legal profession, help to create conditions under which the highest strata of the American judiciary can exert powerful influence on American society in a variety of ways. In Britain, too, where the judiciary is chosen from the ranks of and reflects the status of an independent legal profession, and where legal doctrine is still related to fundamental principles and concepts rooted in the common law tradition of judge-made law, judges' similarly high status is related to their perceived centrality as shapers of law and guardians of its traditions and ideals.

Generally, however, in European continental countries career judiciaries exist. That is to say, judges are not, in general, chosen from the ranks of established legal practitioners but are officials who have undergone a special judicial training with the intention of pursuing a career as a judge rather than as a legal practitioner. In this situation continental judges of code-based civil law systems may see themselves as special state functionaries rather than—as often in Anglo-American systems—as members of an elite stratum of the legal profession. For example, discussions of the German judiciary often strongly stress its 'civil service mentality' (e.g. Kommers 1969; and see Shapiro 1981: 151). In addition, the traditions of code systems and the responsibilities that they place upon judges are seen as different from common law traditions and judicial responsibilities. Different legal traditions, political situations, and professional histories ensure that the status of judges is not uniform throughout contemporary Western industrialised societies.

Furthermore, judiciaries and courts are stratified and differentiated in many ways. Judicial hierarchies may extend from unsalaried volunteer part-time judges such as English magistrates, who may have almost no professional legal training, to the judges of courts of final appeal or ultimate legal review such as the United States Supreme Court, the British House of Lords, or the French *Cour de Cassation,* or to judges of special constitutional courts such as the West German Federal Constitutional Court. Court systems include complex hierarchies of courts of general and special jurisdiction. Tribunals of many kinds which may or may not be included within official definitions of 'courts' pose sociological questions about the scope of judicial systems and the character of adjudicative processes (e.g. Peay 1989). Our concern in this chapter will be to try to identify, in the light of the theory and concepts discussed in earlier chapters of this book, general characteristics of courts and of judicial work which are relatively constant in contemporary Western societies despite differences in the organisation and traditions of the legal systems of these societies.

Concepts of Judge and Court

The concepts of 'judge' and 'court' raise problems of sociological specification only marginally less difficult than those which the concept of profession was seen to raise in Chapter 6. If the essence of the latter problem is that 'profession' is an idea shaped by and used in the struggle between occupational groups rather than a term describing a distinct social phenomenon, the essence of the former is that concepts of 'court' and 'judge' tend to be shaped by political preconceptions. Definitions of 'court' tend to be generalisations from 'common-sense' assumptions about institutions recognised as courts in particular Western societies.

Thus for Theodore Becker, attempting to construct a general functionalist theoretical analysis of courts applicable to all societies: 'A court is (i) a man or body of men (ii) with power to decide a dispute, (iii) before whom the parties or their surrogates present the facts of the dispute and cite existent, expressed, primary normative principles (in statutes, constitutions, rules, previous cases) that (iv) are applied by that man or those men, (v) who *believe* that they should listen to the presentation of facts and apply such normative principles impartially, objectively, or with detachment ... and (vi) that they may so decide, and (vii) as an independent body' (T. L. Becker 1970: 13. Emphasis in original). Becker stresses *impartiality* ('the heart of the judicial process') as essential to the existence of courts (1970: 26); the centrality of *doctrine* in the judicial process (which distinguishes the judge from a mere mediator between the interests of the parties who arranges a compromise of their views); *disputes* as the justification and focus of court work; and *independence* of judicial activity as an essential basis of the court's existence. The importance of judicial independence in traditional conceptions of judge and court is well expressed by an American lawyer Henry Lummis: 'The moment a decision is controlled or affected by the opinion of others or by any form of external influence or pressure, that moment the judge ceases to exist. One who pronounces a decision arrived at even in part by other minds is not a judge ... the courts must be above intimidation, control or influence, or they cease to be courts' (quoted in T. L. Becker 1970: 143).

More recently Martin Shapiro has described the standard 'prototype' or ideal type of courts adopted in much of the literature as involving four elements: (i) an independent judge (ii) applying pre-existing norms (iii) after adversary proceedings (iv) to achieve a dichotomous decision in which one of the parties to the proceedings is assigned the legal right and the other is found wrong (Shapiro 1981: 1). His discussion then seeks to demonstrate that none of these elements holds good for all major judicial systems across the whole range of contemporary and historical societies. Even English judicial experience, which is typically cited as the paragon case of the historical development of a powerful judiciary independent of direct influence from the government of the day, is analysed to show how problematic the notion of 'judicial independence' is. Shapiro writes that by the nineteenth century the 'substantial autonomy' which the English courts had achieved in the seventeenth and eighteenth centuries was 'being broken up by a more effective Parliament. Only laissez-faire concepts of the proper scope of legislation obscured the reality that, once Parliament became the dominant lawmaker, the judges would return to a faithful subordination. The twentieth-century English courts have created a body of administrative law which almost totally subordinates the judges to the discipline of an administrative state' (Shapiro 1981: 124; Hutchinson 1988: ch 4; but cf. Schwartz 1987: 2–3). Shapiro does not deny that English courts enjoy substantial freedom from day-to-day interference by government in particular cases, although government has not hesitated to reverse many court decisions by legislation. His general claim, however, is that the notion of judicial independence 'is so ambiguous and misleading that it cannot serve as a touchstone of "courtness"' (Shapiro 1981: 124–5).

Indeed most of the standard elements of the traditional ideal type of courts raise more problems than they solve, although they offer a starting point for analysis of modern Western judicial systems, at least if some kind of functional analysis of courts is undertaken. To understand what judicial 'independence' can mean it is necessary to look at the relationship between judge and state in theoretical terms and at the conditions under which any such independence can be gained and kept. To consider what judicial 'objectivity' imports we must analyse the tasks that courts can be seen as required to fulfil within the political order. To consider how central 'disputes' are to the work of courts it is important to take account of evidence of the extent of courts' actual concern with disputes and of the extent to which dispute processing is centred on agencies other than those recognised as courts. Finally in considering how far courts' responsibilities with regard to 'doctrine' distinguish them from other institutions for resolving disputes we must consider what exactly those responsibilities are, what contribution courts (at least in contemporary Western societies) are required to make to the development of legal doctrine and, hence, what they contribute to the maintenance or development of particular forms of ideology, as well as of technical devices of regulation and administration available to government.

Most writers see courts as existing to fulfil several functions. In Bredemeier's Parsonian analysis discussed in Chapter 3, the functions of courts are seen as legitimation of political authority, interpretation of policy goals, channelling of roles and expectations, and socialisation. Using other terms reflecting the varied emphases of a wide range of literature we might refer to legitimation, dispute processing, technical aid in administration through the development of relevant doctrine, and elaboration and maintenance of ideology. Undoubtedly most writers on courts see dispute processing as the central focus of the judicial process (e.g. Griffith 1991: 18). In Karl Llewellyn's specification of 'law-jobs' the disposition of 'trouble-cases' is the centrally important job of law and one which in modern Western societies firmly locates the judge at the centre of legal activity (see Chapter 3). Subsequent writers who have sought an equally basic conception of law-related activity have seen dispute processing as its core—the focus that can make possible wide cross-cultural comparisons (Abel 1973; cf. Cain and Kulcsar 1982).

Indeed the idea that the central function of courts is to process disputes is almost universal (e.g. Lieberman, ed, 1984). Shapiro sees the starting point for an understanding of the judicial role in the concept of a 'triad' in which two people in conflict call upon a third to resolve their dispute. This triadic relationship, with its basic appeal to 'common sense' is the fundamental 'social logic of courts, a logic so compelling that courts have become a universal political phenomenon' (Shapiro 1981: 1). Yet the triadic relationship is unstable, for it only appeals to the common sense of the disputants when they consent to this kind of resolution of their conflict, and when the result obtained is broadly satisfactory to both parties in dispute. As Shapiro puts the matter, the triad threatens always to turn into a relationship of two against one (winning party plus adjudicator versus losing party). Hence, the court and its solutions may cease to appear 'valid' or based on 'common sense' to the losing party. As courts become formal mechanisms of adjudication, imposing legal doctrine on the parties' dispute so that one party is 'right' and the other 'wrong', they seem to leave behind the features that provide obvious common-sense consensual justifications for third party resolution of conflict.

These justifying features are associated with the techniques of *mediation* rather than adjudication (Fuller 1971). First, in mediation the parties in dispute typically choose a third party acceptable to both. Secondly, the third party does not seek to impose on the disputants norms drawn from some source external to the conflict but to engineer a compromise of the ideas and demands put forward by the disputants. Thirdly, the mediator consciously strives for the consent of both parties in dispute to the proposals for dispute resolution he or she may put forward, so that neither party is seen as wholly wrong and both can derive satisfaction from the outcome. Between mediation and adjudication stands an intermediate process, *arbitration,* in which the third party's role can be seen as more explicitly directive so that the arbitrator is recognised as a decision-maker with responsibility for determining the rights and wrongs of the dispute, rather than an honest broker for the disputants. Arbitration may be of many kinds. It may be voluntary or binding and where binding norms are imposed by the arbitrator and where the parties are under an obligation to refer their dispute to arbitration, the arbitrator may differ from the judge only in small degree.

In Shapiro's analysis, however, adjudication by courts stands at the opposite end of a continuum from mediation or the even less formalised activity of a mere 'go-between' for the disputants (see also Black and

Baumgartner 1983: 98–107). The legitimacy of courts, as Shapiro understands it, is based on the 'social logic' of the triad, that is, on consent of the disputants. Yet the continuum from go-between to mediation to arbitration to adjudication involves a steady diminution of consent to third party involvement by both parties in dispute and the replacement of this consent by the imposed authority of law—pre-existing norms supported by the power of the state (Shapiro 1981: ch 1). Thus, although courts do seek to gain the consent of the parties by including much more extensive mediatory elements in adjudicative processes than are generally recognised (1981: 8–17), their legitimacy based on their function as dispute-resolving agencies is always unstable in Shapiro's view.

This is a strange conclusion to reach. If the legitimacy of courts is, by their very nature, always in doubt it is hard to see why they have become universal phenomena. Why are such unstable legal institutions nevertheless seemingly essential to developed legal systems? The answer may be that the relationship between courts and dispute processing has been misinterpreted. It is this matter which must now be considered.

Courts and Disputes

Richard Lempert defines disputes as 'controversies involving two (or more) parties, each making a special kind of claim: a normative claim of entitlement' (Lempert 1981: 708). Another definition holds that a dispute is 'a social relationship created when someone (an individual, a group, or an organization) has a grievance, makes a claim, and has that claim rejected' (Kritzer 1981: 510). The problem with seeing dispute processing as central to the work of courts is twofold. First, there are good grounds for saying that the adjudicative process of courts is extremely poorly fitted for dispute resolution. Secondly, there seems to be considerable evidence that a great deal—probably the major part in terms of total number of cases—of courts' work is concerned with matters other than disputes in these senses. Each of these matters will be looked at in turn.

Are Courts Well Fitted for Dispute Resolution?

Shapiro's analysis of the 'social logic' of the triad suggests important reasons for denying that courts are well fitted for resolving disputes. For insofar as the work of courts is held to centre on adjudication and the role of the judge is seen as being to decide the 'rights' and 'wrongs' as between two parties in dispute and to provide a dichotomous solution to their conflict in which one party is held to be right and the other wrong, courts and judges stand at the opposite end of the continuum of dispute settlement from mediation or negotiation through a go-between. They stand at that end of the continuum where consent of both parties to a solution put forward by the third party (judge) is least likely. Consequently the processing of the dispute by the court is unlikely to result in a genuine resolution of it; that is, a solution acceptable to both parties. The dichotomous right/wrong judicial solution is likely to appear as an imposed two-against-one solution which may make continuing relations between the disputants difficult or impossible. This is, of course, a primary reason for the findings of researchers such as Macaulay (see Chapter 1) that many business firms seek to avoid recourse to courts in their dealings with other firms, even when they consider themselves seriously injured by failures on the part of those firms to honour agreements.

A court hearing may escalate a dispute by making it public and focusing attention on it in a way that can often be avoided by using the private and sometimes less complex and protracted proceedings of arbitration. The time and expense involved in court proceedings may seem prohibitive if relatively small amounts of property or compensation are at stake in a dispute. Arbitration procedures have been grafted on to some courts, and small claims courts with simplified procedures and often with restrictions on the use of professional legal counsel are familiar institutions in many legal systems (Whelan, ed, 1990). Yet an ambivalence surrounds them insofar as they exist at the boundaries of state judicial systems, often adopting the presumptions of legal individualism (see Chapter 4) which treat the disputants as autonomous, equal parties before the court, while operating without many of the formal procedures of trial and techniques of legal representation that are assumed to safeguard and express this autonomy and equality in the presentation of each side's case. As Christopher Whelan has noted, there may be an ambiguity in the whole idea of small claims courts as to whether they are essentially a means of extending the effective reach of law and legal controls over social relations, or a forum in which individual grievances can be effectively resolved (Whelan 1990: 232–3).

Furthermore, judicial proceedings 'do not lend themselves well to the consideration of multifaceted disputes ... The adversary proceeding oversimplifies many conflicts, and consequently many disputes are brought to court only as one stage in their ultimate resolution' (Jacob 1984: 12). What have been called 'polycentric problems' (Polanyi 1951: 170ff) are difficult to solve through adjudication since they involve complex networks of relations, like a web in which if any one strand is pulled a complex pattern of adjustment runs through the whole (Fuller 1978: 111–21). In addition, as Vilhelm Aubert has stressed, legal decisions by courts have a 'marked orientation toward the past' (Aubert 1969: 287). They interpret and assess, in terms of legal doctrine, past actions and events, accrued entitlements, established obligations and claims. Yet dispute resolution may also require innovative planning and policy-making to govern future conduct and events.

Given all these difficulties, the court's judgment on the law may perhaps be best seen not primarily as the resolution of a conflict but as an assertion of normative order, a definition in terms of legal doctrine of the way a particular social situation or relationship is to be understood. The successful party in the case may be happy to see the situation in this way, at least in most respects. Losers (if they do not choose, or do not have the opportunity, to appeal to a higher court) must readjust their expectations and perceptions of the situation in accordance with the court's view of it. From this point of view the dispute between litigants is not so much resolved as made no longer significant insofar as the court has greater power to define the relationship between them than do either of the disputants. In this way courts help to fix the accepted meaning of particular kinds of social relationships; the way the relationships are to be interpreted by those involved in them.

Are Disputes Central to the Work of Courts?

The question of how far courts actually are concerned with disputes in which inconsistent claims are actively and publicly asserted by opposed parties has been extensively debated in recent literature. In a longitudinal study of the work of two California courts from 1890 to the 1970s Lawrence Friedman and Robert Percival concluded that the evidence suggested that the primary function of United States trial courts had changed from dispute resolution to the administrative processing of routine cases (Friedman and Percival 1976). Shapiro writes of the American criminal justice system: 'Something over 90 per cent of American criminal cases are settled by a guilty plea or its equivalent, frequently as a result of specific or tacit plea bargaining ... The basic business of American criminal courts is not the triadic resolution of disputes ... Their time is spent disposing of the bodies of those who have pleaded guilty. Thus they are clearly administrators distributing the scarce sanctioning and rehabilitative resources of society among a mass of "applicants".' Given that the element of dispute is, as has been seen, essential to Shapiro's concept of court it is unsurprising that he reaches the conclusion that in 'this sense trial courts have ceased to be courts' (Shapiro 1981: 53; cf. Horowitz 1977: 239–40). In England sample studies have shown that 76 to 93 per cent of defendants in magistrates' courts and 57 to 75 per cent in higher courts plead guilty (McBarnet 1981b: 70). Although discussions of plea-bargaining in England have suggested that the general structure of criminal prosecution in England does not create such an opportunity for putting pressure on defendants to plead guilty as exists under American procedures, Doreen McBarnet has argued in a careful discussion of English and Scottish practice that very strong incentives are nevertheless created to encourage guilty pleas (1981b: ch 4).

Similarly in civil (i.e. non-criminal) proceedings in lower courts much of the court's work is concerned with routine bureaucratic processes in which little or no element of dispute arises (Cain 1986). This is particularly clear in cases in which creditors seek to recover debts. In the overwhelming majority of debt cases dealt with in county courts in England and Wales debtors offer no defence to the creditor's claim and judgment is obtained in an essentially administrative process involving no consideration of merits or requirement of proof of facts. Often the visit of a county court bailiff to execute a warrant for the seizure of property to meet the creditor's claim may be the only personal contact that the debtor has with the court. In an early study of debt enforcement in England, Paul Rock found not only that debtors rarely attend the court hearings, which in theory are an important means of balancing creditors' rights against debtors' capacity to pay, but that the system could not cope with full hearings. One county court registrar remarked: 'A debtor attending is an inconvenient spanner in the works of a delicately balanced time machine. If every debtor turned up and had his affairs fully probed, no judge, in a busy court, would ever get through his list' (quoted in Rock 1973: 184). In America, David Caplovitz's research has painted a similar picture of the very extensive routine administrative debt claims work of lower civil courts in which 'the concept of "judgment" is largely a facade for routinized bureaucratic procedures that have nothing to do with the actions of officials known as "judges"' (Caplovitz 1974: 220).

In a study of the work of an English county court (the lowest level court of exclusively civil jurisdiction in England and Wales) Maureen Cain (1983c) found that in only one quarter of the court's non-familial cases did it settle disputes between two actively participating parties. Only 10.9 per cent of plaintiffs were private citizens, the rest being businesses or public bodies of various kinds, but 83.9 per cent of defendants were private citizens. Enforcement of judgments was regarded by the court personnel as a major part of its work with between a quarter and a third of the court's clerical staff concerned with this. Yet, Cain notes, in over a third of cases judgments were not enforced. Does this suggest that enforcement rather than dispute resolution is the court's actual primary task but is poorly accomplished? This would hardly explain the continuing willingness of large numbers of plaintiffs to use the court. Cain prefers to conclude from the evidence that *judging*—that is, authoritative stating of legal norms in their application to a particular case or type of case—is the primary function of the court and general deterrence is one of the primary motives of court users in taking defendants to court (see also Cain 1986). 'Effectively what the court is doing is continually re-stating the rules, re-stating those entitlements and obligations which constitute the legal basis of use rights ("property") in our society. According to the plaintiffs, failure to have these repeated legal pronouncements would (or could) be interpreted as licence not to pay. Such a licence would amount to a *de facto* change in the rules which constitute use rights ... ' (Cain 1983c: 130; and see Cain 1986: 110–20). Strictly, it is not essential to the social effects of 'judging' in this sense that the judgment be given on the occasion of a particular dispute. Nor is it necessary that every decision of the court be fully enforced if the court's judgment indicates that the law stands on the side of particular interests and therefore legitimises action taken outside the court in support of those interests.

Increasing caseload pressure in the trial courts at the base of judicial hierarchies, coupled with escalating costs of judicial proceedings and complaints of delay in civil and criminal cases, helps to promote administrative efficiency rather than judicial rigour as the dominant virtue sought in the procedures of these courts. None of this is to deny that higher level trial courts and appellate courts are much more centrally concerned with disputes of various kinds, yet the fact that they actually hear and decide a tiny proportion of the total of cases heard by courts in any particular Western legal system should raise doubts as to whether dispute processing is the primary *raison d'être* of judicial systems (Abel 1973: 228) rather than merely providing an appropriate occasion for the fulfilment of other tasks.

In recent years, further longitudinal studies of courts in the United States, and to some extent elsewhere, have suggested an increase in the proportion of genuine disputes brought before trial courts; for example, business firms may be more willing to sue other firms. If this is so, it has been hypothesised that this finding may reflect not so much a change in the character of courts themselves as a change occurring in the social contexts of disputing: perhaps a climate of more intense competition and increasing economic uncertainty, as well as changing attitudes towards alternative methods of airing grievances and seeking redress (Friedman 1990b).

Indirect Dispute Resolution

It can, of course, be persuasively argued that quite irrespective of the number of disputes that are resolved specifically by court decisions, courts contribute in many *indirect* ways to dispute resolution. In a reanalysis of Friedman and Percival's data, Richard Lempert agrees that the mix of judicial business in the courts that Friedman and Percival studied changed over the years but claims that these courts continued to serve their communities as dispute settlement institutions (Lempert 1978). Lempert emphasises the importance of arrangements or agreements made without court intervention but with knowledge of the possibility of action through courts or the availability of judicial recognition of the agreement acting as an incentive to the parties involved in fixing and agreeing terms. Arrangements arrived at in uncontested divorce cases can be suggested as obvious examples. More generally, considerable numbers of cases initiated in courts—for example, personal injury actions—are settled by the litigating parties before being brought to trial (e.g. Genn 1987; Harris et al. 1984: 93ff). This kind of situation is the now well-recognised and much discussed phenomenon of 'bargaining in the shadow of the law' (Mnookin and Kornhauser 1979). Lempert lists seven ways in which courts may contribute to dispute settlement: (i) by defining norms which influence or control the private settlement of disputes; (ii) by ratifying private settlements, providing guarantees of compliance without which one or both parties might have been unwilling to reach such a settlement; (iii) by enabling parties legitimately to escalate the costs of disputing, thereby increasing the likelihood of private dispute settlement; (iv) by providing devices which enable parties to learn about each other's case, thus increasing the likelihood of private dispute settlement by decreasing mutual uncertainty; (v) by enabling court personnel to act as mediators to encourage consensual settlement of disputes; (vi) by resolving certain issues in the case, leaving the parties to agree on the others; and (vii) by authoritatively resolving disputes where parties cannot agree on a settlement.

Lempert's arguments are persuasive. What is most remarkable about these seven contributions of courts to dispute settlement is how few of them fall clearly within the stereotypical image of the court's adjudicatory activities. In general the disparate contributions to dispute resolution which courts may make assume most importance when the adjudicative role is least emphasised. The sixth and seventh items in Lempert's list, which do relate directly to adjudication, apply to a small minority of disputes in society, as the discussion of 'living law' in Chapter 1 indicated. Apart from these, only the first item indicates a judicial contribution (similar in important respects to Llewellyn's concept of preventive channelling of conduct and expectations to avoid friction) that is both central to the general control of disputes in society and that suggests a distinctive output of courts distinguishing them from other governmental agencies. This output is the authoritative exposition and elaboration of legal doctrine.

Insofar as lower courts produce affirmations of legal norms and disseminate legal doctrine, their outputs are of value to court users such as business and public organisations for the reasons indicated by Cain and discussed above. It is easy to extend the argument to see similar interests in affirmation of the norms of criminal law when the state as such is a 'user' of the courts in the specific sense of instituting criminal prosecutions. In both kinds of case it would seem that the primary demands being made upon the court are to affirm and sustain elements of legal doctrine and legal ideology which are for various reasons of importance to those who call upon the court.

If, however, we try to locate judicial work within a broader spectrum of governmental activities it is convenient to talk not in terms of demands addressed to courts but in more abstract functional terms, employing the methods of functional analysis discussed in Chapter 3; that is, not in terms of the expressed purposes of courts or the conscious aims and intentions of judges, or the particular views and requirements of court users but in terms of the contribution that courts can be seen to make to their social and political environment as a part of the machinery of the state (in the sense of the whole apparatus of centralised governmental control and direction of a politically organised society). Thus, at one level (of technical functions), if the affirmation and interpretation of doctrine is seen as a legitimate centrally important part of court work, courts are in a position to determine, clarify or reinforce rules or other technical devices of doctrine which specify how the requirements of collective existence (for example, those sketched by Llewellyn's law-jobs theory) are to be met. At another level (of ideological functions) a functional view of courts might stress their contribution as agencies of government and social control to the maintenance of currents of ideology which legal doctrine shapes, reflects and reinforces and which serve to legitimise government and contribute to social order.

Viewing the matter in this way it becomes possible to begin to see why, despite the fact that the lower courts in Western legal systems deal with vastly more cases than the higher or appellate courts, the latter may properly be seen as of equal or possibly greater sociological significance. Higher courts may for a number of reasons be capable of exerting influence out of all proportion to their share of the total number of cases handled by the court system as a whole. If a primary function of the courts is ideological, what is most important is not whether courts resolve disputes, or how many disputes they process, but what capacity and opportunity they have to exert ideological influence. In this respect, the political and social status of different kinds of court, their relationship with other parts of the state apparatus, the bases of their authority and the nature of their 'independence' are central matters for consideration. So are such matters as the values and occupational expectations that attach to judges and their work, and how far these values and expectations explain the kinds of decisions and interpretations that judges make.

Judicial Behaviour and Organisational Studies of Higher Courts

Appellate Courts, Trial Courts and Legal Realism

It is clear that the variety of statuses, caseloads, jurisdictions and forms of organisation and procedure of particular kinds of courts within any Western legal system makes generalisation about courts hazardous. However, in sociologically oriented 'realist' legal scholarship in the United States in the first half of this century a basic distinction was drawn between trial courts—that is, those concerned with adjudication of cases at first instance—and appellate courts as objects of study. The trial court was seen as typically concerned with the application of relatively settled legal doctrine to the varied fact situations of the numerous cases brought before it. The essential problem for the court was the ascertainment of the legally material facts of the cases heard. The so-called 'fact sceptics' among American legal realists focused on the difficulties of obtaining certainty and predictability in the court's assessment of facts; they raised issues concerning the reliability of witnesses, the 'unscientific' approaches of courts to the gathering, presentation and assessment of evidence, and the 'excesses' of the adversary system of trial (Frank 1949). The law itself, as doctrine applied routinely in many trial court cases, was seen to pose relatively few problems.

The major problem for appellate courts, however, was considered to lie in the uncertainty of the rules of law rather than the facts. Appellate courts, faced with fewer cases and generally having less opportunity—at least in the Anglo-American context—of hearing and assessing all the evidence *de novo* were extensively concerned with points of law argued on appeal. The crucial issue for those realist lawyers dubbed 'rule sceptics' was to understand how judges in such courts came to their decisions on the law. What factors determined how judges interpreted legal rules? Were their decisions predictable as logical extrapolations from existing rules and judicial precedents? Did existing legal doctrine control the judge's decision-making or were judges' actions understandable primarily as expressions of their personal values or attitudes?

On all of these issues the American legal realists—who were lawyers themselves and included among their most prominent spokesmen some judges of considerable renown—tended to prefer the iconoclastic viewpoints. Jerome Frank, a judge of the United States Court of Appeals from 1941 to 1957 and an eloquent apostle of fact scepticism, argued that trial court predictability was probably impossible under existing American modes of trial (Frank 1930; 1949). Among the rule sceptics Karl Llewellyn (1989) saw rules of law not as controlling judges but, at best, as providing guidance for them. So textbook statements of rules could hardly serve as predictions of future judicial decisions. Predictions might be more reliably made by examining what judges do rather than what they say; in other words, by comparing the actual results of cases (that is, who wins, who loses and by how much) to see how far courts favour or disfavour certain interests, values or types of claim in particular kinds of cases. But these patterns of judicial behaviour might not be reflected in legal doctrine, in the reasoning offered by courts to justify their decisions. In any event, the realists argued, there could be many reasons why the judge reached his decision, and legal logic was not necessarily a dominant one. Analysis of legal doctrine often provided a means of rationalising the decision rather than the determinant of it. The Anglo-American doctrine of judicial precedent—the doctrine holding a court bound in interpreting the law to follow previous decisions of superior courts (or sometimes courts of equivalent standing) insofar as those decisions govern legal points at issue in the case—was thus often viewed as of limited significance as a general determinant of the outcome of cases.

Judicial Behaviouralism

What is most interesting in retrospect about the trial court/appellate court or fact scepticism/rule scepticism dichotomy of American legal realism is that the research emphases indicated by it are still clearly reflected in current research on courts (cf. Brigham and Harrington 1989). This is so despite the fact that new theories and methods have reshaped inquiries. Thus, in research on higher courts, emphasis has remained strongly focused on the personality and attributes of the judge. A movement among American political scientists known as judicial behaviouralism has taken the realist hypothesis about the importance of personal values and attitudes of judges and used it as the basis of systematic quantitative analysis of judicial behaviour. Data about the religious affiliations, political views, educational and social backgrounds, and values and attitudes of higher court judges have been extensively subjected to computer analysis in an effort to correlate judges' personal characteristics or views with their decisions in court.

It is not easy to know what to make of this, particularly since a huge industry of research has grown up around the behaviouralist movement in judicial research. The early legal realist literature was obviously polemical in intent; concerned to stir lawyers from complacency and alert them to the need to recognise that analysis of rules would not provide answers to vital moral and political questions about how judges *actually* decide cases and how they *should* decide them. It produced relatively little rigorous empirical research on judicial behaviour in relation to judicial attitudes, values or backgrounds. In its most extreme forms it set out to show that what it saw as the central question about the American judicial process (why courts decide cases the way they do) was unanswerable on the basis of current knowledge, and that lawyers' orthodox answers in terms of legal logic and judicial precedent were of no predictive value whatever. It devoted comparatively little effort to empirical social scientific research that might supply answers.

These characteristics of legal realism suggest a high proportion of crusading rhetoric in the enterprise and a rather limited seasoning of social scientific method. One of the most enduring books to come out of the American legal realist movement, Llewellyn's *The Common Law Tradition* (1960), deliberately distances itself from the shrill rhetoric of some earlier realist writing and stresses the numerous 'steadying factors' operating on judicial decision-making in appellate courts. Precedent is acknowledged as one of these but other factors seen as important include: influences arising from common training and experience of judges; adherence to known techniques of legal argument and legal analysis; the situation of group decision-making where—as is normally the case—an appeal is heard and decided by more than one judge; collective judicial values built into the job of being a judge—certain standards of integrity, impartiality and professional skill; and certain widespread expectations (which Llewellyn calls 'period style') within the legal culture of the time and place as to how judicial responsibilities are to be discharged.

It seems, nevertheless, that the early polemical realist claims, viewed in the light of a productive behaviouralist tradition in other areas of American political science, have been taken with the utmost seriousness by the judicial behaviouralists. Elements of judicial background, attitudes and values have been taken as measurable variables to be subjected to rigorous quantitative analysis and systematically compared with patterns of judicial decision-making. Glendon Schubert, a leading figure in the movement, wrote that it had substantially 'debunked legal principles as factors controlling decisions' (Schubert 1963: 104). The assumption that the personal attitudes and values of judges are the *controlling* factor in judicial decision-making is seen by critics of judicial behaviouralism as plainly evident in much of the work it has produced (T. L. Becker 1970: 29). But it has been charged that the frequent high correlations found in this research between judicial attitudes and judicial behaviour are unconvincing given the looseness of the concept of 'attitude' (what constitutes a distinct and measurable attitude? cf. T. L. Becker 1970: 68–9) and the use of unidimensional attitude scales in many studies (T. L. Becker 1970: 31).

Essentially what behaviouralism has done is to assert, in an extension of the realist polemic, that judges are merely political actors discharging governmental decision-making functions and subject to pressures and constraints not qualitatively different from those existing in other branches of government. As will appear later, this goes in some respects too far, in others not far enough. It goes so far in asserting that judges are merely human—that, to reverse the aphorism, we live under a 'government of men' and not of laws—that it tends to cease to see them as judges at all in any of the distinctive senses that lawyers recognise. At the same time, the strict behavioural approach, seeking measurable correlations between positivistically treated data as the test of research success, makes no attempt to construct a theory of the judicial function. It could hardly attempt to do so since it leaves out of account serious consideration of the meaning content of judicial decisions, the distinctive political nature of the judicial role, and the subjective meaning of judicial work for those engaged in it. These are, after all, hardly measurable phenomena.

Judicial Organisation and Judicial Outlook

The better behavioural studies have certainly taken the organisation of courts to be no less important than the characteristics of the judges who staff them (cf. Jacob 1983). For example, in courts where several judges are involved in the decision of a case, the nature, form and timing of discussions between the judges may be highly relevant to an understanding of how decisions are reached. Even the layout of the court building and the judges' chambers, together with the amount of administrative and legal research assistance available to the judiciary, may have an influence on the extent and kind of interaction that takes place between the judges outside formal case conferences. Mr Justice Powell of the United States Supreme Court described the court as 'perhaps one of the last citadels of jealously preserved individualism ... The informal interchange between [the judges'] chambers is minimal, with most exchanges of views being by correspondence or memoranda. Indeed, a justice may go through an entire term without being once in the chambers of all of the other eight members of the court' (Powell 1976: 1454).

Patterns of formal or informal leadership and of influence among the judges may also be important. Where, as in the United States Supreme Court, typically a single opinion (judgment) is given to express the majority view of the court, the choice of judge to write the opinion may be crucial not only to the way the court's reasoning is expressed but also in determining whether—and if so how many—judges choose to dissent from the court's decision. The power to assign decision-writing (a power which in the United States Supreme Court the Chief Justice holds when he is among the majority) may thus be highly significant (Flango et al. 1986; Abraham 1986: 216–22). In the House of Lords it seems that, although all participating Law Lords are free to write separate opinions, where one member of the court is to write the major opinion in a case this is decided by informal agreement among the judges (Paterson 1982: 92–4).

American studies have examined what David Danelski has called, in discussing the Supreme Court, 'task leadership' and 'social leadership' (Danelski 1967; 1986). Social leaders are judges who act as reducers of tension between the varied personalities of the members of the court; reconcilers and mediators between the other judges whose influence can help to mould collective judicial responses and reduce the likelihood of dissents. Often Chief Justices have taken on such a role. There seems, however, no assumption that the presiding Law Lord in House of Lords cases should adopt any comparable co-ordinating or reconciling position *vis-à-vis* his judicial colleagues (Paterson 1982: 106ff). Task leaders, by contrast, are judges who can strongly influence the actual decision of cases; whose views are likely to weigh particularly heavily among their colleagues. Leadership of this kind depends on 'personality, esteem within the court, intelligence, technical competence, and persuasive ability' (Danelski 1967: 79). Task leaders are likely to be strong personalities and competition between several contenders for leadership in a court may be an important cause of conflict and inefficiency in its work (Danelski 1986). But effective leadership provides a sense of collective purpose and direction. In an important study of the judicial work of the House of Lords, based on extensive interviews with the Law Lords, Alan Paterson has emphasised Lord Reid's personal influence on the collective judicial philosophy of the court in the 1960s and 1970s (1982: chs 6 and 7; cf. Stevens 1979: 468–88). In courts of final appeal such as this, where the total pool of judges is small, where important legal policy decisions have to be taken, and where the judges necessarily have high individual status, the influence of particular judges may clearly be of great importance.

Paterson's study emphasises the importance of collegiate spirit ('the desire for acceptance and esteem from their peer group may be hard to resist', 1982: 33) among the Law Lords who in other respects are necessarily relatively isolated by their role and status from other potential reference groups.[1] On the one hand, judges of high appellate or constitutional courts in contemporary Western societies have considerable independence both collectively and individually; such courts can be appropriate settings for powerful personalities and individual minds. And they can be sites of considerable, if often hidden, judicial conflict (Goldman and Lamb, eds, 1986). On the other, they are constrained by numerous collegiate pressures relating to considerations of their court's

1 Mr Justice Burton described his transition from being a United States Senator to being a member of the Supreme Court (he had had no prior judicial experience when appointed to the court in 1945) as like 'going direct from a circus to a monastery' (quoted in Paterson 1983: 281).

internal efficiency and external authority (Murphy 1964). A high appellate court will not, for example, lightly ignore the views of lower courts (Murphy 1964: ch 4; Paterson 1982: 85–6) and, in the making of decisions whose controversial and far reaching character is clearly recognised by the court, much consideration may sometimes be given to the form of judgment most likely to disarm opposition and result in effective enforcement (e.g. Abraham 1986: 216–7. Cf. Marshall 1989: ch 7).

Phenomenology, Ethnomethodology and Studies of Interaction and Organisation in Lower Courts

Rule scepticism, fired with the image of the Anglo-American appellate judge as a legal oracle, led, understandably, to judicial behaviouralism's emphasis on the judge as a powerful individual political actor. There is an equally significant relationship between the orientation of realist fact scepticism, emphasising the determination of the facts of cases as the central problem of trial court procedure, and modern studies of trial courts importing the methods of phenomenological sociology and ethnomethodology. The legal realists assumed in positivist fashion that the facts were objectively in existence and that the court's problem was to find a means of discovering them. Phenomenological approaches have substituted for this the idea of the 'social construction of reality' in the courtroom, to use Berger and Luckmann's (1967) phrase. The facts of the case—or rather the 'correct', 'official', and accepted meaning or appropriate understanding of actions or situations being judged by the court—are seen as arrived at by processes of interaction within the courtroom. In these processes, labels ('guilty', 'responsibility', 'contract', 'property', 'offence', 'negligence', 'intentional', 'trustee', 'theft' etc.) are attached to situations, actions and individuals, in such a way that the labels are accepted as correct representations of reality. The elusiveness of facts as seen by the realists is reinterpreted in phenomenological and ethnomethodological studies as a situation in which the court *defines* reality by means of the rituals of the civil or criminal trial and the management of courtroom interaction between judges, counsel, witnesses, plaintiffs and defendants. Thus 'law' and 'fact' merge since legal doctrine is part of the apparatus by which reality is defined (cf. Stone 1966: 738ff).

In a much cited early study Harold Garfinkel described the criminal trial as a 'degradation ceremony' in which a carefully managed drama of presentation and examination of evidence, formal procedures, and role playing makes possible the conditions for a successful denunciation of a transgressor of social norms (Garfinkel 1956). Such a denunciation (for which the use of courts offers only one of many possible means, although a particularly important one) is a complex matter, for Garfinkel argues that it involves a change in the total identity of the wrongdoer so that he or she is viewed as 'literally a different and *new* person' (1956: 421) and less favourably than before. This requires many conditions for success, including a detailed convincing presentation and interpretation of the offender's actions 'past, present and prospective' (1956: 422). In this analysis the convicted person (in effect a different being from the unconvicted defendant at the beginning of the trial) is in a strict sense *constituted* by the court and paraded for recognition as such in the world outside the courtroom.

There are clear echoes of Durkheim in Garfinkel's stress on the importance of public denunciation as a means of strengthening social solidarity. More recently, in a similar vein, researchers have analysed the historical importance of confession in legal and religious settings as a ritual by which offenders formally affirm the norms and values they have transgressed (Hepworth and Turner 1982). Further, references in Garfinkel's early paper to the importance of the structuring of verbal interaction in the courtroom point to an area of study which has become of central concern for later ethnomethodological research on courts and other tribunals. The major full length British study in this field, by J. Maxwell Atkinson and Paul Drew (Atkinson and Drew 1979), contains detailed analysis of transcripts of the questioning of witnesses by a Tribunal of Inquiry (the Scarman inquiry into Northern Ireland disturbances in 1969) and of the opening sequences of verbal interaction during an inquest in a Coroner's Court. Analysis of the structure of recorded conversations is used to elucidate such matters as 'the accomplishment of shared attentiveness to court proceedings', 'the management of an accusation' and 'the production of justifications and excuses by witnesses in cross-examination'. It attaches significance to minute detail (for example, the exact positioning of pauses, speech overlaps or interruptions) of the conversations taking place during the hearing. The aim is to show how complex processes of interaction are managed in a courtroom situation to result in (to construct) an acceptable authoritative interpretation of the 'segment of reality' represented by the case being heard. Here, as elsewhere, ethnomethodology's concern is to understand social order and to do so by analysing those small scale situations of interaction (such as court hearings) that reveal conditions under which particular manifestations of order (for example, order in court) are established and maintained.

Often, however, in this kind of research it remains unclear at whom efforts of management of shared meanings and understandings are to be seen as aimed. On the precepts of ethnomethodology it should presumably be the common-sense understandings of participants which are of major, probably sole, importance. However, important studies of courtroom interaction, such as Pat Carlen's work on English magistrates' courts or John Conley and William O'Barr's study of American small claims courts, show that much of what goes on in the court is often meaningless to defendants or understood by them quite differently from the way it is understood by the professional participants (lawyers, police, judges, court officials etc.) in the courtroom drama.[2] The order of the court is, thus, not one which is shaped by nor even necessarily understood by the ordinary citizens who find themselves before it. Nevertheless, litigants who repeatedly encounter the workings of these courts may come to see them in a different light. 'With experience,' remarks Sally Merry in a study of American lower court litigants, 'the court gradually ceases to be a place of awe and fear, one which imposes harsh penalties with inexorable firmness, and becomes a somewhat pliant, if excruciatingly complex, institution, which, with pressure and patience, can sometimes be made to yield help' (Merry 1990: 142).

Atkinson and Drew suggest that ethnomethodological studies may indicate ways of 'humanising the courtroom' to make interaction between laymen (witnesses, defendants and plaintiffs) and court professionals more effective, to improve communication within the courtroom, to make the proceedings less intimidating. Even such matters as the 'ecological arrangements' (Atkinson and Drew 1979: 222ff)—the layout of the courtroom, the places where various participants in the proceedings are required to stand, the identification of various actors by uniform (for example, judges' robes or wigs)—are seen as far from insignificant in this respect. Carlen's more radical analysis claims that the criminal trial in a magistrates' court functions by involving defendants only as far as their presence and participation is necessary to the court's 'plausible public performance of justice' (Carlen 1976b: 64). What seems to be suggested in this view is that the 'construction of social reality' by the trial is a performance for public consumption rather than primarily to persuade the defendant; that insofar as the work of the court is concerned with developing shared understandings of events and actions, it is the public at large whose understandings are to be shaped by the careful labelling and status-altering 'ceremonies' of the courtroom.

In many ways this seems a useful way to understand important aspects of much of the routine work of trial courts. Putting the matter in different (functional) terms we can understand this work not as the production or elaboration of ideology—which, it has been suggested earlier, may be an important aspect of the work of prestigious higher courts—but as routine

2 Carlen 1976b: 81–8; Conley and O'Barr 1990: ch 9. See also Merry 1990: ch 6 on the uses of legal, moral and therapeutic discourses in court. Failures of understanding and distortions of communication may be dramatically intensified where interpreters need to be used in judicial proceedings: see Berk-Seligson 1990.

maintenance of the hegemony of legal ideology. In case after case the trial court reaffirms established legal doctrine and uses it to impose an 'official' meaning on the unending stream of actions and events that are brought to its attention. This is a relatively unglamorous, mundane judicial task, often far removed from the complex decision-making of the higher courts. Yet every trial in which the trial court successfully manages to engineer a 'shared understanding' of events—a *publicly accepted* definition, in conformity with legal ideology, of the conduct or situation upon which the court adjudicates—is an important contribution to the maintenance of the established social order and a successful affirmation of law's legitimacy.

Ideological Functions of Courts

It is clear that both higher and lower court work can be analysed from phenomenological or related perspectives emphasising the negotiation of 'reality' within the courtroom (cf. Paterson 1982: 50) or from a standpoint of sociological positivism (as in judicial behaviouralism) which looks at the 'facts'—data about what courts decide and what observable characteristics judges have—and tries to explain the causes and effects of such facts. It is because the currents of social life appear to swirl incessantly around trial courts with their numerous everyday encounters with creditors, debtors, landlords, tenants, families, police and criminals, that it seems particularly appropriate to understand the trial itself as a confrontation between different social realities. In this setting legal ideology struggles to impose its hegemony on all the varied social relations, claims and expectations brought to the court from the world outside the courtroom door. The relative remoteness of higher courts—dealing with cases often either of a constitutional or political significance that dwarfs the private concerns of litigants, or of a complexity that marks them as the exclusive terrain of expert lawyers—makes it easier to think of these courts as isolated decision-making bodies in which legal decisions are produced by the judges' individual or collective processes of assessment and adjudication and then in effect handed to the outside world to be studied by lower courts, law enforcement officials, and citizens at large.

These considerations, moving towards a recognition of the impact of court work, on the one hand, on everyday perceptions of social life and, on the other, on the business of government, draw us back to functional analysis of courts and to the suggestion earlier in this chapter that ideological functions can be seen to be of major significance in all varieties of court work. This is to say that in so far as court work is *functional* for the maintenance of established social order and political authority it fulfils this function to a considerable extent by the creation, development or maintenance of ideology (cf. Brigham 1987: 204ff). To avoid misunderstanding it is essential to stress the point made in discussion in Chapter 3 that the concepts of 'purpose' and 'function' must be clearly separated. The intentions or motivations of judges, lawyers or other participants in judicial processes are not in issue here. Their varied purposes and those officially ascribed to courts and court procedures are analytically distinct from the functions that can be attributed to courts by virtue of the contribution that their work makes to the political and social environment in which they exist.

The discussion in Chapter 4 indicated that among the major characteristics of ideological thought are the following: first, that it appears 'common sense', obvious and natural, hence not requiring specific justification, but providing a basic structure of perceptions and beliefs in relation to which experience is interpreted; secondly, that this structure of perceptions and beliefs tends to assert its own completeness, timelessness and self-sufficiency, rather than to recognise the permanently provisional character of knowledge as in scientific method; and thirdly, that the claim to completeness and self-sufficiency (which can be considered an understandable search for certainty in an uncertain world) is maintained by emotional commitments which may ultimately justify selective consideration of empirical evidence or the ignoring of inconsistencies in interpretations of experience. Insofar as courts contribute *functionally* through their interpretations, elaborations and justifications of doctrine to the development, maintenance and dissemination of ideology they help to propagate structures of perceptions and beliefs that are foundations of social order. In this way legal ideology founded on legal doctrine contributes to shared understandings and expectations; not so much resolving disputes as defining the limits within which disputes are possible and legitimating particular ways of settling them.

Law Making and Law Finding

Of course, legal doctrine is not timeless but created in contemporary Western societies by definite legislative and judicial acts. Yet basic values and concepts of legal doctrine—'symbols of government', in Thurman Arnold's (1935) phrase, and symbols of the fundamental characteristics of the society—are proclaimed continually by the courts and invoked in interpretation or application of legislation. In civil law countries judicial innovation is typically described as the interpretation of the historic legal codes even where the codes may offer only a few words of terse, abstract prescription upon which extensive new doctrine is built by the courts. In common law countries, and particularly in Britain, the reluctance to admit that judges make law, rather than merely find it in established principle, runs deep. The eminent British judge Lord Radcliffe remarked: 'If judges prefer to adopt the formula—for that is what it is—that they merely declare the law and do not make it, they do no more than show themselves wise men in practice. Their analysis may be weak, but their perception of the nature of the law is sound. Men's respect for it will be the greater, the more imperceptible its development' (1961: 39). Judges, he suggested, should 'keep quiet about their legislative function ... The truth is, in my belief, that the image of the judge, objective, impartial, erudite and experienced declarer of the law that is, lies deeper in the consciousness of civilization than the image of the lawmaker, propounding what are avowedly new rules of human conduct' (1968: 14, 16).

The higher the courts in the judicial hierarchy and in the hierarchy of state institutions, the more difficult it is to reconcile legal policy-making functions of judicial decision-making with the declaratory theory of judging. Thus Paterson describes the internal conflict within the House of Lords in the early 1970s as to whether the court, having in 1966 declared itself no longer bound to follow its own previous decisions, should be open about its judicial innovations or maintain the 'facade' approach advocated by such judges as Lord Ratcliffe (Paterson 1982: chs 6 and 7; cf. Stevens 1979: 617–21). The elaboration of legal doctrine in the face of legislative and social change to maintain the stability—the timeless, common-sense quality—of legal ideology, and hence the conditions of legal domination in Weber's sense and the stability of the legal and social order, is a governmental task requiring the highest levels of judicial skill.

Court and Constitution

The conditions under which this task is performed vary considerably in different Western societies. In the United States, views of the judicial role are strongly influenced by the character and content of the Constitution. Under the constitutional separation of governmental powers the sole authority to interpret the meaning of the often vague words of the Constitution is entrusted to the judiciary. Thus the great power of political decision-making given to the Supreme Court by the open character of constitutional provisions co-existed in the nineteenth century with the idea that judicial review of the constitutionality of legislation and administrative acts amounted merely to the interpretation of already existent law ('Courts are the mere instruments of the law, and can will nothing'; 'the courts ... make no laws, they establish no policy, they never enter into the domain of public action').[3] At the beginning of the twentieth century Mr Justice Holmes declared that the Constitution was 'made for people of fundamentally differing views'; thus it was improper for judges to invoke their own social and economic theories, and they should defer to the democratic will expressed through the legislature.[4] This viewpoint, reiterated in various forms to the present day, is balanced against others: that a constitution is not static but must 'draw its meaning from the evolving standards of decency that mark the progress of a maturing society';[5] that the vagueness of certain constitutional provisions forces the interpreter 'to look beyond their four corners' (Ely 1980: 38).

Where does the Supreme Court claim to find its interpretative values? As John Hart Ely puts the matter in an important discussion of American constitutional adjudication, the search 'purports to be objective and value-neutral; the reference is to something "out there" waiting to be discovered, whether it be natural law or some supposed value consensus of historical America, today's America or the America that is yet to be' (1980: 48; and see Brigham 1987: 36ff). Natural law ideas were, indeed, frequently invoked in Supreme Court decisions to justify a great variety of conflicting value positions throughout the history of the court (Ely 1980: 48–54; Haines 1930), reinforcing legal symbols and legal ideology rather than providing contributions to the technical basis of decisions. More recently, appeals to an assumed societal consensus or shared community values[6] have been evident (cf. Ely 1980: 63–9; Cotterrell 1990b), as have attempts to ground judicial interpretations of constitutional values in tradition and reason. Ely concludes that the only acceptable general criterion for constitutional interpretation—implicit in the Constitution itself—is the necessity of opening and maintaining channels of participation in representative democracy. This, he claims, is acceptable since it relates to procedural matters which judges can sensibly claim to be well equipped to handle and is not inconsistent with democratic ideals.

All of these searches for justification show, in the peculiarly visible judicial politics of the United States Supreme Court, methods by which judges conduct their major ideological task: the construction of doctrine that can be accepted as *self-evidently correct.* There is no unassailably correct moral philosophy or natural law, no compelling empirically demonstrated societal consensus nor any reason to suppose that law is

3 The first quotation is from Marshall CJ, in *Osborn v Bank of the United States* (1824) 9 Wheat 738 at 866; the second an 1894 extra-judicial statement by Brewer J. Both are in White 1982: 417.

4 *Lochner v New York* (1905) 198 US 45 at 76.

5 *Trop v Dulles* (1958) 356 US 86 at 101.

6 E.g. *Furman v Georgia* (1972) 408 US 238 at 314 et seq., per Marshall J (constitutionality of the death penalty).

necessarily founded on such a consensus (cf. Chapter 4), and no absolute virtue in tradition. The attempt to construct such objective criteria of evaluation is, however, part of the never-ending judicial task of demonstrating the authority of legal doctrine and reinforcing the 'common sense' and naturalness of legal ideology.

Variations in the Authority Bases of Judiciaries

In other Western legal systems the environment in which this task is carried out differs. As compared with the reticent 'law finding' self-image of United Kingdom courts, the often relatively explicit law-making of continental judges and of the judges of a constitutional court such as the United States Supreme Court may be explicable in terms of different social bases of judicial authority. We can employ Weber's notions of charismatic and traditional authority (see Chapter 5) here. All judicial work can be thought of as having its authority grounded in some measure in both tradition and charisma. In contemporary Western societies these authority bases supplement the primary *legal* sources of judicial authority (cf. Murphy 1964: 12–13, 17; Weber 1978: 263). Traditional and charismatic judicial authority are available to support legal domination—the authority of law itself as doctrine. In the United States, however, the Supreme Court 'guards' and elaborates the Constitution which provides the basis of legitimacy of government. An important basis of judicial authority, and governmental authority as a whole, in such a system is the *traditional* authority of timeless constitutional principle (cf. Brigham 1987: 168–76); hence the continuing appeal in constitutional analysis to the framers' intentions in an attempt to reconcile the traditional foundations of legitimacy with modern conditions. The Constitution itself is the foundation of political legitimacy; the federal judges derive authority from it and are themselves primarily agents of its authority, with only subordinate elements of charismatic authority of their own. In a sense the Constitution provided a replacement for the traditional basis of judicial authority in the common law (cf. Haines 1932: 22–8, 223–7), a basis which has necessarily become ever more insecure with the decline in the importance of common law as compared with legislation as a source of new law. By contrast, constitutional authority has given the American higher judiciary a special, highly visible, and perhaps increasing, centrality in government (Brigham 1987: ch 2).

Compare the higher judiciary of the United Kingdom, operating under a political order without a written constitution. Lacking authority derived specifically from such a definite historical source, the judiciary guards vital and carefully nurtured characteristics of its own *charismatic* authority—the image of impartiality and objectivity in decision-making, a stance of neutrality and aloofness based on judicial wisdom divorced from all political partisanship, and the highest levels of technical expertise and adjudicatory skill. As compared with its American counterpart, it adopts 'a very formal vision of law' combining careful pragmatism and a distrust for theory with avoidance of anything that looks like policy making (Atiyah and Summers 1987: 348–50). Charismatic elements of authority are supported by the subordinate traditional authority of common law concepts and modes of reasoning. For a great charismatic judge—one whose intellect, learning, manner and intuitions are finely attuned to the requirements of judicial charisma—boldness in judicial utterance is not inappropriate and indeed can provide one of the most powerful forms of reinforcement of legal symbols. But for most judges the maintenance of judicial charisma requires extreme caution in judicial pronouncements and behaviour both on and off the bench.

Judges are to be seen as above all considerations of narrow self-interest. Thus in Britain their salary may well be a great deal less than that which they earned in legal practice (Paterson 1983: 278) and, unlike the position in the United States, a senior judicial post is regarded as a lifetime appointment (a resignation from the bench in order to take another post is regarded as generally unacceptable) (Paterson 1983: 282). The judge occupies a supraprofessional status, in Paterson's view, rather like statesmen, bishops or film stars who have transcended the status of politician, priest or actor respectively (Paterson 1983: 265). It is hardly surprising that charismatic judicial authority should be a tempting resource for government to use by appointing judges to head official inquiries of various kinds: into civil disorders, political scandals, rates of pay and industrial conditions, terrorist activities and numerous other matters (Griffith 1991: ch 2). As with all forms of credit, however, its over-extension can be dangerous. While judicial involvement gives political decision-making an aura of judicial impartiality, it also associates the image of the judiciary with political controversy.

By contrast, the American higher judiciary seems much less dependent on the maintenance of a distinctive judicial charisma. The image of the American judge in this context combines judicial prestige derived from constitutional authority with a much more generalised image of public service. Thus, such judges may well have served some of their career in a legislature or in the executive branch of state or federal government and (as in the case of 40 per cent of all Supreme Court justices appointed since 1789) may have been appointed to high judicial office without any prior experience as a judge (cf. Abraham 1986: 55). Although this kind of judicial background is far from unknown in the history of the English higher judiciary it has now become exceptional and the clear separation of judicial image from politics seems to be more strenuously sought than in the United States.

Zweigert and Kötz (1987: 134) remark that 'France and Germany are alike in not having developed the type of the wise judge which other people find so remarkable in the Anglo-American systems.' E. J. Cohn has described German judges thus: 'The judiciary forms in effect a civil-service-type career holding out security of tenure, statutory independence (which in practice is somewhat less imposing than in theory, owing to numerous rules of detail and traditional habits and arrangements), a reasonable, though not outstanding, social rank and the power to adjudicate upon the failings and disputes of one's fellow men. It is obvious that the type of young man who feels allured by prospects such as these will as a rule not belong to either the most brilliant or to the most strong-willed type' (Cohn 1960: 590). The generally less exalted position of the judiciary as a whole in Western European civil law systems, and its greater apparent direct incorporation within the state establishment do not make its ideological functions different from those of the common law 'wise judge'. The problem of reconciling judicial creativity and doctrinal stability—of portraying the law maker as a law finder—is not essentially different despite differences in doctrinal structures and traditions (Cappelletti 1989: ch 1). Yet continental judges typically hold their authority specifically as technical interpreters of the legal codes and of the legislation that supplements the codes. Historical and constitutional conditions designate their position as that of specialist state functionaries. Their relatively limited prestige as compared with their English counterparts, but nevertheless substantial judicial independence and lack of English judges' need to preserve independent charismatic bases of their authority (illustrated, for example, in the typical absence of an explicit doctrine of judicial precedent in European civil law systems), has often given continental judges considerable freedom to innovate in doctrine 'in a real partnership with the legislature' (Zweigert and Kötz 1987: 274), and has even made possible the phenomenon of the 'radical judge' (e.g. De Haan et al. 1989).

Politicisation of Trials

The ideological work of courts is most clearly revealed in those circumstances where it is hardest to accomplish. Trials have been described earlier from one point of view as situations in which the hegemony of legal ideology is typically affirmed; in which the work of the court depends upon and is aimed towards ensuring that the interpretations of reality offered by legal doctrine prevail and are accepted as objectively 'correct' understandings of events, responsibilities and relationships. From the viewpoint of legal ideology, therefore, no trial in which legally correct procedures have been followed can be properly seen as 'political'. No political choices are seen to be involved in the conduct of the trial. It involves merely the natural, 'commonsense', rational application of doctrine to the facts of the case.

The politicisation of trials occurs, however, either where procedures are deliberately manipulated in ways inconsistent with legal doctrine in order to achieve for political reasons a particular outcome of the trial, or where individuals before the court consciously and explicitly offer fundamental challenges—which are widely recognised as such—to legal ideology. This they may do, for example, by refusing to accept the political impartiality of the court, or by refusing to accept common-sense assumptions about its character as a court and about the appropriate behaviour of those involved in its processes.

Ideological tasks of courts always involve the risk of this occurring. For these tasks to be accomplished effectively court proceedings generally need to be public, not secret, because the presence, or at least potential presence of ordinary citizens is necessary to the claim that the meanings of events and relationships established by the court are indeed accepted by or acceptable to citizens; that is, that legal ideology is indeed successfully affirmed through the trial process. On the other hand, because courts' ideological functions necessitate these conditions, there is always the possibility that the courtroom can be made an arena for the presentation of other ideologies; that, far from legal ideology being affirmed by what takes place in the trial, witnesses or defendants before the court may seize the opportunity to use the court as a forum for political protest, through speeches and deliberate disruption of trial proceedings. By such tactics they defeat the normal elaborate mechanisms of maintenance of ideology by means of courts and use the same mechanisms for different ends. Since the 1960s, these tactics of revolutionary or radical political groups have been familiar in Western societies. Equally, the difficulties created for state authorities by courtroom publicity of politically sensitive matters tempt them to curtail seriously publicity of trials, a strategy which must be self-defeating if carried very far, given the analysis of court work offered in this chapter, and the conditions necessary to success in that work.

Judge and State

The discussion of constitutional interpretation and politicisation of trials in the previous sections should suggest that the often-discussed judicial function of legitimation of government and political processes (e.g. Bredemeier 1962; T. L. Becker 1970: 238–46) is merely one aspect of the wider function of legitimation of the legal and social order as a whole through the maintenance of legal ideology. Both forms of legitimation require that the courts be seen as distanced from other branches of government. Thus, not surprisingly, judicial *independence* is generally seen as essential to the concept of a court although the character of this independence varies in different Western societies (Shapiro 1981: 32–5; Abraham 1986: 41–52). It follows, also, that conflicts may sometimes arise between, on the one hand, a government's short-term need for judicial legitimation of its actions and, on the other, judicial perceptions of the more general long-term need for maintenance of fundamental legal and social values through court decisions. The nature of these judicial perceptions thus becomes a very important matter.

In a controversial study J.A.G. Griffith sought to identify the nature of such perceptions among the British judiciary (Griffith 1991). Griffith analyses judicial development and interpretation of English law in five key areas: industrial relations, civil liberties and personal freedoms, property rights and land use planning, conspiracy law, and a comparison of rights of trade union members against their union with rights of students in disciplinary hearings. He argues on the basis of this evidence that while judges are normally impartial—in other words, they are not usually the victims of conscious prejudice—they are not and cannot be *neutral* in the sense of having no policy interest in the outcome of the cases they decide. This is 'because they are placed in positions where they are required to make political choices which are sometimes presented to them, and often presented by them, as determinations of where the public interest lies; ... their interpretation of what is in the public interest and therefore politically desirable is determined by the kind of people they are and the position they hold in our society: ... this position is a part of established authority and so is necessarily conservative and illiberal' (1991: 319).

Griffith specifies in some detail the content of the collective judicial view in Britain of 'the public interest'. It has three limbs, which he now expresses as 'first, the interest of the state (including its moral welfare); secondly, the preservation of law and order, broadly interpreted; and thirdly, the promotion of certain political views normally associated with the Conservative Party' (1991: 278)[7]. Thus the principal function of the judiciary is 'to support the institutions of government as established by the law' but the judicial view of the public interest may, on occasions, put the judges at odds with the government of the day and result in judicial decisions in opposition to government policy or actions.

Some of the criticism of Griffith's work has merely demonstrated that it dealt powerful blows to some cherished illusions. Everything that has been written in this chapter and in earlier chapters of this book about legal ideology and the mechanisms of its maintenance should indicate that fundamental challenges to these, such as Griffith attempts, are not likely

7 In earlier editions of his book, Griffith included the protection of private property as a specific limb of the public interest, as assumed by the judiciary.

to be received in silence. Nevertheless, there are serious problems with his analysis. The 'sociology' of the book consists of a mixture of simple unelaborated elite theory (judges form part of a small homogeneous group of key decision-makers in public life), and class theory (senior judges' strikingly homogeneous class and educational backgrounds instil common values which are directly reflected in judicial decision-making). In Griffith's view judges are thus bound to be conservative and establishment-supporting. The radicalism of some continental judges is explained on the ground that, in a career judiciary, successful examinees can be appointed to the bench without the need to reveal their political sympathies. The forays of some supreme judiciaries (such as the United States Supreme Court of the 1960s) into 'the positive assertion of fundamental values' on behalf of minorities are not explained at all, and are presumably regarded as incomprehensible aberrations (Griffith 1991: 328). The major problem with the analysis is that Griffith does not offer any theory of judicial functions, nor any analysis of the complex judicial task which maintenance of legal legitimacy poses, nor an analysis of the effects on the carrying out of judicial functions of different bases of judicial authority in different Western societies. Yet, as has already been suggested, these may help to explain judicial activism and judicial restraint as well as the content of judicial law making.

It can be said that as part of the state apparatus the judiciary must 'earn' its privileged position in the hierarchy of state power including its relative independence from direct control by other arms of the state. It does so by making its contribution to maintenance of the stability of the social and political order, first, by providing legal frameworks and legal legitimacy for *government* and government acts and, secondly, by maintaining the integrity of the *legal order* itself—the ideological conditions upon which legal domination depends. At one level the first of these tasks is relatively straightforward in theory if often complex in practice. It involves providing technical devices in the form of legal rules, principles and concepts by means of which social control can be effected, and assessing the use of state power in accordance with rational principles contained in legal doctrine. But this task cannot be achieved without success in the second and much more complex task of maintaining the integrity of the legal order itself. It is in relation to this that judges may differ considerably in their views. Paterson's (1982) discussion of serious differences of view among the Law Lords about the appropriate balance to be struck between, on the one hand, maintaining legal certainty and stability in doctrine by developing it with extreme caution, and, on the other, achieving justice through bold doctrinal innovation, reflects a pervasive dichotomy in judicial work. This is expressed in contrasts between, for example, 'judicial caution' and 'judicial valour'

(Pollock 1929), 'timorous souls' and 'bold spirits'[8] and 'formal style' and 'grand style' (Llewellyn 1960).

Behind this dichotomy stand the contrasting and profoundly ambiguous values of order and justice which are, as was observed in Chapter 5, the foundation of law's legitimacy. Contrary to Weber's claims, legal domination is not self-sustaining but depends on the complex balance of these values as they are perceived by citizens to be embodied in the law; and as legal ideology itself successfully shapes and limits citizens' demands for order and justice. Furthermore, the balance between considerations of formal order and substantive justice in the processes of development of legal doctrine (between Weber's formal and substantive legal rationality) must be related to a wider balance between social order and social justice—in all the complex ways in which these values can be expressed within legal ideology. We cannot here carry this analysis further (cf. Cotterrell 1983b) but only remark on the high levels of judicial craftsmanship required to fulfil successfully the ideological-political tasks of higher courts involved in the elaboration and justification of legal doctrine.

Thus, at the same time as judiciaries support the authority of governmental agencies they must negotiate the perpetual problem of maintaining these balances between values of order and justice within the administration of law and the form and content of legal doctrine. If they are seen to fail in the former task (supporting government) they risk antagonising other arms of the state—executive or legislative—and the possibility of jeopardising conditions of judicial independence and other privileges arising from their position within the hierarchy of state power. If they are seen to fail in the latter (maintaining the integrity of law) they risk criticism and a diminution of their status in the eyes of professional lawyers as well as of citizens. For quite apart from the considerations that bear on the legitimacy of law in the eyes of citizens, it has been seen in Chapter 6 why lawyers have a specific professional commitment to the integrity of doctrine as professional knowledge; a commitment which can justify strong criticism of failures of doctrinal rationalisation. Such a commitment is not necessarily tempered by considerations of state interests. Judges, however, as state functionaries, *cannot* neglect considerations of state interests and these may, on occasions, demand that doctrinal niceties be given short shrift in order to meet particular governmental emergencies.[9]

Finally it is necessary to return to John Griffith's point about the specific conservative values that senior British judges are considered to

8 *Candler v Crane, Christmas & Co* [1951] 2 KB 164 at 178, per Denning LJ.
9 See e.g. *Liversidge v Anderson* [1942] AC 206 and *Hirabayashi v United States* 320 US 81 (1943) (emergency powers of detention in wartime).

espouse and incorporate in their conception of the 'public interest'. It may well be appropriate, as he suggests, to understand important aspects of this in terms of the strikingly homogeneous backgrounds of English higher court judges—a matter which has been fully discussed in the literature (e.g. Griffith 1991: 30–8; Atiyah and Summers 1987: 353–6; Blom-Cooper and Drewry 1972: ch 8)—and their membership of a small integrated elite. But the fundamental character of the central foci of judicial work—legal doctrine and legal ideology itself—must be taken into account. Much that Griffith describes as the political predilections of the judges can be interpreted as aspects of the individualism deeply rooted in legal ideology (see Chapter 4) and strongly supported by certain basic conditions and experiences of legal professional practice particularly in the Anglo-American context (see Chapter 6). Judges who have been appointed to the bench after long years of such practice are surely not unlikely to have their outlook powerfully shaped by the doctrine and ideology they ceaselessly analyse and faithfully serve in their judicial work.

Judicial Hierarchies as Administrative Systems

It follows from the discussion of judges' ambivalent position as an arm of government and, at the same time, as legitimators of the legal and social order necessarily operating 'at arm's length' from government, that the ideological and governmental or administrative tasks of courts are closely intertwined. Studies of courts' administrative tasks emphasise the closeness of judicial functions to those of other arms of the state and indeed in many societies judicial and administrative functions of government have not been institutionally distinguished (Shapiro 1981). By contrast a study of courts' ideological functions necessarily emphasises the distinctiveness of judicial work.

Appeals and Judicial Centralisation

Tensions between administrative and ideological functions arise. The ideological tasks of courts presumably require finality in judicial interpretation so as to maintain the integrity of legal doctrine and legal ideology as a stable structure of reason. However, administrative considerations dictate that modern judicial systems employ processes that seem to *encourage* the publication of judicial disagreements on doctrine, and therefore seem to militate against its acceptance as indisputably 'correct' and authoritative. Provision for appealing cases, perhaps several times, from one court to another so as to seek a reversal of a lower court's decision is a particularly obvious feature of this kind. For example, in England, a person convicted of a criminal offence after trial by a magistrates' court may, in appropriate circumstances, appeal his or her case to the Crown Court or High Court and eventually to the House of Lords. A civil case first dealt with by a county court or the High Court may, in appropriate circumstances, be appealed to the Court of Appeal and thereafter to the House of Lords.

Martin Shapiro has offered perhaps the fullest recent analysis of the administrative importance of appeals systems. He argues that appeal is 'essentially a device for exercising centralized supervision over local judicial officers' (Shapiro 1981: 39). In all legal systems it is 'a device for keeping the strings of legitimacy tied directly between the ruled and the person of the ruler or the highest institutions of government' (1981: 52). Thus appeals systems have been seen to be historically one of the chief means used by continental European regimes to impose a uniform, centralised Roman law on local courts in place of localised customary law (Dawson 1968). By contrast, in England the system of trial courts itself was centralised so less need was felt for a strong mechanism of appeals to impose central government control on trial judges (Shapiro 1981: 39 and ch 2).

The extent of the supervision that processes of appeal provide varies in different Western systems. Historically, English trials used almost entirely oral evidence or relied on jurors' knowledge and so gave rise to a written record containing little factual material. Thus the character of the trial resulted in the examination of the trial record on appeal being necessarily restricted to an examination of the trial court's findings of law. By contrast the full written record of continental proceedings including written evidence facilitated trial *de novo* on appeal—a complete rehearing of the case. Such a system 'tolerated and even encouraged the growth of large governmental bureaucracies, judicial and otherwise' (Shapiro 1981: 39).

Today this simple distinction between Anglo-American and continental procedures is subject to numerous qualifications. Even in those appeal systems where the line between fact and law is theoretically important, it is not easy to draw and Shapiro has drawn attention to the 'pull of appellate courts towards the facts' in the United States, Britain and on the Continent; that is, the tendency of appeal courts to substitute their own findings of fact for those of the trial court even under the guise of legal interpretation (1981: 41ff). He explains this phenomenon in terms of the need for appellate courts to seek legitimacy by appearing as conflict resolvers in particular cases. But it can equally be seen at one level as a matter of the balance of autonomy and control in relations between higher and lower courts which can often engender judicial competition (e.g.

Kommers 1969: 114). At another it reflects the impossibility of rigidly separating doctrine from the facts it interprets in considering the production and maintenance of 'shared understandings' of social reality through judicial work.

Appeals and Legal Legitimacy

Clearly appeal systems operate for the benefit of those who appear before the courts, as well as existing to facilitate overall state administrative control of court systems and the imposition of doctrinal uniformity. Shapiro sees rights of appeal as safety devices for the legal order by which disgruntled losers in court cases can continue to assert their claims without attacking the legitimacy of the legal system. 'Appealing to a higher court entails the acknowledgement of its legitimacy' (Shapiro 1981: 49). Further, even if an appeal is not actually made, its availability is a means of giving the loser an opportunity to adjust gradually to his or her situation and to save face. 'The loser can leave the courtroom with his head high talking of appeal and then accept his loss, slowly, privately, and passively by failing to make an appeal' (1981: 49). In addition it should be noted, however, that the higher in the system of appeals the case is taken the more it tends to become the exclusive preserve of lawyers. Thus it may be easier to explain, in the remoteness of the appeal court environment, that the final outcome is dictated by complex technicalities beyond the understanding of laymen and that these technicalities are necessarily quite distinct from what they—as laymen—understand to be the merits of the case.

Provision for appeal does not seriously disturb legal legitimacy for a variety of reasons. Appeal mechanisms are typically sufficiently complex to be understood fully only by lawyers and perhaps by some laymen involved in making or defending appeals. The exact nature of disagreements between courts or judges is often not widely publicised and rarely fully understood other than by legal professionals. Trial courts in which typically a single judge, perhaps with a jury, delivers judgment provide the major output numerically of legal decisions. Most decisions are not appealed. The results of appeals rarely receive as much publicity as the original trial may have done. Insofar as judicial decisions (trial or appellate) are publicised at all they tend to be noticed in isolation; as single events constituting authoritative pronouncements of law. They are rarely publicised in the way that lawyers analyse them; as occurrences in an endless progression of legal change, to be compared with other judgments and other sources of law to form rational patterns and systems of doctrine.

Thus insofar as judicial development of doctrine contributes to legal ideology disseminated throughout society it often does so by many indirect means: for example, through media publicity given to particular, striking judicial pronouncements, and to the fact of legal validation or invalidation by courts of particular governmental actions or strategies (even when the reasons for judicial decisions are not known or understood by citizens: cf. T. L. Becker 1970: 242–46); through the reflection of judicial reasoning in official justifications given for government policy or administrative action; through the everyday work of law enforcement agencies (see Chapter 8); and especially through the practice of lawyers, carrying doctrine and judicial justifications of it into the advice that they give to clients and the services they provide for them.

Dissents and Multiple Judgments

The view that appellate judgments are aimed primarily at lawyers rather than ordinary citizens seems justified by such empirical evidence as exists. In the United States, surveys have shown that the American public as a whole has very little knowledge of Supreme Court decisions and of the way they are reached (Marshall 1989: 142–5). Paterson's interviews with the Law Lords revealed that, while three of them felt that, where possible, judgments should be intelligible to the man in the street, most wrote their speeches (judgments) with a general audience of lawyers in mind, or to provide guidance or correction for lower courts, or sometimes to influence Parliament or government departments (Paterson 1982: 10–11).

In this light the publication of multiple judgments in appeal cases, and even the publication of dissenting judgments, becomes understandable as part of a dialogue of lawyers, even though it would at first sight appear that both practices are unproductive with regard to the ideological functions of courts. Indeed, where judgments are seen as aimed directly at the public, dissents or less than unanimous multiple judgments may be strongly discouraged as indicating a lack of resolution in the court. Paterson's interviewees felt that single speeches should be given in criminal appeals, and in both the House of Lords and the United States Supreme Court the need for the court to speak with a single clear voice in politically controversial cases is often recognised (Paterson 1982: 98–100; Abraham 1986: 216). In civil law jurisdictions the traditional practice is that there are no separate concurring or dissenting opinions but merely a single judgment of the court, even in appeal courts: 'the standard attitude is that the law is certain and should appear so, and that this certainty would be impaired by noting dissents and by publishing separate opinions' (Merryman 1985: 121).

Quite apart, however, from the advantages of allowing multiple opinions and dissents as ways of improving the technical quality of doctrine in various ways[10] their existence is also an affirmation of judicial independence, and especially of the charismatic image of the wise and fearless judge. As one Chief Justice remarked, dissent 'is some assurance to counsel and to the public that decision has not been perfunctory, which is one of the most important objects of decision-writing' (Chief Justice Stone quoted in Abraham 1986: 215; and see Llewellyn 1989: 59). It is this contribution to charismatic authority which may explain why dissent and independence in opinion writing seem to be particularly institutionalised in British higher courts.

Courts as Policy Makers

We must finally consider one other aspect of the relationship between courts and other branches of the state apparatus. The view that has been taken in this book is that although judges necessarily make law their functions are not typically those of legislators or policy makers but primarily those of rationalisers and elaborators of doctrine in the face of change, and reinforcers and affirmers of established doctrine in dispute cases or in relation to claims brought before them. The extent to which courts can act as effective policy-making bodies is, however, a much discussed topic, particularly in relation to such powerful courts as the United States Supreme Court in which the leeways of constitutional interpretation allow much scope for judicial innovation in rule-making on fundamental social, economic and political issues.

There is indeed clear evidence that some higher courts are treated as essentially legislative or policy-making bodies, at least in certain circumstances. 'Today's brief [before American appellate courts] on an environmental, desegregation, apportionment or welfare issue frequently contains exactly the same data in exactly the same format as would a presentation to a congressional committee' (Shapiro 1981: 44). In the United States the so-called 'Brandeis brief'—the presentation to a court by counsel of statistical or social scientific evidence rather than or in addition to purely legal doctrinal arguments—has been extensively used since its explicit recognition by the Supreme Court as a valid forensic

10 For example, a powerful dissent may force the majority opinion to take account of its strongest arguments; and concurring opinions may elucidate additional justifications, limitations or implications of the court's decision. Cf. Abraham 1986: 212ff; Danelski 1986: 36–44; Paterson 1982: 100ff.

technique in 1908.[11] To a limited extent such evidence is admitted in some British courts. An analysis by V. G. Rosenblum (Abraham 1986: 245) of the use of social scientific evidence in the United States Supreme Court during five terms between 1954 and 1974 found that reliance was placed on this kind of evidence (although it was not always crucial in reaching the decision in the case) in about one third of the approximately 1270 majority, concurring or dissenting opinions delivered in a total of 601 cases. Rosenblum found that, among disciplines, political science was most often relied upon (43 per cent of cases), followed by economics (20.1 per cent), sociology (18.8 per cent), psychology (9.4 per cent), history (4 per cent), anthropology (1.3 per cent) and 'others' (3.4 per cent). By far the heaviest use of such material was in legislative apportionment, criminal procedure, racial discrimination and election law cases.

The issues surrounding the use of such evidence in courts have been much discussed. Its introduction makes explicit a primarily policy-making judicial role because the court is asked to lay down rules on the basis of an expressed judgment of social or economic desirability or necessity. Judges and professional lawyers are typically ambivalent in their attitudes to such a judicial role, although for different reasons. For judges the ambivalence arises from the necessity of trying to balance ideological and governmental judicial functions. The use by courts of the kind of evidence, and the kind of reasoning, that legislators and administrators use threatens to undermine the perceived distinctiveness of judicial analysis and justification which underlies courts' ideological functions. At the same time, particularly in societies where constitutional restraints on legislative power are important, the pressure on courts to govern may be hard to resist. In the United States, the example of the school desegregation cases, the willingness of legislators to let courts 'take the heat' in controversial issues, the easing of procedural requirements governing jurisdiction and *locus standi*, and the development of far-reaching but immediate judicial remedies have been suggested as reasons for the increasing demands made on courts (Horowitz 1977: 9–12).

For legal professions, ambivalence about explicit judicial policy-making arises, on one side, from professional commitment to the purity of legal doctrine as a knowledge system (see Chapter 6) and, on the other, from lawyers' interest in winning cases which impels them to seek to use whatever means of persuasion a court will show itself prepared to heed. Thus, counsel's role in certain kinds of cases may become not so much that of an advocate of particular interpretations of doctrine as that of a

11 *Muller v Oregon* (1908) 208 US 412 (constitutionality of statute limiting women's work in certain establishments to a maximum of 10 hours per day). The technique is named after the counsel (later Supreme Court Justice) Louis D. Brandeis who successfully employed it in the *Muller* case.

choreographer and co-ordinator of expert witnesses who are able to present, as directed, complex statistical or scientific material in support of particular policies being advocated, and in opposition to other expert witnesses testifying in court for the other side (Chesler et al. 1988: chs 4 and 5).

Numerous features of the structure of judicial work can make explicit policy-making in the courts hazardous, in some measure, to their legitimacy and to that of the law they develop. Alongside familiar claims of usurpation of legislative functions within a representative democracy by undemocratic judicial systems are arguments about the nature of the adversary process with its binary oppositions in which normally one side must win and the other lose (Eisenberg 1976), a situation hardly conducive to a balancing of many considerations in policy formation (Fuller 1978). A broad view of the social policy issues and consequences of a decision is hard to obtain in a deliberately limited context of analysis of rights of the litigating parties (Horowitz 1977: 34–5, ch 7). Other arguments stress that the courts' approach to ascertainment or specification of facts is necessarily different from the scientific procedures of data gathering (Lévy-Bruhl 1964: 150–2) that are assumed to be the appropriate basis of rational policy-making.

Courts do not, in any event, have the resources to gather social data in the systematic and wide-ranging manner considered necessary for rational governmental policy-making (Horowitz 1977: 45–51). Many commentators on the use of social scientific or statistical evidence in the courts have argued the inability of courts to assess critically this kind of evidence or to monitor its collection and presentation in a forensic setting (e.g. Cahn 1955). As an American judge put it: 'One expert tells us one thing and another seemingly equally qualified expert testifies to the contrary... if we're overwhelmed by a mass of statistical data somebody still has to make the choice.... The judge has to make that choice' (quoted in Chesler et al. 1988: 92–3). In addition there is the general problem in judicial law-making—writ large when judges appear as explicit legislators—of safeguarding the interests of litigants. Where their dispute is used by the court as an occasion to introduce on policy grounds new rules overturning the legal situation on which they relied and on which the rights they assert are grounded the court may be seen as causing litigants considerable injustice. This problem has given rise to much analysis throughout this century (Stone 1966: 658–67) of the potentialities of the controversial concept of 'prospective overruling' by which new judicially created rules may be made prospective in effect while the rights of the parties are decided according to the previously established law.[12]

12 Cf. *Jones v Secretary of State for Social Services* [1972] AC 944: *Linkletter v Walker* (1965) 381 US 618.

Perhaps most serious of all limitations on social or economic policy-making by courts is their inability to monitor the consequences of their decisions (Horowitz 1977: 264). Although judicial activism has often been justified on the ground that democratic legislatures tend to be overburdened and slow to act to remedy specific problems which could be dealt with by courts, the fact remains that Western courts can only hand down decisions when a case is brought before them and, in principle, only on the issues arising in that case. In this sense they are passive rather than active in approach to their governmental role and their policy-making is necessarily 'piecemeal' (Horowitz 1977: 35–45). They cannot follow through decision-making with frequent adjustments of policy to take continuous account of a feedback of information about the effects of their actions (Horowitz 1977: 51–6).

Of course, it can be said that in many of these respects legislatures and administrative agencies show no less serious failings, either because they too lack the resources to formulate and implement policy in a rational manner or because they choose not to use available resources appropriately to do so. Nevertheless the point remains that, if, as the analysis in this chapter suggests, courts have other, specific responsibilities with regard to providing legitimation of the legal and social order, there are special risks to their success as legitimators if they are seen to act too much like these other agencies. Visible failures by courts in explicitly governmental (that is, policymaking or 'legislating') roles which they undertake, or even a too conspicuous success which reveals them as 'merely' agencies of government rather than specialist interpreters and implementers of legal doctrine, may be damaging to their legitimacy and perhaps ultimately in some circumstances to that of the legal order as a whole, especially where the primary basis of judicial authority is charismatic. Balzac must have been well aware of these legitimating functions of courts when he wrote: 'to distrust the judiciary marks the beginning of the end of society. Smash the present patterns of the institution, rebuild it on a different basis ... but don't stop believing in it' (quoted in Kirchheimer 1961: 175).

Postscript on Functional Analysis of Courts

In this chapter a variety of sociological approaches to the study of courts has been outlined. In the latter part of the chapter, however, one approach, the analysis of courts in terms of their functions in relation to other institutions—a form of functional analysis—has been used specifically to examine the relationship between the courts and other parts of the state apparatus. Its use may serve as a limited illustration of the applicability of functional approaches in the sociological study of law. Before closing this chapter, however, it is important to stress some limitations of the scope of functional analysis in the context of study of courts.

In Chapter 3 it was argued that functional analysis is a probably essential part of sociological method but one with important limitations. To recognise those limitations it is essential to make clear that this kind of analysis highlights only certain aspects of relationships between social phenomena viewed in terms of the postulated conditions under which these phenomena co-exist. Thus, it cannot be assumed that courts invariably successfully fulfil the functions that can be seen as determining their position within their political and social environment. Neither can it be supposed that all aspects of courts and their work can be adequately explained in terms of postulated functions. Nor can it be assumed that other institutions cannot exist to fulfil these functions. Nor can any judgment be made from this analysis as to whether the functions are desirable or undesirable.

Yet, as has been seen earlier, functional analysis in sociology tends seemingly inevitably to the assumption that stability—the successful integration of functions—is normal and it measures the reality it observes against this model of stability. The functional method thus provides a framework for looking at aspects of social reality from a certain perspective of order. As long as it is borne firmly in mind that this offers only *one* limited perspective on society the temptation to accept, as comprehensive, theories of law or of society built entirely from this perspective can be avoided. The functional approach is appropriate to look at certain facets of relationships between particular institutions or processes. As we saw in Chapter 3, when it is used for more than this—as the basis of a comprehensive social theory—the particular assumptions of order and integration on which the method is based have a tendency to get out of hand.

8 The Enforcement and Invocation of Law

Whether we think of law as state (or lawyers') law or in some wider terms encompassing more than lawyers' law, we assume that it must have sanctions—specific forms of pressure or inducement—available to ensure compliance; that law constitutes an order that is enforceable and, in general, enforced. Thus for Weber the mark of a *legal* order is 'the presence of a staff engaged in enforcement', a body of persons whose activities demonstrate that compliance with the demands of law is not optional but compulsory (Weber 1954: 5; 1978: 34). For Ehrlich social pressure is usually a sufficient sanction to guarantee law in the wide sense in which he understands the term 'law' (see Chapter 1). For Hoebel, seeking to derive a concept of law applicable to societies of many different kinds, simple and complex, 'law has teeth, teeth that can bite if need be, although they need not necessarily be bared' (Hoebel 1954: 26).

Sanctioning processes and institutions of law may be formal or informal, specialised or unspecialised, distinctively focused or diffuse, rudimentary or highly developed depending on the kind of society, social systems or social groups whose law is under consideration and, of course, on the concept of law adopted. Further, there may be many different kinds of sanctions, enforcement processes and enforcement agencies focused on different parts of a legal order. In the legal systems of contemporary Western states this is invariably the case. In these legal systems a variety of highly developed enforcement agencies exists. They include, particularly, police, with responsibility for the general enforcement of criminal law, and many different regulatory bodies, inspectorates and commissions charged with the enforcement and overseeing of particular areas of legislation. Behind the police power of the state stands ultimately its military power, relatively rarely employed in aid of general policing in peacetime conditions in contemporary Western societies, yet clearly available and used to counter what are perceived as serious threats of civil disorder, for example as a result of strikes (Jeffery and Hennessy 1983).

This chapter is concerned with enforcement and enforcement agencies of state law in contemporary Western societies. Its purpose is not to *describe* law enforcement but (as with the previous two chapters on legal professions and courts) to consider ways in which empirical material on legal institutions can illuminate theoretical issues about law discussed in the earlier chapters of this book.

Institutional Commitments to Legal Doctrine

The coercive aspects of state law are inseparable from its ideological and instrumental aspects. The state reaches into society by means of enforcement agencies. These apparently seek to *impose* the demands and outlook (cognitive and evaluative ideas) expressed in legal doctrine on citizens and their social and economic relationships. Everyone is assumed to know the law and the state holds out sanctions intended to create incentives for citizens to find out the law's demands and comply with them.

But the channels of legal coercion are not the same as the channels of law's ideological effects. They are, in general, maintained by different personnel. In Western societies an institutionalised division of labour exists between enforcement agencies (for example, police, inspectorates, regulatory commissions) and courts. Often the outlook on the law and on the task of law enforcement held within these agencies differs considerably from that of the courts with which they have dealings. As will appear, this can lead to tensions and even hostility or resentment arising from divergent institutional goals. Lawyers—the practising legal profession—are in yet another different position with professional commitments distinct from the occupational and institutional commitments of the judiciary and of enforcement 'staffs'. Since in this book we have taken law to mean primarily legal doctrine in its institutional settings, what is of particular significance is the relationship of these institutions of enforcement, adjudication and legal professional practice, and their personnel, to law in this sense. In other words, what are their specific *commitments* to law?

In Chapter 6 it was argued that the lawyer's typical commitment is not merely to order but to *legal* order founded on predictable, manageable doctrine. In this sense commitment to the integrity of legal doctrine, for a variety of reasons which have been discussed, is typically a central commitment of professional lawyers in contemporary Western societies. As we saw in Chapter 7, however, the judge's relationship with law as doctrine is more problematic. Although a centrally important task of the judicial process is the affirmation and development of legal doctrine so as to present it as a rational, comprehensive and coherent system, this task must also be reconciled with short-term demands for support from other arms of the state: for example, demands for legitimation of current government policy and for technical aid in implementing it; and even demands from many quarters that the courts themselves become directly involved in policy formation, 'legislating' as an arm of government.

Enforcement agencies may be of many different kinds and may have many different kinds of commitment depending especially on the external sources of their authority, their internal organisation and resources, and the nature of their enforcement task and the environment in which it is to be accomplished. In very general terms it can be said that the police, seeing themselves as 'front line' defenders of established social order against the numerous immediate threats to it arising from particular disturbances, are not primarily concerned with the more subtle contributions to social order arising from maintenance of legal ideology and the integrity of legal doctrine. Thus, as will appear, the demand for 'order' can be separated in the context of police work from the demand for 'law', law being treated as (and its utility assessed by police in terms of) a means towards order as an end. The result is a potential tension between maintenance of legality and fulfilment of the police task of social control. It will be argued in this chapter that police commitment to 'order' in a certain sense takes precedence over police commitment to maintenance of the integrity of legal doctrine.

The variety of other kinds of agencies concerned with law enforcement makes it impossible to generalise about their primary commitments. Depending on their nature and situation these boards, commissions, and inspectorates may have primary commitments to 'law' or to 'order', to the promotion of particular governmental policies, or of particular public interests (for example, prevention of discrimination on the grounds of race or sex), or private interests (for example, business self-regulation through trade associations to maintain an acceptable public image of business). In this chapter our concern will be to outline and compare those aspects of the commitments of various kinds of enforcement agencies that bear on the relation of their work to law as institutionalised doctrine.

Enforcing Law and Invoking Law

If we take law to mean legal doctrine created by agencies of the state to regulate society, enforcement of this law is naturally the concern of the state. In the field of criminal law responsibility for enforcement is assumed by the state. However, in relation to civil (i.e., in this context, non-criminal) law such as the rules of contract and civil liability (tort or delict) the state typically merely provides facilities for enforcement while relying on the citizen to initiate action to make use of these facilities (for example, for primarily compensatory remedies such as damages) (cf. Summers 1971).

Any sociologically significant clear line between these situations is, however, hard to draw. Literature on the 'mobilisation' of law—that is, the manner and circumstances in which law is called upon and deliberately employed in solving social or personal problems—stresses the close links between the capacity of state agencies to enforce law and the willingness of citizens to call upon these agencies (Black 1973; 1970). Donald Black writes: 'Complainants are the most invisible and they may be the most important social force binding the law to other aspects of social organization' (Black 1970: 748). Empirical research in the United States shows that most police arrests occur as a result of citizen complaints (Black 1971). In a recent study of a division of the Devon and Cornwall Constabulary, police were found most often to cite information from victims, witnesses and members of the public as the major factor in solving the crimes they had investigated (Morgan 1990: 52–3). Studies in Britain of local government consumer law enforcement agencies and environmental health officers have shown that these rely heavily on complaints from members of the public although they expose a considerable amount of unlawful activity through their own initiative (Hutter 1988: 97–103; Cranston 1979: ch 3). Citizens' willingness to *invoke* law—that is, to call upon it for aid in securing their private interests—thus often seems essential to effective *enforcement* of law by state agencies.

Further if some (civil) law is by its nature left unenforced unless citizens choose to invoke it, so the concerns of government or particular state agencies may, as will be seen in this chapter, require that even criminal law not be rigorously enforced. Thus criminal prosecution authorities (Hall Williams, ed, 1988; Moody and Tombs 1983) and also regulatory agencies concerned, for example, with pollution control, health and safety in factories and trading standards may exercise considerable discretion in deciding what kinds of breaches of the law should be brought before courts. Even where specialised criminal prosecution authorities seek to minimise discretion (cf. Blankenburg and Treiber 1985) they must rely on enforcement or detection agencies to bring cases to their notice. In Britain it is still, in most cases, a matter for the police to take the initial decision as to whether criminal proceedings should be instituted.[1] Conversely modern agencies concerned with law enforcement often have responsibility for the institution or supervision of civil actions (for example, in Britain, the Commission for Racial Equality and the Equal Opportunities Commission). Sometimes, as in the case of consumer agencies in Britain concerned with trading standards, this responsibility may be in addition to responsibilities with regard to enforcement of criminal law. In addition, individual citizens may have

1 Prosecution of Offences Act 1985, s. 3(2)a.

a strong personal interest in the invocation of criminal law and in England private prosecutions of some offences are still possible.

The distinction between public law and private law represents in legal thought the distinction between 'state' and 'civil society' in classic social theory. Yet we have seen (especially in Chapter 4) that various writers now point to the erosion of this distinction with the intrusion of state controls into 'private' spheres in numerous subtle and complex ways, and with the 'extension' of the state through a variety of institutions—for example, the family—associated with the private sphere (e.g. Donzelot 1980).[2] The clear relevance of these arguments in the present context is to the numerous different statuses of governmentally co-ordinated policy-implementing agencies. Many of these are substantially or partially autonomous bodies existing in various relations with central government (e.g. De Smith 1989: ch 12). They make the boundaries of the state, thought of as the institutionalised concentration of political power, extremely difficult to draw.

Further, the fact that enforcement and invocation of law may be best thought of as two sides of social control which cannot be clearly separated suggests that law enforcement is best understood not so much as the direct control of citizens' conduct by state agencies as a much more diffuse form of social control maintained by action at *all* 'levels' of society, from that of the individual citizen complainant to that of centralised state administrative and regulatory agencies. Thus, again, the intimate connection between law's ideological and coercive effects is stressed, since both are seen as operating and being maintained at numerous social levels.

Yet it cannot for a moment be assumed that this social control and the manner in which it operates are uniform throughout society. We have already considered sources of resistance to the mobilisation of state law that are located in the strength and effectiveness of 'living law' systems of various kinds (see Chapter 1). The jurisdiction of enforcement agencies may be centralised, local, government controlled, quasi-autonomous or (for example, in trade associations) private. As this jurisdiction 'fans out' from the power centres of the state to the private reaches of civil society enforcement agencies are faced with demands for accommodation to the living law of various sectors of society. Thus studies of British regulatory agencies concerned, for example, with pollution control and environmental health show the agencies taking careful account of the pressures shaping normal business practice in deciding how to enforce law against business firms (Hutter 1988: 59, 92ff; Richardson 1983). Studies of trade association and business-sponsored consumer complaint handling agencies in the United States have shown that these serve to defuse pressures for more stringent state

2 See further ch 9.

law controls on business at the same time as they apply a living law favourable to business interests (Greenberg and Stanton 1980: 223–4; Eaton 1980: 252, 267).

This takes us to the last general point to be made here as regards the relationship between enforcement and invocation. For many reasons, which will emerge in this chapter, economically powerful actors (especially large business enterprises) have much greater control over the manner in which law is enforced than do other actors. In addition, they have much greater opportunities to control, in furtherance of their own perceived interests, processes set in motion by their invocation of law. These are matters that will be examined by comparing aspects of police organisation and police work with corresponding aspects of the work of other enforcement agencies. First, however, it will be necessary to consider in more detail the ways in which law is invoked.

Opportunity and Incentive to Invoke Law

What determines whether law will be invoked? Many studies in Britain and elsewhere have pointed to the fact that even where citizens recognise that they have a problem or grievance they often do not see it as a matter for which law can provide redress (e.g. Harris et al 1984: 75–6, 69–70). The German social theorist Niklas Luhmann, in discussing what he calls the 'thematisation' of law, sees many factors as determining whether this thematisation occurs; that is, whether the specifically *legal* aspects of a situation become a topic of communication or controversy. Luhmann stresses that communication about respective interests can take many forms—assume many thematisations—not just legal ones and that what he calls a 'thematisation threshold' has to be crossed before interaction or communication within the framework of legal claims takes place. Heightened risks arising from resort to legal argument—of conflict, breakdown of interaction, or lack of control by the parties of the course of interaction between them—create a resistance to crossing this threshold (Luhmann 1981). Luhmann's approach goes some way towards explaining why, as Macaulay (1963) found, contracts may be made in a business environment frequently with little regard to their formal legal validity (Blegvad 1990). The object is to use prior planning of interaction between the parties so as to *prevent* the thematisation of law, not to facilitate it.

Factors Inhibiting the Effective Voicing of Grievances

Law frequently requires what the sociologist Howard Becker (1963) refers to as 'whistle blowers' to set its institutional machinery in motion by drawing breaches of law to the attention of appropriate authorities. But research has shown many reasons why citizens are often reluctant or unable to 'blow the whistle' on illegalities of which they are victims or of which they have knowledge. Complexity of legal and administrative systems is often stressed as a major reason. An eminent United States Supreme Court judge once remarked: 'The increasing complexities of our governmental apparatus at both the local and the federal levels have made it difficult for a person to process a claim or even to make a complaint. Social security is a virtual maze; the hierarchy that governs urban housing is often so intricate that it takes an expert to know what agency has jurisdiction over a particular complaint; the office to call or official to see for noise abatement, for a broken sewer line, or a fallen tree is a mystery to many in our metropolitan areas'.[3] These remarks in an American context are applicable to other Western legal and administrative systems. Citizens' fear of or bewilderment at the real or assumed complexities of rules and procedures is often coupled with their reluctance to approach lawyers and others who could provide help in understanding the complexities (Harris et al. 1984: ch 2).

The poor and inarticulate, in particular, lack knowledge and opportunity to complain against abuses. David Greenberg's study of dispute handling by a retail store in the Washington 'ghetto' found that customers often could not gain access to information about their own accounts so as to find out whether they were being overcharged on their monthly payments (Greenberg 1980). In Britain, national surveys show 'that many consumers who think that they have experienced consumer problems fail to complain, lack a rudimentary knowledge of their legal rights, and are ignorant of official bodies such as consumer agencies, which may be able to assist them' (Cranston 1979: 5). Again, accident victims may not consider approaching a lawyer for help unless they are already convinced about the legal strength of their claim. Yet many potential claimants have only minimal relevant legal knowledge and rely on advice from other non-lawyers (Harris et al. 1984: ch 2). In this context, trade unions are a most valuable source of information and advice. Access to information necessary for effective invocation of law may be particularly difficult when it relates to highly technical regulation of complex processes, for example, in pollution control (Richardson 1983: 88, 124). Nevertheless many enforcement agencies do make considerable efforts to publicise the rights and duties established by the law that they are required to enforce.

Complaining has its costs. In an influential book on complaint behaviour Albert Hirschman concluded that 'voicing' complaints is usually considerably more costly in time, trouble, effort and often money

3 *Johnson v Avery* (1969) 393 US 483 at 491, per Douglas J.

than either putting up with the situation or terminating dealings with the party at fault ('exiting') and making substitute arrangements with others (for example, buying from another supplier of consumer products or services as a result of dissatisfaction with the original supplier). 'Voice' will thus be the exception rather than the rule in cases of dissatisfaction in the marketplace. It may, however, be chosen in preference to 'exit' in some circumstances: for example, when 'exit' is impossible because of the unavailability of alternative sources of supply, or where there is a reasoned expectation that the offending organisation will be motivated and able to remedy its performance as a result of complaint (Hirschman 1970).

William Felstiner (1974) has similarly argued that 'avoidance' ('limiting the relationship with the other disputant sufficiently so that the dispute no longer remains salient') carries significantly lower costs in what he calls 'technologically complex rich societies' (TCRSs) than either adjudication or mediation as means of dealing with dissatisfaction. The cost of avoidance is always a reduction in the content of a relationship truncated or terminated. This is a relatively low cost if the relationship relates only to a single interest of the dissatisfied party. Because in TCRSs many relationships beyond family ties are of this kind whereas in 'technologically simple poor societies' they are typically multiplex or many sided, avoidance is a typical response to dissatisfaction in TCRSs. Although Festiner thinks that, on the whole, this is a beneficial consequence of market freedom in Western TCRSs the costs of avoidance are nevertheless seen as considerable where unorganised individuals are prejudiced by the actions of large organisations of which they are not members.

Reluctance to 'voice' does certainly seem widespread. Ross Cranston (1979: 59), referring to British surveys, states: 'Most consumers who, in their own view, have cause to complain do not do so. There is a widespread toleration of faulty goods.' Again, many crime victims avoid contacting police for help (e.g. Morgan 1990: ch 10). A major British study of redress for accidental injuries found that nearly 90 per cent of all accident victims in the survey failed to obtain any damages for their injuries through the legal system, the vast majority of victims never having sought any legal advice (Harris et al. 1984: 50–1, 65). The American Bar Foundation's mid-1970s study of lawyer use found that less than 10 per cent of people involved in a dispute with a seller of consumable goods over a major purchase seek legal help (Curran 1980: 12). Barbara Curran writes of the study: 'No general alternative resources emerged for problems encountered in the marketplace. Indeed except where real property was involved or wages threatened, approximately three quarters of the consumers either tried to handle such matters on their own without legal or other help or simply did nothing at all about such problems' (1980: 12). Such a situation does not, however, necessarily reflect low avoidance costs. Felstiner's thesis has been criticised principally on the ground that he underestimates the usual costs of avoidance (Danzig and Lowy 1975; cf. Felstiner 1975). Both the costs of taking effective action to secure redress *and* the costs of avoidance may be so high that the only solution seems to be to swallow one's pride, stifle one's anger and take no action or, at most, to make ineffectual complaints without invoking legal or other 'official' channels of redress (cf. Addiss 1980).

Other writers have stressed less tangible but important constraints on voicing of grievances and invocation of law. In a conservative and conformist culture complainants are often made to feel deviant (Nader and Shugart 1980: 67–8). Victims of accidents at work frequently blame themselves for, or view fatalistically, injury and illness (Hale and Pérusse 1977). More generally, self-blame may often be a way of avoiding the risks accompanying complaining (Coates and Penrod 1981) and attribution of fault to others may occur only after the prospect of claiming has arisen (Harris et al. 1984: ch 4). Richard Abel writes that 'To assert a claim is to render oneself vulnerable by admitting that one has been injured or bested and by acknowledging weakness (at least if the adversary is an equal or superior). Many ... [people] find that very difficult to do, ... particularly men, which may explain why there is a disproportionate number of women complainants before informal institutions. The claimant also opens himself to further reverses if the claim is denied and may be blamed for initiating the conflict or advancing the complaint' (Abel 1982: 286). In addition an aggrieved person is unlikely to complain against an oppressor upon whom he or she is dependent. Greenberg's study of a retail store in the poorest area of Washington DC showed that customers were very unlikely to complain about the store's malpractices. How could they when no other store would grant them, living on only a small income of welfare payments, the credit they depended upon to buy merchandise? (Greenberg 1980; cf. Cranston 1979: 59). Similarly, fear of disrupting important relationships (for example, with employers, landlords, local authorities, neighbours or friends) may deter accident victims from pursuing claims for compensation (Harris et al. 1984: 74–5, 115).

Seeking Help from Law

Even if action is taken for redress of grievances this may not lead to 'thematisation' as a legal controversy. Quite apart from complainants' typical reluctance to litigate, a persistent consumer complainant, for example, may be 'bought off' by an offending business in a settlement explicitly designed by the business to prevent litigation which could result in an undesirable legal precedent against particular business practices. Further, 'private law making' through use of limiting or exclusion clauses in contracts has often provided a means by which a business could exclude by standard form contracts the possibility of thematisation by its customers of problems as legal. Thus while many complainants are reluctant to cross the 'thematisation threshold' of law, equally those complained against may have effective means of preventing the legal thematisation of a controversy.

Certain types of problem, however, appear to be generally recognised as legal, involve sufficient risk to make lawyer use worthwhile, are typically problems of the kind encountered by the favoured categories of lawyer clientele and hence the subject of well-developed lawyer expertise, or do not require the maintenance of continued relations between the parties in dispute. Such factors may strongly influence the thematisation of problems as legal matters. Lawyer use provides a partial index of this thematisation. The American Bar Foundation survey found that lawyer use in the United States varied widely according to problem type, from less than one per cent of persons complaining of racial or sex discrimination in jobs to 85 per cent of those drafting wills. More than 50 per cent of people with estate planning or divorce problems consulted lawyers, 37 per cent in real property matters, 31 per cent in settling a spouse's estate, 16 per cent in personal injury and property damage cases, 15 per cent in claims against governmental agencies and 12 per cent for breaches of constitutional rights and for consumer problems generally (but only 7 per cent for major difficulties with sellers of consumer goods) (Curran 1980).

The 'Users Survey' of the Royal Commission on Legal Services in England and Wales found that 15 per cent of its respondents had consulted a lawyer in the previous year, 22 per cent within two years, one third within five years, and slightly more than one half at some time during their lifetime. Only 9 per cent of respondents in the previous year recalled an occasion when they considered that consulting a lawyer might have been helpful but decided against it.[4] Various studies in America have found the extent of individuals' income and property to be the major determinant of their contacts with lawyers. But there is no reason to suppose that 'have-nots' have fewer legal problems than 'haves' (Carlin and Howard 1965), and the experience of law centres or neighbourhood law firms hardly indicates a lack of demand for legal advice and services. Indeed there seems considerable demand in those areas of problems in relation to which ordinary private practice lawyers are consulted only by a small minority of grievants. Lawyer use provides only a very imperfect index of the extent of public recognition of

4 Cmnd 7648 (1979) Vol I paras 4–15, Vol II paras 8–14, 8–371.

problems as legal, though it does indicate some important 'thresholds' of opportunity, ability and incentive to invoke law.

The American legal scholar Marc Galanter has explored aspects of these thresholds in an important essay examining reasons why certain categories of litigants are able to invoke law far more effectively than others (Galanter 1974). Galanter distinguishes what he calls 'repeat players' (who frequently litigate) from 'one shotters' (who rarely do so). The repeat players of law are not necessarily the 'haves' of society, although in the American legal system (and presumably in other Western legal systems) this tends to be the case since only the economically powerful can normally afford to litigate regularly. Repeat players are typically (but by no means always) businesses and one shotters are typically ordinary citizens. By virtue of their familiarity with litigation, repeat players often have advance knowledge and expertise relevant to litigation and informal relationships with legal and other officials (cf. Jacob 1969: 100). They obtain generally better lawyers and more continuity in legal advice, 'better record keeping, more anticipatory or preventive work, more experience and specialized skill in pertinent areas, and more control over counsel' (Galanter 1974: 114). They are in a position to devise their transactions to fit the relevant legal rules and so benefit from them. One shotters use lawyers typically in such matters as criminal, divorce or personal injury cases. The non-repeating nature of their demands encourages a mass processing by lawyers of cases so that, as an earlier American study concluded, 'only a limited amount of time and interest is usually expended on any one case—there is little or no incentive to treat it except as an isolated piece of legal business. Moreover, there is ordinarily no desire to go much beyond the case as the client presents it, and such cases are only accepted when there is a clear-cut cause of action; i.e., when they fit into convenient legal categories and promise a fairly safe return' (Carlin and Howard 1965: 385; cf. Genn 1987: 66ff).

Galanter argues that his study defines a position of advantage in the legal arena and shows 'how those with other advantages tend to occupy this position of advantage and to have their own advantages reinforced and augmented thereby' (Galanter 1974: 103). The familiar tendency of small claims courts to become dominated by debt collection actions by business plaintiffs is a particularly striking confirmation of the general argument (Caplovitz 1974: ch 11; cf. Whelan 1990: 212–7). Galanter's broad distinction between the position of repeat players and one shotters and Carlin and Howard's sweeping statements about the mass processing of one shotter claims are coloured by the strong orientation of the American legal profession to business interests. Nevertheless, in Britain, Maureen Cain (1983c) sees her study of county court work as confirming the utility of the Galanter analysis and makes a further distinction between 'national repeat players' (large national firms) and 'local repeat players' (local firms regularly bringing cases before particular courts). The latter particularly enjoy the advantages of informal relations with local legal officials. Similarly, Hazel Genn sees the Galanter thesis as particularly appropriate to her study of personal injury litigation in Britain 'despite the fact that the repeat players... are the defendants' in these cases; but the situation and interests of lawyers, as well as those of plaintiffs and defendants, are significant factors in determining the outcome of cases (Genn 1987: 26).

Invoking Law in Support of Collective Interests

Attempts by citizens to invoke law in support of broad public or community interests encounter quite different special problems. An individualist ethos tends to reinforce the idea of each protecting his own, not responsible for any general aspect of *public* welfare. This idea is, as has been seen in earlier chapters, expressed in legal doctrine itself. It is reflected particularly, however, in the difficult legal problems surrounding the concept of *locus standi* or 'standing'—that is, the nature of the personal interest which individual litigants must have in the outcome of litigation to entitle them to have their legal action heard by a court. This is especially important as regards law relating to broad public interests—for example, environmental law—rather than particular individual rights. Litigants must normally show that they have some individual interest in enforcement of the law. In the United States, Britain and other Western European countries rules of standing have been loosened in various ways to recognise broader interests which litigants may have in clarification and enforcement of law but much uncertainty surrounds the legal issues (e.g. Cappelletti 1989: 272ff; Schwartz 1987: ch 4).

The individualist orientation of Western law is reflected also in the difficulty of successfully bringing *collective* claims before the courts. In many cases where the general interest of a section of society demands clarification or enforcement of law but litigation by individuals is deterred by cost in financial or other terms, a collective claim on behalf of the whole class or category of the population affected, or by a self-selected sample, may seem an appropriate strategy for invoking the law. In the United States class actions have been effectively used in bringing collective claims before courts (Yeazell 1987: ch 9). Other Western legal systems have come to recognise similar devices or other procedures producing some of the benefits of class actions; for example, the bringing of 'test' cases before courts (e.g. Prosser 1983). In England, representative actions on behalf of individuals sharing a common grievance and a common interest can be brought. All of these methods seem, however, in important respects anomalous within the established pattern of individual legal claims. Even in the United States, important limitations on the availability of class actions have been created by the courts. The extension of the scope of legal action beyond individual claims, like the extension of *locus standi,* is fraught with numerous legal doctrinal, ideological and practical difficulties (e.g. Cappelletti 1989: ch 7; Feldman 1992).

Types of Enforcement Agencies

We must now return to consideration of agencies of law enforcement. Their variety is such that generalisation is extremely difficult. Enforcement of general criminal law is typically the responsibility of police. In Western legal systems, including the English and Scottish systems, criminal prosecution decisions are usually taken by special centralised or local state prosecution agencies (e.g. Hall Williams, ed, 1988; Moody and Tombs 1983) although these clearly rely to a considerable extent on the way in which police decide to conduct their inquiries. Prosecution practice as well as more general enforcement policy (arising from the organisation of police forces) may, therefore, be relatively centralised or decentralised in different Western states.

In Britain the enforcement of large areas of what is often called 'regulatory law' (concerned, for example, with industrial safety, environmental pollution or consumer protection) is entrusted to central or local government agencies or inspectorates of many different kinds. A historical distinction can be drawn between the development of 'efficiency' and 'enforcement' inspectorates (Rhodes 1981: ch 1), the former concerned with overseeing efficient provision of public services such as education, sanitation, police and fire services and prisons, the latter concerned primarily with checking compliance with law on such matters as conditions of work and trading standards. On this view efficiency inspectorates are part of the state's administrative system by which central and local government are related (Rhodes 1981: 11). Enforcement inspectorates may be a part of central government (for example, Her Majesty's Inspectorate of Pollution, operating under the Environmental Protection Act 1990) or of local government (for example, consumer agencies and environmental health departments); or they may be organised into quasi-autonomous public bodies such as the Health and Safety Executive (concerned with enforcement of industrial safety regulations) set up by the Health and Safety at Work (etc.) Act 1974, or the National Rivers Authority (concerned with enforcing water pollution regulation) established by the Water Act 1989.

In fact an important part of law enforcement or supervision of the working of law is now entrusted to what have been called 'quasi-nongovernmental organisations' (or 'quangos'). In this context they can be thought of as agencies, usually with a diversity of functions, not directly incorporated into the structure of central or local government but carrying out designated public responsibilities. Those agencies of this kind that are centrally concerned with law enforcement and the implementation of legislative policy typically have similarities with the longer established independent regulatory commissions of the United States (Cushman 1941), characterised by quasi-judicial powers to evaluate the behaviour of the regulated, quasi-legislative powers to set standards and rules, powers of investigation and enforcement, and often powers to conduct research and monitor the effectiveness of legislation. Examples of such agencies in Britain are the Civil Aviation Authority (Baldwin 1985), the Commission for Racial Equality and the Equal Opportunities Commission. Their apparent 'arm's length' relationship with the major structures of local or central government has many advantages for government, in particular that of reducing its direct responsibility for the conduct of implementation and enforcement of particular areas of law. On the other hand, the formal legal status of enforcement agencies gives very little guidance as to the degree of actual autonomy in organisation and decision-making that they possess.

As a sub-category of enforcement agencies, regulatory agencies (which will be used hereafter as a general term for agencies of enforcement and supervision of law other than police) are typically concerned with enforcement of criminal law, or with criminal law and the supervision or instigation of some civil actions. Why should some criminal law enforcement be entrusted to these kinds of enforcement agencies while other criminal law enforcement is the task of police? Two reasons are typically offered. First, special agencies are required where law enforcement requires particular specialised knowledge, either of the environment in which the law is to be enforced or of the nature of the activities to be policed. Thus the control of industrial pollution requires special knowledge of both the industrial processes involved and the practical means by which compliance with law can be achieved. Weights and measures regulation became the concern of special agencies rather than the police as methods of measuring improved and precise technical standards could be developed. Nevertheless there are areas of law, policed by regulatory agencies, that require little specialised knowledge and, equally, specialised areas of traffic law enforced by the ordinary police (Rhodes 1981: 206–7).

Secondly, a distinction is often drawn between so-called 'real crime', which is the concern of the police, and regulatory offences, controlled by regulatory agencies, which—though technically criminal—lack the moral stigma of 'ordinary' crime such as offences against persons or property. The distinction between 'real crime' and regulatory offences is one which it will be necessary to look at in more detail but for the moment it is enough to say that, whatever the basis of the distinction, it is inadequate as an exact characterisation of the difference between the objects of law enforcement by police and regulatory agencies. Many road traffic offences, for example, are seen as regulatory offences rather than 'real crime' yet are the concern of the police (Elliott and Street 1968: ch 5).

Both of these suggested reasons for a 'dual' system of law enforcement based on police and regulatory agencies hint at an important distinction between most police work and most work of regulatory agencies. Police work is overwhelmingly concerned with the criminal acts of ordinary citizens. Regulatory agencies are typically concerned with the control of business firms' behaviour. Sociological studies show that although police work and regulatory agency work are subject to many common occupational and organisational pressures they also differ fundamentally as a result of the different *environments* in which they are required to enforce law. Although there can be no simple general explanation of the reasons for allocation of law enforcement between different kinds of agencies of enforcement many historical studies have clearly shown that the nature of regulatory law and regulatory agencies has been determined by the interaction between pressures for control of business activities and equally powerful pressures from business communities to limit and determine the kinds of controls imposed upon them. In this respect business pressure has usually been extremely successful in limiting the scope of legal control or the effectiveness with which control can be exercised.[5] Again, many of the most important differences in general approaches to law enforcement adopted by different kinds of agencies can be explained in terms of the kinds of situation and the sections of society to be policed, and the resources (including resources of authority and prestige) available to the enforcement agency. In the rest of this chapter aspects of the typical situations and strategies of regulatory agencies and police will be considered, so as to provide a basis for comparisons between these two major categories of enforcement agencies.

Regulatory Agencies and Their Strategies

One of the clearest lessons to emerge from studies of regulatory agencies is the difficulty of isolating law enforcement activities or objectives from much wider tasks and aims. Although in Britain local government inspectorates and some central government ones are largely concerned

5 Numerous studies have shown this. See e.g. Paulus 1974 and Kolko 1963 on food and drugs legislation in Britain and America, respectively; Gunningham 1974 on anti-pollution legislation; Carson 1974 and 1980 on industrial health and safety legislation in Britain; McCormick 1979 on American antitrust legislation.

with ensuring the observance of specific legislative requirements, few are concerned exclusively with this aim (Rhodes 1981: 173). Among the factors contributing to broadening of agency concerns beyond mere policing are: the need of government for information and advice on the working of legislation and on the utility of legislative policy—a need which agencies and their personnel are often in the best position to satisfy; the desire of enforcement agency staff for enhanced professional status through the development and use of special expertise—for example in advice-giving to businesses; the wording of legislative provisions giving significant discretion to enforcement agents or requiring interpretation of the policy of the legislation; and the need to negotiate extensively with business on practical strategies for securing effective implementation of the law (Rhodes 1981: 163–4, 172–3).

Thus studies in Britain show that advice-giving, primarily to regulated business communities, is a major activity of consumer agencies (Cranston 1979: 5, 28–31), anti-pollution authorities (Richardson 1983: 128–30) and environmental health officers (Hutter 1988: 92–3). Further, an enforcement inspectorate with substantial autonomy, long established traditions of practice and a high level of special expertise may come to see itself as following its own long-term strategies for implementation of legislative policy and contributing substantially to the practical interpretation of that policy (Rhodes 1981: 152, 162–3). Thus, one criticism of such a body—the former Alkali and Clean Air Inspectorate—with virtually a century of specialised experience and authority, was that, while lacking economic expertise, it had taken upon itself the making of *economic* decisions in interpreting whether 'best practical means' were used by businesses to avoid polluting activities (Rhodes 1981: 154).[6] Thus law enforcement cannot be taken in isolation from the interpretation of policy.

The Use of Prosecution and Publicity

The methods of law enforcement available to regulatory agencies are typically varied and carefully graduated, ranging from the use of administrative sanctions such as notices issued by the agency requiring compliance with the law, through court enforceable orders, to actual prosecution of offences. In the relatively confrontational atmosphere of some regulatory activity in the United States the practice or threat of prosecution may be important and not infrequent (Vogel 1986: 21), but in Britain prosecution by regulatory agencies is relatively rare. For example, in one year, 48,300 weights and measures offences detected in

6 The functions of the Alkali Inspectorate have now been subsumed within those of Her Majesty's Inspectorate of Pollution, operating under the Environmental Protection Act 1990.

the Greater London area produced only 204 prosecutions. Of 21,430 infringements of the Trade Descriptions Act 1968 discovered over a six month period, 1,003 were prosecuted, 5,885 led to cautions and 14,542 were resolved by giving advice to the businesses involved (Cranston 1979: 101). W.G. Carson (1970), studying factory legislation enforcement in south-east England, found that in less than 4 per cent of 3,800 contraventions of the law known to inspectors was a prosecution either instituted or threatened. In 1967 the Alkali Inspectorate's chief inspector declared that 'only on three occasions in the last forty seven years have court proceedings been brought' by it (Gunningham 1974: 66). A study of local authorities' reports in 1970–74 indicated that on average only 2 to 5 per cent of contraventions of the Clean Air Acts resulted in prosecutions. 'Clearly, with whatever assiduity the enforcement agencies seek out offenders, criminal prosecution is not regarded as a normal part of the enforcement process' (Richardson 1983: 62).

Genevra Richardson's study of anti-pollution law enforcement policy and practice in two British regional water authorities[7] found that the agency personnel saw prosecution as not very useful for special deterrence—that is, to deter particular wrongdoers—because of the frequent inappropriateness of available legal sanctions (fines too low, or in some cases too high) for the particular case. However, general deterrence of law breaking through exemplary prosecutions of carefully chosen cases was seen as the most appropriate use of prosecution (1983: 139–41). By contrast, Bridget Hutter's study of environmental health officers found that the rare prosecutions they instituted were aimed at special rather than general deterrence (Hutter 1988: 68). Nevertheless, one of the enforcement officers Ross Cranston interviewed in his study of British consumer agencies remarked: 'if you get a good conviction against one spiv, you create a ripple in the pond. Other people get to know about it and they will slow up. You can't prevent it all, you can only slow them up' (Cranston 1979: 174). The assumption is thus that despite the difficulties of deterrence theory as applied to ordinary criminal behaviour (see Chapter 5), business organisations act on rational calculation and therefore take account of legal sanctions in assessing the costs of their actions (e.g. Chambliss 1967).

It follows from the predominant emphasis on general deterrence that publicising prosecutions and offenders is often seen as of great importance (Braithwaite 1989: 125–7). In Richardson's 'Northern Authority' the agency lawyers always informed their public relations department of hearing dates to allow the local press to be alerted (Richardson 1983: 141), but it seems that consumer agencies often have not used publicity effectively (Cranston 1979: 144). In some countries legislation has

7 The major regulatory responsibilities of regional water authorities were transferred to the National Rivers Authority by the Water Act 1989.

sometimes specifically provided for publication of reports of court judgments on breaches of consumer law (Nader and Shugart 1980: 97–8) although such provisions have rarely been significant in practice. However, in Britain and elsewhere official publicity has been given to names of businesses offending against particular regulations (Cranston 1979: 143–44).

Cranston justifiably remarks, however, that publicity 'is a two-edged sword for consumer agencies, for there is an argument that it may encourage greater violation. For example, publicity of a conviction may reveal that penalties for flagrant breaches of consumer legislation are trivial or that only the most serious transgressors are prosecuted. It may actually disseminate knowledge in the business community about how a legal provision can be successfully avoided. Publicity may show a consumer agency in an unfavourable light and undermine its public image of effectiveness. For example, it may become obvious that an agency has not prosecuted offences under consumer law in the past, that it prosecutes trivial cases, or that on this occasion it has been tardy in taking action' (1979: 145; cf. Richardson 1983: 142–43). Similar risks attach to the publicised activity of any regulatory agency, particularly if it cannot rely on firm support for its policy and practice from courts, government or other state agencies with the power to influence the success of its actions and general opinion with regard to them.

Thus, within the range of graded strategies available to regulatory agencies, advice, cajoling, patient negotiation, the maintenance of subtle pressure (for example, through increase in the number of inspections), implied or expressed threats, and bargaining to avoid a threatened prosecution are employed (and see Hawkins 1984). Actual prosecution, with all its risks and difficulties, is typically the rarely used extremity of this range.

Discretion in Enforcement

Clearly there is often very considerable regulatory agency discretion to decide on the kind of enforcement action to take. Hutter (1988: 159–61) found that significant differences in prosecution practice as between local authority environmental health departments reflected important differences in enforcement philosophy. Richardson (1983: 135) also found that the incidence of prosecutions varied markedly between the two regional water authorities she studied and between divisions within them. There was no evidence of a clear inter-authority policy on prosecution. Similarly Cranston found wide variation in consumer agency prosecution practice and, again, an absence of formal prosecution policy (1979: 56–7, 170). When prosecutions were brought they tended to be 'watertight' cases so that prosecution was successful in the vast majority of instances; and differences in prosecution rates were partly explained by different investigatory practices, some agencies detecting many more infringements than others (1979: 116, 76). In Richardson's study, relatively high levels of prosecution in one authority were associated with the nature of the locality policed (with a large number of firms in a heavily industrialised area), and with a prosecution tradition in the enforcement agency that made the process of prosecution more familiar and less daunting than for the other agencies studied.

These findings with regard to regulatory agencies are reminiscent of those of numerous studies of police work emphasising that crime rates, based on prosecutions or offences known to the police, may be much more important as indicators of police law enforcement activity and policy, and of the extent of police effectiveness in gathering information on law breaking, than as indicators of actual levels of crime (e.g. Black 1970). In regulatory agency work (and equally if not more so in police work) extensive discretion by the enforcement agency mediates between the rules of law and their practical significance for the regulated. One important difference between some regulatory agency work (especially that concerned with pollution control) and police work, however, is that the authority to set and interpret legal 'standards' of behaviour for the regulated (in the sense of definitions of the limits of permissible conduct) is often given explicitly to regulatory agencies in a way that is not done with the police. The orthodox justification of this is that, where regulatory agencies are concerned with the control of complex technical industrial practices, norms of appropriate business behaviour must be framed and interpreted in the light of specialised and changing technical and scientific knowledge.

Although variations in legal recognition of enforcement agency discretion are of considerable doctrinal importance, not too much should be made of these distinctions from a sociological viewpoint. Of primary importance is the necessarily very extensive discretion involved in *all* law enforcement activity. This is partly a consequence of the need for careful allocation of regulatory agency and police resources. For both kinds of agency 'full' enforcement of law is realistically an impossibility given available resources. Consequently agency policy determined in the 'higher ranks' will direct enforcement activity in certain directions rather than others.

Equally, however, the 'lower ranks' who are dealing on a daily basis with the regulated population of businesses (in the case of inspectors of regulatory agencies) or citizens (in the case of police officers) work out a *modus vivendi* in their dealings with members of this population; a set of practices and procedures based on enforcement agents' stereotypes of the regulated population and experience of practical law enforcement. We shall need to look at the nature of these stereotypes in relation to both police work and regulatory agency work. But the reason why such lower rank practices and the attitudes on which they are based are so important is that lower ranks in enforcement agencies tend to have a large measure of independence in the way they deal with cases.

While this is a characteristic of police work strongly emphasised in sociological literature, control of lower ranks within the hierarchy of regulatory agencies is likely to be easier than in police organisations (cf. Hutter 1988: 138–40). This is because of regulatory agencies' generally less clearly defined occupational culture, the less central position in the regulatory task of virtually unsupervisable field work, and usually less immediacy and urgency in enforcement action so that the progress and handling of cases can be more easily overseen. Nevertheless, studies of regulatory agencies note the significant scope for independent action by lower ranks; the emphasis on the need for decisions 'on the ground' by inspectors with first-hand knowledge of the particular case; and the ability of lower ranks to shape significantly the treatment of cases by the way their case reports are framed (Hutter 1988: 141–3; Richardson 1983: 81, 187; Cranston 1979: 80–1).

Regulatory Agencies and Their Environment

Many sociological studies of organisations emphasise that for an organisation to survive it must come to terms with the environment in which it exists, and with its own internal requirements of integration, order and motivation. Thus the aims and activities of the organisation will if necessary be adapted to ensure its survival; to neutralise or divert pressures upon it from internal and external sources. This, of course, strongly suggests a structural functionalist outlook on organisations (cf. Chapter 3, above) so that, in the manner of Parsonian social systems, they have to satisfy certain functional requisites for their survival.

There are, of course, other ways of looking at the organisational situation. In a Weberian 'action' perspective, emphasis is on the interaction of organisation members within the organisation and with outsiders, and on the ways in which patterns of interaction develop and are given meaning by those involved in them, so that the nature of the organisation and its activities is determined by these interactions rather than by the 'official' descriptions and designations of organisation goals and practices. More radical analyses stress the position of organisations within the wider power structures of society, placing less emphasis on the organisation's 'negotiation' of its position in relation to other centres of organised power and much more on its integration, as part of the extension of bureaucracy in social life, within state or other large scale power structures. From a Marxist perspective the concern is likely to be to replace a focus on bureaucratic power with a focus on the organisation of capital—the structure of primarily economic power—and on the ways in which organisations of various kinds are linked to the power of capital throughout society.

When applied to enforcement agencies (that is, both regulatory agencies and police) these various theoretical approaches emphasise different aspects of the agency's relationship with its environment. Functionalism may tend to exaggerate agency autonomy in solving its problems of existence, while Marxist approaches may suggest less independence in regulatory agencies than empirical studies seem to indicate. Approaches that stress the complexities of interaction between the agency and its environment and the ways in which attitudes and outlooks of agency personnel are shaped by experience in dealing with that environment and in interacting with the regulated population seem particularly enlightening in explaining law enforcement activity.

Relationships with the Regulated Community

Numerous studies of American regulatory agencies describe the way in which they are 'captured' by the business enterprises they purport to regulate, or are overcome by bureaucratic constraints (e.g. Bernstein 1955). Thus they may come to adopt an outlook on the law similar to that prevalent in the regulated community, or become ineffectual. Among the major reasons given are: first, that agencies recruit personnel who have gained expertise through experience in industry but have also necessarily developed strong sympathies with the outlook prevalent in the industry; secondly, industry recruits personnel from the administrative staff of agencies so agency staff are aware of potential rewards from co-operation and do not wish to alienate industry; thirdly, day-to-day contact between agency staff and businessmen leads to an assimilation of viewpoints; and fourthly, agencies often require the political support of business leaders and their political contacts to guarantee agency funding and authority. The American judge William O. Douglas once went so far as to propose that all regulatory agencies should be abolished and reconstituted every 10 years to prevent permanent industry capture (Nader 1980: 33).

Whatever the adequacy of the 'capture' analysis in the United States, there is doubt as to whether it can easily be applied to comparable regulatory agencies in Britain. Robert Baldwin's study of the British Civil Aviation Authority, a body concerned with regulating and promoting the airline industry and safeguarding consumer interests, concluded that the Authority was not dependent on the goodwill of the industry for essential data, its key personnel were not tied to the industry by career concerns or allegiance to industry policies, and there was no evidence that its decisions were influenced by fear of industry pressure (Baldwin

1985: 219–31). Comparisons of environmental regulation strategies in the United States and the United Kingdom have emphasised a more confrontational and legalistic relationship between regulators and regulated in the former as compared with the latter. As a result, it is claimed, certain mechanisms of resistance and strategies of 'capture' by the regulated are much more strongly developed in the United States, as responses to regulatory agencies' coercive methods of control (Vogel 1986). Yet 'capture' is also facilitated by the informal relationships between regulators and regulated encouraged when agencies adopt co-operative or conciliatory approaches (Ayres and Braithwaite 1991).

The situation and mode of operation of large-scale American regulatory agencies such as the Federal Trade Commission and the Securities and Exchange Commission are certainly very different from those of most British regulatory agencies. In the latter context relationships between regulators and regulated seem more a matter of compromise than of 'capture'. Analyses of American agencies have stressed a variety of factors shaping agency policy, including the ideologies of agency personnel, the legal and political mandate of the agency, the social and political organisation of regulation, and its potential economic impact (e.g. Kagan 1978: ch 4). In Britain, however, Richardson and her colleagues found that limited agency resources were seen by agency personnel as more important in promoting a policy of accommodation with the regulated community than concern about the law's effects on business interests (Richardson 1983: 97). Undoubtedly some British research does show external pressures seriously undermining law enforcement. W.G. Carson's important study of the enforcement of industrial safety legislation on North Sea oil installations paints a disturbing picture of intense political pressures to maximise oil production acting against attempts to police effectively safety arrangements on oil rigs. In addition, powerful business organisations, which because of their foreign ties were reluctant to accept British legal controls, were sometimes able to hinder enforcement activity in a direct manner, for example by making inspection of facilities extremely difficult (Carson 1981).

More typical, it seems, however, is a situation of partial accommodation between the agency and its regulated community. 'We're not on opposite sides of the fence,' remarked a British consumer agency officer in talking about food manufacturers. 'We both want the same thing—the offering of food in a proper state. That's what we want and that's what they want,' (quoted in Cranston 1979: 29). Agencies can shield business from the full force of the law by advice-giving rather than prosecution. Their activities also reinforce business respectability through the affirmation of standards. In return, agencies depend on business goodwill. Offering advice that business will accept is less costly in scarce resources than prosecution. And, as the American studies affirm, business may actually offer protection and support to regulatory agencies on the basis that worse might befall business interests without the agency's sympathetic approach to enforcement. Further, some business enterprises, particularly the larger or longer established organisations, may find the policing activities of the agency valuable in controlling competitors (cf. Cranston 1979: 29–30; Carson 1974). The entire regulatory process is seen by regulatory agencies to depend on co-operation, goodwill and mutual appreciation of problems. As the Alkali Inspectorate's chief inspector put the matter: 'Abating air pollution is a technological problem—a matter for scientists and engineers, operating in an atmosphere of co-operative officialdom. Great care has to be exercised by all to prevent the development of adversary attitudes' (quoted in Rhodes 1981: 145).

It is very difficult to find an adequate criterion of effective law enforcement. Nevertheless serious doubts can be expressed as to whether in Britain the accommodative approach leads to optimum enforcement. The Alkali Inspectorate, in particular, was subjected to the severest criticism for its lack of effective action. Public outcry or independent scientific investigation sometimes forced action to control pollution caused by particular firms even where the Alkali Inspectorate had approved the practices involved (Gunningham 1974: 67–8). Carson's (1970) study of Factory Inspectorate files between 1961 and 1966 on a sample of firms in south-east England showed 3,800 offences recorded by the Inspectorate during this period with every firm having at least one violation recorded against it. Nevertheless only 1.5 per cent of enforcement decisions taken were for prosecution, and prosecution was very rare even for firms offending several times. All firms prosecuted pleaded guilty and received fines averaging £50. The Inspectorate's major response in the remaining cases was to write a letter indicating what was wrong with the firm's conduct and how it might be improved. As regards consumer agencies, Cranston (1979: 174) argues that they and the law they enforce have an effect on business but 'many breaches of consumer law pass undetected, and even when detected often continue because sufficiently vigorous action is not taken.'

Reasons for Policies of Accommodation

What explains the policy of accommodation which is so clearly revealed in virtually all studies of regulatory agencies? Six factors, at least, seem of major significance. First is the general inadequacy of agency resources to confront the problem of business regulation, particularly where control depends upon costly research and testing (Cranston 1979: 75, 109; Richardson 1983: 105–6) or where attempts are made to control large business organisations which can often call upon considerable resources to defend themselves against any threats to their operations.

This difficulty in proceeding against the biggest firms partly explains why the 'history of corporate legislation enforcement is a history of penalizing the small fish whilst letting the big ones escape' (Box 1983: 74). Several North American studies show both the relative leniency with which law breaking by large firms is treated and the relatively more serious character of their law breaking (e.g. Clinard and Yeager 1980; Goff and Reasons 1978). In Britain Cranston found that consumer agency legal proceedings against large business firms were sometimes discontinued by agencies when a firm had the resources to contest the proceedings effectively and showed it was determined to do so (1979: 125–6). The problem of imbalance of power and resources becomes painfully obvious when multinational corporations are involved (e.g. Carson 1981), so that whole operations can be moved from one country to another partly to avoid burdensome legal controls. In these circumstances rigorous law enforcement may entail economic consequences far beyond anything a particular enforcement agency can countenance.

Secondly, available sanctions against law breaking are usually highly inadequate (Hutter 1988: 71–2, 75–80; Richardson 1983: 142–3; Cranston 1979: 45–6). Fines may often be sufficiently low to constitute mere licence fees for illegal conduct. Studies of crime in business environments have long drawn attention to the tendency to deal with law breaking through civil proceedings or administrative sanctions rather than criminal prosecution. The standard justification of the situation is that the stigma of being subjected to the legal process as a law breaker is a powerful sanction for middle-class business executives with reputations and social and business contacts to maintain. Severe criminal sanctions are therefore unnecessary. The justificatory argument is unconvincing, however. The tendency to decriminalise such conduct lessens stigma. Further, there is no substantial evidence that significant stigma arises from conviction for offences in the business environment in the way that it may arise in relation to other crime. On the contrary, there is even some evidence that offenders prosper (Box 1983: 52–3).

Thirdly, the often insecure basis of agency authority tends to encourage agencies to adopt accommodatory policies. As has been noted earlier, agencies may need the support of business to protect themselves from political pressures, as well as to maintain an image of effectiveness despite the limited resources available to them to pursue uncompromising enforcement activity. In the United States, many studies trace the complex interconnections of business and political influence. David Serber's study of the Policy Services Bureau of the California Department of Insurance describes a low status agency subject to powerful control by political superiors who have, themselves, strong informal ties with the regulated insurance industry. In such circumstances the agency's capacity to conduct formal investigations is reduced by political pressure and a policy of co-operation with business is seen as the only means by which the agency can operate (Serber 1980).

Fourthly, agency personnel often complain of a lack of support and understanding from the courts: of the inadequacy of fines imposed; and of the courts' lack of appreciation of practical problems of enforcement and of the realities of the business world (Hutter 1988: 72–4; Cranston 1979: 46–9). In such circumstances it is unsurprising that they should favour policies of accommodation and seek to avoid adversarial situations which may be resolvable only by prosecution.

Fifthly, lack of clear, unequivocal public support for regulatory agencies' work encourages caution and a co-operative approach (e.g. Hutter 1988: 184–6). In an important essay on business crime Vilhelm Aubert suggested that lack of strong public support for business regulation reflects citizens' difficulty in appreciating the complexity of the issues involved. A public outcry at, for example, a breach of price control regulations is unlikely until there is a general 'acceptance of relatively complicated means-ends hypotheses from modern economic science' (Aubert 1952: 266). There are considerable difficulties in achieving full recognition that breaches of factory safety regulations, or failure to meet product specifications (for example, in car manufacture) may be potentially far more harmful than many forms of 'ordinary' crime. Nevertheless, evidence suggests that public attitudes to offences in business contexts are changing. In Britain, trade union concern with factory safety law enforcement has increased significantly since the 1960s, as has general public pressure for more adequate environmental protection; and, in recent decades, 'consumer consciousness' has developed in many forms. It is claimed that research in the United States has shown a significant raising of the public rating of the seriousness of corporate crime (Box 1983: 65–6).

Finally, accommodatory agency policies are encouraged by the complexity of the circumstances in which regulatory and other business offences occur. Often a fine line exists between observance and breach of the law. The inevitability of change in technological and business circumstances has to be taken into account in regulatory law through a degree of flexibility in legal provisions (cf. Richardson 1983: 22–3; Hutter 1988: 60–1). Thus while some regulation is highly particularised it is usually paralleled by discretionary regulation (cf. Chapter 5) allowing adaptation in law enforcement and administration to changing circumstances. Often considerable difficulties may exist in determining issues of causation, of allocation of responsibility, and of culpability. These factors make law enforcement a matter often attended by uncertainty or debate and again encourage strategies of negotiation and agreement with the regulated.

Regulation and 'Real Crime'

What significance do the circumstances discussed in the previous sections have for sociological analysis of law? First, they help to define what law means in business practice, because as many writers stress, the existence of extensive agency discretion in law enforcement, coupled with the authority that many agencies have to establish regulatory standards, creates a situation in which enforcement practice determines the *effective meaning* of law for the regulated. Thus, where matters are not brought before courts it is enforcement agency personnel and not judges who settle the shared understandings that constitute actual regulation (Cranston 1979: 44–5). In this situation state law encounters and interacts with what, following Ehrlich, we might call the living law of business communities. Enforcement practice represents an accommodation between different normative systems.

Secondly, legal ideology itself is influenced by these situations of enforcement and the social, economic and political conditions they reflect. Regulatory agencies rationalise their relations with business through a particular view of law and crime which takes account of particular problems of law enforcement in the business field. This view treats offences by business executives and business firms as *different in nature* from other criminal offences, despite the general requirement of modern Western legal doctrine that criminal acts not be defined by reference to different economic statuses of actors. Thus regulatory offences and other business crimes tend to be distinguished from what is seen as 'real crime' such as murder, theft or other criminal offences committed in non-business contexts. Regulatory offences are considered in some respects less serious and less deserving of moral stigma than 'real crime'.

The stereotypes that agency personnel have of business firms and business executives (Hawkins 1984: ch 6; Richardson 1983: 124–6; Cranston: 1979: 32–9) reinforce the distinction between regulatory offences and 'real crime' and its relevance in justifying agency policies. Most business people are seen as law-abiding and respectable, though occasionally requiring advice and guidance (Hutter 1988: 61–6). Some are recognised as having strong, honestly held views on proper business conduct. A tiny minority is seen as 'black sheep', 'amoral calculators', 'unscrupulous', 'rogues' or 'cowboys'. Only these are likely to be considered 'real' criminals or potential ones. As we shall see, this favourable view of the regulated community contrasts sharply with the strongly negative view that police tend to take of the community they regulate. Further, as with the opposite police view, the regulatory agency view of the regulated is extremely resistant to change. To some extent it influences the kind of investigatory action that agencies take, with strong emphasis on a small minority of 'rotten apple' businesses and sometimes a lack of attention to more widespread and widely accepted but questionable practices (cf. Cranston 1979: 33). The different stereotypes of the regulated that police have justify for them, and encourage, a far more assertive, watchful, suspicious and crisis conscious approach to their tasks.

While the 'real crime' idea is important to regulatory agencies as a rationalisation and guide for conduct it is by no means confined to them. Indeed it is a part of legal ideology accepted by citizens and supported by the pronouncements of judges,[8] despite being inconsistent with legal doctrine, which does not make a general distinction of this nature between types of offences. In fact it derives from a complex interaction of social and economic circumstances focusing on law enforcement rather than on doctrinal interpretation. What lies behind the 'real crime' concept is a complex amalgam of perceptions and beliefs. Part of its basis, however, is a reluctance to put 'respectable citizens', found guilty of offences committed while engaged in socially useful pursuits, in the same category as the 'criminal classes'. Regulatory offences are often thought of as offences of inadvertence rather than wilful wrongdoing. Undoubtedly many of these are offences of strict liability because of the difficulties involved in proving intention or assigning blame. However, the exclusion of other offences from 'real crime' does not entirely depend on absence of individual culpability, for many road traffic offences involving intentional action or negligence by the offender and considerable risk of harm to others are similarly treated as not 'normal crimes' in the view of many people (Elliott and Street 1968: ch 5; Ross 1960). Equally, many breaches of anti-pollution legislation that are treated as regulatory offences are the result of deliberate policy by a firm's management on discharge of industrial waste.

Neither is a concept of *mala in se* (action intrinsically wrong rather than merely prohibited) useful in distinguishing real crime, for this merely begs the question of what criteria make some actions intrinsically wrong, and, for example, why the deliberate or reckless selling of bad foodstuffs with the attendant risk of serious harm to consumers is not obviously 'intrinsically wrongful'. Perhaps we come closer to an answer when we note that 'real crime' tends to be crime committed by identifiable individuals against other identifiable individuals. Harm caused to the public at large (for example, through tax evasion) or harm caused by remote corporate enterprises rather than particular identifiable human offenders seems to be more difficult to accept as normal crime. But these characteristics may be merely an expression of a deeper basis on which

8 See e.g. *Sherras v De Rutzen* [1895] 1 QB 918 at 922, per Wright J (acts 'not criminal in any real sense, but ... which in the public interest are prohibited under a penalty'); *Alphacell v Woodward* [1972] AC 824.

moral judgments are made. After all, the fact that harm is caused not to individuals but to society as a whole by fraudulent obtaining of social security benefits does not prevent this behaviour being generally fiercely condemned. Durkheim's notion that crime is to be defined by reference to the *conscience collective* (Chapter 3)—as an expression of moral sentiment binding society together—founders, as we have seen (Chapter 4), on the impossibility of identifying the scope of any such consensus. What exist instead are important currents of ideas that justify the existing social order and portray it as natural. The popular conception of crime represents, above all, an accommodation to the fact of actual inequalities of power and influence of different sections of the population.

The primary importance of studies of regulatory agencies for the sociological understanding of law is to emphasise that practices and strategies of law enforcement necessarily take account of distributions of power and influence in society that are excluded from explicit recognition in legal doctrine. In addition, those conditions exert a 'feedback' influence on legal ideas (most clearly through the notion of 'real crime'), introducing subtle modifications in thought which help to avoid the contradictions that can arise when legal doctrine is confronted with the social conditions it is supposed to regulate.

Police and Law

We must turn now from regulatory agency law enforcement to consider the law enforcement work of police. Police constitute one particularly important kind of enforcement agency, that which is typically most visible to citizens, has the largest personnel[9] and is entrusted with the most general range of criminal law enforcement. Like regulatory agencies, police forces are faced with internal problems of organisation and motivation, and external problems of adaptation to the environment in which they exist. To continue to function they must protect the social and political bases of their authority and the flow of resources upon which they depend. To do this they must demonstrate an adequate degree of success in the tasks allotted to or assumed by them. These tasks constitute police work. Like members of any other occupational group police seek to shape or interpret the work they do in ways that make it personally satisfying. In addition, as organisations, police forces seek to define their tasks in ways that emphasise the vital necessity of police work to society and the unique qualifications of police to perform that work.

9 In England and Wales there are approximately 126,000 regular police. Rhodes (1981: 234ff) calculated that, at the time of his study, there were some 18,000 enforcement or efficiency inspectors attached to more than 40 British regulatory agencies.

Numerous studies of police work now exist. Our concern here, as in considering regulatory agencies, is with the relationship between enforcement activities and law thought of as institutionalised legal doctrine. So we need to examine aspects of police work that parallel the features of regulatory agency work already considered, and to note some important general contrasts between these forms of enforcement agency. This section will sketch the nature of police commitments to law. Subsequent sections will attempt to summarise the major factors that influence these commitments.

Law and Order

Studies of police show that, strictly speaking and contrary to general belief, police objectives are not primarily those of law enforcement. Historically, modern police emerged as a force for maintaining peace and social order. They were seen as in competition with other order maintaining forces such as the military services (Gleizal 1985: 30–6; Manning 1977: 90–1). In eighteenth-century Europe police forces 'were above all a weapon wielded in the defense of governments in power and, thus, essentially a weapon of political control' (Bittner 1975: ix). The importation into England from France of the word 'police' at the beginning of the eighteenth century carried with it the primary associations of surveillance and control of citizenry. However, the legitimacy of modern police as a permanent agency entitled to use force to control the civil population depended on police acting within the constraints laid down by law (Gleizal 1981: 369–79).

Thus the central focus of police work has always been the maintenance of social order (Brogden 1982) but its modern legitimacy depends upon law. Enforcement of law constitutes a means to the end of order maintenance, rather than an end in itself (Skolnick 1975: ch 1). Even this may, however, be overstressing the importance of law for police work. Peter Manning (1977: 41) argues that 'the legitimation of the police in terms of legal authority flows from the power of the state and citizens' deference to it rather than from the law as an independent entity'. He writes that a preliminary definition of policing must be 'analytically separated' from law and that the legal basis of policing in Anglo-American societies is not essential to its nature and is 'only occasionally related to the police function' (1977: 39). As we noted when considering lawyers' attitudes to law and order in Chapter 6, the concepts of law and order are not necessarily mutually supportive as they are so often assumed to be in political rhetoric (Skolnick 1975: 7–8). Commitment to law (legal order) may be antagonistic to the maintenance of certain kinds of social order (for example, order based on arbitrary or unpredictable use of power). Conversely a commitment to maintenance of order in society and the control of disturbances may give rise to impatience with legal niceties that seem to stand in the way of effective control.

Police Discretion

This somewhat tangential relationship between police and iaw is reflected in many aspects of police work and police attitudes. The working legal knowledge of police is likely to be restricted to the law governing those situations they routinely police (Manning 1977: 113–14). This is hardly surprising in view of the complexity of the law and rapid changes in it, but it highlights the point that while lawyers and judges are analysing rules, the police task is to make immediate decisions on action whatever the complexity of legal issues.

Discretion in deciding how to enforce the law, or indeed whether to do so in particular cases, is a necessarily fundamental aspect of police work (Klockars 1985: ch 5; Skolnick 1975: ch 4). Police lack the resources even to attempt 'full' law enforcement. Decisions on allocation of resources have to be made within the police organisation; and decisions must be made every day by police on patrol as to whether and how to intervene in the situations that they encounter. Equally these decisions about enforcement reflect the primary police commitment to maintenance of order. They involve a recognition that optimal strategies for peace keeping or order maintenance are *incompatible* with an attempt to enforce the law rigorously on every occasion. In a study of arrest practices, Donald Black (1971: 1106) concluded that police 'are lenient in their routine arrest practices, they use their arrest power less often than the law would allow' and that the probability of arrest increased with the seriousness of the offence, the strength of evidence available to the police officer, the relational distance between complainant and suspect, and disrespectful behaviour by the suspect to police.

Discretion in law enforcement gives police, like regulatory agency personnel, considerable scope to draw upon their own image of the regulated population in making enforcement decisions. The views that police have of various sections of the population are highly relevant in understanding how law is enforced. And, just as regulatory agency policy determines the practical meaning of law for most purposes, so, because 'the application of the law depends to a large extent on the definition of the situation and the decision reached by the patrolman, he, in effect, makes the law; it is his decision that establishes the boundary between legal and illegal' (Niederhoffer 1967: 60–1), except in those numerically rare cases where the police exercise of discretion—the decision to act or not to act—is challenged in a court.

Further, police discretion influences the recording of crime and its consequent presentation as criminal statistics (Black 1970). In situations where the initiative for enforcement lies with the police this is clear. Most police law enforcement activity arises, however, from citizens' action in bringing a matter to police attention (Black 1970; 1971; 1972). In such cases discretion may arise in deciding whether to treat an occurrence as a crime, in deciding what criminal charges are relevant, in deciding which offence, if any, the suspect is to be charged with, and in deciding whether to bargain with the suspect over charges (Manning 1977: 131).

Police sometimes seek to 'correct' the legal position. Wayne La Fave's American study of police arrest practices showed that because the police he studied did not consider laws governing prostitution were adequate they used harassment strategies of arrest without intention to prosecute to achieve the kind of control of the situation they considered necessary, despite the legal position (La Fave 1965). Similarly use of violence beyond what is legally permissible is sometimes justified by police as a means of punishing disrespect shown to them, obtaining information (Morgan 1990: ch 12), showing police power (cf. Waddington 1991: ch 6) or controlling hardened criminals (cf. Westley 1970; Smith and Gray 1983: 87–90). Jerome Skolnick concluded from his observations of an American city force that 'norms located within police organisation are more powerful than court decisions in shaping police behaviour, and that actually the process of interaction between the two accounts ultimately for how police behave' (Skolnick 1975: 219).

This observation in an American context has been confirmed by Simon Holdaway's (1983) account of work in a British police force in which he served as a sergeant. Holdaway sees the occupational culture of lower rank policemen as central in defining what counts as proper behaviour in the job for them. Law is only one of the influences on this occupational culture which is shaped by the environment of police work and the nature of the police organisation. He quotes a senior officer: 'There are two important things about police work. First, policemen must be willing to cut corners or else they would never get their job done. Secondly, it's because policemen have been happy to gild the lily that the law has been administered in this country' (1983: 8). In this context cutting corners means dispensing with some legal formalities; 'gilding the lily' is a well-known euphemism for 'adjustments, refinements and corrections' made to evidence to render the suspect's guilt more obvious before a court (Holdaway 1983: 113; Smith and Gray 1983: 224–30).

Pressures Towards Legality and Illegality

In extreme cases, as Holdaway describes, refining evidence can extend to 'verballing'. The use of 'verbals' in evidence before a court is plainly illegal, because a verbal is 'an oral statement of admission or incrimination which is invented by the arresting or interviewing officer and attributed to a suspect' (Holdaway 1983: 108). In discussing verballing, Holdaway is at pains to point out that 'the costs of being found out are very considerable' and that in his sub-division, which he calls Hilton, 'many officers—indeed most—do not entertain its use ... The number of officers who might verbal a suspect is impossible to assess; it is difficult to separate attitudes expressed in conversation from action, rumour from fact. Nevertheless, verballing remains acceptable for some, and despite a firm and general unwillingness to "fit people up" with evidence, the structure of the work group as a team and the values of trust and secrecy [within it] combine to provide a setting in which it is possible for an officer to verbal' (Holdaway 1983: 118, 119). What is most important, in this context, is Holdaway's presentation of clear evidence from numerous statements of police officers that police culture treats verballing as justifiable in certain circumstances.

The Policy Studies Institute's report on the London Metropolitan Police concluded at the beginning of the 1980s that 'outright fabrication of evidence is probably rare ... our findings strongly suggest that departure[s] from rules and procedure affecting evidence are far more common than outright fabrication and have a far more significant effect on the quality of the evidence that goes before the courts' (Smith and Gray 1983: 229). This may still be the situation but the quashing on appeal in recent years of a string of convictions in Britain founded on police evidence shown to be unreliable has demonstrated in a most public and dramatic manner instances of what have been, at the very least, highly suspect or irregular police practices. General procedures for tape recording of police interviews with suspects at police stations were introduced by the Police and Criminal Evidence Act 1984. These and other reforms have undoubtedly affected police practice, but it is too early to say how far they have removed or curtailed pressures towards the production and presentation of false, misleading or oppressively obtained evidence (see Willis et al. 1988; Morgan 1990: ch 14; cf. Smith and Gray 1983: 229).

Nevertheless, police in contemporary Western societies clearly see themselves, and are seen, as centrally concerned with upholding the law. Thus a distinction is drawn between what police view as petty, technical or misconceived legal rules which are considered to obstruct police work, and other law, especially that defining crimes and requirements of public order, which provides basic legitimacy for police action in maintaining social order and which, in this respect, is central to police work (cf. Skolnick 1975: 197). Further, pressures for police professionalisation depend on reinforcing police legitimacy and authority and so tend to encourage emphasis, particularly from higher ranks, on police commitment to the rule of law.

The point of referring to police ambivalence towards law is not to denigrate police work. '[O]rder, legality and justice ... are ambiguous terms in any social system. But what philosophers, social scientists, and lawyers have argued over for centuries, the police must do every day' (Reiss and Bordua 1967: 33). The point is that police attitudes to law reflect a number of the dilemmas of policing, especially for the lower ranks. Law enforcement and peace keeping are two distinct tasks. While the first is reasonably definable in scope, the second is not. It does not indicate clear limits for police concerns (Bittner 1967). Thus the police must continually define and redefine 'order' in relation to everyday situations and reconcile their practical definitions of order, forged in experience, with their legal powers. Apparent tolerance of verballing reflects different views of law and legal processes as between police and courts, and frequent feelings of frustration on the part of the police at what they see as the inadequacies of the law and of judicial processes (Westley 1970: 76–86). In their view these sometimes, perhaps often, allow known criminals to escape punishment. 'He's as guilty as sin, so why not fit him up? He's a dangerous, violent animal', one London detective constable remarked of a notorious local criminal (Smith and Gray 1983: 225; cf. Holdaway 1983: 112–13).

Just as regulatory agency officials often criticise what they see as courts' lack of understanding and sympathy with their difficulties, so do police probably to a much greater extent (cf. Skolnick 1975: chs 9 and 10). Police resent what they see as lawyers' tricks and legal technicalities hindering them from doing their job, which they define primarily as fighting crime. Their occupational commitments are typically different from those of lawyers or judges. A 'jurisdictional conflict'—that is, a conflict between professional claims to define problems and the means of their solution—exists between police and those who must legally evaluate their conduct (Reiss 1971: 125–8).

Thus, it has to be recognised that many of the everyday breaches of law that occur in police work are not the result of bad policing by bad policemen.[10] They are encouraged as part of ordinary 'good' policing by organisational demands, police occupational culture, and the primary police commitment to order. In short they are built into the job as it is presently defined by police organisation and culture.

10 Police corruption, which is the subject of numerous studies (e.g. Punch 1985), is a different matter. It involves acceptance by policemen of personal rewards for action they are required to undertake anyway as part of their job, or for ignoring or tolerating actions they are required as police to prevent. Thus law is betrayed in the interest of personal profit (Reiss 1971: 169), rather than subordinated to what are seen as the legitimate order-maintenance aims of police work. On corruption in regulatory agency practice see e.g. Ayres and Braithwaite 1991.

Police Work and Police Organisation

How far does police organisation determine the nature of police law enforcement? Police literature emphasises the strongly hierarchical, apparently quasi-military style of police organisation. 'In principle and in rhetoric, a police organisation is one characterized by strict subordination, by a rigid chain of command and, more doubtfully, by a lack of formal provision for consultation between ranks' (Reiss and Bordua 1967: 48). Sociological studies highlight its bureaucratic character (Chatterton 1989; Gleizal 1985: 64–5; Cain 1973: 169–70; Niederhoffer 1967: 11ff). The official aims of police organisations are clearly set by the higher ranks. The orientation and methods of police organisation may vary considerably, depending on the attitudes and policies of particular chief and senior police officers. Thus, in the United States, James Q. Wilson has distinguished three styles of policing associated with different kinds of police organisation. These are 'watchman style' (oriented to maintenance of the existing social and political order of the locality), 'legalistic' (oriented to law enforcement as such) and 'service style' (oriented to serving the respectable population of the locality). While the last mentioned is seen as characteristic of suburban policing, the other two are associated with urban police organisations (Wilson 1968). Among the general aims of police organisation, however, is the enhancement of police status and influence in society; an objective which depends ultimately—as for all occupations—on professionalisation.

Professionalisation can be considered as an occupational group's successful claim, based on the assertion of special knowledge or skills and effective self-regulation in the public interest, to a degree of monopolisation of practice in a particular field (see Chapter 6). For the police, professionalisation depends upon the claim to expertise and efficiency in order-maintaining tasks and specifically in crime fighting; that is, the maintenance of social order as defined by the criminal law. The then Commissioner of the London Metropolitan Police Force declared in 1977, 'I suppose you could sum it all up by saying that in Britain certainly, and I have no doubt elsewhere, the time has come when the police are abandoning their artisan status and are achieving, by our ever-increasing variety of services, our integrity, our accountability and our dedication to the public good, a status not less admirable than that of the most learned and distinguished professions' (Mark 1977: 42). Professional status provides a justification for self-regulation rather than external control, and for the claim of the police to be heard in political debate, including especially debate on changes in the law they enforce. In this way the police commitment to order through enforcement of law 'feeds back' into demands to reshape law in the service of order.

Professionalisation stresses police commitment to the rule of law as the basis of police authority. At the same time it tends to encourage the isolation of the police in society. It emphasises the unique expertise of the police in combating crime. As expertise is stressed so accountability to and reliance upon citizens seems less important. The maintenance of order becomes a task for experts. To some extent, then, developments in police organisation have meshed with the evolution of more authoritarian and centralised state control in Western societies (Gleizal 1981: 377). The development of increasingly sophisticated police technology for surveillance and control is both an expression of increasing police professionalisation and autonomy, and a reflection of contemporary state demands for guarantees of social order.

The countercurrent towards 'community policing' (Schaffer 1980; Horton and Smith 1988: ch 7)—the attempt to take police back into the community and to foster liaison between police and social services, schools and community organisations—is not inconsistent with professionalisation and the police demand for autonomy from external control. It reflects well-grounded fears about the capacity of police to fight crime without information and support from citizens. In addition it represents an attempt to put police relationships with local communities on a specific professional basis. Thus, on one view of police professionalisation, police are to be seen as 'social diagnosticians. Their role is to recognise social crises or their incipient causes and to activate other social agencies where expertise is needed' (Alderson 1973: 45). But much controversy and diversity of views exists in the most senior ranks of police as to how the varied components of the police role are to be presented in terms of an integrated police 'philosophy' (Reiner 1991: ch 6).

Two points need to be made about everyday police work in relation to these aspirations to professionalisation based on expert practice. First, police efficiency, like regulatory agencies' efficiency in law enforcement, is extremely difficult to measure (cf. Horton and Smith 1988: ch 2). What criteria are appropriate? Undoubtedly arrests are taken, within the police organisation, to be a major criterion of competence and effort in police work. Some arrests—for example, for drunkenness, gross indecency or football violence—are easily made and serve to boost a policeman's efficiency record (Holdaway 1983: 59–61, 83). However, perhaps because they represent little real challenge they may be regarded as unsatisfactory (Smith and Gray 1983: 61ff). 'However, a "crime arrest" is interpreted as *the* act that keeps chaos at bay, a view fuelled by the centrality of the figures for arrest and charge, the major measure of police performance' (Holdaway 1983: 83; Smith and Gray 1983: 56–61).

This is a disturbingly artificial and arbitrary test of success, yet organisational structure demands some 'objective' means of assessing the work of law enforcement agents. For regulatory agency personnel, the test tends to be the amount of paperwork completed and the extent of energetic co-operative dealings with business (Richardson 1983: 185) or the number of inspections and the amount of plant inspected (Cranston 1979: 78). Measures of success tend to detach themselves from the main directions of law enforcement work, since so much that is important about it is impossible to quantify. Nevertheless these kinds of criteria, dictated by organisational imperatives, exert strong influence on the way law enforcement is carried out. For example, although walking the beat has the advantage of lessening the distance between police and community and may have very considerable intelligence advantages for the police, the use of cars is favoured partly because it allows the police to get more work; to find more incidents that will give rise to specifically recordable police action, especially arrests (Holdaway 1983: 135).

Secondly, the claim to special police expertise is undermined by the sheer range and diversity of tasks that police are required to undertake. Many studies emphasise that crime related work constitutes a minor part of police activity. Police resources are used in crime control, but equally in settling quarrels, dispersing or controlling crowds, rescuing children, transporting elderly people, quietening noisy neighbours, saving a person from drowning, supervising the transfer of a mental patient and many other tasks (Morgan 1990: ch 1; Shapland and Vagg 1988: 35–40). Maureen Cain's British study found an amazing variety of tasks assumed by rural police. Yet urban police had a lower proportion of actual crime work in their daily routine, despite the relative triviality of crimes in the rural context, since rural police had more control over and involvement in criminal investigations than did ordinary police officers in the urban context (Cain 1973: ch 2, 71). Brian Morgan's recent research on police work in a division of the Devon and Cornwall Constabulary suggests a similar picture: 35 per cent of a total of 20,469 matters dealt with by police over a 12 month period were related to ordinary crime (excluding traffic offences); 33 per cent were of a 'service' nature (relating, for example, to lost or found property, fire or flood accidents, straying animals, death or illness, among numerous other categories); 18 per cent concerned maintenance of public order and 14 per cent were traffic-related matters (Morgan 1990: 4–6).

Despite this situation, police define crime control as the heart of policing; the central area of their expertise (e.g. Shapland and Vagg 1988: 156–7). Yet even in this area the claim to professional control of specialised expert practice is problematic. Manning writes without qualification: 'there is ample evidence that the police have little if any effect on the amount of crime present in any society ... they cannot control crime' (Manning 1977: 19). The implication is that social conditions, not police activity, determine crime levels. The effect of various policing styles in deterring serious crime remains controversial (cf. Sampson and Cohen 1988) but there is little evidence that traffic stops and police action taken against traffic offenders have significant long-term effects on accident rates or driving practices although dramatic short-term effects of law enforcement drives have been recorded (Ross 1984). Neither is it easy to stress crime detection as the pre-eminent test of success. Most crimes remain unsolved. Most cases involving arrest are 'solved' in the sense that the person responsible is known to the complainant or the police at the time the matter comes to police attention; and a large proportion of other crimes solved by arrest is made up of previously unsolved crimes to which an arrested person confesses having been arrested for a different offence (Reiner 1985: 121–2).

Against general influences on police work handed down 'from above'—from the managerial strategies and policy formulations of higher ranks of police organisations—must be set the powerful influences 'from below'; from the rank and file officers. Sociological studies of police emphasise that despite the appearance of strong hierarchical control in police organisations, lower ranks have considerable autonomy in day-to-day work (Morgan 1990: ch 7; Gleizal 1985: ch 4; Holdaway 1983). The major part of this work is by its nature almost unsupervisable; hence the importance of on-the-spot discretion, as well as the enduring problem of achieving efficient management control in police organisations (cf. Horton and Smith 1988). It is in the lower ranks that what can be called police culture is nurtured. It provides the basis of solidarity and informs the exercise of discretion by rank and file police officers. Thus it provides a very important key to the understanding of law enforcement practices.

Police Culture

While the occupational culture of police as described in Anglo-American literature is complex and multifaceted, its major components bearing on attitudes to law enforcement can be briefly sketched. Numerous American studies describe the police's image of society and especially of the regulated locality—the world seen from the police station or patrol car—as that of an environment hostile to them and always on the verge of chaos (Westley 1970: ch 3; Wilson 1968). Holdaway's study of British urban police strongly emphasises this police view. The image of the 'thin blue line' of police ranged against forces of disintegration in society is a police self-image. 'Hilton's police perceive space, place and the local population as part of a world potentially erupting into disorder. No sense of conspiracy lies behind this view; Hilton simply remains on the brink of inevitable chaos, and the police save it from sliding over the edge'

(Holdaway 1983: 37, 44–6). Comparable views of society's moral disintegration or decline are common also in the highest police ranks (Reiner 1991: 140, 169, 194–200). On the other hand, although Cain found that the image of a hostile public was held by the urban British police she studied, rural police did not share it but they often sought to distance themselves from what they saw as a claustrophobic and demanding community environment (1973: 104).

The police image of themselves as a front line force against disorder in a society often naive, ungrateful or mendacious (Manning 1977: 117) reinforces both secretiveness and intense solidarity in police organisations. Much police work is tedious and unexciting, but police culture exaggerates the elements of excitement—fights, car chases, situations of danger—treating these as central elements of the job (e.g. Smith and Gray 1983: 51–6). In this way definitions of what is important or worthwhile in police work are reinforced in the occupational culture. Similarly the 'outside world' is interpreted in terms of stereotypes of sections of the population which reflect collective experience, attitudes continually expressed among and influencing lower ranks, and collective myths (cf. Manning 1977: 35) reinforced in jokes and conversation. In particular, sections of society are categorised in terms of their assumed attitude to the police or the threat they are seen to pose to order (e.g. Reiner 1985: 94–7). Lawyers tend to be viewed with suspicion for reasons that have been discussed earlier (Holdaway 1983: 72–4). So, it seems, are businessmen. Police tend to be wary of the special favours that may be asked of them by such people (Westley 1970: 70–2); for example, where attempts are made to enlist active police help in industrial conflicts (e.g. Kahn et al. 1983: 95–6). Criminals, too, are seen in distinct categories in terms of police culture.

Police attitudes to socio-economic position tend to be complex. The distinction between 'respectable people' and others which the Policy Studies Institute's report on the London Metropolitan Police found to be widely accepted within the force does not correlate directly with commonly used class labels (Smith and Gray 1983: 162ff). Police officers themselves tend to be of upper-working-class or lower-middle-class origin. They typically distinguish between so-called 'slag' and respectable working-class people, and between 'the vulgar, flashy or newly-rich' and the 'solid middle class' or the 'real aristocracy'. 'Slag' refers to people who lead disorganised or unconventional lives and are therefore thought to be likely to be involved in crime. Commonly accepted social class indicators such as occupation, education and accent help to determine whether a person is so labelled by police but 'people who are dependent on drugs, people living in communes or squats, people with extreme or unusual political views and (possibly) people with unusual sexual habits may all be regarded as "slag"' (Smith and Gray 1983: 163, 164).

Research indicates that in making judgments about these and numerous other elements within the population, police invoke absolutist moral attitudes. They tend to presuppose that the values they adopt express a natural consensus of society shared by all decent citizens; only deviants of one kind or another do not accept these values. Similarly they see themselves as serving in a politically neutral way ('delivering a uniform product') a state that, on the whole, neutrally serves all citizens (Reiner 1991: 210; Manning 1977: 102, 112). In this way policing, like at least some forms of regulatory agency practice, tends to reflect strong values deeply rooted in the occupational culture of lower ranks (cf. Hutter 1988: 117–20).

Police and Race Relations

No aspect of police outlook has received as much attention in Anglo-American literature as attitudes to race and to particular minority ethnic groups. There is now abundant evidence of the widespread expression of very strong racial prejudice among police in Britain (Smith and Gray 1983: ch 4: Holdaway 1983: 66–71; Gordon 1983). In the United States racial prejudice among police has been explicitly recognised as a problem for much longer (e.g. Kephart 1957; Bayley and Mendelsohn 1969). Some studies have suggested that the extent of this prejudice may be not appreciably greater than that in the section of the population from which the police are drawn (Bayley and Mendelsohn 1969: 144ff). Equally it has been suggested in American studies that there is no evidence that police racial prejudice is responsible for differential arrest rates as between blacks and whites (Black and Reiss 1970; Lundman et al. 1978). It is argued that since police exercise of discretion in arrest is strongly affected by the 'respectfulness' of the suspect, blacks are arrested more often because they appear to show the police less respect (Black 1971). Again, studies of police misconduct in the United States, particularly with regard to excessive use of force, suggest that while socio-economic class has a significant bearing on the matter 'race is not an issue' (Reiss 1971: 144–56).

It seems clear, however, at least from British studies, that police experience with minorities cannot fully explain racialist attitudes that are strongly reinforced in the occupational culture, and often expressed in extreme form. Rather these attitudes inform the way situations involving members of racial or ethnic minorities are interpreted by police. The determinants of attitudes are undoubtedly very complex. However, racialism together with a strong attraction towards 'order' as a fundamental value, forms part of the detailed characterisation, in a famous study by Theodor Adorno and his colleagues (Adorno et al. 1950), of what they term the 'authoritarian personality'. This characterisation has been used in analysis of the culture of American police (Niederhoffer 1967: ch 5).

The implication that can be drawn from this kind of analysis is that racialist attitudes may form part of a broader and relatively integrated outlook sympathetic to or encouraged by the occupational emphasis on order.

Although most studies are cautious in claiming that racial attitudes influence actual police behaviour, it seems hard to imagine that, given the scope of police discretion, this is never the case (cf. Jefferson 1988; Piliavin and Briar 1964). The Metropolitan Police study, which extensively documents the expression of racialist attitudes within the police, concludes that 'we are fairly confident that there is no widespread tendency for black or Asian people to be given greatly inferior treatment by the police'. However the statement is qualified in six ways. First, blacks are much more likely to be stopped by police than are whites and there are strong indications that this situation influences the attitudes of blacks to police; secondly, police strongly associate crime with blacks (cf. Bayley and Mendelsohn 1969: 195); thirdly, police are sometimes reluctant to act energetically to assist Asians because they see them as a 'closed community'; fourthly (echoing American research), police differential treatment of minority groups is usually attributable to causes other than racialism; fifthly, where large numbers of black people are in confrontation with police (as in the 1981 Brixton riots in London) the ethnic factor will be a focus for police hostility; and, finally, for some police officers racial prejudice may indeed be the chief reason for bad behaviour on some occasions (Smith and Gray 1983: 128–29).

Enforcement and Law

It seems clear that the occupational outlook of police, like that of regulatory agency personnel, has an important bearing on the way law is enforced. But we must conclude this chapter with a stronger claim than that. Because of the existence of enforcement discretion, and sometimes of legally authorised discretion in setting standards for compliance with law (as in the case of some regulatory agencies), enforcement practice actually determines the effective content and meaning of law for many practical purposes within the regulated population. Similarly the results of serious attempts by citizens or organisations to invoke law may indicate for them the effective meaning and content of the law they have attempted to use. Thus, to the picture which has been created in previous chapters of mechanisms by which legal doctrine and legal ideology are produced and disseminated, a further important element must be added. Enforcement and invocation are also part of these mechanisms. The decision to enforce, or to invoke law, and the manner in which that decision is carried into effect, mark the point of impact of state law as a normative order on the numerous other normative orders (systems of 'living law' in Ehrlich's sense) that exist in contemporary Western societies.

The experience of law enforcement and of law invocation feeds into citizens' perceptions of law. Further, as in the case of the distinction between 'real crime' and regulatory offences, the socio-economic conditions affecting enforcement and invocation of law influence not only the opinion of citizens, but the way legal doctrine is viewed by courts. In addition, police and regulatory agency personnel's professionalisation based on the claim to special expertise contributes to a situation in which enforcement agencies can powerfully influence the legislation they enforce. Thus it is misleading to see legal doctrine as the exclusive preserve of courts or lawyers. Its creation, interpretation and application are all strongly influenced by the agencies of enforcement associated with it and by the varying degrees of power and opportunity that individuals, organisations and social groups have to invoke it.

9 The Prognosis for Law

In previous chapters we have considered broad theoretical analyses of the position of law in contemporary Western societies. We have also discussed empirical studies of the effects of law, social factors influencing the creation of laws, the organisation of professional practice of law, adjudication, and the enforcement and invocation of law. The concern throughout has been with issues of the present; with the current situation of law in society. The sociology of law seeks to explain the nature of law in terms of the empirical conditions within which legal doctrine and institutions exist in particular societies or social conditions. As a study aimed at the explanation of social phenomena through analysis of systematically organised empirical data it must concern itself centrally with understanding law as it is, rather than as it might or should be.

Nevertheless, even when the focus is on understanding the actual conditions of the present, this sociologically oriented literature—particularly the part of it that explicitly takes up major issues of contemporary social theory—necessarily involves interpreting the past. Equally it can hardly avoid speculating on the future of law. 'Present' cannot be separated from 'past' and 'future' as a distinct object of analysis if a serious attempt is made to understand why contemporary law and legal institutions have their present form, and what processes are at work shaping law in contemporary Western societies.

Such a dynamic or historical perspective implies complex problems of interpretation: interpretation of experience in terms of what is most significant for the future; in terms of what seem central and what peripheral aspects of the social phenomena under consideration. These matters of interpretation can hardly be uninfluenced by the personal values of the interpreter and by the climate of thought in which he or she works. Yet to make sense of the present we must put it into a perspective that assesses directions of change or conditions of stability.

Ideally, other extensions of the range of study are required. To make an already large subject reasonably manageable, the concerns of this book have been wholly restricted to aspects of the law and legal institutions of some contemporary Western European and North American societies. It is, however, clear that a deeper understanding of the condition of law in these societies would require comparisons with the situation of law in very different contexts—for example, those of Third World societies or the rapidly changing former state socialist societies of Eastern Europe.

Further, the concern of this book has been entirely with law *within* nation states; that is, it has been concerned primarily with state law and much less centrally with the possibility of conceptualising law so as to include, within the concept, normative systems other than state law, but existing within the territory of the nation state. What has not been considered but is again of great importance is the increasing 'internationalisation' of law; the extent to which the law of the nation state is being subordinated to or powerfully influenced by international or supranational legal regimes (for example, that of the European Community) (Cain 1983d). Equally this internationalisation of law reflects the internationalisation of economic systems: the growth of multinational corporations; the extension of consumer markets, production systems, investment, loan relationships and complex structures of economic domination and dependency beyond national boundaries; all in all, the vastly increased international power of capital in the contemporary world. To discuss these extremely important developments adequately, as well as to make useful comparisons of contemporary Western state legal systems with those of other contemporary societies, would require far more space than is available here.

It remains the case that, for the present, state law—that is, the law of the nation state created, interpreted and applied by state agencies—can plausibly be considered the most central and fully developed form of law in Western societies. As a form of regulation it has sufficient significance, complexity and sociological interest in its own right to justify detailed theoretical and empirical analysis in temporary isolation from wider considerations of other legal forms. It is therefore natural that the literature of the sociology of law developed in contemporary Western societies should be largely focused on state law in these societies.

But, as has already been remarked, sociological analysis of the present situation of law cannot be isolated from an interpretation of directions of change in law and its social context. Consequently the sociologically oriented literature on law contains views of law's future that are primarily views on the future of state law rather than detailed considerations of the emergence or extension of quite different legal forms. In this final chapter, our concern is to consider themes in the sociological literature on contemporary Western law that suggest the prognosis for state law in this context; in other words, to consider how far sociological analysis of the present characteristics and problems of state law in Western societies may indicate directions of development of this law and of the conditions under which it exists. And this attempt to plot law's transformations will lead to some final reflections on sociology of law itself in a time of legal change.

The main themes to be discussed have made their appearance in various ways in previous chapters. The discussion here is intended primarily to draw together matters previously treated separately and so to show the connections between them. Each of these themes points to problems of contemporary legal organisation which, in some of the literature, are seen as 'crises' of law or legal order. Most of the themes and problems are closely interrelated. Together they sketch a picture of change in the very foundations of Western law. Some elements in the foreground of this picture are in sharp focus while other parts are necessarily only vague, ambiguous or unidentifiable outlines on a distant horizon.

The Scope of Law and Legal Authority

Throughout this book the idea of the 'autonomy' of Western law from other aspects of society has been discussed from many viewpoints. Is it appropriate to speak not merely of autonomy but of *isolation* or alienation of law within the society it is supposed to regulate; of a divorce of law from popular needs and the conditions of broad popular acceptance? The theme of a 'crisis of legal legitimacy' has been discussed in Chapter 5. It has been one of the foremost themes of contemporary sociologically oriented writing on Western law. In this context, however, it is important to consider it alongside the closely connected theme of the expansion of legal regulation and the increasing use of legal processes in these societies—the legal 'explosion' as some American writers have called it (cf. Galanter 1986).

Thus state law seems to extend into an increasing range of fields (Galanter 1992: 13–4). As it does so it supplements or perhaps replaces other mechanisms of control (mores, informal understandings governing social relations, community or neighbourhood networks and institutions, family responsibilities) that are often assumed to have clearer and more deep-rooted bases of legitimacy (e.g. Habermas 1986). The American sociologist Austin Turk notes that as law is brought into a field of social relations it becomes a 'contingency which must be met'. Individuals or organisations find it necessary to gain or increase control over legal resources if only to neutralise law as a weapon that an opponent might use. Pressure to settle disagreements through voluntary negotiation and agreement may be lessened by the availability of law. Otherwise legal pressures may lead to premature termination of open conflict without full resolution of differences, so that future conflicts are more likely, and likely to be worse (Turk 1976). In a sense law 'expropriates' disputes from the parties involved, removing not only methods of resolving conflicts but also the conflicts themselves from the control of citizens (Christie 1977) so that they take on a different character from that which the participants understood. Law intrudes increasingly into social life, but it does so as an alien force; a contingency to be taken into account; an imposition and control upon, rather than an expression of, spontaneous social relations.

In Chapter 3 some of the problems involved in thinking of law as an integrative mechanism of social solidarity were considered. Many writers stress law's antipathy to community. Community is traditionally thought of as the life of a social group (probably relatively small) characterised by shared beliefs and values, direct and many-sided relationships between members, and action between members based on principles of reciprocity (Taylor 1982: 25–38). It thus emphasises the co-operative, egalitarian and participatory aspects of social life. But it is argued that 'the pull of the legal solution is always to the rule of the few and the legal solution is the enemy of full participatory democracy' (Bankowski and Nelken 1981: 267). Thus the extension of law involves the further decline of community solidarity. And the apparently increasing tendency to litigate—the discarding of living law systems of resolving or containing disputes in favour of reliance on state legal solutions—is a symptom of this decline.

For many writers law's acceptability depends on its restriction within a limited field. Robert Nisbet (1975: 240) writes: 'Law is vital ... but when every relationship in society becomes a potentially legal relationship, expressed in adversary fashion, the very juices of the social bond dry up, the social impulse atrophies.' The pressing contemporary problem is considered to be the excessive 'juridification of social spheres' (Teubner, ed, 1987). For Jürgen Habermas (1986), law is a support, protection and stabilising structure for the 'life world' within which values, motivations and initiatives of individuals are born and nurtured. But, as a directing instrument or medium, it threatens to crush, through 'violent abstraction', the moral subtleties, local meanings and diversity of individual life. The central critique uniting these kinds of views expressed by writers with widely varying conceptions of an ideal social order is that law, although increasing its scope and reach into society, cannot replace—but may destroy—the spontaneous processes by which social stability and change can be brought about through interaction between members of society.

Habermas (1976) has stressed the impossibility in contemporary Western societies of continuing to base the legitimacy of law and political systems on the objective existence of a 'gapless' all-embracing system of rationally made legal rules providing a framework for purpose rational action. He sees this basis of legitimacy, which Weber described in terms of legal domination, as actually depending on the particular conditions and free-market values of liberal capitalism. Today, however, the state and its legal order does far more than provide this 'neutral' system of rules. It manages and directs economic and social life and it derives its legitimacy primarily from its success in these management tasks (Habermas 1976: 36–7). As was seen in Chapter 5, Habermas considers that certain inherent problems of capitalist socio-economic order which make management success by the state in the economic sphere highly problematic (1976: 45–6) provide the conditions for possible legitimation crises.

But other views are possible. The recent adoption by Western governments of policies and forms of rhetoric that deny or underplay any 'steering' role of the state in relation to social or economic conditions may be a way of safeguarding legitimacy. The state explicitly seeks to absolve itself of responsibility for economic performance, unemployment levels, etc. The continued legitimacy of regimes and of the regulation they produce is achieved not by actually giving up steering functions—which, in contemporary conditions, can be discarded in Western societies only to a strictly limited extent without chaos ensuing—but by a*ppearing* to do so (cf. Cotterrell 1988). The regulated population is to be convinced that crises are not the state's responsibility but are, for example, the result of natural processes of the market or worldwide trends. This is, in a sense, an attempt to *simulate* optimal conditions of legal domination in societies whose regulatory structures and demands are, as noted in Chapter 5, rather too complex to allow those conditions actually to be created.

Another perspective on this, which implies that the strategy can be successful up to a point, is provided by evidence suggesting that people judge the legitimacy of legal institutions in terms of perceived fairness of procedures rather than substantive outcomes of cases (Tyler 1990). On the basis of this evidence, it would seem that legal institutions are still viewed very much within the terms of Weberian legal domination: law is seen as providing a predictable, stable framework for purpose-rational activity. All that is asked of law is that it 'hold the ring' as individuals negotiate their own social and economic relationships. But behind judgments about the fairness of procedures are assumptions about what the procedures are for and what kinds of opportunities and possibilities for purpose-rational action are reasonably and realistically to be expected. In other words, judgments of fairness of procedures may be enough to make legal institutions acceptable as long as the balance of order and justice these institutions are thought to embody is considered to be natural, inevitable, desirable or the best that can be hoped for (see pp. 171–6, above).

In this context, changes in the forms of contemporary regulation are of great importance. We have noted, in Chapter 5, the development of discretionary and particularised regulation which challenges the rule of law as a component of legal ideology. Not only is the reach of regulation extending but its boundaries increasingly seem unclear as state regulation intertwines with business self-regulation, legal standards merge with scientific standards, and discretion and rule reinforce each other to extend regulatory jurisdictions into realms of policy formulation often beyond the purview of judicial review. In addition, doctrine is produced, interpreted and applied not only by legislatures and courts, but in the operation of enforcement agencies (Chapter 8) and in the professional mediation and negotiation of legal strategies in lawyer-client interaction (Chapter 6). Law seems to extend its regulatory scope deeper into society, but much of this extension is by means that cannot be understood as the application of Weberian formal rationality or the fulfilment of the promise of the rule of law. As regulation extends in scope it tends to discard many characteristics (predictability, formality, stability, generality, systematicity) that seemed to underpin its acceptability. Hence, legal regulation seems to become more alien within citizens' experience, at the same time as it confronts that experience in ever more detailed and intimate ways.

Informalism, Delegalisation and Access to Law

One kind of response to law's isolation or alienation is to argue the need for devices, procedures and institutional reforms to make law more accessible; to make the invocation of law easier and more worthwhile for a much wider range of citizens. Some of the major obstacles that stand in the way of invocation of law were discussed in Chapter 8. Much literature, particularly in the United States, has, however, been less concerned with increasing citizen access to existing legal institutions than with the possibility of changing legal institutions to bring them closer to citizens. It analyses the possibilities and practice of creating new or modified legal institutions operating in a much less formal manner than, for example, ordinary courts and providing 'popular justice' in a relatively inexpensive form and often in locations much more accessible to potential users. Developments of this kind have been seen as part of a wide-ranging reaction against formal legal institutions which has been labelled 'informalism'. Although this has become of particular importance in contemporary Western legal systems, and especially in the United States, it is neither new nor restricted to these systems.

From one point of view, the supplementation of formal institutions such as courts with an array of informal neighbourhood dispute resolution institutions appears as an *extension* of the legal system. But because this extension typically emphasises compromise, mediation and negotiation in dispute processing, rather than full reliance on formal rules and formal procedures it can also be seen as part of a trend towards 'delegalisation'; the removal of some areas of social problems or social relations from the control of legal rules and procedures. In this specific sense it is sometimes seen as part of an apparent counter-trend of *reduction* of the scope of state law.

Some commentators view the general development of 'popular justice' institutions as benign: breaking down law's isolation from community and modifying the system of legal institutions to provide means of dispute resolution widely available to citizens; a necessary provision for those many people who realistically can neither litigate in ordinary courts, nor merely cut their losses and terminate the relationship that has given rise to a dispute (e.g. Danzig and Lowy 1975; and see Whelan 1990). However, other writers see the extension of the legal system through informal institutions primarily as increasing the scope of state power; a development that has the effect of extending the reach of the state and its mechanisms of control deeper into society.

Thus, Christine Harrington's study of a Kansas City neighbourhood justice centre, an agency dealing informally with minor criminal and civil cases, shows that harassment and assault cases accounted for 63 per cent of disputes referred to the centre, and 88 per cent of cases in these categories were referred by prosecutors, judges or police (Harrington 1985: 115–7). The agency appeared as one to which the criminal justice system could offload 'trivial' but relatively troublesome cases for simple processing. These kinds of cases were numerically far more significant in the agency's workload than were disputes not already being dealt with by legal institutions or officials, and which therefore might otherwise not have been processed within the legal system. The agency was thus easing the existing burden of the legal system rather than making possible the resolution of further categories of disputes. Equally, the effectiveness of the informal mediation system (for example, as regards ensuring the participation of the parties) depended on its relationship with the formal legal system. Harrington concludes: 'The coercion and authority of police, prosecutors, and judges are essential elements to the institutional existence of neighbourhood justice centres' (1985: 170). Indeed, community justice programmes are often viewed as a way of increasing the scope of judicial administration of dispute processing at a much lower cost than would be involved in an extension of the ordinary system of courts. The increased provision is considered necessary to reduce caseload pressure on the courts and to deal with increasingly vocal criticisms of citizens' lack of access to the legal system.

It has been argued that informal justice facilitates more extensive state control because it removes the possibility of effectively asserting strict legal rights (Abel 1981b: 256ff). Where mediation, compromise and negotiation are the essential techniques of dispute processing, the exercise of power either by the state or citizens is not channelled through and controlled by legal rules. It operates diffusely and is not subject to formal control. Hence in such a situation rules and rights cannot be set up against the powerful. An agreed compromise is likely to reflect the will of the dominant party in any dispute (Fiss 1984; Genn 1987). It is precisely for this reason that those populations (such as members of various ethnic minority groups) typically finding themselves in positions of relative social disadvantage and powerlessness as against other populations in a society are likely to see formality, rather than informality, in legal and administrative processes as advantageous, since it may hamper blatant discrimination in adjudication, arbitration or mediation, and it may have some potential for excluding from dispute resolution the influence of social statuses that are wholly irrelevant to the issue in dispute (Williams 1991: ch 8). Members of majority populations may find value in informal processes that are cheap, speedy and allow more disputes to be settled in less intimidating ways than the formal processes of law allow; but minorities 'will want the safety that comes from structure, rights and rules' (Delgado 1988: 412; but cf. Black 1989). Thus reliance on rights through formal processes can be, in some respects, a defence and a weapon of socially excluded or marginalised groups (Hunt 1990). As was seen in Chapter 4, law in the form of predictable rules organises and channels power, but in doing so it imposes important conditions on the use of power; conditions which the relatively powerless may be able to exploit.

Boaventura de Sousa Santos has tried to explain, in Marxist terms, the 'striking contrast' in contemporary Western societies between the tendencies to informalism and community justice strategies, on the one hand, and the simultaneous but seemingly opposite movement towards a return to legalism in criminal justice and penal policy (Santos 1982). The decline of treatment policies—involving individualised clinical decision-making approaches to treatment of particular criminal offenders or categories of offenders—has been accompanied by the re-establishment of a 'justice model' for correction of offenders. The latter stresses the importance of 'just deserts' and strict application of general legal rules to ensure justice in punishing criminals for their crime (e.g. Von Hirsch 1976; and see Chapter 5). Why is it that some areas of social control show a decrease in state use of rule-governed formal institutions while other areas show renewed emphasis on formality and rule?

Santos sees three elements in contemporary Western law. He calls these 'rhetoric' (based on persuasion through argument around socially accepted ideas and circumstances), 'bureaucracy' (based on professional knowledge, general formal rules and hierarchically organised procedures), and 'violence' (based on the use or threat of physical force). Over the past two centuries of legal development rhetoric has been displaced by bureaucracy and violence but the growth of informalism shows its re-emergence. Informalism has returned the element of rhetoric to law. But the formal aspects of the legal system centre on bureaucracy and violence. Santos argues that 'bureaucracy and violence are being concentrated in those legal fields that correspond to the core areas of political domination' where law's major function is to define the 'enemies' of society and disperse them by excluding or neutralising them. But 'rhetoric is being expanded in legal fields that correspond to the periphery of political domination, where their main function is to define the enemy as non-enemy and to disperse that enemy through mechanisms of trivialisation and integration' (Santos 1982: 257).

Santos' dichotomy may be too stark to explain complex legal policies, but it raises the possibility that very different legal strategies exist in different areas of the legal system, corresponding primarily to what he sees as different aspects or areas of political domination. In core areas of domination the line between state and civil society is sharp and state power is clearly defined in rules and formal procedures. In the periphery of political domination, however, state power is diffuse, the line between state and non-state may be hard to draw, and state control combines with and makes use of numerous informal controls in social life. 'In other words, the state is expanding in the form of civil society, and that is why the dichotomy of state and civil society is no longer useful, if ever it was' (1982: 262; and see Santos 1985: 302ff). Recently, Santos has further elaborated the idea of a core and periphery in legal systems, emphasising more generally that legal resources are refined and focussed in core areas and more diffuse, limited and undeveloped at the periphery. He now describes the core of 'bourgeois state legality' not merely as the area in which domination over 'enemies' of civil society is most crucial but also as that in which essential mechanisms of civil society are provided, such as the facility to make contractual agreements (Santos 1987: 292ff).

Other writers have, of course, emphasised the importance of the particular structural location of formality and informality in any legal order. Weber's historical discussion of the sociological significance of two levels of the English legal system (the relative formality and predictability of adjudication in the higher courts and the relative informality and discretionary justice of the courts of justices of the peace) in the heyday of capitalist development offers a familiar example. Santos' discussion, however, with its different emphasis, relates questions of formality and informality to issues about the relationship between state and civil society and about the nature of power in contemporary Western societies. These issues are central to contemporary discussions of the prognosis for law and must now be outlined.

State, Civil Society and the Diffusion of Power and Control

The contrast in nineteenth-century social theory between 'civil society' and 'state', although used in a variety of ways, broadly suggested a clear distinction between, on the one hand, a civil realm of social relations governed by private transactions between individuals based on the concepts of contract and private property and, on the other, a political realm in which the members of society are recognised as citizens with relations defined by reference to political organisation and political obligation. It drew a relatively clear line between private and public spheres of social life; and between relationships based on the free pursuit of individual self-interest and relationships structured through state power and control. The idea, present in Santos' writings, that the distinction between state and civil society, or political and private realms of social life, is breaking down is a familiar one in recent social theory.

This perceived breakdown is described in many different ways. Some writing, like Santos', emphasises the extension of the reach of the state into the private sphere through the use of informal devices harnessing what remain of structures of community life (for example, mediation or neighbourhood organisation) in the service of political control. The French Marxist philosopher Louis Althusser (1971) developed the influential thesis of the state acting through what he termed 'ideological state apparatuses' (ISAs) which are to be understood as far more extensive and pervasive than the parallel repressive apparatuses of the state (police, military organisation etc.). Althusser sees the state (and—in more concrete terms—those who wield political power within it) as exerting or capable of exerting ideological control over society by means of direct or indirect influence on a great variety of institutions: churches, education, the family, political parties and organisations, trade unions, the media, cultural institutions, as well as the law (which Althusser sees, in conformity with the tradition of Marxist analysis, as simultaneously an ideological and repressive apparatus of the state). To this extent all of these institutions, which are traditionally associated wholly or partly with civil society, are ISAs. The state works, or can work, through them, co-ordinating their effects so as to guarantee the maintenance of the established social and economic order.

The extension of state power and control by formal and informal means is a theme of much Marxist writing. For example, Thomas Mathiesen's discussion of what he calls the 'absorbent state' (Mathiesen 1980) describes many ways in which the state can exert control by subsuming within itself possible sources of dissent and opposition. Nevertheless, an argument might be made that, especially since the beginning of the 1980s, governmental strategies in many Western societies have been aimed at *strengthening* civil society by establishing clear boundaries of state activity, removing many previous legal structures of intervention in private economic arrangements, and generally, according to the political slogan, 'getting the state off the backs of the people'. To this extent the state-civil society divide might appear not as further eroded but as deliberately re-established. However, this development can be seen in a different light. We have earlier noticed reasons why the legitimacy of law and government might be strengthened by the apparent withdrawal of government from direct regulation of, and hence responsibility for, economic conditions. Yet evidence suggests that despite much rhetoric about the withdrawal of the state from interference with the economy, a very great deal of state direction occurs (e.g. Thompson 1984b). The rhetoric of liberalisation goes along with considerable state involvement. In this way civil society seems to be strengthened only by being further invaded (Cotterrell 1988). The networks of interdependence that characterise contemporary economic life are increasingly complex and extensive and the state appears indispensable to regulate the conditions that maintain this sometimes fragile and vulnerable interdependence.

Further, Santos' idea that fundamentally different forms and strategies of regulation can be applied to different populations within contemporary Western societies provides a reminder that the recreation of civil society may be achieved not only through its invasion by state regulation but also by the control of sectors of society that may threaten it. Thus, a 'consensual authoritarianism' (Norrie and Adelman 1989) accepting and even welcoming state control and surveillance of widening areas of life—especially those areas in which society's 'have nots' seem to pose a threat to the orderly relationships of civil society—may come to be a characteristic attitude of many ordinary beneficiaries of civil society.

In an incisive discussion of the contemporary capitalist state, the French writer Nicos Poulantzas (1978) has stressed an important tendency paralleling extensions of state control. Poulantzas notes that as the scope of the state has expanded, with numerous levels of central and local administration, the tendency for dissent and conflict to develop *within* this state structure has grown. It has always been misleading to think of the personnel of the numerous branches of the state apparatus as necessarily united in outlook and strategies. But with a significant increase in the size of administrative bureaucracies, and a greater variety of agencies existing on the vague borderline between public and private spheres of life, the state has increasingly mirrored within itself the conflicts of civil society (Poulantzas 1978: 241–7). Thus Poulantzas sees an internal weakening of the state occurring simultaneously with its external strengthening. Hence, those controlling the higher levels of the state apparatus feel the need to extend stricter control over lower levels to maintain the cohesiveness of an unwieldy political-administrative state structure.

Poulantzas discusses these ideas about problems of control and co-ordination only in general terms of the state apparatus as a whole. But they can, of course, be related specifically to the legal system as a particular part of this apparatus. The problem of control of lower ranks of personnel, or lower levels of the legal apparatus, by higher ranks or levels has been considered in several connections in earlier chapters. The system of appeals in the hierarchy of the courts was discussed in these terms in Chapter 7; the relationships between higher ranks and lower ranks in enforcement agencies, including the police, were considered in Chapter 8; and the relations of various sections or groups within legal professions were discussed in the context of an analysis of the idea of professional unity in Chapter 6. From those discussions it might be suggested that the possibility of firm hierarchical control depends to a considerable extent on the amount of discretion necessarily involved in the activities to be controlled, and also on the possibility of higher ranks obtaining sufficiently detailed knowledge of the actions of lower ranks to make control feasible and effective.

For example, judicial decisions in modern Western trial courts are, in comparison with many administrative decisions of lower rank administrators, relatively formalised and visible. The decision reached is delivered and recorded in a way that makes its details accessible not only to higher levels of the judicial hierarchy (especially appeal courts) but also to citizens and their legal advisers. In addition, reasons for the decision must usually be made explicit at the time it is made. In this situation, information on lower rank decision-making is available to higher ranks in the judicial hierarchy in considerable detail and control of lower levels by higher is thereby facilitated. Compare the problems of control of enforcement agency lower ranks' decision-making, which were discussed in Chapter 8. Here, the necessarily considerable discretion vested in agency personnel makes strict control by higher ranks difficult. Further, since the decision-making process in law enforcement does not need to be public in the way that the judicial function typically demands, it is more difficult for higher ranks (especially in the police) to obtain objective verifiable information about the nature and circumstances of lower ranks' decisions. Thus the conditions of hierarchical control differ within different institutional elements of the legal system.

Emphasis on the pervasiveness of power in numerous forms, and on the inappropriateness of attempting to analyse power relations in contemporary Western societies in terms of a strict separation of state and civil society, or public and private spheres, is in no way restricted to Marxist writing. One of the most important recent contributions to analysis of power has been that of the French scholar Michel Foucault. Foucault sees power as an ubiquitous feature of social life. 'Power is everywhere; not because it embraces everything, but because it comes from everywhere' (Foucault 1979: 93). In contrast to the generally negative and critical analysis of power which is central to Marxist theory, Foucault sees power as essential to social life, the means by which all that is useful is accomplished socially. Thus while much social theory links power specifically with the state or with economic relations, Foucault sets it free as a general concept applicable in the analysis of all social structures and relations. Different kinds of institutions—schools, factories, prisons, hospitals, armies—have different institutional objectives; they are concerned with producing different kinds of effects or outputs. But they are related by common 'techniques of discipline'—that is, modes of organisation and control of individuals and their behaviour—which are fundamentally uniform in character despite the variety of institutions in which they exist. Power exerted through these institutions arises from the intersection of productive capacity and disciplinary techniques.

Existing in this very general form, power is in no way limited to that which is expressed through law. Essential to Foucault's analyses are: the idea that power is an irreducible and fundamental characteristic of social life; that discipline offers a basic conceptual category necessary to the understanding of power in present societies; that the state is to be seen as a linking together of micropowers—the numerous forms of power existing at all levels of social life; and that, consequently, power is not a derivation from the state but the state is the crystallisation and organisation of the dispersed forms of power that are ubiquitous in social life.

This kind of thinking encourages a recognition that power can be expressed within the state in numerous forms of administration and surveillance. Welfare administration and control, and the organisation of family life can be interpreted as some of many fields in which power is dispersed and yet ordered within the state's 'overall strategy' (cf. Foucault 1980: 142; Donzelot 1980). Equally, like the Marxist analyses discussed earlier, Foucault's approach casts doubt on any possibility of maintaining a clear analytical separation of society into a public and a private realm if we are to understand the complexities of organisation and control in contemporary societies.

The Breakdown of Legal Autonomy?

The idea of the diffusion of power in many forms leads us to a further theme in contemporary writing: that of the breakdown of legal autonomy; of the dissolution of law as a distinct form of regulation and of the legal system or legal order as a social phenomenon distinguishable from other forms of social control.

To claim any such breakdown or dissolution may seem fanciful in a situation where, in all contemporary Western societies, highly developed legislative, judicial and law enforcement agencies exist and where legal practice is highly professionalised. However, the discussion in Chapter 5 of debates on the future of the rule of law and of the growth of new forms of regulation hinted at this theme. Indeed it is present in many varieties of contemporary thought about law. Pashukanis' Marxist legal theory interpreted law as reaching its most perfect formal development in capitalist society—but saw it as fated to disappear in socialist society where it would be gradually replaced by administrative procedures. More recent Marxist writers, however, have seen the same kind of process occurring within capitalist society itself. Poulantzas notes that: 'From the punishable offence laid down by a universal and general Act of Parliament, we are moving towards the suspicious circumstance whose contours are administratively defined by supple, malleable and particularist regulation ... Thus, while the law is evidently not defunct, it is undergoing a clear *retreat*' (Poulantzas 1978: 220. Italics in text). Increasingly, executive acts are taking the place of legislative acts as the basis of state control and 'the relative distinction between legislative and executive power is becoming less sharp' (Poulantzas 1978: 218).

Non-Marxist observers see similar tendencies towards the decline or marginalisation of legal form as such. Foucault suggests, though with some ambiguity (cf. Santos 1985: 325–6), that state law as a specific regulatory form has been increasingly displaced by a variety of disciplinary powers founded on scientific or technical knowledges (Foucault 1979: 89; 1980: 103–8). Kamenka and Tay (1978: 49) note that, at least in the common law world, lawyers have tried to maintain specifically legal concepts, attitudes and procedures 'by distinguishing law from regulation, courts from tribunals, justice from administration. Today—and this is part of the crisis—the distinction becomes less and less tenable.' Nonet and Selznick argue that as 'law becomes more open-textured, as its sources are enriched, as its cognitive competence is raised, legal casuistry loses its distinctiveness.' Autonomous law (that is, the kind of law associated with a distinctive autonomous legal system) in decline creates the possibility of responsive (or purposive) law which is seen by Nonet and Selznick as both an ideal and a stage of legal historical development. 'With purposive law there is a decline of artificial reason, a convergence of legal and policy analysis, a reintegration of legal and moral judgment and of legal and political participation' (Nonet and Selznick 1978: 89, 110).

Legal analysis today can hardly be separated from analysis of government policy and its implementation. Thus, although it would be quite wrong to suggest that 'pure' logical legal analysis, of the kind referred to in the introduction to this book has become unimportant to the lawyer's concerns, it is increasingly supplemented and occasionally replaced by argument from policy; that is, argument in terms of governmental aims, social utility, moral claims or economic welfare. Concepts of core and periphery can again be pressed into service. One writer refers to a core of legal thought in which 'law feels natural, secure (unchallenged), unadulterated by incompatible paradigms or rationalities', and a periphery where 'everything is opposite: law feels awkward, bureaucratic and challenged both by other forms of thought and other kinds of experts'. Yet, at the core, law seems also 'abstract, socially inconsequential, obsolescent; while the periphery seems modern, relevant, substantive, powerful' (Clune 1989: 189).

As has been noted earlier, law's perceived identity crisis is expressed partly in terms of regulatory overload, 'legal pollution' (Teubner 1987: 3), excessive juridification of society (Teubner, ed, 1987) and a general belief that inherent limits of legal regulation can no longer be specified. The uncertainty of boundaries between public and private spheres, state and civil society, law and administration, legal principle and public policy is seen as undermining law's integrity and dissolving away its specific competences. What results, on this view, is a jumble of regulation, indeterminate in form, unprincipled in substance, chaotic in strategies and processes. In Chapter 2 and elsewhere, we have noted the development of legal autopoiesis theory as related, in part, to these observations about law. The theory clearly recognises the complexity of contemporary regulation; indeed, it seems to remain agnostic about the specific form or substance of legal regulation. But legal autopoiesis theory insists that, as a system of communication, law is necessarily narrowly specialised within the array of sub-systems of complex modern societies. Thus, legal discourse is not the discourse of planning, policy, administration, technology, efficiency or morality. It is solely the discourse of legality and illegality, operating a binary code (right/wrong) in specifically legal terms. Viewed in this way, law in modern conditions retains not only autonomy but also the capacity to reproduce endlessly its own discourse without subversion from other discourses. It transforms all signals from its environment—economic, scientific, technological, cultural or political events, developments and demands—into its own specific terms. In this way law is neither undermined nor fragmented. But its autonomy must be understood in new ways.

Autopoiesis theory may, however, be less an explanatory theory of law's contemporary character than a framework for justifying and elaborating certain defences against contemporary threats to law's autonomy. Teubner has suggested that law 'thinks' in its own distinctive ways (Teubner 1989). But a contrasting view might be that legal reasoning is 'ignorant' and cannot cope with the many modern forms of knowledge to which it must relate. Thus, reliance on expert scientific evidence in trials may produce professionally embarrassing miscarriages of justice when the characteristics or limits of this evidence are insufficiently understood. And lawyers may struggle to maintain the hegemony of their own professional knowledge in situations where it is confronted directly by other social knowledge (for example, concerning child welfare) that might seem, from the lawyer's standpoint, threatening, vague or hard to assess in the terms in which it is presented (cf. King and Piper 1990). Certainly the consequence may be that law seems, from one viewpoint, like an autopoietic, self-referential communication system. But from another viewpoint law—as a distinctive professional knowledge of lawyers or as the rational system of general rules fundamental to the ideal of the rule of law—appears highly vulnerable, relating defensively to a great variety of scientific, social, cultural and political knowledge fields and expertises from which legal doctrine and institutions cannot be insulated.

Nevertheless it may well be premature, as suggested in Chapter 5, to bewail the imminent passing of the rule of law, of government through known formally established general legal rules. Even if regimes increasingly claim legitimacy on the grounds of their relative success in managing economic problems, as Habermas suggests, it seems very doubtful whether such claims have done more than supplement a basic reliance on legal domination in Weber's sense (the authority of a seemingly comprehensive system of rationally developed and fairly applied legal rules) as the foundation of legitimacy. If so, there would seem to be definite limits on the replaceability of rules by administrative discretion in policy implementation and formulation if social order and its foundations of legitimacy are to be maintained in Western societies. The rule of law may well thus continue in the necessarily compromised, thoroughly imperfect form in which it has existed from the beginning of the modern era; that is, with numerous detractions from and exceptions to its vague principles but nevertheless as a basic ideological framework. Its existence and the limits on its realisation reflect the balance of formal and substantive rationality in law that is always present in any system that makes use of rules as an instrument of government.

On the other hand, contemporary technological developments have greatly extended the capacity of the state to control and direct society by means of both highly particularised regulation and broad discretionary regulation, rather than by means of clearly defined legal rules governing general categories of cases. Modern information technology with its revolutionary effects on the ability of state agencies to amass, store, transmit and retrieve vast amounts of data on individual citizens and circumstances has made it increasingly possible for state agencies to take specific individualised administrative decisions with regard to particular citizens and their situations. To some extent, indeed, part of the justification of general rules—that of limiting the range of facts to be taken into account in decision-making in order to make the decision-making process manageable—is disappearing. The ability to sort, store and retrieve quickly almost unlimited amounts of information and vastly to increase the range of variables that can be taken into account in administrative decision-making is clearly within sight.

A longer term perspective on law's autonomy is hard to establish. It would, however, seem to require some assessment of the present and possible relationships between state law and other forms of normative regulation. Gurvitch, using a concept of juridical pluralism that recognises many levels of law in society (cf. Chapter 1), calls the legal systems of contemporary Western societies—somewhat ominously—'transitory systems'. He sees many centres of economic power struggling for dominance and for a 'new jural equilibrium' with the state. A fragmentation of the normative order of society is occurring as the normative systems of various groups and sectors of society reflecting actual power relations and economic conditions not directly expressed in state law 'take their revenge'—as Gurvitch puts it—upon the state monopoly of law which, in his view, reached its apex at the end of the nineteenth century (Gurvitch 1947: 222). 'The development of organised capitalism (joint-stock companies, cartels, trusts), of trade unionism, of collective labour agreements, simultaneously breaks up the principles of national sovereignty and the autonomy of will, as well as freedom of contract. The aforementioned institutions express themselves in organised social law which competes with the framework of State law' (1947: 223). The tensions and conflicts of economic life, which shape actual patterns of social interaction and the varied systems of normative expectations governing them (what Gurvitch terms 'social law'), eventually challenge the authority of state law, which is seen as remote from and insensitive to these realities.

Gurvitch refuses to predict the future, arguing only that one possibility, the development of increasingly authoritarian regimes, is necessarily hostile to 'jural culture'; that is, 'to the safeguarding of the autonomy of social control through law as contrasted with other spheres of control and regulation' (1947: 225). On the other hand, the opposite possibility, a tendency towards pluralistic democracy is most favourable to maintenance of jural culture. Pluralistic democracy would involve the integration in a complete system of the 'social law' of the various groups and industrial sectors of society without the destruction of their autonomy. But such an integration would be possible only on democratic socialist principles; through an organisation of society in the common interest which nevertheless recognises the autonomous interests and concerns of its component groups and their members. Gurvitch sees this development (or else the authoritarian state) as the only real solution to the 'anarchy' of an economy and society divided between mutually hostile interest groups.

There are, of course, strong echoes of Durkheim in Gurvitch's prescriptions. In particular there is the same suggestion that the solution to the disorder and friction of contemporary societies may lie in removing the gulf that exists between the individual and the state, by promoting systems of regulation that exist at many levels in society and are to be linked or co-ordinated without destroying or distorting them (cf. Hirst, ed, 1989). Durkheim expresses this in terms of a vast delegation of legislative power to intermediate organisations existing between state and individual. Such a proposal may hardly be practicable as it stands.

But, more generally, the isolation of state law from the lives of individual citizens might be remedied by *co-ordinating*, rather than replacing, living law systems through state law and forms of law-making delegated from the state (Cotterrell 1988). This would not necessarily involve accepting any living law system *in toto*—since collective needs of society as a whole may require the modification of the regulatory systems of particular sections of society. But it would involve taking systematic account of the integrity of rule systems (and associated systems of values, attitudes and beliefs) of particular social groups or categories of citizens as well as of the interests reflected in and shaped by those values and outlooks. Like Gurvitch, I see such an approach as necessarily socialist because the recognition and co-ordination of many levels of regulation based on living law or social norms of particular groupings could only be seen to be in the interest of all if great disparities of private economic power were deliberately removed by means of the power of the state.

The Future of Legal Individualism

Another closely related theme of contemporary discussion in sociologically oriented literature on law to which we must refer is that of the future of legal individualism. In earlier chapters (especially Chapter 4) the dominance of an individualist outlook in modern Western law has been stressed. From the standpoint of Pashukanis' Marxist legal theory individualism is part of the very *essence* of law because law is a particular form of the relationship between commodity owners; the private property owner is the fundamental legal subject. The general form of law (expressed in terms of rights and duties of legal subjects) is seen as a generalisation of the relationship between individual commodity owners in the market. From this standpoint then, law can be nothing other than a form of the relationship between isolated self-interested individuals; it is the means by which these isolated atoms of capitalist society are linked—not so as to form a community or social unity based on solidarity but for specific limited purposes by means of legal agreement or for the preservation of a basic framework of order for the pursuit of individual self-interest.

In Chapter 4 some aspects of legal individualism as an important element in legal ideology in Western societies were considered, together with some challenges to it and consequent adaptations in legal doctrine. It remains, however, an extremely difficult and important question to ask how far Western law can evolve beyond its more or less exclusive emphasis on individuals and their personal rights and responsibilities, and recognise collective claims, rights and duties (cf. Cappelletti 1989: ch 7), or various kinds of communal structures as a focus of legal regulation.

As has been seen in Chapter 4, the recognition in law of corporate legal persons such as business enterprises existing in the form of joint-stock companies allows individualist legal reasoning to be applied to organisations by the device of treating the corporate group as if it were an individual actor. Thus the most economically significant legal actors today are undoubtedly organisations rather than individual citizens. The joint-stock company as a legal person can own property, make contracts, and be held responsible in civil or criminal law for its corporate actions.

This is, however, not the same thing as a general legal recognition of collective rights or claims. These rights or claims can be understood as representing the similar motivation to invoke law of a number of individuals united by common interests or concerns (for example, the common concern of members of an ethnic minority group to assert a right to legal protection from discrimination on grounds of their race or ethnicity; or the common interest of women workers in a particular industry to assert a right to promotion prospects or rates of pay equal to those of men engaged in similar work). A legal perspective that sees only the individual and individual rights and duties is seriously limited in its ability to evaluate claims whose weight depends particularly on the *extent* of the social problem they reflect; on the range of individuals affected and on the nature of the social environment in which the individual's claim arises (e.g. Lustgarten 1986). Legal individualism cannot take adequate account of the manner in which relationships and claims between individuals are often determined by relationships between large social groups; of the extent to which the position of individuals is often merely a reflection of the conditions of a much larger social environment. A court is often reluctant to take account explicitly of the interests of large numbers of people not represented as individuals before it.

Class actions and other forms of collective representation in legal claims before courts are examples of attempts to overcome the limits of legal individualism. As the line between law and policy blurs, the balancing of individual rights and duties by law seems no longer adequate but must be supplemented by an emphasis on law as distributor of benefits and burdens within society. Such a change of emphasis directs attention to collective claims and obligations. The themes discussed earlier in this chapter—the suggested demise of legal autonomy, the extension of the state and the blurring of the distinction between state and civil society, and the perceived isolation of state law and its techniques from conditions of life and aspirations of many citizens—are complemented by demands that law accommodate certain collective aspirations as well as individual claims. There is a close connection between all of these perceived developments. Individualism tends to be associated with the idea of a clearly defined realm of civil society, a realm of autonomous individuals freely pursuing their individual aims. As the idea of a clear separation of state and civil society (of public and private, or of political and personal spheres) becomes more problematic, many of the assumptions of legal individualism tend also to be challenged. Legal individualism seems a part of legal ideology in which the contradictions between legal doctrine and the changing social environment in which it is applied are breaking through the calm surface of legal ideas.

It is important to ask, however, what kinds of collective claims or aspirations press for aid and recognition from law. While contemporary Western legal systems recognise a strictly limited range of collectivities as having legal personality, they also notice in various ways in legal doctrine the existence of diverse social and economic groups or population sections (for example, welfare claimants, consumers, employees, children, women or members of religious or ethnic groups that may suffer discrimination). Yet, on the whole, legal doctrine has retained its individualistic outlook. The effect of this has been that where law addresses specific sections of a population its strategy is generally to create conditions, interests or claims for members of these sections that purport to set them as individuals in some abstract condition of equality in relation to the rest of the population. For members of particular population groups law, with its stance of abstract individualism, may even offer a means of escape from a ghetto-like community existence. In other words, law's blindness to structures of community may be liberating. Law's promise of individual rights is seen, for example, as a means of escape from 'impoverished forms of "community" forced on women' by fathers, husbands and sexual harassers (Olsen 1984: 430). Harlon Dalton writes of ethnic minorities in America: 'No matter how smart or bookish *we* were, we could not retreat from the sights, sounds, and smells of the communities from which we came' (Dalton 1987: 439). The promise of individualistic law applied to all is a promise of a world of secure social interaction beyond these communities. As Sally Merry found in a recent study, law with its assumption of distanced, measured and limited social relations may be for some people moving from American city neighbourhoods to the suburbs a welcome and sufficient substitute for the violence and claustrophobic controls of neighbourhood life (Merry 1990: ch 8). Law provides escape from the repressions or limitations of existing communities. But despite all this, legal individualism ensures that, for the present, contemporary Western law contributes in only the most limited ways to realising possibilities for more open communal structures that might be superimposed over the privatised lifestyles often considered typical of contemporary Western societies.

A Postmodern World?

What do all of these themes and tensions in contemporary law add up to? Is it possible to generalise from them about the present condition of law in society? This book has sought to characterise in a sociological perspective the law of 'modern' Western societies. But what should 'modern' be taken to mean, as we notice numerous transformations of law's forms, scope, identity and tasks highlighted in this chapter and illustrated throughout this book? Perhaps the legal world of Durkheim, Weber, Marx and the other classic social theorists must now be recognised as no longer modern in any meaningful sense; or perhaps 'modernity' as understood in much of the social theory and legal sociology discussed in these pages now appears as a historical phase that is passing.

What might justify such a conclusion? One version of the story of legal modernity can be told in the following terms. Modern law is the law of the *Rechtsstaat*. Freeing itself from traditional roots in culture, and discarding old common law ideas of legal doctrine as an expression of communal values or timeless wisdom, law became recognised as *a technical instrument of rational government* for modern states. As such it served a modern 'urge to re-make the world', grounded in the discovery of that world's contingent, changeable character (Bauman 1992: xii–xiii). This law appeared morally and intellectually *autonomous* (both in the sense of its distinctiveness as a governmental tool and its superiority over and independence from other competing normative systems in society). It seemed *comprehensive* (modern law could be used to cover all contingencies and provide man-made solutions to all problems of order); *unified and systematic* as a body of doctrine linked by its formal rational qualities (a structure of human reason subduing chaos and contingency); and *principled* as a consistent expression of essential conditions of social life (law embodied the values of modern civilisation, the product of human progress).

But this legal modernity contained its own contradictions. For example, the assumed autonomy of state law from other normative systems, such as morality or 'living law', set up a tension with the idea of law as embodying values rooted in modern civilisation. Furthermore, the idea of law as a technical instrument of government coexisted uneasily with that of law as a rational system of doctrine, since law-as-instrument implies attention always to concrete effects of law in society (emphasising the character of law as a medium of power), while law-as-doctrinal-system implies attention always to abstract relationships between legal ideas (emphasising the character of law as a structure of reason). The Diceyan notion of the rule of law balanced these elements only precariously, assuming that unfettered parliamentary sovereignty would be exercised in ways that would allow legal doctrine to preserve its character as a predictable, reliable, coherent framework of rational order within which individual citizens could find spheres of secure freedom of action.

If this sketch of 'modern' law is adopted, what can be said to have happened to legal modernity? We have noted the fragmentation of legal form in discretionary and particularised regulation; the apparent invasion of legal reason and doctrine by 'non-legal' knowledges and the array of policy demands pressed on legal doctrine and legal institutions; the unclear boundaries of state law reflected in the extension of informalism and the proliferation of forms of regulation; and the widespread belief that modern law has become overloaded and unprincipled. This image of overload and lack of principle suggests that law's effectiveness as a means of 'remaking the world' is put seriously into question. Law does not now appear as a means of creating order and stability from the contingency and transience of patterns of social life; instead it seems to mirror that contingency and transience. Living law systems begin, in Gurvitch's phrase, to 'take their revenge' on state law, reasserting their claims to integrity and independence, but without offering any normative systems comparable in scope with and so able to replace that of state law.

It might be said that state law has achieved total regulatory supremacy and freedom—freed from traditional cultural ties, moral groundings, limits of form and substance, and the imperatives of presenting itself as a doctrinal system—at the precise moment when its limited regulatory capabilities and moral hollowness have become inescapably obvious. It has become 'postmodern' law, freed from the constraints of modern form while still rooted in this form; and regulating, through a mass of piecemeal, ever-changing technicalities, a social world no longer susceptible to control and interpretation through comprehensive rational systems and timeless forms and structures of order. The modern illusion of the control of contingency through reason has been shattered.

A view of modern law and its transformations approximating to that sketched above provides the context for much recent literature addressing what it calls the 'postmodern' condition of contemporary law. But this literature usually seems less concerned with explaining the empirical conditions or consequences of these postmodern legal transformations than with elaborating in various ways the moral dilemmas of contemporary law and society that they are seen to pose. Postmodernism, as reflected in a great profusion of 'postmodernist' commentary on society and culture, is thus not so much a state of affairs as a state of mind (Bauman 1992: vii) widespread in contemporary Western societies. It is characterised by a loss of faith not only in all moral absolutes (which modern law's separation from moral moorings had already at least implicitly recognised) but also in the possibilities of rational transformation of social life (hence also in orthodox forms of politics centred on the state) and, most fundamentally, in the power of science as an instrument of social improvement. Postmodern thought extends the ideas of complexity, fragmentation, transience and localised rationality—all of which can be associated with contemporary law—to most features of present existence. One result is a rejection of all claims that 'truth' can be attained through philosophy or science. As Jean-Francois Lyotard has expressed the matter, 'grand narratives' have lost their credibility (Lyotard 1984: 37).

In a postmodern view, however, contemporary law may acquire ever greater symbolic or rhetorical power, whatever might be said of its technical effectiveness. This is because it is now revealed as the quintessentially postmodern form of social knowledge—explicitly constructed (for example, through deliberate legislation or judicial pronouncements), transient and disposable (continually subject to change and intellectually important only insofar as it remains practically applicable), and highly localised (relating to numerous specific, usually narrowly defined circumstances and valid only in relation to them). Thus, postmodernist legal theory has highlighted law's significance as symbolism and rhetoric; its capacity to provide effective, if morally empty, means of communication in a world that is losing faith in other discourses (e.g. Goodrich 1990). It is possible to see tendencies in some recent literature to resurrect the idea of law itself as social science (cf. Murphy 1991) or to explore traditions of social thought antedating modern social science and located in legal reasoning and legal speculation (Kelley 1990).

Wherever this may take us, it seems doubtful at present that it will lead to a more precise understanding of law as an empirical phenomenon, if only because in most postmodernist and related literature the specific empirical contexts in which law as doctrine is developed, interpreted, enforced or invoked rarely receive detailed analysis. One gains little sense of who creates, interprets and applies law and against whom, or of the particular processes and situations of interaction in which legal doctrine and legal consciousness are formed. Most postmodernist writing on law appears to avoid all concern with empirical study of specific social contexts of legal doctrine or institutions, or with theory aimed directly at empirical explanation. This is not to deny that it illustrates, sometimes in highly effective ways, important characteristics of legal rhetoric. But it often resorts, deliberately, to rhetoric itself in characterising law. Thus, the claim that law, as a form of knowledge, dominates social existence is sometimes sustained by broad assumptions about the autonomy of law, 'its own history, its own interpretive techniques and its own meta-language of methodology' (Goodrich 1987: 169), although these assumptions are undermined by the very empirical observations about contemporary law that make a postmodernist perspective persuasive in important respects.

At present it seems to me doubtful whether we should talk of a qualitatively different postmodern condition of Western law or whether the transformations of law noted in this book are merely a further working out in ever more complex social conditions of a relationship that has existed at least since the time of the classic social theorists: the relationship between law as the technical instrument and channel of governmental and private power and law as professional knowledge, rational doctrine and legitimating ideology. But it is clear that, as Zygmunt Bauman (1992) has explained, sociology in interpreting postmodernity necessarily continues to stand on a 'modern' terrain since its commitment remains a commitment to some idea of scientific enlightenment through generalising explanations, systematically developed on the basis of empirical observation and experience. Bauman also stresses certain changes of perspective which he thinks sociology must make in order to recognise the essentially new conditions of postmodern social life. The social world should no longer be seen as a 'cohesive totality' (1992: 54) but as complex, infinitely changeable and diverse, and contingently ordered; the centrality of consumption rather than production in influencing the key features of postmodern existence should be emphasised, as should the significance of individual autonomy and freedom of choice rather than social determination; and concepts such as 'system', and even 'society', might best be discarded since they imply firm structure, definite limits and a kind of solidity and fixity in social life that is belied by contemporary experience (1992: ch 9).

Sociology of Law as Critique

If the character of sociology of law is properly understood it requires, in my view, no fundamental paradigm-shift such as Bauman advocates for sociology (which he plainly treats as an academic discipline of professional sociologists). If sociology of law is portrayed, as this book has sought to portray it, not as an academic discipline or sub-discipline with specific methodological or theoretical commitments, but as a continually self-reflective and self-critical enterprise of inquiry aspiring towards ever broader perspectives on law as a field or aspect of social experience, it follows that it cannot be constrained within particular social theories, concepts of system or structure, images of 'society', or, indeed, visions of 'truth'. Neither is sociology of law constrained methodologically by its drive to broaden partial perspectives on legal experience. The search for broader perspectives through theoretical interpretation of experience is a never-ending process of stumbling, hesitant and always painfully limited—yet genuine—enlightenment. It occurs not in some rarefied realm of 'pure science' but in specific historical conditions where conflicts of knowledge and understanding are fought out (Cotterrell 1986).

It must also necessarily be a process that distills and respects local, partial perspectives rather than replaces them. Thus, localised understandings of social experience (for example, arising in a particular lawyer-client confrontation, a particular kind of legal practice, or a litigant's specific experiences of courtroom procedures), which postmodernism sees as the characteristic knowledges of contemporary society, are not discarded or trivialised when the effort is made to see them systematically, reflexively and self-critically in a broader view. A broader perspective interprets and contextualises these knowledges or perspectives, but is, itself, grounded in, enriched by, and ultimately validated by, the partial or limited experiences and knowledges subsumed within it. Thus, the idea of sociology of law as 'science' is complex. Science, in this context, is an aspiration. But it is not an aspiration to bind the world in categories of understanding so tight that all sense of choice, contingency and diversity is lost. Nor is it an aspiration only to ever greater specialisation in pursuit of rigour, so that, as postmodernist critiques suggest, science fragments into incommensurable discourses that defeat communication between different kinds of scientific specialists no less than between lay citizens. Instead, science in this context is the aspiration continually to extend understanding of law by means of ceaseless observation, questioning, comparison and synthesis of legal experience, using methods that are consistently and systematically empirical, self-conscious and open about the value commitments they entail, and aimed at theoretical generalisation to develop provisional frameworks for interpreting, contextualising and relating partial, local perspectives on experience.

At the end of the nineteenth century when Durkheim set out very deliberately to establish sociology as a science comparable with the natural sciences, he associated scientific method and scientific rigour with specialisation and sought to give sociology status in the academy by presenting it as the ally and expression of this specialisation of modern life (cf. Durkheim 1984: 2–4). Now, a century later we can compare postmodernism's harsh judgment on science as a network of specialisms. Science has lost its capacity to enlighten ordinary citizens as it has become so intricate and esoteric that only the masters of sub-specialisms of specialisms within scientific disciplines can follow selected pathways through science's knowledge-mazes (cf. Bauman 1992: 37). Sociology of law must aim to interpret complexity, rather than replicate it or hide within it; it must seek to reveal the broadest significance of the social details it studies, to build bridges between the legal experience of individuals and of different social groups, to construct perspectives that connect disparate specialised or localised knowledges. It cannot be satisfied with 'a localised, particularistic, and strategic science' (cf. Sarat 1990b: 164) even though much of its material will derive from localised, particularistic and strategic studies.

Austin Sarat has recently written that in contemporary conditions social science cannot be 'powerful or authoritative enough to end arguments. Yet it continues to keep alive the hope that science can serve as a tool of persuasion, albeit a limited one' in a world of diverse values, perspectives, and criteria of evaluation (Sarat 1990b: 165). The reason for insisting on sociology of law's orientation to broaden perspectives on legal experience is that this is what gives it some potential for enlightenment, persuasion, and effective critique of existing knowledge, including its own knowledge. If science is not powerful and authoritative enough to end arguments, we can still recognise that some forms of knowledge are more powerful than others. Perhaps it can be said that knowledge relating to a certain field is provisionally valid for individuals if it explains or seems consistent with their personal experience in that field, explains or seems consistent with data relating to that field that they accept as reliable, and accounts plausibly for other competing explanations of this data and experience by seeming to them to provide a more rigorous, more comprehensive, or more detailed and richer explanation or elaboration of data and experience. This assumes validity to be conferred not by society or scientific communities but by individuals who confront 'scientific' knowledge claims with their own experience and knowledge. It recognises also that receptivity to knowledge claims, like experience itself, is mediated by ideology. But, as was suggested in Chapters 4 and 5, since ideological thought is shaped in experience the possibility exists also for it to be subverted by experience, and by knowledge claims that provide powerful clarifications or elaborations of existing experience and understandings.

This book has emphasised law's ideological significance. Legal ideology, like all ideology, presents its categories of knowledge as obvious, 'common sense'; natural, adequate and complete within their field. Yet sociology of law reveals that law does not provide the autonomous structure of understanding, the coherent system of values or the securely independent discourse of legality that is often associated with it. In focussing on the central institutions of state law—professional organisation; adjudication by courts; and processes and agencies of enforcement—an attempt has been made to show the weakness of law's claims to autonomy, its interpenetration at all levels with more general structures of governmental power, wider currents of ideology, and diverse but often interconnected forms of knowledge usually considered external to law. In this sense, contemporary Western law is fragile. Yet, in emphasising this fragility, sociology of law also makes it possible to focus clearly on the primary sources of law's strength and security, also revealed in these central legal institutions. Modern law's strength is as a technical instrument of government, and as a medium of power. Legal ideas, as a framework of understandings of the character of social life, are moulded in numerous situations and processes of social interaction—in confrontations in the courtroom, negotiations in lawyers' offices, the resolution or containment of disputes in neighbourhood settings, the bargaining practices of regulatory agencies, the elaboration of police culture, and so on. Nevertheless, the character of law as institutionalised doctrine is most strongly shaped by coercive state power which stands in the shadows or sometimes clearly in view in all those settings where state law is invoked or impossible to avoid. Power in this sense is not dispersed but organised and structured through law. Thus, it seems to make sense to focus on it initially in what appear to be its most central locations, as this book has sought to do (but cf. Silbey 1991: 828–30).

Sociology of law reveals, however, the contradictions and limitations of the mediation of power through law. It reveals the ambivalent relationships between law as governmental instrument and law as a form of knowledge or reason whose integrity supports the legitimating ideal of the rule of law. Consequently sociology of law offers warnings to the powerful about tensions that seem inherent in the modern career of state law. Its message may be that contemporary legal regulation is in urgent need of new sources of moral authority which can only be obtained by building more effective participatory processes into the remote structures of the modern state. The overreach of law into society, which many contemporary observers describe, may be the consequence of regulatory practices that have lost all sense of the moral conditions of life of the regulated and see only the technical problems that the complexity of contemporary societies poses. Yet to remove state regulation might be only to replace complexity with chaos, so that power is exercised in social and economic life not only without the precision and predictability that law sometimes provides, but without the legal constraints that make it worthwhile for the relatively powerless to seek co-operation rather than conflict, accommodation rather than revolt.

On the other hand, what can sociology of law say directly to the relatively powerless, the 'have nots' of contemporary Western societies? Perhaps it can speak to them only through its efforts to make its critique of law's self-images a part of everyday understanding outside the academy and the professional world of law. Despite all the obstacles to achieving this in relation to a field such as contemporary law, characterised by intricacy, technicality and professional mystique, sociology of law's most effective strategy will again be its permanent search for broadened perspectives. Above all, this involves the effort to portray and interpret the localised, yet very powerful knowledges and practices of the professional and political world of state law, in ways that enable them to be confronted by understandings of power, morality and social order arising in the experiences of ordinary citizens in many situations and conditions of life.

Notes and Further Reading

In the following notes sources included in the list of text references are cited by author and date only. The same abbreviations of periodical titles as in the list of text references are used.

Introduction: Theory and Method in the Study of Law

Lawyers' conceptions of law: the distinction drawn in the text between normative legal theory and empirical legal theory is discussed in detail in Cotterrell 1989, especially chs 1 and 8.

Sociology and law: as long as 'sociology' is understood in the broad sense developed in the text, my view corresponds with Durkheim's when he wrote: 'My aim has been precisely to introduce... [the sociological idea] into those disciplines from which it was absent and thereby to make them branches of sociology' (Durkheim 1982, p. 260). If, however, sociology is conceived as merely another academic discipline this view becomes simply an unacceptable academic imperialism. Useful accounts of the early historical development of the sociology of law can be found in Gurvitch 1947; Timasheff 1939; R. Pound 'Sociology of Law' in G. Gurvitch and W. E. Moore (eds) *Twentieth Century Sociology* 1945; Carbonnier 1978. On the development and present scope of research in sociology of law in various countries see V. Ferrari (ed) *Developing Sociology of Law: A World-Wide Documentary Enquiry* 1990. Other recent surveys include J. van Houtte (ed) *Sociology of Law and Legal Anthropology in Dutch Speaking Countries* 1985; G. Wilson *Socio-Legal Research in Germany* 1980; R. Tomasic *The Sociology of Law* 1985 (a trend report first published in 33 Current Sociology, No. 1). See also e. g., for France, Carbonnier 1978, pp. 126–32 and *passim,* and A.-J. Arnaud *Critique de la raison juridique* 1981; for Italy, T. Pitch 'Sociology of Law in Italy' (1983) 10 J Law & Soc 119 and Comment (1984) 11 J Law & Soc 135–6; for Scandinavia, H. Hyden 'Sociology of Law in Scandinavia' (1986) 13 J Law & Soc 131; for Poland, A. Kojder and J. Kwasniewski 'The Development of the Sociology of Law in Poland' (1985) 13 Int J Soc L 261, and G. Skapska 'The Sociology of Law in Poland: Problems, Polemics, Social Commitment' (1987) 14 J Law & Soc 353. For retrospective views of the extensive development of American 'law and society' studies see e. g. F. J. Levine 'Goose Bumps and "The Search for Signs of Intelligent Life" in Sociolegal Studies: After Twenty-Five Years' (1990) 24 Law & Soc Rev 7; A. Sarat and S. S. Silbey 'The Pull of the Policy Audience' (1988) 10 Law and

Policy 97; L. M. Friedman 'The Law and Society Movement' (1986) 38 Stanford Law Review 763; R. L. Abel 'Redirecting Social Studies of Law' (1980) 14 Law & Soc Rev 805.

Sociological positivism versus 'interpretive sociology': the major statements of Donald Black's theories are in Black 1976 and Black 1989. See also D. Black (ed) *Toward a General Theory of Social Control* Vols 1 and 2 1984. For critiques of his approach to sociology of law see A. Hunt 'Behavioural Sociology of Law' (1983) 10 J Law & Soc 19; D. F. Greenberg 'Donald Black's Sociology of Law: A Critique' (1983) 17 Law & Soc Rev 337 (Comment by A. V. Horwitz at 369; and reply by Greenberg at 385). More sympathetic recent discussions include M. Cooney 'Behavioural Sociology of Law: A Defence' (1986) 49 Mod L Rev 262; L. A. Hembroff 'The Seriousness of Acts and Social Contexts: A Test of Black's Theory of the Behavior of Law' (1987) 93 Am J Soc 322; D. P. Doyle and D. F. Luckenbill 'Mobilizing Law in Response to Collective Problems: A Test of Black's Theory of Law' (1991) 25 Law & Soc Rev 103 (but stating findings contrary to Black's predictions). For other studies testing Black's hypotheses about law's behaviour see citations in Doyle and Luckenbill's paper and in Black 1989, p. 108. Black's influence is apparent also in the ideas of measurement of law adopted in M. Silberman's *The Civil Justice Process: A Detroit Area Study* 1985 and in the view of social control underlying M. P. Baumgartner's *The Moral Order of a Suburb* 1988.

On 'understanding' approaches in sociology: modern developments of this approach are found in sociological writings which have been influenced by phenomenological philosophy: see e.g. Berger and Luckmann 1967 which draws particularly on the work of Alfred Schutz. A further development, deriving primarily from the work of the American Harold Garfinkel, is in what has come to be called ethnomethodology: see J. M. Atkinson 'Ethnomethodological Approaches to Socio-legal Studies' in Podgorecki and Whelan (eds) 1981. Recent ethnographic studies of the formation of legal consciousness in social interaction have also been particularly important. See, especially, literature cited in text of and notes to the sections on 'Microsociological Approaches' in Chapter 5 and 'Phenomenology, Ethnomethodology and Studies of Interaction and Organisation in Lower Courts' in Chapter 7. Writing at about the same time as Weber, the Polish jurist Leon Petrazycki similarly argued that study of social action required empathetic introspection by the observer to gather the subjective meaning attached to the action by the observed. In 1907 he wrote: 'One who did not, through his own experience, know of hunger, thirst, anger, joy, and the like would, in general, be incapable of knowing these psychic phenomena ... hence he could not understand the corresponding behaviour, bodily movements or speeches of others ... The same is true as to legal phenomena. A man suffering from absolute legal idiotism—that is to say, complete inability to have legal experiences—could not possibly know what law is or understand the human conduct evoked thereby' (Petrazycki 1955, pp. 14–15). Cf. Hart 1961, pp. 55–6 and 86–7 on the 'internal aspect' of rules.

Chapter 1: The Social Basis of Law

Folkways and Mores: Sumner (1840–1910) held a chair of political and social science at Yale University from 1872 until his death. Previously he had studied at Yale and later been a tutor in mathematics and Greek and a minister of the Protestant church. On Sumner generally, see e.g. Hinkle 1980; R. Hofstadter *Social Darwinism in American Thought* 1955, ch 3; and L. A. Coser's acute brief critique in Bottomore and Nisbet (eds) 1979, pp. 294–8. Sumner's stress on organic legal development parallels and supports his legal politics, best encapsulated in the statement that 'the most difficult problem in respect to liberty under law is now what it has always been, to prevent the law from overgrowing and smothering liberty' *Earth Hunger and Other Essays* (1913) 1980 edn, p. 166. For an interpretation of Sumner's views on law see H. V. Ball, G. E. Simpson and K. Ikeda 'Law and Social Change: Sumner Reconsidered' (1962) 67 Am J Soc 532. Compare with Sumner's view of law as emerging from folkways and mores, Carbonnier's discussion of the relationship between *règles d'automatisme, régularites* and *règles d'obligation* in Carbonnier 1988, pp. 94–8; and Paul Bohannon's idea of law as a double institutionalisation of custom in 'The Differing Realms of the Law' reprinted in Evan (ed) 1980, pp. 3–11.

Law and Culture: Savigny (1779–1861) taught at Marburg and Berlin and was Prussian Minister of Legislation from 1842 to 1848. He produced major writings on Roman law and its history. For further discussion of his work see Böckenförde 1991, ch. 1; Stone 1966, ch 2. For a detailed account of the legal and political context and consequences of the debate on codification in Germany in the nineteenth century see M. John *Politics and Law in Late Nineteenth-Century Germany: The Origins of the Civil Code* 1989. The major themes of Savigny's early polemic against codification (Savigny 1831) are restated and elaborated in Savigny 1867, especially ch 2.

Legal ideas and 'shared understandings': on the cultural relativity of legal and moral concepts see M. Mead 'Some Anthropological Considerations Concerning Natural Law' (1961) 6 Natural Law Forum 51; H. Allen 'One Law for All Reasonable Persons?' (1988) 16 Int J Soc L 419 (sexist cultural assumptions contained in the common law concept of reasonableness). The concept of legal culture is developed by analogy with that of political or civic culture, a familiar idea in political science since the early 1960s. See G. Almond and S. Verba *The Civic Culture* 1963; Almond and Verba (eds) *The Civic Culture Revisited* 1980; L. H. Fuchs *The American Kaleidoscope: Race, Ethnicity and the Civic Culture* 1990. Cf. H. W. Ehrmann, *Comparative Legal Cultures* 1976. See also Atiyah and Summers 1987 pp. 411–5.

Ehrlich's Polemic Against Legal Positivism: On Bentham's and Austin's legal philosophies in relation to the political context of their time see generally Cotterrell 1989, ch 3. Even within the common law world important variations exist in the relationship between judge-made law and legislation. Thus, D. L. Horowitz writes that in England the struggle between these two legal sources was an 'unequal battle, the outcome perhaps foreordained by the Glorious Revolution, which settled the issue of parliamentary supremacy', but in the

United States 'the outcome remains in doubt. A written Constitution, in need of judicial interpretation; a separation of powers that made each branch [of government] in theory the equal of the others; a profound distrust of popular legislative majorities: a strong current of natural rights: and a transplanted common law tradition partly antedating the embodiment of natural right in Parliament: these were among the elements which sustained the creative lawmaking of judges' (Horowitz 1977, p. 2).

Ehrlich (1862–1922) studied and taught law originally at the University of Vienna. From 1897 until his death he was a professor of law at Czernowitz, his birthplace, in the province of Bukovina. His major work on the sociology of law, *Fundamental Principles of the Sociology of Law* (Ehrlich 1936), was first published in German in 1913. Some of its main themes are summarised in his posthumously published essay 'The Sociology of Law' (1922) 36 Harv L Rev 130. For recent discussion of Ehrlich's theories see K. Ziegert 'The Sociology behind Eugen Ehrlich's Sociology of Law' (1979) 7 Int J Soc L 225; D. Nelken 'Law in Action or Living Law? Back to the Beginning in Sociology of Law' (1984) 4 Legal Studies 157; H. Rottleuthner 'Three Legal Sociologies: Eugen Ehrlich, Hugo Sinzheimer, Max Weber' in A. Febbrajo et al. (eds) *European Yearbook in the Sociology of Law 1988* 1988. On Ehrlich's influence in the United States see A. Nussbaum 'Fact Research in Law' (1940) 40 Col L Rev 189, citing many references in earlier literature. Enthusiastic pioneer advocacy of Ehrlich's ideas in the common law world is found in W. H. Page 'Professor Ehrlich's Czernowitz Seminar of Living Law' in *Proceedings of the 14th Annual Meeting of the Association of American Law Schools* 1914 pp. 46–75: 'the possibilities of our common-law system seem almost exhausted....New materials must be sought for the revival and development of the common law, or for the codification which is the next step in an era of legislation; and a most fertile field for these materials is that which Professor Ehrlich calls the living law' (p. 75). An acute early critique of Ehrlich is in P. Vinogradoff 'The Crisis of Modern Jurisprudence' in his *Collected Papers* 1928, vol 2.

The idea of a plurality of legal orders which is central to Ehrlich's work attacks not only the legal positivist distinction between law and non-law but also the assumption of a unitary source of legal authority within lawyers' law. Critics of Austin noted that the Austinian concept of sovereignty as the single source of authority of all laws within a legal system led to intractable problems in analysis of federal legal systems such as that of the United States where law derives from national organs and from those of the separate states. The problem is not confined to federal systems. Many legal systems can be seen as consisting of several levels or regions of law possessing autonomous or semi-autonomous bases of authority. This diversity is not rendered insignificant by the existence of a distinct hierarchy of legal sources within the legal system as a whole. Cf. H. W. Arthurs *'Without the Law': Administrative Justice and Legal Pluralism in Nineteenth-Century England* 1985.

Law as the Framework of Social Life: On state responses to duelling see also F. Billacois *The Duel: Its Rise and Fall in Early Modern France* 1990, especially ch 10 on 'Opposition to the Duel: The State' and pp. 208–12. For recent research on compliance with tax laws see K. W. Smith and K. A. Kinsey 'Understanding

Taxpaying Behavior: A Conceptual Framework with Implications for Research' (1987) 21 Law & Soc Rev 639.

Empirical Studies of the Living Law: Published research that can be regarded as concerned with living law in Ehrlich's sense is very extensive. Among recent studies of normative order largely independent of state law in diverse social settings see e. g. R. C. Ellickson *Order Without Law: How Neighbors Settle Disputes* 1991; M. P. Baumgartner *The Moral Order of a Suburb* 1988; Greenhouse 1986. S. Henry *Private Justice* 1983 stresses the interpenetration of state law and private justice systems. Cf. S. P. Menefee *Wives For Sale: An Ethnographic Study of British Popular Divorce* 1981. Studies inspired by, related to or commenting on Macaulay's seminal 'non-contractual relations' paper (Macaulay 1963) include: Beale and Dugdale 1975; S. Macaulay 'Elegant Models, Empirical Pictures, and the Complexities of Contract' (1977) 11 Law & Soc Rev 507; R. Lewis 'Contracts Between Businessmen: Reform of the Law of Firm Offers and an Empirical Study of Tendering Practices in the Building Industry' (1982) 9 J Law & Soc 153; T. Daintith 'The Design and Performance of Long-Term Contracts' in T. Daintith and G. Teubner (eds) *Contract and Organisation* 1986; Vincent-Jones 1989; Blegvad 1990; Friedman 1990b. For Macaulay's own reassessment of his original findings, which also brings out some of the politics of research on living law see his 'An Empirical View of Contract' [1985] Wisconsin Law Review 465. For views of legal-business relations from the lawyer's standpoint see S. Wheeler 'Lawyer Involvement in Commercial Disputes' (1991) 18 J Law & Soc 241.

Mere Polemic?: On the integrity of living law: L. E. Trakman 'Frustrated Contracts and Legal Fictions' (1983) 46 Mod L Rev 39 discusses disruptive effects of judicial imposition of implied contract terms in circumstances where business practice provides adequate but different solutions. On the advantages to businessmen of arbitration as compared with litigation see e.g. Goode 1982, pp. 971–2; and Mr Justice Kerr 'International Arbitration v. Litigation' (1980) Journal of Business Law 164. But cf. A. H. Hermann *Judges, Law and Businessmen* 1983, pp. 197–241: 'Arbitration, believed to be cheaper, faster, less formal and a more common-sense method of resolving disputes, has lost almost all of these advantages' (p. 197). The cause, in Hermann's view, is primarily the formalisation of the arbitration process—in a sense its colonisation by the official legal system; see further Chapter 9 on informal processes as an extension of the official legal system. See also Lord Justice Kerr 'Commercial Dispute Resolution: The Changing Scene' in M. Bos and I. Brownlie (eds) *Liber Amicorum for Lord Wilberforce* 1987 which highlights both the important considerations of 'consumer satisfaction' (p. 125) that inspired the liberalising Arbitration Act 1979 and also the strikingly legalistic framework of present international arbitration. Cf. F. A. Mann 'Private Arbitration and Public Policy' (1985) 4 Civil Justice Quarterly 257 expressing a lawyer's worries that arbitration is insufficiently controlled within the state legal system.

For recent examples of 'legal impact' research see J. S. Legge jr 'Reforming Public Safety: An Evaluation of the 1983 British Seat Belt Law' (1987) 9 Law and Policy 17; M. Gysels et al. '(In)equality of Husband and Wife in Patrimonial

Matters' (1987) 15 Int J Soc L 29; M. D. Laurence, J. R. Snortum and F. E. Zimring (eds) *Social Control of the Drinking Driver* 1988; Ross 1984; S. I. Singer and D. McDowall 'Criminalizing Delinquency: The Deterrent Effects of the New York Juvenile Offender Law' (1988) 22 Law & Soc Rev 521; Hayden 1989; M. Friedland, M. Trebilcock and K. Roach *Regulating Traffic Safety* 1990. For a critical discussion of impact research on United States Supreme Court decisions see Brigham 1987, ch 7.

The Problem of the Concept of Law: Legal pluralism: see Carbonnier 1978, pp. 208–18; Carbonnier 1988, pp. 16ff; and for recent pluralist conceptions of law M. Galanter 'Justice in Many Rooms: Courts, Private Ordering, and Indigenous Law' (1981) 19 Journal of Legal Pluralism and Unofficial Law 1; P. Fitzpatrick 'Law and Societies' (1984) 22 Osgoode Hall Law Journal 115; Fitzpatrick 1983; Santos 1985; J. Griffiths 'What is Legal Pluralism?' (1986) 24 Journal of Legal Pluralism 1; Santos 1987; S. Merry 'Legal Pluralism' (1988) 22 Law & Soc Rev 869; G. Teubner 'Two Faces of Janus: Rethinking Legal Pluralism' Cardozo Law Review (forthcoming). On Gurvitch see MacDonald 1979; and cf. the harsh assessment by A. Hunt in S. Spitzer (ed) Research in Law and Sociology vol 2, 1979, 169–204, which also discusses Timasheff's work. On Petrazycki see e.g. J. Gorecki (ed) *The Sociology and Jurisprudence of Leon Petrazycki* 1975. The so-called French institutionalist jurists saw society as composed of numerous institutions each with its own law. See A. Broderick (ed) *The French Institutionalists: Hauriou, Renard, Delos* 1970; and Stone 1966, ch 11, where the related ideas of the Italian jurist S. Romano are also discussed. Hostility to the assumption of state dominance of law is particularly marked in the early twentieth century writings of the French jurist Léon Duguit. Duguit, a disciple of Durkheim, saw law as an expression of social solidarity rather than as the imperatives of the state. See Duguit 'Objective Law' (1920) 20 Col L Rev 817, (1921) 21 Col L Rev 17, 126, 242; and on Durkheim see Chapter 3. Llewellyn's legal pluralism is discussed in Chapter 3.

Law as coercive order: emphasis on sanctions as the hallmark of the legal is characteristic of much literature in legal theory, sociology and anthropology. In anthropology, A. R. Radcliffe-Brown adopted the jurist Roscoe Pound's definition of law as social control through the systematic application of the force of politically organised society. Radcliffe-Brown sees sanctions as legal 'when they are imposed by a constituted authority, political, military or ecclesiastic'. In the absence of such sanctions obligations are customary or conventional but not legal (*Structure and Function in Primitive Society* 1959, pp. 208, 212). Within Marxist theory the fragmentary writings of the Italian Antonio Gramsci sometimes adopt a broad and, in this context, highly unusual view of law as identified by its sanctioning capacities and in no way limited to being the instrument of governmental agencies. Gramsci usually seems to be writing of what law *could be* in revolutionary practice, however, rather than of what it is: see Cain 1983b.

Dispute processing: an important and detailed statement of an analytical approach focused on 'disputes' is Abel 1973, which is considerably more cautious in its claims than much subsequent 'disputes' literature. For perceptive criticisms of the assumptions in this literature see Cain and Kulcsar 1982, and their 'Introduction: the Study of Disputes' in Cain and Kulcsar (eds) 1983. See further Chapter 7.

Law as doctrine: some research has used a relatively narrow and explicitly value-laden concept of 'legality' as a basis for sociological study, most notably in analysing police work (Skolnick 1975) and industrial relations (Selznick 1969): see Chapter 3. By contrast, in such works as Edelman 1979 a study of legal doctrine is used in a Marxist theoretical framework as the means of revealing important ideological effects of law: see further Chapter 4.

Chapter 2: Law as an Instrument of Social Change

Modern Law and Modern State: On the development of the modern state see e. g. J. Anderson (ed) *The Rise of the Modern State* 1986; Mann 1984; Poggi 1978. The concept of 'civil society' is elaborated in different ways in the writings of, for example, Saint-Simon, Adam Ferguson, Hegel and Marx. The distinction between state and civil society, developed particularly in Hegel's early-nineteenth-century writings is a consistent theme in much social theory: see Keane 1988. In Hegel's analysis, civil society is the intermediate phase between the intimate, close-knit relationships of family life and the universal public interest and perspective of the state. It is the sphere in which individuals' private interests embodied in property and contract are freely pursued under a framework of law. In broad terms, then, civil society can be identified as the social sphere in which individuals pursue their own isolated self-interest; the state can be identified with the public realm of common interest. See especially G. W. F. Hegel *Philosophy of Right* (transl. T. M. Knox) 1952, Part 3 (ii) and (iii). See further Chapter 4 and Chapter 9.

Social Change: On Renner's theories of legal and social change see e.g. P. Robson 'Renner Revisited' in E. Attwooll (ed) *Perspectives in Jurisprudence* 1977; and on Renner in the political and intellectual context of his times see M. E. Blum *The Austro-Marxists 1890-1918: A Psychobiographical Study* 1985 chs 2, 3 and 10.

The Limits of Effective Legal Action: See also R. Summers *Instrumentalism and American Legal Theory* 1982, ch 12; W. M. Evan 'Organizations and the Limits of Effective Legal Action' in Evan 1990; Allott 1980. Pennock and Chapman (eds) 1974 contains essays from various disciplinary perspectives. Studies of the genesis of legislation are beyond the scope of this book but for their relevance for inquiries about the kinds of policy which may inform law making and law enforcement and the related conditions of acceptance of new legislation see e.g. Gusfield 1963; Paulus 1974; Carson 1974; Gunningham 1974; Kolko 1963; McCormick 1979.

Making People Good Through Law?: A useful study, which also summarises the findings of much previous research on the effects of law on attitudes, is J. Colombotos 'Physicians and Medicare: A Before-After Study of the Effects of Legislation on Attitudes' (1969) 34 Am Soc Rev 318. See also, among other empirical studies, N. Walker and M. Argyle, 'Does the Law Affect Moral Judgments?' (1964) 4 Brit J Crim 570 (no significant evidence of influence of knowledge of legal position on attitudes); L. Berkowitz and N. Walker 'Laws and Moral Judgments' (1967) 30 Sociometry 410 (knowledge of the legal position is much less significant in changing moral judgments than is knowledge of a consensus of opinions among peers); N. Walker and C. Marsh 'Does the Severity of Sentences Affect Public Disapproval?' in N. Walker and M. Hough (eds) *Public Attitudes to Sentencing* 1988 (no evidence that variation in severity of punishment affects degree of disapproval of the sanctioned behaviour); J. Andenaes 'The Moral or Educative Influence of Criminal Law' (1971) 27 Journal of Social Issues No. 2, 17. For a recent examination of efforts to enforce laws against alcohol and drug use, gambling and prostitution in the United States see M. Woodiwiss *Crime, Crusades and Corruption: Prohibitions in the United States, 1900–1987* 1988. See also J. J. Rumbarger *Profits, Power, and Prohibition: Alcohol Reform and the Industrializing of America, 1800–1930* 1989.

Legislative Strategies for Promoting Social Change: On indirect effects of law through the shaping of social institutions see G. B. Melton and M. J. Saks 'The Law as an Instrument of Socialization and Social Structure' in G. B. Melton (ed) *The Law as a Behavioral Instrument* 1986. See further e.g. R. S. Summers, *Instrumentalism and American Legal Theory* 1982 ch 8; J. Morison 'How to Change Things with Rules', and S. Livingstone 'Using Law to Change a Society: The Case of Northern Ireland', in S. Livingstone and J. Morison (eds) *Law, Society and Change* 1990. R. J. Bonnie 'The Efficacy of Law as a Paternalistic Instrument' in Melton (ed), above, is a wide-ranging survey of the effects of legal strategies in various fields. On important differences between methods and styles of legislation in the United Kingdom and the United States see Atiyah and Summers 1987, ch 11.

Some Prerequisites for Effective Legislation: On race and sex discrimination legislation in Britain see Lustgarten 1986; J. Gregory *Sex, Race and the Law: Legislating for Equality* 1987; C. McCrudden, D.J. Smith and C. Brown *Racial Justice at Work* 1991. And on the extension of civil rights in the United States: L. S. Greene 'Twenty Years of Civil Rights: How Firm a Foundation? (1985) 37 Rutgers Law Review 707 (offering a relatively positive assessment of the social effects of civil rights legislation); N.C. Amaker *Civil Rights and the Reagan Administration* 1988; M. R. Belknap *Federal Law and Southern Order: Racial Violence and Constitutional Conflict in the Post-Brown South* 1987. See also G. N. Rosenberg *The Hollow Hope: Can Courts Bring About Social Change?* 1991 (a generally negative assessment of efforts through courts to engineer major social change in the United States). On the use of rewards to achieve compliance see e. g. M. Friedland, M. Trebilcock and K. Roach *Regulating Traffic Safety* 1990, ch 3.

Limitations of 'Law and Social Change' Studies: See D. Nelken 'Beyond the Study of Law and Society?' (1986) American Bar Foundation Research Journal 323 (identifying themes of disillusionment with efforts to assess law's effects 'on society').

A Note on Autopoiesis Theory: Teubner (ed) 1988 provides a convenient guide to current debates around legal autopoiesis theory. Among recent writings on law by Luhmann see e. g. Luhmann 1986; 'The Sociological Observation of the Theory and Practice of Law' in A. Febbrajo et al. (eds) *European Yearbook in the Sociology of Law 1988* 1988; Luhmann 1988a; Luhmann 1988b; 'Law as a Social System' (1989) 83 Northwestern University Law Review 136. Among recent writings by Teubner on autopoiesis see sources referred to in the text and 'Hypercycle in Law and Organisation: The Relationship between Self-Observation, Self-Constitution and Autopoiesis' in Febbrajo et al. (eds) *European Yearbook*, above. For critique see Rottleuthner 1989; and reply by S. C. Smith (1991) 19 Int J Soc L 321. See also King and Piper 1990, and M. King 'Child Welfare Within Law: The Emergence of a Hybrid Discourse' (1991) J Law & Soc 303 (using autopoiesis theory to analyse confrontation between legal and child welfare discourses); and on the problems and limits of law as a 'steering mechanism' in society, T. Daintith (ed) *Law as an Instrument of Economic Policy: Comparative and Critical Approaches* 1988.

Chapter 3: Law as an Integrative Mechanism

Function and Purpose in Law: Merton 1968 is an elaborate and sophisticated analysis of theoretical and methodological implications of the use of the concept of 'function' in sociology and anthropology. Merton's distinction between manifest and latent functions broadly parallels the distinction between purpose and function in the text. For effective criticism of the idea of laws as expressions of the will or purpose of legislators see K. Olivecrona *Law as Fact* 2nd edn, 1972. In modern normative legal theory, the need for 'purposive' interpretation of law has been most vigorously championed in the writings of the American jurist Lon Fuller. Fuller writes: 'We must ... be sufficiently capable of putting ourselves in the position of those who drafted a rule to know what they thought "ought to be". It is in the light of this "ought" that we must decide what the rule "is"': (1958) 71 Harv L Rev 630, 666.

Discussions of functional method in sociology are innumerable. See e.g. H. Bredemeier 'The Methodology of Functionalism' (1955) 20 Am Soc Rev 173; K. Davis 'The Myth of Functional Analysis as a Special Method in Sociology and Anthropology' (1959) 24 Am Soc Rev 757; R. P. Dore 'Function and Cause' (1961) 26 Am Soc Rev 843. For an influential statement from the standpoint of anthropology see A.R. Radcliffe-Brown 'On the Concept of Function in Social Science' in his *Structure and Function in Primitive Society* 1952 and cf. the different interpretation of B. Malinowski 'The Functional Theory' in *A Scientific Theory of Culture and Other Essays* 1944. Critical discussions of functional method are listed in the notes to 'Functionalism as Social Theory', below, and see W.E. Moore 'Functionalism' in Bottomore and Nisbet—(eds) 1979; also A. Giddens 'Functionalism—*Après la lutte*' in his *Studies in Social and Political Theory* 1977; J. C. Alexander (ed) *Neofunctionalism* 1985.

A Law-Centred Conception of Social Cohesion—Pound: Roscoe Pound (1870–1964) was a dominating figure in American legal scholarship throughout much of the first half of the twentieth century. David Wigdor's excellent biography *Roscoe Pound—Philosopher of Law* 1974 clearly shows the uneasy combination in Pound's thinking, as expressed in his prolific writings, of a sympathy for legal reform and an adherence to traditional professional legal values emphasising organic legal development by common law methods. The latter tendency eventually came to dominate Pound's outlook: see Cotterrell 1989, ch 6. Despite his continually self-proclaimed 'sociological' sympathies he stayed on the sidelines of social science and because of his failure to connect his ideas with the developing literature of modern sociology the burgeoning social scientific study of law has tended to pass by the ideas in his writings with little comment. Pound's *magnum opus* is his five volume *Jurisprudence* 1959. A good survey of Pound's work in relation to social scientific analysis of law is contained in A. Hunt *The Sociological Movement in Law* 1978, ch 2. Some of Pound's central concepts are applied or analysed in social scientific studies in Hoebel 1954, Hartzler 1976 and R. Quinney *The Social Reality of Crime* 1970.

Law and Solidarity in Modern Society—Durkheim: The influence of Durkheim (1858–1917) on many aspects of social science remains extensive and profound. As the pioneer of sociology in France he taught at the University of Bordeaux for fifteen years before being appointed to a chair at the Sorbonne in Paris. S. Lukes *Emile Durkheim* 1973 is an excellent account of his life and work. For contrasting recent efforts to build directly on Durkheim's sociological theory see e. g. S. G. Mestrovic *The Coming Fin de Siècle: An Application of Durkheim's Sociology to Modernity and Postmodernism* 1991; F. Pearce *The Radical Durkheim* 1989; J. C. Alexander (ed) *Durkheimian Sociology: Cultural Studies* 1988. His most important discussion of law is in Durkheim 1984, his first book, originally published in France in 1893. Also important are Durkheim 1982; *Professional Ethics and Civic Morals* 1957; 'Two Laws of Penal Evolution' (1973) 2 Economy and Society 285; and *The Elementary Forms of the Religious Life* 1915. There is a convenient set of extracts from his writings on law in S. Lukes and A. Scull (eds) *Durkheim and the Law* 1983, and from his writings on politics and the state in A. Giddens (ed) *Durkheim on Politics and the State* 1986. Durkheim's views on law are discussed in detail in Hunt *Sociological Movement*, above, ch 4; and see also R. Reiner 'Crime, Law and Deviance: The Durkheim Legacy' in S. Fenton *Durkheim and Modern Sociology* 1984. There is an extensive literature on his theories of crime and punishment: see especially Garland 1990, chs 2 and 3. Among many critiques of Durkheim's conception of legal development from predominantly repressive to predominantly restitutive law see especially L. S. Sheleff 'From Restitutive Law to Repressive Law' (1975) 16 European Journal of Sociology 16; and Schwartz and Miller 1964. With several such studies, however, there is a problem of misunderstanding the limited scope and exact nature of Durkheim's legal concepts which are formulated for the specific purpose of his discussion of social solidarity in *The Division of Labour*: on this see Cotterrell 'The Durkheimian Tradition in the Sociology of Law' (1991) 25 Law & Soc Rev 923. The significance of professional and occupational groups for organic solidarity is detailed by Durkheim especially in *Professional Ethics*, above.

Universal Functions of Law? Llewellyn: The law-jobs conception was first fully expressed in Llewellyn 1940 in which important ideas have to struggle through unnecessarily opaque prose. The conception has been influential in some anthropological studies and is applied to legal analysis most notably by Llewellyn and E.A. Hoebel in *The Cheyenne Way* 1941 and in Hoebel 1954, both of which contain brief summaries of the law-jobs analytical scheme.

Social System and Social Structure: Parsons: Parsons (1902–1979) is the most influential American sociological theorist of the twentieth century. He spent almost all of his teaching career at Harvard University, initially in the Department of Economics but moving to the newly formed Department of Sociology in 1931. Parsons' earliest comprehensive statement of the conception of social system is contained in his *The Social System* 1951 which is, however, extremely difficult for anyone lacking substantial prior knowledge of sociological theory and concepts. His later social theory including the central concepts discussed in the text is best summarised in the twin volumes *Societies* 1966 and *The System of Modern Societies* 1971. For assessments see e.g. K. Menzies *Talcott Parsons and the Social Image of Man* 1977; S. P. Savage *The Theories of Talcott Parsons* 1981; F. Bourricaud *The Sociology of Talcott Parsons* 1981; R. J. Holton and B. S. Turner *Talcott Parsons on Economy and Society* 1986; R. Robertson and B. S. Turner (eds) *Talcott Parsons: Theorist of Modernity* 1991. The relation of Parsons' ideas on norms and values to Durkheim's concepts is clearly brought out in Parsons 1960b.

The Autonomy of Law in Western Society: Parsons' discussions of law are scattered through his prolific writings and the summary in the text is pieced together from many sources. Among the main ones dealing specifically with law are Parsons 1954b; 1960a, chs 4 and 5; 1962; and 1964; together with the 1966 and 1971 works cited in notes to the previous section. There are two generally less useful later papers: 'Law as an Intellectual Stepchild' in H.M. Johnson (ed) *Social System and Legal Process* 1978; and 'Law and Sociology—A Promising Courtship?' in A.E. Sutherland (ed) *The Path of the Law from 1967* 1968. See also Parsons 1977.

Durkheim's fears about the moral basis of cohesion in contemporary societies are most clearly expressed in *Elementary Forms*, above, which has been called (see R. Nisbet's introduction to the 1976 edition) 'one of the most powerful justifications of the functional indispensability of religion to society ever written.'

The Legal Profession and Its Functions: For Durkheim's views on the importance of professions in modern society see *Professional Ethics*, above; and cf. H. Perkin *The Rise of Professional Society: England Since 1880* 1989 (on the political and moral significance of the development of professional society). For Parsons' views see especially Parsons 1939 and 1954b and his essay 'Professions' in D. Sills (ed) *International Encyclopedia of the Social Sciences* vol 12, 1968.

Parsons' writings frequently make use of the four square AGIL diagram (see text Fig. 1) as a way of representing functional sub-systems and their relations in any social system. The location of internal system-problems of a legal system in this way is, however, my own synthesis from Parsons' remarks on the functions of the legal profession in maintaining and enhancing the authority and autonomy of the legal system. For commentary on functionalist approaches in the sociology of legal professions, see Abel 1988, pp. 25–30 or Abel 1989a, pp. 34–9. See further Chapter 6.

The Legal System as a Sub-System of Society: It is not difficult to correlate Bredemeier's four 'outputs' of law into the other three societal sub-systems (two to the polity) with Llewellyn's four law-jobs, but to do so adds important dimensions to the law-jobs not apparent in Llewellyn's formulation.

On the use of social scientific and statistical evidence in courts see Chapter 7.

Law and Equal Opportunity: An Empirical Test of Parsonian Theory: Cf. Parsons' paper 'Full Citizenship for the American Negro?' in Parsons 1967. For another study of the Massachusetts Commission see J. L. Jowell *Law and Bureaucracy: Administrative Discretion and the Limits of Legal Action* 1975.

Functionalism as Social Theory: For the claim that functional analysis is the fundamental method of sociology, see K. Davis 'Myth of Functional Analysis', above; and for the view that it 'leaves human beings out of the picture', see G. Homans 'Bringing Men Back In' (1964) 29 Am Soc Rev 808; D. H. Wrong 'The Oversocialized Conception of Man in Modern Sociology' (1961) 26 Am Soc Rev 183 and postscript in his *Skeptical Sociology* 1976. A.W. Gouldner's *The Coming Crisis in Western Sociology* 1971 is a detailed analysis of and attack on the conservative orientations of Parsonian theory. Parsons' mature conception of power is set out in 'On the Concept of Political Power' in Parsons 1967 and for a critique see A. Giddens '"Power" in the Writings of Talcott Parsons' in his *Studies in Social and Political Theory* 1977. For a general assessment of functionalism in relation to studies of law see Wilkinson 1981.

The Integrative Functions of Law: Although specifications of law's functions vary greatly, the general conception of its integrative tasks is assumed in much literature, old and new. See e.g. P. Vinogradoff *Common Sense in Law* 1914, pp. 46ff. Podgorecki 1974 elaborates integrative functions of law (especially pp. 274–5). Gurvitch 1947 and Timasheff 1939 both stress these functions.

Chapter 4: Law, Power and Ideology

The Consensus Constituency: See further e.g. M. Mann *Consciousness and Action Among the Western Working Class* 1973; D. Gallie *Social Inequality and Class Radicalism in France and Britain* 1983; Held 1987, pp. 196–201. In representative democracies elections provide the most visible and formalised expressions of popular will, but are not necessarily the most reliable. Thus, levels of political participation can be interpreted in opposite ways. A low level might indicate general satisfaction or extensive alienation. Political apathy (e.g. non-voting) has been interpreted by some writers as harmful to consensus-based democracy, by others as protecting it by keeping authoritarian, ignorant or extreme political views (shown in some studies to be associated with apathy about political processes) out of effective politics. See e.g. Lipset 1960, pp. 121–22, 218; B. Ginsberg and M. Shefter *Politics by Other Means: The Declining Importance of Elections in America* 1990. Equally, in the case of those who vote, it is not easy to assess what exactly they are voting for or against, and why.

Symbolic Functions of Law: On law as a reservoir of symbols see also, among recent studies, W. E. Conklin *Images of a Constitution* 1989 (discussing constitutions as images, products of 'the legal community's imagination'); L. Baas 'The Constitution as Symbol' (1980) 8 American Politics Quarterly 237. On the political uses of symbols: H. Gunnlaugsson and J. F. Galliher 'Prohibition of Beer in Iceland: An International Test of Symbolic Politics' (1986) 20 Law & Soc Rev 335; C.D. Elder and R.W. Cobb *The Political Uses of Symbols* 1983; M. Edelman *Politics as Symbolic Action* 1971; Gusfield 1963; and, for a historical study, Carson 1974. On police discretion under the Police and Criminal Evidence Act 1984 see R. Baldwin 'Regulation and Policing by Code' in M. Weatheritt (ed) *Police Research: Some Future Prospects* 1989. For other research on the effects of the Act see K. Bottomley, C. Coleman, D. Dixon, M. Gill and D. Wall 'The Detention of Suspects in Police Custody: The Impact of the Police and Criminal Evidence Act 1984' (1991) 31 Brit J Crim 347.

Marx: Repressive and Ideological Functions of Law: Marx (1818–1883), the son of a successful lawyer, was born in Trier in Germany and studied law and philosophy at the universities of Bonn and Berlin. Unable to secure a university teaching position he devoted his life to journalism, political activity and private study. He settled in London in 1849, having been exiled from Germany and expelled from France for his political activities. The major writings on law of Marx and his close collaborator Friedrich Engels are conveniently collated in Cain and Hunt (eds) 1979. Collins 1982 offers a lucid discussion of some main themes and problems in Marxist legal theory. For other commentary see e. g. Hunt 1991; Cotterrell 'Conceptualizing Law' (1981) 10 Economy and Society 348. The most valuable reference resource on Marxist thought as a whole is L. Kolakowski's encyclopedic *Main Currents of Marxism* 1981.

Law, Class and Power: Neither Marx nor Engels ever clearly defined the concept of class, despite its centrality in their theory. See e.g. Kolakowski, above, vol 1, pp. 352–8. For recent discussion of the utility of the concept of social class see e. g. E. O. Wright *Classes* 1985; Wright, ed, 1989; Bottomore 1991; R. Miliband *Divided Societies: Class Struggle in Contemporary Capitalism* 1989; S. G. McNall, R. F. Levine and R. Fantasia (eds) *Bringing Class Back In: Contemporary and Historical Perspectives* 1991. For the judiciary's recognition of its own class biases the best known source is Lord Justice Scrutton's statement in 'The Work of the Commercial Courts' (1923) Cambridge Law Journal 6, 8.

On the concept of power: see e.g. D. Wrong *Power: Its Forms, Bases and Uses* 1979; S. Lukes *Power* 1974; P. Bachrach and M. S. Baratz *Power and*

Poverty: Theory and Practice 1970. On elite theory and pluralist political theory: see e. g. Held 1987, ch 6; O'Leary and Dunleavy 1987, chs 2, 4 and 6. Modern studies of ruling elites: e.g. J. Scott *Who Rules Britain?* 1991; Mills 1956; G.W. Domhoff *The Powers That Be* 1979; Miliband 1969; J. Howorth and P.G. Cerny (eds) *Elites in France* 1981; also Mathiesen 1980 on empirical evidence of the relationships between legal elites and other economic and political leaders. In Mills' famous study, above, lawyers are seen as the professional 'go-betweens' who help to unify the power elite.

Bias and inequalities in the administration of law: see generally Cranston 1985, ch 3. For a sample from numerous recent studies: I. Brown and R. Hullin 'A Study of Sentencing in the Leeds Magistrates' Courts: The Treatment of Ethnic Minority and White Offenders' (1992) 32 Brit J Crim 41 (race not a significant factor in use of custodial sentences or in range of non-custodial sentences applied); G. Mair 'Ethnic Minorities, Probation and the Magistrates' Courts' (1986) 26 Brit J Crim 147 (finding limited evidence of differences along racial lines in use of alternatives to custody); NACRO Race Issues Advisory Committee *Black People and the Criminal Justice System* 1986 (evidence of differential use of alternatives to custody); Gordon 1983 (evidence of racial bias in policing in Britain); M. A. Walker 'The Court Disposal and Remands of White, Afro-Caribbean and Asian Men (London, 1983)' (1989) 29 Brit J Crim 353; T. Bennett 'The Social Distribution of Criminal Labels' (1979) 19 Brit J Crim 134 (social class of offender as determinant of police action), but cf. criticism of this study in 21 Brit J Crim 27. P. Gordon 'Black People and the Criminal Law: Rhetoric and Reality' (1988) 16 Int J Soc L 295 surveys much literature on black citizens' experience of the criminal justice system. On gender bias and differential treatment of women see e. g. S. McLean and N. Burrows (eds) *The Legal Relevance of Gender* 1988; D. Elliott *Gender, Delinquency and Society* 1988 (gender bias in juvenile justice); P. Carlen and A. Worrall (eds) *Gender, Crime and Justice* 1987; M. Eaton *Justice for Women? Family, Court and Social Control* 1986 (routine processes of summary justice reinforce women's social position); cf. L. Gelsthorpe *Sexism and the Female Offender: An Organizational Analysis* 1989 (images of female offenders are mediated by organisational factors not necessarily linked directly to sexist ideology); D.P. Farrington and A.M. Morris 'Sex, Sentencing and Reconviction' (1983) 23 Brit J Crim 229 (sex of defendant not a direct influence on severity of sentencing in an English magistrates' court).

Among American literature see e. g. D. C. Baldus, G. Woodworth and C. A. Pulaski jr. *Equal Justice and the Death Penalty: A Legal and Empirical Analysis* 1990 (death sentence more likely where victim is white rather than black in Georgia); M. S. Zatz 'The Changing Forms of Racial/Ethnic Biases in Sentencing' (1987) 24 Journal of Research in Crime and Delinquency 69; M. L. Radelet and G. L. Pierce 'Race and Prosecutorial Discretion in Homicide Cases' (1985) 19 Law & Soc Rev 587; D. Weisburd et al. 'Class, Status, and the Punishment of White-Collar Criminals' (1990) 15 L & Soc Inq 223 (class position of defendant has independent influence on judicial sentencing behaviour); E. Rapaport 'The Death Penalty and Gender Discrimination' (1991) 25 Law & Soc Rev 367; C. K. Gillespie *Justifiable Homicide: Battered Women, Self-Defense, and the Law* 1989 (harsh judicial treatment of battered women who kill their tormentors). On the class backgrounds of judges and lawyers see Chapters 6 and 7: and on inequalities of access to law see Chapter 8 ('Opportunity and Incentive to Invoke Law').

Law and Ideology: For applications, refinements, and extensions of the conception of the nature of ideology advocated in this section, and further developed throughout this book, see e. g. Harrington 1985, Brigham 1987, S. A. M. Galligan 'Law, Gender and Ideology' in A. Bayefsky (ed) *Legal Theory Meets Legal Practice* 1988, C. B. Harrington and B. Yngvesson 'Interpretive Sociolegal Research' (1990) 15 L & Soc Inq 135. For a critique of my development of this conception specifically within the framework of this book see Silbey 1991. See also Cotterrell 1983a; 1983b; 1988; 1990b. Alan Hunt has elaborated similar views of the character of legal ideology and its importance. For his powerful theoretical analysis see 'The Ideology of Law: Advances and Problems in Recent Applications of the Concept of Ideology to the Analysis of Law' (1985) 19 Law & Soc Rev 11. Recent theoretical studies of ideology include I. Mészáros *The Power of Ideology* 1989; R. Boudon *The Analysis of Ideology* 1989; J. B. Thompson *Ideology and Modern Culture* 1990; T. Eagleton *Ideology: An Introduction* 1991; J. B. Thompson *Studies in the Theory of Ideology* 1984. C. Sumner *Reading Ideologies* 1979 is a difficult but useful discussion of relationships between law and ideology.

'Structuralist' analyses of law and ideology: see especially Althusser 1971; Edelman 1979; Poulantzas 1978; Mathiesen 1980. Hirst 1979 chs 2 and 3 provide an excellent summary and critique of Althusser's seminal contribution to development of the concept of ideology. On Althusser generally, see G. Elliott *Althusser: The Detour of Theory* 1987. Somewhat related to these modern structuralist approaches are the ideas of thc Italian Marxist Antonio Gramsci. Gramsci, like Althusser, sees the realm of ideas as a terrain of class struggle significant in its own right and the mechanisms of moral, political and intellectual leadership—what he calls 'hegemony'—as providing the means by which a dominant class can rule in modern Western societies by consensus (by shaping the ideas which form the consensus) rather than coercion. For the relevance of Gramsci's fragmentary writings for legal theory see Cain 1983b; M. Benney 'Gramsci on Law, Morality and Power' (1983) 11 Int J Soc L 191; Hunt 1990. On 'class instrumentalist' analysis: see especially Collins 1982.

Pashukanis: see Pashukanis 1978 and E.B. Pashukanis *Selected Writings on Marxism and Law* (ed P. Beirne and R. Sharlet) 1980. For a perceptive study see A. Norrie 'Pashukanis and the "Commodity Form Theory"' (1982) 10 Int J Soc L 419; and, for an unusual recent discussion from a liberal standpoint, N. Simmonds 'Pashukanis and Liberal Jurisprudence' (1985) 12 J Law & Soc 135. Pashukanis' work has been influential in German Marxist analyses of the state: see generally J. Holloway and S. Picciotto (eds) *State and Capital* 1978.

Legal Individualism: R. L. Abel 'A Critique of American Tort Law' (1981) 8 Brit J Law & Soc 199 notes the stress in the law of tort on individual responsibility and the rejection of affirmative duties (e.g. duty to rescue) 'a rejection that asserts that *each* man is an island, sole unto himself': p. 206. See also on tort law Friedmann 1972, ch 5. Friedman 1990a argues that individualism in general is being transformed into a modern idea of the uniqueness of human beings and that much contemporary law directly expresses this idea. It might equally be said, however, that much of this law is necessary because of the declining scope of free initiative (in other words, the declining capacity to act as a unique being) in increasingly complex Western societies: see further Chapter 9. The lack of strong cultural supports for individual life may be such that the scope of individual action needs to be legally marked out for individuals in increasingly explicit and detailed ways.

Contract and agreement: see e.g. Atiyah 1979; M. Horwitz *The Transformation of American Law 1780–1860* 1977. On the history of standard form contracts see Prausnitz 1937. The employment contract: on the social, economic and political background of the doctrine of common employment in United States labour law see Friedman and Ladinsky 1967; and for its history and consequences in English law see P.W.J. Bartrip and S.B. Burman *The Wounded Soldiers of Industry* 1983, pp. 103ff. The rule weakened and was abolished with the development of a standardised compensation system involving calculable risks for business, and which business accepted because of rising litigation costs and the threat of more radical reforms.

On the application of ordinary contract principles to marriage and cohabitation arrangements: see generally L. J. Weitzman *The Marriage Contract: Spouses, Lovers and the Law* 1981; and e. g. E. Kingdom 'Cohabitation Contracts: A Socialist-Feminist Issue' (1988) 15 J Law & Soc 77 (recognition of cohabitation arrangements on ordinary contractual principles gives flexibility to design varied arrangements free of status constraints associated with the marriage form); R. L. Deech 'The Case Against Legal Recognition of Cohabitation' (1980) 29 International and Comparative Law Quarterly 64 (cohabitation agreements should not be legally recognised in ways that would bring them closer to the status contract of marriage; rather the latter should be brought closer to an individualistic purpose contract); M. M. Schultz 'Contractual Ordering of Marriage: the New Model for State Policy' (1982) 70 California Law Review 204. Historical transformations of the legal institution of marriage are traced in Stone 1990; Phillips 1988. On the changing situation of the family as 'a private arena' see F. R. Elliot 'The Family: Private Arena or Adjunct of the State' (1989) 16 J Law & Soc 443; R. Dingwall and J. M. Eekelaar 'Families and the State: An Historical Perspective on the Public Regulation of Private Conduct' (1988) 10 Law and Policy 341; M. McIntosh 'The Family, Regulation, and the Private Sphere' in McLennan et al. (eds) 1984.

Since the concept of private property is central to legal individualism, advocacy of extension or entrenchment of important social policies or welfare benefits has had particular impact when these issues of collective welfare have been framed in terms of arguments about individual property rights, as notably in C. Reich 'The New Property' (1964) 73 Yale L J 733. On the 'new property' thesis see also Glendon 1981; R. Baldwin and D. Horne 'Expectations in a Joyless Landscape' (1986) 49 Mod L Rev 685; D. Kettler 'Legal Reconstitution of the Welfare State: A Latent Social Democratic Legacy' (1987) 21 Law & Soc Rev 9, 16–25. Debates about the centrality of the concept of individual rights in contemporary law are considered in Chapter 9. On the individualist ideology of the French and German civil codes see Zweigert and Kötz 1987, pp. 95–6, 149–50.

Law in Corporate Society: On the sociological significance of debates about corporate personality see Friedmann 1967, ch 34. Hallis 1930 provides a detailed discussion of theories of corporate personality. On the relationship between legal controls and corporate business activity see also F. Pearce and S. Tombs 'Ideology, Hegemony, and Empiricism: Compliance Theories of Regulation' (1990) 30 Brit J Crim 423; H. J. Glasbeek 'Why Corporate Deviance Is Not Treated as a Crime: The Need to Make "Profits" a Dirty Word' (1984) 22 Osgoode Hall Law Journal 393. On law and corporate organisation see D. Sugarman and G. Teubner (eds) *Regulating Corporate Groups in Europe* 1990; H. Collins 'Ascription of Legal Responsibility to Groups in Complex Patterns of Economic Integration' (1990) 53 Mod L Rev 731 (problems in regulating complex economic groups and associations resulting from law's focus on individual responsibility). Jessop 1982 is an excellent survey of Marxist theories of the state. On corporatist theory see e. g. A. Cawson *Corporatism and Political Theory* 1986; G. Lehmbruch and P. C. Schmitter (eds) *Patterns of Corporatist Policy-Making* 1982; P. C. Schmitter and G. Lehmbruch (eds) *Trends Toward Corporatist Intermediation* 1979; and in relation to legal analysis J. T. Winkler 'Law, State and Economy: The Industry Act 1975 in Context' (1975) 2 Brit J Law & Soc 103.

State and Individual: The increasing intrusiveness of the state in individual lives through technological and administrative innovation and surveillance and control through welfare systems is a pervasive theme of much recent literature. See e.g. S. Hall 'Reformism and the Legislation of Consent' in the National Deviancy Conference's *Permissiveness and Control* 1979; Donzelot 1980 (on state and family); Elliot 'The Family: Private Arena or Adjunct of the State', above; R. Matthews '"Decarceration" and the Fiscal Crisis' (on penal policy) in the NDC's *Capitalism and the Rule of Law* 1979; S. Uglow *Policing Liberal Society* 1988, ch 6; Santos 1982; M. Foucault *Discipline and Punish* 1977 and Foucault 1979; Mathiesen 1980. But cf. R. Matthews 'Decarceration and Control: Fantasies and Realities' (1987) 15 Int J Soc L 39. See also P. Hillyard and J. Percy-Smith *The Coercive State: The Decline of Democracy in Britain* 1988. For a subtle analysis of relationships between changing penal and social control strategies and the evolution of the modern welfare state see D. Garland *Punishment and Welfare: A History of Penal Strategies* 1985. On the relevance of Foucault's work for analysis of law see Chapter 9. Claims that the classic distinction in social theory between state and civil society is ceasing to be relevant in modern conditions are discussed in Chapter 9.

The Problem of Economic Determinism: Among recent efforts to reinterpret or reconstruct Marxist theory see E. O. Wright, A. Levine and E. Sober *Reconstructing Marxism: Essays on Explanation and the Theory of History* 1992; J. Larrain *A Reconstruction of Historical Materialism* 1986. Cohen 1978 is a very well argued attempt to solve some of the problems of the base-superstructure metaphor. A. Cutler, B. Hindess, P. Hirst and A. Hussain *Marx's 'Capital' and Capitalism Today* 1977 is a seminal work attempting to reformulate Marxist concepts in a radical manner.

Chapter 5: The Acceptance and Legitimacy of Law

The Experience of Law: Positivist Approaches and KOL Studies: On KOL studies see generally, Podgorecki et al. 1973; and for a critique e.g. Bankowski and Mungham 1976, pp 18–23. On law and popular opinion see also generally Gibson and Baldwin (eds) 1985; and Marshall 1989 on opinion and the United States Supreme Court (and numerous citations to literature therein). See also e. g. N. Walker and M. Hough (eds) *Public Attitudes to Sentencing: Surveys from Five Countries* 1988.

Legal Socialisation: E. S. Cohn and S. O. White *Legal Socialization: A Study of Norms and Rules* 1990; J. L. Tapp 'Jury Service as Legal Socialization' in Gibson and Baldwin (eds) 1985; S. Macaulay 'Images of Law in Everyday Life: The Lessons of School, Entertainment, and Spectator Sports' (1987) 21 Law & Soc Rev 185; G. B. Melton 'The Significance of Law in the Everyday Lives of Children and Families' (1988) 22 Georgia Law Review 851; A. Chase 'Toward a Legal Theory of Popular Culture' [1986] Wisconsin Law Review 527; G. A. Caldeira 'Children's Images of the Supreme Court: A Preliminary Mapping' (1977) 11 Law & Soc Rev 851. Cf. S. Milgram *Obedience to Authority* 1974 (reporting experiments demonstrating general disposition to obey recognised figures of authority). On Gilligan's work see L. K. Kerber et al. 'Viewpoint: On *In a Different Voice*: An Interdisciplinary Forum' (1986) 11 Signs 304; E. C. Dubois et al. 'Feminist Discourse, Moral Values and the Law—A Conversation' (1985) 34 Buffalo Law Review 11.

Deterrence and Compliance with Law: For a general overview of concepts and research see J. P. Gibbs 'Deterrence Theory and Research' in G. B. Melton (ed) *The Law as a Behavioral Instrument* 1986. On certainty and severity of sanctions: among numerous recent studies see e. g. Klepper and Nagin (1989) (perceived risk of criminal prosecution significantly deters non-compliance with tax laws); Paternoster 1989 (perceptions of certainty, though not severity, have some deterrent effect; but far less significant than social costs and other considerations in influencing conduct); D. E. Lewis 'The General Deterrent Effect of Longer Sentences' (1986) 26 Brit J Crim 47 (lengthening of sentences has some deterrent effect); R. E. L. Watson 'The Effectiveness of Increased Police Enforcement as a General Deterrent' (1986) 20 Law & Soc Rev 293 (increased perception of risk of punishment for breach of car seat belt law reduces non-compliance); J. Braithwaite and T Makkai 'Testing an Expected Utility Model of Corporate Deterrence' (1991) 25 Law & Soc Rev 7 (certainty of detection relates to compliance with regulation by chief executives of small organisations, but no evidence of deterrent effect of certainty or severity of punishment); C R. Tittle *Sanctions and Social Deviance: The Question of Deterrence* 1980. Cf. R. Paternoster et al. 'Perceived Risk and Social Control: Do Sanctions Really Deter?' (1983) 17 Law & Soc Rev 457 (effect of perceived sanctions on criminal involvement is minimal once the effects of moral attitudes and informal sanctions are isolated from effects of state sanctions); and Braithwaite 1989, ch 5; Ross 1984.

Microsociological Approaches: Social Interaction and Legal Consciousness: One of the clearest and most influential attempts to sketch a general sociology from a phenomenological perspective is Berger and Luckmann 1967. T. Luckmann (ed) *Phenomenology and Sociology* 1978 reprints several seminal essays particularly on the philosophical foundations of phenomenological sociology. Los 1981 summarises some tenets of phenomenological approaches in sociology.

On ethnomethodological study of law, see especially J. M. Atkinson 'Ethnomethodological Approaches to Socio-Legal Studies' in Podgorecki and Whelan (eds) 1981. On ethnomethodology generally the classic source is H. Garfinkel *Studies in Ethnomethodology* 1967. Specific studies related to law, apart from those cited in the text of this section, include Garfinkel 1956; A. V. Cicourel *The Social Organisation of Juvenile Justice* 1968; Atkinson and Drew 1979. See further Chapter 7.

Studies of popular legal consciousness: apart from sources cited in the text of this section see e. g. C. J. Greenhouse 'Courting Difference: Issues of Interpretation and Comparison in the Study of Legal Ideologies' (1988) 22 Law & Soc Rev 687; J. Brigham 'Rights, Rage and Remedy: Forms of Law in Political Discourse' (1987) 2 Studies in American Political Development 303; C. B. Harrington and S. E. Merry 'Ideological Production: The Making of Community Mediation' (1988) 22 Law & Soc Rev 709; Brigham 1987; S. E. Merry 'Everyday Understandings of Law in Working-Class America' (1986) 13 American Ethnologist 253; Merry 'Rethinking Gossip and Scandal' in D. Black (ed) *Toward a General Theory of Social Control* Vol. 2 1984.

Instrumental Acceptance of Law: Max Weber: Weber (1864–1920) studied and taught law before gravitating by way of economics and economic history to sociology. He taught at the Universities of Berlin, Freiburg, Heidelberg and Munich but ill health after 1896 virtually terminated his teaching career though not, except temporarily, the prodigious output of studies ranging over numerous fields which made him a legendary figure in his lifetime. On his life, Marianne Weber's *Max Weber: A Biography* (1975; republished with a new introduction 1988) is fascinating and indispensable. The volume of literature on Weber is immense and ever increasing. Among the most valuable recent general introductions to his work are D. Käsler *Max Weber: An Introduction to His Life and Work* 1988 and M. Albrow *Max Weber's Construction of Social Theory* 1990. Also useful are R. J. Holton and B. S. Turner *Max Weber on Economy and Society* 1989; W. Mommsen *The Political and Social Theory of Max Weber* 1989; B. S. Turner *Max Weber: From History to Modernity* 1992. W. Hennis *Max Weber: Essays in Reconstruction* 1988 is an important corrective to most understandings of Weber in contemporary sociological writing, showing that the main thrust of his work cannot be confined within academic sociology's disciplinary preconceptions or boundaries. Weber 1949 contains his major texts on the methodology of sociological inquiry. Weber 1954 collates, in an excellently edited volume, major texts on law from his *magnum opus*, *Economy and Society* (Weber 1978).

The most detailed analysis of Weber's sociology of law is A. Kronman *Max Weber* 1983. See also e. g. S. M. Feldman 'An Interpretation of Max Weber's

Theory of Law: Metaphysics, Economics, and the Iron Cage of Constitutional Law' (1991) 16 L & Soc Inq 205; H. J. Berman 'Some False Premises of Max Weber's Sociology of Law' (1987) 65 Washington University Law Quarterly 758; D. M. Trubek 'Max Weber's Tragic Modernism and the Study of Law in Society' (1986) 20 Law & Soc Rev 573; Trubek 'Reconstructing Max Weber's Sociology of Law' (1985) 37 Stanford Law Review 919 (reviewing Kronman); Cotterrell 1983b; papers by M. Cain and by P. Beirne in volumes 3 (1981) and 2 (1979) respectively of *Research in Law and Sociology*, edited by S. Spitzer. For a valuable survey of literature bearing on the question of the significance of legal doctrinal developments for capitalist development, see D. Sugarman 'Law, Economy and the State in England 1750–1914: Some Major Issues' in Sugarman (ed) 1983.

Legality and Legitimacy: On Weber's 'England problem' see A. Hunt *The Sociological Movement in Law* 1978, pp. 122–28; Kronman, above, pp. 120ff; D. Trubek 'Max Weber on Law and the Rise of Capitalism' [1972] Wisconsin Law Review 720. It has been argued that Weber's stress on the need for 'calculability' in state law as a basis of economic activity is misleading in that through the private law-making device of the contract, economic actors can produce the balance of flexibility and precision they require as well as agreeing on their own means of interpretation or adjudication of differences. What is necessary from state law is thus only a minimum apparatus of support for this normative framework of calculability created by commercial actors themselves: see Ferguson 1980. Ewing 1987 suggests that this was, more or less, Weber's own view.

On exchange theory in sociology see H. C. Bredemeier 'Exchange Theory' in Bottomore and Nisbet (eds) 1979; and for a useful discussion in relation to law, A. Heath 'The Principle of Exchange as a Basis for the Study of Law' in Podgorecki and Whelan (eds) 1981.

On Weber's analysis of legal domination see generally D. Campbell 'Truth Claims and Value-Freedom in the Treatment of Legitimacy: The Case of Weber' (1986) 13 J Law & Soc 207; Cotterrell 1983b; Barker 1990, ch 3. On the empirical utility of concepts of legitimacy, see A. Hyde 'The Concept of Legitimation in the Sociology of Law' [1983] Wisconsin Law Review 379, which argues that there is no evidence that law contributes significantly to popular acceptance of social norms as legitimate, and that the concept of legitimacy is unenlightening as a foundation for explaining the degree of stability of a legal system; C. A. McEwen and R. J. Maiman 'In Search of Legitimacy: Toward an Empirical Analysis' (1986) 8 Law and Policy 257; and e. g., among much literature in political sociology, F. D. Weil 'The Sources and Structure of Legitimation in Western Democracies: A Consolidated Model Tested with Time-Series Data in Six Countries Since World War II' (1989) 54 Am Soc Rev 682.

The Meaning of the Rule of Law: Literature on the rule of law is immense. Among recent general discussions of the substance of the doctrine from a variety of standpoints see e.g. A. C. Hutchinson and P Monahan (eds) *The Rule of Law: Ideal or Ideology?* 1987; N. Luhmann *Political Theory in the Welfare State*

1990, ch 6; N. Bobbio *The Future of Democracy: A Defence of the Rules of the Game* 1987, ch 7; V. Aubert *Continuity and Development in Law and Society* 1989, ch 2; J. Jowell 'The Rule of Law Today' in J. Jowell and D. Oliver (eds) *The Changing Constitution* 2nd edn 1989; L. Lustgarten 'Socialism and the Rule of Law' (1988) 15 J Law & Soc 25; J. Raz *The Authority of Law* 1979, ch 11. F. Neumann *The Rule of Law: Political Theory and the Legal System in Modern Society* 1986 is a detailed study of the evolution of the doctrine in Western thought and an assessment of its significance in twentieth century political and social conditions.

On magistrates' justice in Britain see H. Parker, M. Sumner and G. Jarvis *Unmasking the Magistrates* 1989 (reporting an extensive study of sentencing decisions and concluding that 'magistrates have a sublime disregard for the principle of treating like cases alike. Most did not even refer back to their own previous decisions, much less those of their colleagues, and even less to decisions made in other localities': p. 117). See also R. J. Henham *Sentencing Principles and Magistrates' Sentencing Behaviour* 1990; J. W. Raine *Local Justice: Ideals and Realities* 1989; S. Brown *Magistrates at Work: Sentencing and Social Structure* 1991. Cf. D. M. Provine *Judging Credentials: Nonlawyer Judges and the Politics of Professionalism* 1986 on American lay judges. On the inequality of citizens before the law see generally Cranston 1985, ch 3.

The Transformations of Modern Law: On discretionary regulation see also Adler and Asquith (eds) 1981; Galligan 1986. On the 'resurgence' of status bases of legal regulation see e.g. M. Barkun 'Law and the New Ascriptive Groups' in R. Gambitta et al. (eds). *Governing Through Courts* 1981 stressing 'the rising legal and political importance attached to birth-related or biologically grounded aspects of personality identity for example, race, ethnicity, gender, sexual orientation, and physical handicaps.' Cf. Kahn-Freund 1967; Rehbinder 1971; M. Minow *Making All the Difference: Inclusion, Exclusion, and American Law* 1990, ch 5. The *locus classicus* of arguments for the legal recognition of statuses providing security in the holding of major contemporary forms of wealth or guarantees of wellbeing (e. g. jobs, welfare entitlements, occupational licences and franchises) is Reich's 'New Property' essay, cited in notes to 'Legal Individualism' in Chapter 4, above.

Sociological Explanations of Changes in the Form of Western Law: Among the works cited in the text Kamenka and Tay 1975 is primarily descriptive, usefully providing a typology of change. On Luhmann's systems theory see Luhmann 1982; and W. T. Murphy 'Modern Times: Niklas Luhmann on Law, Politics and Social Theory' (1984) 47 Mod L Rev 603.

Legal Legitimacy After the Rule of Law?: G. Teubner 'Substantive and Reflexive Elements in Modern Law' (1983) 17 Law & Soc Rev 239 compares the views of legal development offered by Nonet and Selznick, on the one hand, and Habermas and Luhmann, on the other. On Nonet and Selznick's 'responsive law' see also Galligan 1986, pp. 99–106. See also, generally, D. Kettler 'Legal Reconstitution of the Welfare State: A Latent Social Democratic Legacy' (1987) 21 Law & Soc Rev 9. For Habermas' ideas, P. Dews (ed) *Habermas:*

Autonomy and Solidarity 1986 (a volume of interviews) and R. Roderick *Habermas and the Foundations of Critical Theory* 1986 are accessible introductions. Among Habermas' many works *The Theory of Communicative Action* Vol. 1 1984 and Vol. 2 1987 is a major statement of his developed social theory. Habermas 1975 contains his analysis of legitimation problems of the contemporary state in Western societies and his critique of Weber's views on legal domination. Cf. C. Sumner 'Law, Legitimation and the Advanced Capitalist State: The Jurisprudence and Social Theory of Jürgen Habermas' in Sugarman (ed) 1983. Some of his current views on law are set out in Habermas 1986; and see K. Raes 'Habermas' Approach to Law' (1986) 13 J Law & Soc 183. On Habermas' influence on legal studies see W. T. Murphy 'The Habermas Effect: Critical Theory and Academic Law' (1989) Current Legal Problems 135.

Ideology, Personal Values and Support for Law: On perceived fairness of procedures as a basis of acceptance of law see also E. A. Lind and T. R. Tyler *The Social Psychology of Procedural Justice* 1988; Tyler 'What Is Procedural Justice? Criteria Used by Citizens to Assess the Fairness of Legal Procedures' (1988) 22 Law & Soc Rev 103; Tyler 'The Role of Perceived Injustice in Defendants' Evaluations of Their Courtroom Experience' (1984) 18 Law & Soc Rev 51; J. D. Casper, T. R. Tyler and B. Fisher 'Procedural Justice in Felony Cases' (1988) 22 Law & Soc Rev 483; Gibson 1989; T. R. Tyler and K. Rasinski 'Procedural Justice, Institutional Legitimacy, and the Acceptance of Unpopular U. S. Supreme Court Decisions: A Reply to Gibson' (1991) 25 Law & Soc Rev 621.

On E. P. Thompson's view of the rule of law see also A. Merritt 'The Nature and Function of Law: A Criticism of E. P. Thompson's *Whigs and Hunters*' (1980) 7 Brit J Law & Soc 194; Sugarman 1981; A. Hunt 'Dichotomy and Contradiction in the Sociology of Law' (1981) 8 Brit J Law & Soc 47, 67–72. Many other writers, criticising 'informalism' and administrative discretion, have similarly argued that reliance on formal rules can be a weapon of the oppressed: see Chapter 9.

Chapter 6: Professional Guardianship of Law

What is a Legal Profession?: On the sociology of the professions see generally e. g. Abbott 1988; Freidson 1986; Larson 1977; Dingwall and Lewis (eds) 1983; and, on the emergence of professions, W. Prest (ed) *The Professions in Early Modern England* 1987 (considering occupational organisation and status of doctors, lawyers, clergy, soldiers, teachers, and estate stewards). Abel and Lewis (eds) 1989 presents valuable recent theoretical essays on the sociology of legal professions.

Professional Unity and the Stratification of Legal Work: The literature on the sociology of legal practice is now immense. Citations in this and the following sections are, in the main, limited to a small sample of relatively recent publications. On the organisation of legal practice in continental European countries see generally R. L. Abel and P. S. C. Lewis (eds) *Lawyers in Society. Vol 2: The Civil Law World* 1988; and A. West 'Reforming the French Legal Profession: Towards Increased Competitiveness in the Single Market' (1991) 11 Legal Studies 189 (on changing formal professional divisions). Rueschemeyer 1973 is a detailed comparative study of the work, organisation, and social, economic and political environment of lawyers in the United States and in Germany. On the social structure of the American legal profession Heinz and Laumann 1982 is the most instructive recent study. See also Nelson 1988 and Galanter and Palay 1991 (on large law firms); Spangler 1986 (on salaried lawyers, corporate staff counsel, civil service attorneys, lawyers in large law firms, and legal services advocates); A. Chayes and A. H. Chayes 'Corporate Counsel and the Elite Law Firm' (1985) 37 Stanford Law Review 277; E. O. Laumann, J. P. Heinz et al. 'Washington Lawyers and Others: The Structure of Washington Representation' (1985) 37 Stanford Law Review 465. Cf. J. Hagan et al. 'Class Structure and Legal Practice: Inequality and Mobility Among Toronto Lawyers' (1988) 22 Law & Soc Rev 9. Abel 1989a is an excellent overview of the sociology of legal practice in the United States, and its companion volume Abel 1988 is an equally valuable compendium of sociological knowledge about the legal profession in England and Wales. Podmore 1980 reports a survey and analysis of English solicitors' involvement in community and political activities but is most useful for its extensive summary of literature bearing on the sociology of lawyers. See also Blacksell et al. 1991 on lawyers in rural Britain; and W. Bishop 'Regulating the Market for Legal Services in England: Enforced Separation of Function and Restrictions on Forms of Enterprise' (1989) 52 Mod L Rev 326.

Official Values of Legal Practice: Recently the 'decline of professionalism' and the rise of a relatively unrestrained business ethos has been a theme of much literature on legal practice. See e. g. R. L. Abel 'The Decline of Professionalism' (1986) 49 Mod L Rev 1; Abel 'Between Market and State: The Legal Profession in Turmoil' (1989) 52 Mod L Rev 285; C. Glasser 'The Legal Profession in the 1990s: Images of Change' (1990) 10 Legal Studies 1. For reasons given in the text, this development seems to me unlikely, in the short term at least, to lead to the discarding of constraints on practice that underpin lawyers' ability successfully to claim a specific professional status; nevertheless the increased pressures of competition in many fields of legal work will probably ensure that these constraints are pushed to their limits. See also I. Szelenyi and B. Martin 'The Legal Profession and the Rise and Fall of the New Class' in Abel and Lewis (eds) 1989 (suggesting that deprofessionalisation is being followed by reprofessionalisation in new forms).

On legislative changes aimed at promoting competition and liberalising legal practice arrangements in Britain see M. Partington 'Change or No-Change? Reflections on the Courts and Legal Services Act 1990' (1991) 54 Mod L Rev 702. For somewhat comparable developments in France see West 'Reforming the French Legal Profession', above. See also B. Dickson 'Legal Services and Legal Procedures in the 1990s' in S. Livingston and J. Morison (eds) *Law, Society and Change* 1990. On advertising by lawyers see, in addition to the references in the text, G. Quinn 'The Right of Lawyers to Advertise in the Market for Legal Services: A Comparative American, European and Irish Perspective' (1991) 20 Anglo-American Law Review 403; C. N. Mitchell 'The Implicit Regulation and Efficiency of Lawyer Advertising' (1982) 20 Osgoode Hall Law Journal 119.

Client Interests and 'Public Interest': On social class and legal representation see e.g. Carlin and Howard 1965; Galanter 1974; McDonald (ed) 1983, Part 2; Cain 1983a; McConville and Mirsky 1987; M. McConville and C. L. Mirsky 'The State, The Legal Profession and the Defence of the Poor' (1988) 15 J Law & Soc 342. On lawyer/client negotiations see Genn 1987 (negotiation of settlements in personal injury cases); A. Sarat and W. L. F. Felstiner 'Law and Strategy in the Divorce Lawyer's Office' (1986) 20 Law & Soc Rev 93 (lawyers' methods of reducing client expectations); Sarat and Felstiner 1988 (confrontation between lawyers' and clients' expectations and understandings).

Professional Knowledge: See especially Freidson 1986; Abbott 1988, pp. 52–8; Larson 1977, pp. 40-7; T. C. Halliday 'Knowledge Mandates: Collective Influence by Scientific, Normative and Syncretic Professions' (1985) 36 British Journal of Sociology 421; Halliday *Beyond Monopoly: Lawyers, State Crises, and Professional Empowerment* 1987, ch 2; Morison and Leith 1992. Cf. R. L. Abel and P. S. C. Lewis 'Putting Law Back into the Sociology of Lawyers' in Abel and Lewis (eds) 1989, pp. 501–13; R. Posner 'The Decline of Law as an Autonomous Discipline: 1962–1987' (1987) 100 Harv L Rev 761 (discussing the diversity of forms of knowledge now applied in legal analysis). For recent comment on reliance on technical or scientific expert knowledge in trials see M. N. Howard 'The Neutral Expert: A Plausible Threat to Justice' [1991] Criminal Law Review 98 and J. R. Spencer 'The Neutral Expert: An Implausible Bogey' *ibid* 106.

The Effects of Lawyers on the Law: On lawyers' position in social class structures see sources cited in the text and e.g. Rueschemeyer 1973, ch 3; P. McDonald 'The Class of '81: A Glance at the Social Class Composition of Recruits to the Legal Profession' (1982) 9 J Law & Soc 267; Podmore 1980, pp. 30–3, 90–3. For a powerful historical critique of the 'unofficial values' of elites within the United States legal profession, see J. S. Auerbach *Unequal Justice: Lawyers and Social Change in Modern America* 1976.

On women in legal professions see also C. Menkel-Meadow 'Feminization of the Legal Profession: The Comparative Sociology of Women Lawyers' in Abel and Lewis (eds) 1989; D. Podmore and A. Spencer 'The Law as a Sex-Typed Profession' (1982) 9 J. Law & Soc 21; R. Chester *Unequal Access: Women Lawyers in a Changing America* 1985; C. F. Epstein *Women in Law* 1981; R. Pearson and A. Sachs 'Barristers and Gentlemen: A Critical Look at Sexism in the Legal Profession' (1980) 43 Mod L. Rev 400. On women in the professions generally see A. Spencer and D. Podmore (eds) *In a Man's World: Essays on Women in Male-Dominated Professions* 1987. See also R. Jack and D. C. Jack *Moral Vision and Professional Decisions: The Changing Values of Women and Men Lawyers* 1989.

On the representation of minority groups in legal professions see generally R. Dhavan, N. Kibble and W. Twining (eds) *Access to Legal Education and the*

Legal Profession 1989; S. Gouldbourne *Minority Access to the Legal Profession: A Discussion Paper* 1985; H. Amoo-Gottfried 'Racism within the Legal Profession' Law Society's Gazette, January 6th 1988, p. 10; P. Cohen 'Racial Discrimination among Solicitors' LAG Bulletin, May 1982, p. 11, and 'Bar Racism on Trial' LAG Bulletin, April 1982, p. 6; D. Holley and T. Kleven 'Minorities and the Legal Profession: Current Platitudes, Current Barriers' (1987) 12 Thurgood Marshall Law Journal 299 (providing detailed information on the United States position); G. R. Segal *Blacks in the Law: Philadelphia and the Nation* 1983. See also M. King and C. May *Black Magistrates* 1985. Williams 1991 is a powerfully eloquent, richly anecdotal and theoretically sophisticated observation of racism in law and society, written from the vantage point of a black American law professor.

The literature on lawyers' influence in politics and government is very extensive. Halliday *Beyond Monopoly*, above, provides an instructive and detailed account of the influence of the Chicago Bar Association on the framing of state legislation and in state government. See also Podmore 1980, chs 3 and 4 and the numerous sources there cited. On professional socialisation and professional attitudes see e.g. J. C. Foster 'The "Cooling Out" of Law Students: Facilitating Market Cooptation of Future Lawyers' in R. Gambitta et al. (eds) *Governing through Courts* 1981.

On law centres and public legal services see M. Stephens *Community Law Centres: A Critical Appraisal* 1990; J. Cooper and R. Dhavan (eds) *Public Interest Law* 1986, especially Part 3; J. Cooper *Public Legal Services* 1983 which offers detailed analyses of developments in Britain, the United States and the Netherlands; B. Garth *Neighbourhood Law Firms for the Poor* 1980. On factors in German legal culture which hamper the development of public interest law practice see E. Blankenburg 'Some Conditions Restricting Innovativeness of Legal Services in Germany' in Blankenburg (ed) 1980. On class actions see further Chapter 8.

On the radicalisation of professional practice, see S. A. Scheingold *The Politics of Rights* 1974: Scheingold 'The Politics of Rights Revisited' in Gambitta et al. (eds) *Governing Through Courts* 1981; S. M. Olson 'The Political Evolution of Interest Group Litigation' in the same volume; Scheingold 'Radical Lawyers and Socialist Ideals' (1988) 15 J Law & Soc 122; A. F. Ginger and E. M. Tobin (eds) *The National Lawyers' Guild* 1988.

Chapter 7: Judges, Courts, Disputes

On the variety of Western judicial systems and their political and social environments see generally e.g. Shapiro 1981; Abraham 1986; T. L. Becker 1970; Merryman 1985, chs 6 and 13; Zweigert and Kötz 1987, pp. 123ff and 265ff.

Concepts of Judge and Court: On triadic relationships and their instability see K. H. Wolff (ed) *The Sociology of Georg Simmel* 1950. For further discussion in a legal context see V. Aubert 'Competition and Dissensus: Two Types of Conflict and of Conflict Resolution' (1963) 7 Journal of Conflict Resolution 26; Black and Baumgartner 1983. On adjudication see Fuller 1978. On mediation see Fuller 1971; S. S. Silbey and S. E. Merry 'Mediator Settlement Strategies' (1986) 8 Law and Policy 7.

Courts and Disputes: For a useful general survey of issues and research see R. Cranston 'What Do Courts Do?' (1986) 5 Civil Justice Quarterly 123. On disputes see generally Abel 1973 which takes dispute processing as its focus but clearly recognises that the ability of courts to resolve disputes is limited; B. Yngvesson and L. Mather 'Courts, Moots and the Disputing Process' in Boyum and Mather (eds) 1983; Felstiner 1974; S. E. Merry 'Going to Court: Strategies of Dispute Management in an American Urban Neighborhood' (1979) 13 Law & Soc Rev 891 (court functions as a sanctioning rather than dispute settlement forum). See further Chapter 8 on invocation of law.

On small claims courts see Whelan (ed) 1990; Lord Chancellor's Department *Civil Justice Review: Small Claims in the County Court* 1986; N. Vidmar 'The Small Claims Court: A Reconceptualization of Disputes and an Empirical Investigation' (1984) 18 Law & Soc Rev 515; C. A. McEwan and R. J. Maiman 'Mediation in Small Claims Court: Achieving Compliance through Consent' (1984) 18 Law & Soc Rev 11. A. Mulvaney and D. S. Greer 'Small Claims: The Northern Ireland Experience' (1987) 6 Civil Justice Quarterly 56; B. A. Moulton 'The Persecution and Intimidation of the Low-Income Litigant as Performed by the Small Claims Court in California' (1969) 21 Stanford Law Review 1657. On 'polycentric' problems see also P. Weiler 'Two Models of Decision-making' (1968) 46 Canadian Bar Review 406.

Are disputes central to the work of courts?: see also e. g. A. W. Alschuler 'Mediation with a Mugger: The Shortage of Adjudicative Services and the Need for a Two-Tier Trial System in Civil Cases' (1986) 99 Harv L Rev 1808 (numerous lawsuits occur but insufficient opportunities exist for full adjudication to vindicate claims and clarify legal principles); S. Daniels 'Continuity and Change in Patterns of Case Handling: A Case Study of Two Rural Counties' (1985) 19 Law & Soc Rev 381 (decline in proportion of cases decided by full trial in U.S. state courts); D. M. Engel 'Legal Pluralism in an American Community: Perspectives on a Civil Trial Court' [1980] American Bar Foundation Research Journal 425 reporting that few defendants filed an answer to plaintiff's complaint, in only one in every ten civil cases did a trial take place and 'in the remainder, the judge for the most part confined himself to approving and signing documents drafted beforehand by counsel' (p. 433); Cain 1986; R. Kagan 'The Routinization of Debt Collection: An Essay on Social Change and Conflict in the Courts' (1984) 18 Law & Soc Rev 323 (sharp decline in number of contested debt cases results from increased costs of litigation in comparison with costs of alternative strategies). On the work of trial courts in a variety of Western countries see 'Longitudinal Studies of Trial Courts' (1990) 24 Law & Soc Rev No. 2 (special issue).

Indirect dispute resolution: W. McIntosh '150 Years of Litigation and Dispute Settlement: A Court Tale' (1981) 15 Law & Soc Rev 823 is a study of civil litigation in a state general jurisdiction trial court in the United States over a 150 year period. McIntosh agrees with Lempert that analysis of court functions need not rest solely on the results of formal case resolution and concludes that 'neither socio-economic development nor increasing costs of litigation have withered the dispute resolution function' (p.823). The nature of judicial involvement in dispute resolution has changed over time but 'instead of becoming irrelevant to dispute settlement, the court seems to have altered its role to de-emphasise direct intervention and adjudication at trial, which might serve to escalate disputes unnecessarily, and toward encouraging adversaries to settle' (p. 842). See also M. L. Schwartz 'The Other Things that Courts Do' (1981) 28 University of California at Los Angeles Law Review 438; M. Galanter 'The Radiating Effects of Courts' in Boyum and Mather (eds) 1983; J. W. Hurst 'The Functions of Courts in the United States 1950-1980' (1981) 15 Law & Soc Rev 401. On the role of courts in case settlement see M. Galanter '...A Settlement Judge, Not a Trial Judge: Judicial Mediation in the United States' (1985) 12 J Law & Soc 1; K. F. Röhl 'The Judge as Mediator' (1985) 4 Civil Justice Quarterly 235. Cf. Fiss 1984.

Judicial Behaviour and Organisational Studies of Higher Courts: On American 'realist' scholarship see W. Twining *Karl Llewellyn and the Realist Movement* 1973: W. E. Rumble *American Legal Realism* 1968. For classic expositions of 'rule scepticism' see K. Llewellyn 'A Realistic Jurisprudence: The Next Step' (1930) 30 Col L Rev 431, 'Some Realism About Realism' (1931) 44 Harv L Rev 1222, and Llewellyn 1989; and for expositions of 'fact scepticism' see Frank 1930 and 1949.

Judicial Behaviouralism: For a brief outline of the development of the behavioural orientation in judicial research see C. H. Pritchett 'The Development of Judicial Research' in J. B. Grossman and J. Tanenhaus (eds) *Frontiers of Judicial Research* 1969. Pritchett's *The Roosevelt Court* 1948 pioneered the systematic study of judicial attitudes and small group interaction in quantitative analysis of Supreme Court voting patterns.

For modern behavioural and organisational studies of judges see G. Schubert *Quantitative Analysis of Judicial Behavior* 1959; Schubert (ed) *Judicial Decision-Making* 1963; Schubert *The Judicial Mind* 1965; Grossman and Tanenhaus (eds), above; D. J. Danelski and G. Schubert (eds) *Comparative Judicial Behavior* 1969; Schubert *The Judicial Mind Revisited* 1974; D. Robertson 'Judicial Ideology in the House of Lords: A Jurimetric Analysis' (1982) 12 British Journal of Political Science 1; C. N. Tate 'Personal Attribute Models of the Voting Behavior of U. S. Supreme Court Justices...' (1981) 75 American Political Science Review 355; H. J. Spaeth and M. F. Altfeld 'Influence Relationships within the Supreme Court: A Comparison of the Warren and Burger Courts' (1985) 38 Western Political Quarterly 70; Goldman and Lamb (eds) 1986; J. R. Schmidhauser (ed) *Comparative Judicial Systems* 1987; Marshall 1989 (on the impact of public opinion on judicial decision-making); S. S. Ulmer 'Are Social Background Models Time-Bound?' (1986) 80 American Political Science Review 957. Murphy 1964 is an excellent study of judicial strategy and organisation in the United States Supreme Court. T. L. Becker 1970 and Stone 1966, pp. 687–96 offer useful assessments of judicial behaviouralism.

On the backgrounds of British judges: Griffith 1991, pp. 30–8; C. N. Tate 'Paths to the Bench in Britain' (1975) 28 Western Political Quarterly 108; Paterson 1983. J. R. Schmidhauser 'The Justices of the Supreme Court: A Collective Portrait' (1959) 3 Midwest Journal of Political Science 1 offers a comprehensive survey of the social backgrounds of United States Supreme Court justices since 1789.

Phenomenology, Ethnomethodology and Studies of Interaction and Organisation in Lower Courts: See also W. L. Bennett and M. S. Feldman *Reconstructing Reality in the Courtroom* 1981 which analyses the American criminal trial as a 'storytelling' process in which competing counsel seek to convince judge and jury of the plausibility of their version of events. Such matters as the skills of the 'storyteller' and the language-use rules that determine the plausibility of the story are more significant in determining the outcome of the trial than the attitudes or values of judge or jury. B. S. Jackson *Law, Fact and Narrative Coherence* 1988 argues that pragmatics of courtroom interaction and particular narrative models largely determine the court's official views of reality. Cf. J. D. Jackson 'Law's Truth, Lay Truth and Lawyers' Truth: The Representation of Evidence in Adversary Trials' (1992) 3 Law and Critique 29 (the form of 'truth' that emerges in the courtroom is essentially produced by lawyers, rather than by interaction and negotiation between professional and lay participants in the trial); Conley and O'Barr 1990 (on the interaction between different judicial approaches to decision-making and different kinds of outlook of litigants on their problems); Merry 1990 (on confrontation between litigants' conceptualisation of claims and problems and lawyers' understandings); Berk-Seligson 1990 (on the transformation or impoverishment of litigants' or witnesses' testimony through translation in the courtroom). See also P. Rock 'Witnesses and Space in a Crown Court' (1991) 31 Brit J Crim 266; R. Dunstan 'Context for Coercion: Analyzing Properties of Courtroom "Questions"' (1980) 7 Brit J. Law & Soc 61; C. Nesson 'The Evidence of the Event? On Judicial Proof and the Acceptability of Verdicts' (1985) 98 Harv L Rev 1357 (on the importance to the trial process of the social acceptability of verdicts); W. M. O'Barr and J. M. Conley 'Litigant Satisfaction versus Legal Adequacy in Small Claims Court Narratives' (1985) 19 Law & Soc Rev 661. See also K. Bumiller 'Fallen Angels: The Representation of Violence Against Women in Legal Culture' (1990) 18 Int J Soc L 125 (symbolic representation of women in a rape trial). On the construction of events in memory see e.g. G. L. Wells and E. F. Loftus (eds) *Eye Witness Testimony: Psychological Perspectives* 1984.

Ideological Functions of Courts: On constitutional interpretation see further e.g. F. Hase and M. Ruete 'Constitutional Court and Constitutional Ideology in West Germany' (1982) 10 Int J Soc L 267 (the court maintains the 'constitutional coalition' and limits and depoliticises conflicts by referring them to 'the universally accepted constitutional value system'). On natural law bases of constitutional interpretation see in addition to the text references e.g. T. C. Grey 'Origins of the Unwritten Constitution: Fundamental Law in American Revolutionary Thought' (1978) 30 Stanford Law Review 843; J. W. Gough *Fundamental Law in English Constitutional History* 1955. John Brigham (1987) has applied the kind of approach suggested in the text in considering the contribution of United States Supreme Court decisions to the shaping of legal ideology.

Variations in the authority bases of judiciaries: on judicial authority see also R. A. Posner *Cardozo: A Study in Reputation* 1990 (discussing general determinants of judicial reputation); Cotterrell 'Realism, Pragmatism and the Appellate Judge' (1991) 54 Mod L Rev 594; Cotterrell 1990b (on different ideological foundations of judicial authority); W. Hurst 'Who is the Great Appellate Judge?' (1949) 24 Indiana Law Journal 394. For a comparison of styles and backgrounds of American and British judges see Atiyah and Summers 1987 ch 12.

Politicisation of trials: see R. Christenson (ed) *Political Trials in History: From Antiquity to the Present* 1991; Christenson *Political Trials: Gordian Knots in the Law* 1986; T. L. Becker (ed) *Political Trials* 1971: Kirchheimer 1961; S. E. Barkan 'Criminal Prosecutions in the Southern Civil Rights and Vietnam Antiwar Movements' in S. Spitzer (ed) *Research in Law and Sociology* vol 3, 1980; Z. Bankowski and G. Mungham 'Political Trials in Contemporary Wales' in Bankowski and Mungham (eds) *Essays in Law and Society* 1981.

Judge and State: For an eminent judge's assessment of Griffith's thesis see Lord Devlin 'Judges, Government and Politics' (1978) 41 Mod L Rev 501. For discussion of the political status of English judges in comparison with those of other Western countries see e.g. Shapiro 1981, ch 2; A. A. Paterson 'Judges: A Political Elite?' (1974) 1 Brit J Law & Soc 118; and more generally S. Shetreet and J. Deschenes (eds) *Judicial Independence* 1985. J. L. Waltman and K. M. Holland (eds) *The Political Role of Law Courts in Modern Democracies* 1988 provides summaries of the constitutional position, structure and political situation of judiciaries in a range of Western societies. See also P. Robertshaw 'Judicial Politics Within the State' (1980) 8 Int J Soc L 201; and on the history of conceptions of judicial independence, M. J. C. Vile *Constitutionalism and the Separation of Powers* 1967.

Judicial Hierarchies as Administrative Systems: The hierarchical ordering of systems of adjudication is considered in detail in M. R. Damaska *The Faces of Justice and State Authority: A Comparative Approach to the Legal Process* 1986, where, however, it is contrasted with a concept of coordinate organisation which the author associates with some Western judicial systems; see also Damaska 'Structures of Authority and Comparative Criminal Procedure' (1975) 84 Yale L J 480. On the relationship between appeals and the administrative and legitimating functions of higher courts see Shapiro 1981, ch 1. See also Shapiro 'Appeals' (1980) 14 Law & Soc Rev 201 on the variety of appeals systems in different legal systems. On dissents and their importance see Danelski 1986 and many of the papers in Goldman and Lamb (eds) 1986; Abraham 1986, pp. 212-5; K. H. Nadelmann 'The Judicial Dissent' (1959) 8 Am J Comp L 415; J. R. Kaufman 'Chilling Judicial Independence' (1979) 88 Yale L J 681. On separate opinions see Abraham 1986, pp. 215–6; Llewellyn 1989, pp. 52–61. On dissents and multiple judgments in the House of Lords see Paterson 1982, pp. 96–121.

Courts as Policy Makers: See R. A. Posner *The Problems of Jurisprudence* 1990 for an American federal judge's theoretical elaboration of appropriate judicial approaches to policy matters. For a view from within the senior British judiciary see P. Devlin *The Judge* 1979, ch 1. On the use of social scientific evidence by courts see Chesler et al. 1988; J. Monahan and L. Walker 'Social Authority: Obtaining, Evaluating and Establishing Social Science in Law' (1986) 134 University of Pennsylvania Law Review 477; J. Sanders, B. Rankin-Widgeon, D. Kalmuss and M. Chesler 'The Relevance of "Irrelevant" Testimony: Why Lawyers Use Social Science Experts in School Desegregation Cases' (1982) 16 Law & Soc Rev 403; Collins 1978; P. L. Rosen *The Supreme Court and Social Science* 1972; A. H. Grundman 'School Desegregation and Social Science: The Virginia Experience' in R. J. Simon (ed) *Research in Law and Sociology* vol 1, 1978. For an early statement see W. F. Willcox 'The Need of Social Statistics as an Aid to the Courts' (1913) 47 American Law Review 259.

For an attempt at empirical assessment of the United States Supreme Court as a policy-making institution see Marshall 1989 ch 7; and for an empirical study of effects on court legitimacy of policy-making by the judiciary see W.F. Murphy and J. Tanenhaus 'Public Opinion and the United States Supreme Court: A Preliminary Mapping of Some Prerequisites for Court Legitimation of Regime Changes' in Grossman and Tanenhaus (eds), above. A. S. Miller 'Public Confidence in the Judiciary' in his *The Supreme Court: Myth and Reality* 1978 offers a more speculative discussion. On the consequences of explicit judicial policy-making see also N. Glazer 'The Judiciary and Social Policy' in L. J. Theberge (ed) *The Judiciary in a Democratic Society* 1979.

Chapter 8: The Enforcement and Invocation of Law

Enforcing Law and Invoking Law: On prosecution and prosecutorial discretion see e.g. Hall Williams (ed) 1988; G. Mansfield and J. Peay *The Director of Public Prosecutions: Principles and Practices for the Crown Prosecutor* 1987 (on the operation of the DPP's office prior to the Prosecution of Offences Act 1985 establishing the Crown Prosecution Service); A. Ashworth 'The "Public Interest" Element in Prosecutions' [1987] Criminal Law Review 595; Moody and Tombs 1983 (a study of the Scottish procurator fiscal). On police-prosecutor relationships in the United States see M. M. Feeley and M. H. Laserson 'Police-Prosecutor Relationships: An Interorganizational Perspective' in Boyum and Mather (eds) 1983. On the relationship between informal social controls and citizens' willingness to draw crimes to the attention of police see Shapland and Vagg 1988.

Opportunity and Incentive to Invoke Law: M. Cappelletti (ed) *Access to Justice* Vols 1–4 1978–9 offers a detailed international survey of the conditions of invocation of law in a variety of legal systems.

Factors inhibiting the effective voicing of grievances: see generally Harris et al. 1984; N. Vidmar 'Seeking Justice: An Empirical Map of Consumer Problems and Consumer Responses in Canada' (1988) 26 Osgoode Hall Law Journal 757; R. E. Miller and A. Sarat 'Grievances, Claims and Disputes: Assessing the Adversary Culture' (1981) 15 Law & Soc Rev. 525; W. L. F. Felstiner, R. L. Abel and A. Sarat 'The Emergence and Transformation of Disputes: Naming, Blaming, Claiming' (1981) 15 Law & Soc Rev 631; K. O.

Boyum 'The Etiology of Claims: Sketches for a Theoretical Mapping of the Claim-Definition Process' in Boyum and Mather (eds) 1983.

Seeking help from law: see e.g. Genn 1987; H. L. Ross *Settled Out of Court: The Social Process of Insurance Claims Adjustments* 2nd edn 1980, an important American study of the processing and consequences of insurance claims; H. M. Kritzer *Let's Make a Deal: Understanding the Negotiation Process in Ordinary Litigation* 1991; Merry 1990; H. M. Kritzer 'Propensity to Sue in England and the United States of America: Blaming and Claiming in Tort Cases' (1991) 18 J Law & Soc 400 (differences in willingness to litigate in personal injury claims in England and Wales and in the United States are attributable to fundamental cultural differences); and cf. comment by S. Lloyd-Bostock at pp. 428ff.

On the thesis that 'the "haves" come out ahead' in litigation see also M. Galanter 'Afterward: Explaining Litigation' (1975) 9 Law & Soc Rev 347; C. Wanner 'The Public Ordering of Private Relations: Part 2—Winning Civil Court Cases' (1975) 9 Law & Soc Rev 293 (government and business litigants tend to fare better than individuals); B. Atkins 'A Cross-National Perspective on the Structuring of Trial Court Outputs: The Case of the English High Court' in J. R. Schmidhauser (ed) *Comparative Judicial Systems* 1987 (similar findings in a study in Britain); S. Wheeler et al. 'Do the "Haves" Come Out Ahead? Winning and Losing in State Supreme Courts, 1870–1970' (1987) 21 Law & Soc Rev 403 (stronger parties do have litigational advantage over weaker parties but generally the advantage is small). On patterns of court use see e. g. R. Cranston 'What Do Courts Do?' (1986) 5 Civil Justice Quarterly 123, 128–30.

Invoking law in support of collective interests: on class actions see Yeazell 1987, which considers the topic in an extremely broad historical perspective; 'The Sociology of Class Actions: A Symposium' (1982) 57 Indiana Law Journal 371–458. Cappelletti 1989, ch 7 is essentially an edited reprint of material from volume 3 of *Access to Justice*, above, without significant updating, but remains a very useful comparative study of various methods of pursuing 'public interest' claims through litigation.

Types of Enforcement Agencies: Rhodes 1981 provides a useful survey of types of enforcement and efficiency inspectorates in Britain. On some important recent developments in structures of regulation see e. g. J. Gibson 'The Integration of Pollution Control' (1991) 18 J Law & Soc 18; M. Purdue 'Integrated Pollution Control in the Environmental Protection Act 1990: A Coming of Age of Environmental Law?' (1991) 54 Mod L Rev 534; R. Macrory 'The Privatisation and Regulation of the Water Industry' (1990) 53 Mod L Rev 78.

Regulatory Agencies and Their Strategies: See generally K. Hawkins and J. M. Thomas (eds) *Enforcing Regulation* 1984. For British material see especially Hutter 1988; Hawkins 1984; Richardson 1983; Cranston 1979; and e. g. J. Rowan-Robinson, P. Q. Watchman and C. R. Barker *Crime and Regulation: A Study of the Enforcement of Regulatory Codes* 1990; M. Weait 'The Letter of the Law? An Enquiry into Reasoning and Formal Enforcement in the Industrial Air Pollution Inspectorate' (1989) 29 Brit J Crim 57; Y. Brittan *The Impact of Water Pollution Control on Industry: A Case Study of Fifty Dischargers* 1984; P. B.

Beaumont 'The Limits of Inspection: A Study of the Workings of the Government Wages Inspectorate' (1979) 57 Public Administration 203. See also B. M. Hutter 'Variations in Regulatory Enforcement Styles' (1989) 11 Law and Policy 153 (examining variations in accommodative approaches of agencies); J. Braithwaite, J. Walker and P. Grabosky 'An Enforcement Taxonomy of Regulatory Agencies' (1987) 9 Law and Policy 323 (identifying seven types of agency in terms of their enforcement strategies). R. Cranston 'Regulation and Deregulation: General Issues' (1982) 5 University of New South Wales Law Journal 1 offers a convenient survey of literature on a variety of aspects of business regulation. On publicity as a sanction see B. Fisse and J. Braithwaite *The Impact of Publicity on Corporate Offenders* 1983. On prosecution decisions see K. Hawkins '"Fatcats" and Prosecution in a Regulatory Agency: A Footnote on the Social Construction of Risk' (1989) 11 Law and Policy 370.

Regulatory Agencies and Their Environment: See also e.g. P. C. Yeager *The Limits of Law: The Public Regulation of Private Pollution* 1990; S. Gräbe 'Regulatory Agencies and Interest Groups in Occupational Health and Safety in Great Britain and West Germany: A Perspective from West Germany' (1991) 13 Law and Policy 55; B. M. Hutter and P. K. Manning 'The Contexts of Regulation: The Impact upon Health and Safety Inspectorates in Britain' (1990) 12 Law and Policy 103. See generally e.g. M. T. Hannan and J. Freeman *Organizational Ecology* 1989.

Regulation and 'Real Crime': For an interesting study of what citizens think of as 'really criminal' see Shapland and Vagg 1988, pp. 81–6. See also I. Loveland 'Policing Welfare: Local Authority Responses to Claimant Fraud in the Housing Benefit Scheme' (1989) 16 J Law & Soc 187 (discussing attitudes of local authority officials); S. Uglow 'Defrauding the Public Purse: Prosecuting in Social Security, Revenue and Excise Cases' [1984] Criminal Law Review 128; R. Smith 'Who's Fiddling?: Fraud and Abuse' in S. Ward (ed) *DHSS in Crisis: Social Security—Under Pressure and Under Review* 1985; D. Cook *Rich Law, Poor Law: Different Responses to Tax and Supplementary Benefit Fraud* 1989; M. Levi *Regulating Fraud: White-Collar Crime and the Criminal Process* 1987 (discussing investigation and prosecution of fraud by police and other enforcement agencies); J. McEwan, 'Tax Evasion: Is it Treated Too Leniently?' (1981) 45 Conveyancer 114; P. Knightley *The Vestey Affair* 1981 (on calculated major tax avoidance). For a detailed study of differential enforcement of criminal law in Britain against business landlords and against individual landlords see D. Nelken *The Limits of the Legal Process. A Study of Landlords, Law, and Crime* 1983. See also C. Corbett and F. Simon 'Police and Public Perceptions of the Seriousness of Traffic Offences' (1991) 31 Brit J Crim 153 (police and public largely agree on seriousness of various traffic offences).

Police and Law: Sociological literature on the police is now very extensive. For valuable general discussions see e.g. Reiner 1985; M. Stephens *Policing: The Critical Issues* 1988; Klockars 1985; Gleizal 1985; Holdaway 1983; Skolnick 1975; Bittner 1975; Cain 1973; Brogden 1982; Westley 1970; Wilson 1968;

Manning 1977. For accounts of policing in various Western European countries see J. Roach and J. Thomaneck (eds) *Police and Public Order in Europe* 1985.

Law and order: the order maintaining role of police is graphically illustrated in M. Brogden *On the Mersey Beat: Policing Liverpool Between the Wars* 1991; and on the variety of historical factors shaping the social control orientations and strategies of policing in Britain see Brogden 'An Act to Colonise the Internal Lands of the Island: Empire and the Origins of the Professional Police' (1987) 15 Int J Soc L 179. See also C. Elmsley *Policing and its Context: 1750–1870* 1983, ch 8. For an excellent attempt to synthesise diverse explanations of the historical origins of modern policing in Britain see Reiner 1985, ch 1. On the legal accountability of police see e. g. T. Jefferson and R. Grimshaw *Controlling the Constable: Police Accountability in England and Wales* 1984.

Police discretion: cf. P. K. Manning and K. Hawkins 'Police Decision-Making' in M. Weatheritt (ed) *Police Research: Some Future Prospects* 1989; P. Southgate *Police-Public Encounters* (Home Office Research Study, No. 90) 1986. For a Canadian study see R. V. Ericson *Reproducing Order: A Study of Police Patrol Work* 1982.

Pressures towards legality and illegality: Gleizal 1985, ch 6 discusses the ambivalent relations of policing and law in France. R. Baldwin 'Regulation and Policing By Code' in M. Weatheritt (ed) *Police Research: Some Future Prospects* 1989 considers effects of the Police and Criminal Evidence Act 1984 on policing in Britain. On police corruption see Punch 1985.

Police Work and Police Organisation: The most detailed recent British empirical study is the Policy Studies Institute's four volume report on the London Metropolitan Police, *Police and People in London* (1983). See especially vol 3, *A Survey of Police Officers* by D. J. Smith. For a theoretical perspective see Brogden 1982. On police professionalisation see also e.g. N. J. Greenhill 'Professionalism in the Police Service' in D. W. Pope and N. L. Weiner (eds) *Modern Policing* 1981. On police effectiveness in fighting crime see S. Uglow *Policing Liberal Society* 1988, ch 4; J. Q. Wilson and B. Boland 'The Effect of the Police on Crime' (1978) 12 Law & Soc Rev 367. On the political voice of the police see e.g. Reiner 1991; M. Kettle 'The Politics of Policing and the Policing of Politics' in P. Hain (ed) *Policing the Police* vol 2, 1980; Mark 1977; Reiner 'Fuzzy Thoughts: The Police and Law-and-Order Politics' (1980) 28 Sociological Review 377. On police technology and its uses see e.g. M. Stephens *Policing: The Critical Issues*, above, ch 3; Waddington 1991; G. P. A. Fraser 'The Applications of Police Computing' in Pope and Weiner (eds), above; D. Campbell 'Society Under Surveillance' in Hain (ed), above; S. Manwaring-White *The Policing Revolution: Police Technology, Democracy and Liberty in Britain* 1983. On police power in defence of the state see e.g. R. Eveleigh *Peace-Keeping in a Democratic Society* 1978; T. Bunyan *The History and Practice of the Political Police in Britain* 1976; and, for an interesting historical perspective, T. Bowden *Beyond the Limits of Law* 1978. On community policing see also e.g. Stephens *Policing*, above, ch 4.

Police Culture: See S. Holdaway 'Discovering Structure: Studies of the British Police Occupational Culture', and N. G. Fielding 'Police Culture and Police

Practice', both in Weatheritt (ed) *Police Research*, above; Holdaway 1983; Fielding *Joining Forces: Police Training, Socialisation and Occupational Competence* 1988; Smith and Gray 1983; Stephens *Policing*, above, ch 5. On policemen's attitudes see also e.g. C. J. Vick 'Explaining Police Pessimism', and R. C. A. Adlam, 'The Police Personality', both in Pope and Weiner (eds), above; A. Colman and P. Gorman 'Conservatism, Dogmatism, and Authoritarianism in British Police Officers' (1982) 16 Sociology 1. R. Graef *Talking Blues: The Police in Their Own Words* 1990 and M. Baker *Cops: Their Lives in Their Own Words* 1985 provide fascinating raw data on police culture in Britain and the United States, respectively. See also C. Norris 'Avoiding Trouble: The Patrol Officer's Perception of Encounters with the Public' in Weatheritt (ed), above. Police and Race Relations: see generally E. Cashmore and E. McLaughlin (eds) *Out of Order? Policing Black People* 1991; Jefferson 1988; Reiner 1985, pp. 124–36; S. Holdaway 'Race Relations and Police Recruitment' (1991) 31 Brit J Crim 365. Cf. Hutter 1988, pp. 113–5 on environmental health officers' dealings with and attitudes towards various ethnic groups.

Chapter 9: The Prognosis for Law

The Scope of Law and Legal Authority: On the complex patterns of expansion of litigation in the United States see e. g. M. Galanter 'Reading the Landscape of Disputes: What We Know and Don't Know (and Think We Know) About Our Allegedly Contentious and Litigious Society' (1983) 31 University of California at Los Angeles Law Review 4; Friedman 1985; Galanter 1986 and commentaries on this paper in (1986) 46 Maryland Law Review by B. R. Civiletti, D. B. Dobbs, J. J. Phillips, M. J. Saks and R. J. Samuelson. Galanter 1992 is a convenient survey of evidence of the more general expansion of law in Western societies.

Informalism, Delegalisation and Access to Law: See generally on informalism R. L. Abel (ed) *The Politics of Informal Justice* Vols 1 and 2 1982; and, for a historical perspective on informalism in the United States, Harrington 1985, ch 2. Among recent discussions: R. Matthews (ed) *Informal Justice?* 1988, including Maureen Cain's paper 'Beyond Informal Justice' on the need to distinguish different kind of informal justice settings some of which provide liberating possibilities; C. B. Harrington and S. E. Merry 'Ideological Production: The Making of Community Mediation' (1988) 22 Law & Soc Rev 709 (emphasis on achieving consensual process in mediation conflicts with ideology of community justice).

State, Civil Society and the Diffusion of Power and Control: On the extension of state controls in civil society see notes to Chapter 4 ('State and Individual'). On the theoretical inadequacy of the distinction between state and civil society in contemporary Western conditions see e. g. B. Frankel *Beyond the State? Dominant Theories and Socialist Strategies* 1983. Foucault's works most directly relevant to the sociology of law are Foucault 1979; 1980; and *Discipline and Punish* 1977. For discussion see e.g. J. Palmer and F. Pearce 'Legal Discourse and State Power: Foucault and the Juridical Relation' (1983) 11 Int

J Soc L 361; Hutchinson 1988, ch 9; G. Turkel 'Michel Foucault: Law, Power and Knowledge' (1990) 17 J Law & Soc 170. On Foucault's work as a whole, H. L. Dreyfus and P. Rabinow *Michel Foucault: Beyond Structuralism and Hermeneutics* 1982 is especially useful.

The Breakdown of Legal Autonomy?: See also Posner 'The Decline of Law as an Autonomous Discipline' cited in notes to Chapter 6, above. For efforts to analyse the ways in which the autonomy of legal discourse is asserted in contemporary conditions see D. Nelken 'The Truth about Law's Truth' in A. Febbrajo (ed) *European Yearbook of the Sociology of Law*, new series, Vol. 2 (forthcoming); Teubner 1989; Cotterrell 1986; King and Piper 1990.

The Future of Legal Individualism: There is now an extensive literature debating the merits of reliance on rights, despite all their associations with legal individualism, as a transformative political strategy. For recent discussions see Hunt 1990; J. Fudge and H. Glasbeek 'The Politics of Rights: A Politics with Little Class' (1992) 1 Social and Legal Studies 45; K. W. Crenshaw 'Race, Reform, and Retrenchment: Transformation and Legitimation in Antidiscrimination Law' (1988) 101 Harv L Rev 1331; P. Hirst 'Law, Socialism and Rights' reprinted in his *Law, Socialism and Democracy* 1986, ch 2. On the problems and possibilities of conceptualising collective rights in contemporary law see also T. Campbell *The Left and Rights* 1983. On the utility of rights arguments in promoting the interests of ethnic minorities see the symposium 'Minority Critiques of the Critical Legal Studies Movement' (1987) 22 Harvard Civil Rights-Civil Liberties Law Review, No. 2 (papers by R. Delgado, M. J. Matsuda, P. J. Williams and H. L. Dalton); responses by A. Freeman and M. J. Horwitz in (1988) 23 Harvard Civil Rights-Civil Liberties Law Review, No. 2; and Delgado 1988. On privatised social relations see M. P. Baumgartner *The Moral Order of a Suburb* 1988.

A Postmodern World?: For useful indications of diverse contemporary thought about the 'postmodern condition' see Lyotard 1984; Z. Bauman *Legislators and Interpreters: On Modernity, Postmodernity and Intellectuals* 1987; D. Harvey *The Condition of Postmodernity* 1989; A. Heller and F. Feher *The Postmodern Political Condition* 1989; A. Callinicos *Against Postmodernism: A Marxist Critique* 1989; Z. Bauman *Modernity and Ambivalence* 1991; S. Lash *Sociology of Postmodernism* 1990; Bauman 1992. On the impossibility of philosophical 'truth' see especially R. Rorty *Philosophy and the Mirror of Nature* 1980. Among varied recent contributions to postmodernist legal theory see e. g. Goodrich 1990; A. Carty (ed) *Post-Modern Law: Enlightenment, Revolution and the Death of Man* 1990; A. Woodiwiss *Social Theory After Postmodernism: Rethinking Production, Law and Class* 1990, especially Part 3 'Rethinking Law'; C. Douzinas and R. Warrington *Postmodern Jurisprudence* 1991; J. M. Balkin 'Deconstructive Practice and Legal Theory' (1987) 96 Yale L J 743; J. W. Singer 'The Player and the Cards: Nihilism and Legal Theory' (1984) 94 Yale L J 1.

Sociology of Law as Critique: My comments in this section are intended partly as a clarification in the light of Susan Silbey's (1991) thoughtful and detailed critique of this book's emphasis on sociological study of law as institutionalised doctrine, and on courts, lawyers and enforcement agencies as foci for considering the nature of legal ideology. Silbey argues that these emphases build a conservatism into the book's outlook which undermines its potentially liberating conception of law's contribution to the development and maintenance of currents of ideology. More general debates about the possibility and character of a critical sociology of law have been conducted in the United States in recent years. See especially D. M. Trubek 'Where the Action Is: Critical Legal Studies and Empiricism' (1984) 36 Stanford Law Review 575; S. Silbey and A. Sarat 'Critical Traditions in Law and Society Research (1987) 21 Law & Soc Rev 165; D. M. Trubek and J. Esser '"Critical Empiricism" in American Legal Studies: Paradox, Program, or Pandora's Box' (1989) 14 L & Soc Inq 3; Sarat and Silbey 'The Pull of the Policy Audience' (1988) 10 Law and Policy 97; C. B. Harrington and B. Yngvesson 'Interpretive Sociolegal Research' (1990) 15 L & Soc Inq 135; Sarat 1990b; Esser and Trubek 'From "Scientism Without Determinism" to "Interpretation Without Politics": A Reply to Sarat, Harrington and Yngvesson' (1990) 15 L & Soc Inq 171.

Abbreviations

Am J Comp L	American Journal of Comparative Law
Am J Soc	American Journal of Sociology
Am Soc Rev	American Sociological Review
Brit J Crim	British Journal of Criminology
Brit J Law & Soc	British Journal of Law and Society (continued as the Journal of Law and Society)
Col L Rev	Columbia Law Review
Harv L Rev	Harvard Law Review
Int J Soc L	International Journal of the Sociology of Law
J Law & Soc	Journal of Law and Society
L & Soc Inq	Law and Social Inquiry
Law & Soc Rev	Law and Society Review
Law Q Rev	Law Quarterly Review
Mod L Rev	Modern Law Review
Soc Prob	Social Problems
Yale L J	Yale Law Journal

References

Abbott, A. (1988) *The System of Professions: An Essay on the Division of Expert Labor* (Chicago: University of Chicago Press).

Abel, R. L. (1973) 'A Comparative Theory of Dispute Institutions in Society' 8 Law & Soc Rev 217–347.

(1979) 'Delegalization: A Critical Review of its Ideology, Manifestations, and Social Consequences' in E. Blankenburg et al. (eds) *Alternative Rechtsformen und Alternativen zum Recht* pp. 27–47 (Opladen: Westdeutscher Verlag).

(1981a) 'Law in Context, the Sociology of Legal Institutions, Litigation in Society' in R. Luckham (ed) *Law and Social Enquiry* pp. 34–75 (Uppsala: Scandinavian Institute of African Studies; New York: International Centre for Law in Development).

(1981b) 'Conservative Conflict and the Reproduction of Capitalism: The Role of Informal Justice' 9 Int J Soc L 245–67.

(1982) 'The Contradictions of Informal Justice' in R. L. Abel (ed) *The Politics of Informal Justice* Vol I pp. 267–320 (New York: Academic Press).

(1988) *The Legal Profession in England and Wales* (Oxford: Basil Blackwell).

(1989a) *American Lawyers* (New York: Oxford University Press).

(1989b) 'Comparative Sociology of Legal Professions' in Abel and Lewis (eds) (1989) pp. 80–153.

Abel, R. L. and Lewis, P. S. C. (eds) (1989) *Lawyers in Society. Vol. 3: Comparative Theories* (Berkeley: University of California Press).

Abraham, H. J. (1986) *The Judicial Process: An Introductory Analysis of the Courts of the United States, England, and France* (5th edn, New York: Oxford University Press).

Addiss, P. (1980) 'The Life History Complaint Case of Martha and George Rose: "Honoring the Warranty"' in Nader (ed) (1980) pp. 171–89.

Adler, M. and Asquith, S. (eds) (1981) *Discretion and Welfare* (London: Heinemann).

Adorno, T. W., Frenkel-Brunswick, E., Levinson, D. J. and Sanford, R. N. (1950) *The Authoritarian Personality* (New York: John Wiley edn 1964).

Alcock, P. (1989) '"A Better Partnership Between State and Individual Provision": Social Security Into the 1990s' 16 J Law & Soc 97-111.

Alderson, J. C. (1973) 'The Principles and Practice of the British Police' in J. C. Alderson and P. J. Stead (eds) *The Police We Deserve* pp. 39–54 (London: Wolfe).
Allen, C. K. (1964) *Law in the Making* (7th edn, Oxford: Oxford University Press).
Allott, A. (1980) *The Limits of Law* (London: Butterworths).
Althusser, L. (1969) *For Marx*, transl. by B. Brewster (London: New Left Books edn 1977).
(1971) 'Ideology and Ideological State Apparatuses' reprinted in L. Althusser *Essays on Ideology* pp. 1–60 (London: Verso, 1984).
Antunes, G. and Hunt, A. L. (1973) 'The Impact of Certainty and Severity of Punishment on Levels of Crime in American States: An Extended Analysis' 64 Journal of Criminal Law and Criminology 486–93.
Arnold, T. W. (1935) *The Symbols of Government* (New York: Harcourt Brace and World edn 1962).
(1937) *The Folklore of Capitalism* (Westport, Conn.: Greenwood Press rep. 1980).
Atiyah, P. S. (1979) *The Rise and Fall of Freedom of Contract* (Oxford: Oxford University Press).
Atiyah, P. S. and Summers, R. S. (1987) *Form and Substance in Anglo-American Law: A Comparative Study of Legal Reasoning, Legal Theory, and Legal Institutions* (Oxford: Oxford University Press).
Atkinson, J. M. (1971) 'Societal Reactions to Deviance: The Role of Coroners' Definitions' in S. Cohen (ed) *Images of Deviance* pp. 165–91 (Harmondsworth: Penguin Books).
(1978) *Discovering Suicide: Studies in the Social Organisation of Sudden Death* (London: Macmillan).
(1981) Book Review, 9 Int J Soc L 101–6.
Atkinson, J. M. and Drew, P. (1979) *Order in Court: The Organisation of Verbal Interaction in Judicial Settings* (London: Macmillan).
Aubert, V. (1952) 'White-Collar Crime and Social Structure' 58 Am J Soc 263–71.
(1966) 'Some Social Functions of Legislation' 10 Acta Sociologica 98–120.
(1969) 'Law as a Way of Resolving Conflicts: The Case of a Small Industrialised Society' in L. Nader (ed) *Law in Culture and Society* pp. 282–303 (Chicago: Aldine).
Ayres, I. and Braithwaite, J. (1991) 'Tripartism: Regulatory Capture and Empowerment' 16 L & Soc Inq 435–96.
Bagehot, W. (1963) *The English Constitution* (Fontana edn, London: Collins).
Baker, J. H. (1990) *An Introduction to English Legal History* (3rd edn, London: Butterworths).

Baldwin, J. and McConville, M. (1979a) *Jury Trials* (Oxford: Oxford University Press).

(1979b) 'Plea Bargaining and the Court of Appeal' 6 Brit J Law & Soc 200–18.

Baldwin, R. (1985) *Regulating the Airlines: Administrative Justice and Agency Discretion* (Oxford: Oxford University Press).

Bankowski, Z. and Mungham, G. (1976) *Images of Law* (London: Routledge and Kegan Paul).

Bankowski, Z. and Nelken, D. (1981) 'Discretion as a Social Problem' in Adler and Asquith (eds) (1981) pp. 247–68.

Barker, R. (1990) *Political Legitimacy and the State* (Oxford: Oxford University Press).

Bauman, Z. (1992) *Intimations of Postmodernity* (London: Routledge).

Bayley, D. H. and Mendelsohn, H. (1969) *Minorities and the Police: Confrontation in America* (New York: Free Press).

Beale, H. and Dugdale, T. (1975) 'Contracts Between Businessmen: Planning and the Use of Contractual Remedies' 2 Brit J Law & Soc 45–60.

Becker, H. S. (1963) *Outsiders: Studies in the Sociology of Deviance* (New York: Free Press).

(1970) 'The Nature of a Profession' in H. S. Becker *Sociological Work* pp. 87–103 (Chicago: Aldine).

Becker, T. L. (1970) *Comparative Judicial Politics: The Political Functionings of Courts* (Chicago: Rand McNally).

Bedau, H. A. (1979) 'The Death Penalty in the United States: Imposed Law and the Role of Moral Elites' in S. B. Burman and B. E. Harrell-Bond (eds) *The Imposition of Law* pp. 45–68 (London: Academic Press).

Bell, D. (1973) *The Coming of Post-Industrial Society: A Venture in Social Forecasting* (New York: Basic Books).

Bentley, A. F. (1908) *The Process of Government* (Cambridge, Mass.: Harvard University Press edn 1967).

Berger, M. (1952) *Equality by Statute: Legal Controls over Group Discrimination* (New York: Columbia University Press).

Berger, P. L. and Luckmann, T. (1967) *The Social Construction of Reality* (London: Allen Lane).

Berk-Seligson, S. (1990) *The Bilingual Courtroom: Court Interpreters in the Judicial Process* (Chicago: University of Chicago Press).

Berle, A. A. and Means, G. C. (1933) *The Modern Corporation and Private Property* (New York: Transaction Books edn 1991).

Bernstein, M. H. (1955) *Regulating Business by Independent Commission* (Princeton: Princeton University Press).

Bernstein, R. (1985) *Beyond Objectivism and Relativism: Science, Hermeneutics, and Praxis* (Philadelphia: University of Pennsylvania Press).

Beyleveld, D. (1982) 'Ehrlich's Analysis of Deterrence' 22 Brit J Crim 101–23.
Bittner, E. (1967) 'The Police on Skid Row: A Study of Peace Keeping' 32 Am Soc Rev 699–715.
(1975) *The Functions of the Police in Modern Society: A Review of Background Factors, Current Practices, and Possible Role Models* (New York: Jason Aronson).
Black, D. J. (1970) 'The Production of Crime Rates' 35 Am Soc Rev 733–48.
(1971) 'The Social Organization of Arrest' 23 Stanford Law Review 1087–111.
(1972) 'The Boundaries of Legal Sociology' 81 Yale LJ 1086–100.
(1973) 'The Mobilization of Law' 2 Journal of Legal Studies 125–49.
(1976) *The Behavior of Law* (London: Academic Press).
(1989) *Sociological Justice* (New York: Oxford University Press).
Black, D. J. and Baumgartner, M. P. (1983) 'Toward a Theory of the Third Party' in Boyum and Mather (eds) (1983) pp. 84–114.
Black, D. J. and Reiss Jr., A. J. (1970) 'Police Control of Juveniles' 35 Am Soc Rev 63–77.
Blacksell, M., Economides, K. and Watkins, C. (1991) *Justice Outside the City: Access to Legal Services in Rural Britain* (Harlow: Longman).
Blankenburg, E. (ed) (1980) *Innovations in the Legal Services* (Cambridge, Mass.: Ölgeschlager, Gunn & Hain).
Blankenburg, E. and Schultz, U. (1988) 'German Advocates: A Highly Regulated Profession' in R. L. Abel and P. S. C. Lewis (eds) *Lawyers in Society. Vol. 2: The Civil Law World* pp. 124–49 (Berkeley: University of California Press).
Blankenburg, E. and Treiber, H. (1985) 'The Establishment of the Public Prosecutor's Office in Germany' 12 Int J Soc L 375–91.
Blegvad, B.-M. (1990) 'Commercial Relations, Contract, and Litigation in Denmark: A Discussion of Macaulay's Theories' 24 Law & Soc Rev 397–411.
Blom-Cooper, L. and Drewry, G. (1972) *Final Appeal: A Study of the House of Lords in its Judicial Capacity* (Oxford: Oxford University Press).
Blumberg, A. (1967) 'The Practice of Law as Confidence Game: Organizational Cooptation of a Profession' 1 Law & Soc Rev No. 2, 15–39.
Böckenförde, E.-W. (1991) *State, Society and Liberty: Studies in Political Theory and Constitutional Law*, transl. J. A. Underwood (Oxford: Berg).
Bottomore, T. (1991) *Classes in Modern Society* (2nd edn, London: Harper and Collins).

Bottomore, T. and Nisbet, R. (eds) (1979) *A History of Sociological Analysis* (London: Heinemann).
Bourlet, A. (1990) *Police Intervention in Marital Violence* (Milton Keynes: Open University Press).
Box, S. (1983) *Power, Crime and Mystification* (London: Tavistock).
Boyum, K. O. and Mather, L. (eds) (1983) *Empirical Theories About Courts* (New York: Longman).
Braithwaite, J. (1989) *Crime, Shame and Reintegration* (Cambridge: Cambridge University Press).
Bredemeier, H. (1962) 'Law as an Integrative Mechanism' in Evan (ed) (1962) pp. 73–88.
Brigham, J. (1987) *The Cult of the Court* (Philadelphia: Temple University Press).
Brigham, J. and Harrington, C. B. (1989) 'Realism and Its Consequences: An Inquiry into Contemporary Sociological Research' 17 Int J Soc L 41–62.
Brogden, M. (1982) *The Police: Autonomy and Consent* (London: Academic Press).
Brown, H. P. (1986) *The Origins of Trade Union Power* (Oxford: Oxford University Press).
Cahn, E. (1955) 'Jurisprudence' 30 New York University Law Review 150–169.
Cain, M. (1973) *Society and the Policeman's Role* (London: Routledge and Kegan Paul).
(1983a) 'The General Practice Lawyer and the Client: Towards a Radical Conception' in Dingwall and Lewis (eds) (1983) pp. 106–30.
(1983b) 'Gramsci, the State and the Place of Law' in Sugarman (ed) (1983) pp. 95–117.
(1983c) 'Where Are the Disputes? A Study of a First Instance Civil Court in the UK' in Cain and Kulcsar (eds) (1983) pp. 119–33.
(1983d) 'Introduction: Towards an Understanding of the International State' 11 Int J Soc L 1–10.
(1986) 'Who Loses Out on Paradise Island: The Case of Defendant Debtors in County Court' in I. Ramsay (ed) *Debtors and Creditors: A Socio-Legal Perspective* pp. 101–46 (Abingdon: Professional Books).
Cain, M. and Hunt, A. (eds) (1979) *Marx and Engels on Law* (London: Academic Press).
Cain, M. and Kulcsar, K. (1982) 'Thinking Disputes: An Essay on the Origins of the Dispute Industry' 16 Law & Soc Rev 375–402.
Cain, M. and Kulcsar K. (eds) (1983) *Disputes and the Law* (Budapest: Akademiai Kiado).

Campbell, C. M. and Wiles, P. (1976) 'The Study of Law in Society in Britain' 10 Law & Soc Rev 547–78.
Caplovitz, D. (1974) *Consumers in Trouble: A Study of Debtors in Default* (New York: Free Press).
Cappelletti, M. (1989) *The Judicial Process in Comparative Perspective* (Oxford: Oxford University Press).
Carbonnier, J. (1978) *Sociologie Juridique* (Paris: Presses Universitaires de France).
(1988) *Flexible droit: textes pour une sociologie du droit sans rigueur* (6th edn, Paris: Librairie Générale de Droit et de Jurisprudence).
Carlen, P. (1976a) 'The Staging of Magistrates' Justice' 16 Brit J Crim 48–62.
(1976b) *Magistrates' Justice* (London: Martin Robertson).
Carlin, J. E. (1962) *Lawyers on Their Own: A Study of Individual Practitioners in Chicago* (New Brunswick: Rutgers University Press).
(1966) *Lawyers' Ethics: A Survey of the New York City Bar* (New York: Russell Sage Foundation).
Carlin, J. E. and Howard, J. (1965) 'Legal Representation and Class Justice' 12 University of California at Los Angeles Law Review 381–437.
Carson, W. G. (1970) 'White Collar Crime and the Enforcement of Factory Legislation' 10 Brit J Crim 383–98.
(1974) 'Symbolic and Instrumental Dimensions of Early Factory Legislation: A Case Study in the Social Origins of Criminal Law' in R. Hood (ed) *Crime, Criminology and Public Policy* pp. 107–38 (London: Heinemann).
(1980) 'The Institutionalization of Ambiguity: Early British Factory Acts' in G. Geis and E. Stotland (eds) *White Collar Crime: Theory and Research* pp. 142–73 (London: Sage).
(1981) *The Other Price of Britain's Oil: Safety and Control in the North Sea* (Oxford: Martin Robertson).
Chambliss, W. J. (1966) 'The Deterrent Influence of Punishment' 12 Crime and Delinquency 70–5.
(1967) 'Types of Deviance and the Effectiveness of Legal Sanctions' Wisconsin Law Review 703–19.
(1973) 'Introduction' in W. J. Chambliss (ed) *Sociological Readings in the Conflict Perspective* pp. 1–38 (Reading, Mass.: Addison-Wesley).
(1978) 'Toward a Political Economy of Crime' in Reasons and Rich (eds) (1978) pp. 191–211.
Chan, J. B. L. and Hagan, J. (1982) *Law and the Chinese in Canada* (Toronto: University of Toronto Centre of Criminology).

Chatterton, M. R. (1989) 'Managing Paperwork' in M. Weatheritt (ed) *Police Research: Some Future Prospects* pp. 107–36 (Aldershot: Avebury).

Chesler, M. A., Sanders, J. and Kalmuss, D. S. (1988) *Social Science in Court: Mobilizing Experts in the School Desegregation Cases* (Madison: University of Wisconsin Press).

Chiricos, T. G. and Waldo, G. P. (1970) 'Punishment and Crime: An Examination of Some Empirical Evidence' (1970) 18 Soc Prob 200–17.

Christie, N. (1977) 'Conflicts as Property' 17 Brit J Crim 1–15.

Clark, J. and Wedderburn, Lord (1983) 'Modern Labour Law: Problems, Functions and Policies' in Lord Wedderburn, R. Lewis and J. Clark (eds) *Labour Law and Industrial Relations* pp. 127–242 (Oxford: Oxford University Press).

Clinard, M. B. and Yeager, P.C. (1980) *Corporate Crime* (New York: Free Press).

Clune, W. H. (1989) 'Legal Disintegration and a Theory of the State' in C. Joerges and D. M. Trubek (eds) *Critical Legal Thought: An American-German Debate* pp. 187–208 (Baden-Baden: Nomos Verlagsgesellschaft).

Coates, D. and Penrod, S. (1981) 'Social Psychology and the Emergence of Disputes' 15 Law & Soc Rev 655–80.

Cohen, G.A. (1978) *Karl Marx's Theory of History: A Defence* (Oxford: Oxford University Press).

Cohen, J., Robson, R. A. H. and Bates, A. (1958) *Parental Authority: The Community and the Law* (Westport, Conn.: Greenwood Press rep. 1980).

Cohen, S. (1980) *Folk Devils and Moral Panics: The Creation of the Mods and Rockers* (2nd edn, Oxford: Martin Robertson).

Cohn, B. S. (1967) 'Some Notes on Law and Change in North India' in P. Bohannon (ed) *Law and Warfare: Studies in the Anthropology of Conflict* pp. 139–59 (Garden City, NY: Natural History Press).

Cohn, E. J. (1960) 'The German Attorney: Experiences with a Unified Profession (I)' 9 International and Comparative Law Quarterly 580–99.

Collins, H. (1982) *Marxism and Law* (Oxford: Oxford University Press).

Collins, S. (1978) 'The Use of Social Research in the Courts' reprinted in Evan (ed) (1980) pp. 563–75.

Conley, J. M. and W. M. O'Barr (1990) *Rules Versus Relationships: The Ethnography of Legal Discourse* (Chicago: University of Chicago Press).

Cooper, R. (1987) 'Contracts, Crime and Agrarian Conflict: From Slave to Wage Labour on the East African Coast' in F. Snyder and D. Hay (eds) *Labour, Law and Crime: An Historical Perspective* pp. 228–52 (London: Tavistock).

Cornish, W. R. and Clark, G. de N. (1989) *Law and Society in England 1750-1950* (London: Sweet and Maxwell).
Corwin, E. S. (1936) 'The Constitution as Instrument and as Symbol' 30 American Political Science Review 1071–85.
Coser, L. A. (1956) *The Functions of Social Conflict* (London: Routledge and Kegan Paul).
Cotterrell, R. B. M. (1983a) 'The Sociological Concept of Law' 10 J Law & Soc 241–55.
(1983b) 'Legality and Political Legitimacy in the Sociology of Max Weber' in Sugarman (ed) (1983) pp. 69–93.
(1986) 'Law and Sociology: Notes on the Constitution and Confrontations of Disciplines' 13 J Law & Soc 9–34.
(1988) 'Feasible Regulation for Democracy and Social Justice' 15 J Law & Soc 5–24.
(1989) *The Politics of Jurisprudence: A Critical Introduction to Legal Philosophy* (London: Butterworths).
(1990a) 'Sociology of Law in Britain: Its Development and Present Prospects' in V. Ferrari (ed) *Developing Sociology of Law: A World-Wide Documentary Enquiry* pp. 779–803 (Milano: Giuffre).
(1990b) 'Law's Images of Community and Imperium' in S. S. Silbey and A. Sarat (eds) *Studies in Law, Politics, and Society: A Research Annual. Vol. 10* pp. 3–27 (Greenwich, Conn.: JAI Press).
Cranston, R. (1979) *Regulating Business: Law and Consumer Agencies* (London: Macmillan).
(1985) *Legal Foundations of the Welfare State* (London: Weidenfeld and Nicolson).
Curran, B. (1980) 'Research on Legal Needs: Patterns of Lawyer Use and Factors Affecting Use' in Blankenburg (ed) (1980) pp. 9–18.
Cushman, R. E. (1941) *The Independent Regulatory Commissions* (New York: Oxford University Press).
Dahl, R. A. and Tufte, E. R. (1974) *Size and Democracy* (Oxford: Oxford University Press).
Dalton, H. L. (1987) 'The Clouded Prism' 22 Harvard Civil Rights-Civil Liberties Law Review 435–47.
D'Amato, A. (1983) 'Legal Uncertainty' 71 California Law Review 1–55.
Danelski, D. J. (1967) 'Conflict and its Resolution in the Supreme Court' 11 Journal of Conflict Resolution 71–86.
(1974) 'The Limits of Law' in Pennock and Chapman (eds) (1974) pp. 8–27.
(1986) 'Causes and Consequences of Conflict and Its Resolution in the Supreme Court' in Goldman and Lamb (eds) (1986) pp. 21–49.
Danzig, R. and Lowy, M. J. (1975) 'Everyday Disputes and Mediation in the United States: A Reply to Professor Felstiner' 9 Law & Soc Rev 675–94.

Davis, K. C. (1969) *Discretionary Justice: A Preliminary Inquiry* (Urbana: University of Illinois Press edn 1971).

Dawson, J. B. (1982) 'The Exclusion of Unlawfully Obtained Evidence: A Comparative Study' 31 International and Comparative Law Quarterly 513–49.

Dawson, J. P. (1968) *The Oracles of the Law* (Ann Arbor: University of Michigan Law School).

Delgado, R. (1988) 'Critical Legal Studies and the Realities of Race—Does the Fundamental Contradiction Have a Corollary?' 23 Harvard Civil Rights-Civil Liberties Law Review 407–13.

Denning, Lord (1982) *What Next in the Law?* (London: Butterworths).

D'Entrèves, A. P. (1967) *The Notion of the State* (Oxford: Oxford University Press).

De Haan, W., Silvis, J. and Thomas, P. A. (1989) 'Radical French Judges: *Syndicat de la Magistrature*' 16 J Law & Soc 477–82.

De Smith, S. A. and Brazier, R. (1989) *Constitutional and Administrative Law* (6th edn by R. Brazier; Harmondsworth: Penguin).

De Tocqueville, A. (1945) *Democracy in America*, transl. by H. Reeve (revised and corrected edn, New York: Knopf).

Devlin, Lord (1965) *The Enforcement of Morals* (Oxford: Oxford University Press).

Dicey, A. V. (1905) *Lectures on the Relation Between Law and Public Opinion in England During the Nineteenth Century* (London: Macmillan).

(1959) *Introduction to the Study of the Law of the Constitution* (10th edn, London: Macmillan).

Dingwall, R. (1976) 'Accomplishing Profession' 24 Sociological Review 331–49.

Dingwall, R. and Lewis, P. (eds) (1983) *The Sociology of the Professions: Doctors, Lawyers and Others* (London: Macmillan).

Dixon, D. (1991) *From Prohibition to Regulation: Bookmaking, Anti-Gambling, and the Law* (Oxford: Oxford University Press).

Dixon, D., Coleman, C. and Bottomley, K. (1989) 'Consent and the Legal Regulation of Policing' 17 J Law & Soc 345–62.

Dixon, D., Bottomley, A. K., Coleman, C. A., Gill, M. and Wall, D. (1989) 'Reality and Rules in the Construction and Regulation of Police Suspicion' 17 Int J Soc L 185–206.

Dodd, E. M. (1943) 'From Maximum Wages to Minimum Wages: Six Centuries of Regulation of Employment Contracts' 43 Col L Rev 643–87.

Donzelot, J. (1980) *The Policing of Families: Welfare Versus the State*, transl. by R. Hurley (London: Hutchinson).

Doo, L.-W. (1973) 'Dispute Settlement in Chinese-American Communities' 21 Am J Comp L 627–63.

Dror, Y. (1959) 'Law and Social Change' 33 Tulane Law Review 787–802.

(1970) 'Law as a Tool of Directed Social Change: A Framework for Policy-Making' 13 American Behavioral Scientist 553–59.

Dunleavy, P. and O'Leary, B. (1987) *Theories of the State: The Politics of Liberal Democracy* (London: Macmillan).

Durkheim, E. (1960) 'Sociology and its Scientific Field', transl. by K. Wolff, in Wolff (ed) (1960) pp. 354–375.

(1969) 'Individualism and the Intellectuals', transl. by S. and J. Lukes, reprinted in W. S. F. Pickering (ed) *Durkheim on Religion: A Selection of Readings with Bibliographies and Introductory Remarks* (London: Routledge and Kegan Paul, 1975) pp. 59-73.

(1982) *The Rules of Sociological Method and Selected Texts on Sociology and its Method,* transl. by W. D. Halls (London: Macmillan).

(1984) *The Division of Labour in Society,* transl. by W. D. Halls (London: Macmillan).

Dworkin, R. (1986) *Law's Empire* (Cambridge, Mass.: Harvard University Press).

Eaton, M. (1980) 'The Better Business Bureau: "The Voice of the People in the Marketplace"' in Nader (ed) (1980) pp. 233–81.

Edelman, B. (1979) *Ownership of the Image: Elements for a Marxist Theory of Law*, transl. by E. Kingdom (London: Routledge and Kegan Paul).

Edelman, M. (1964) *The Symbolic Uses of Politics* (Urbana: University of Illinois Press).

Ehrlich, E. (1936) *Fundamental Principles of the Sociology of Law,* transl. by W. L. Moll (New York: Arno Press edn 1975).

Eisenberg, M. A. (1976) 'Private Ordering Through Negotiation: Dispute Settlement and Rulemaking' 89 Harv L Rev 637–81.

Elliott, D. W. and Street, H. (1968) *Road Accidents* (Harmondsworth: Penguin).

Ely, J. H. (1980) *Democracy and Distrust: A Theory of Judicial Review* (Cambridge, Mass.: Harvard University Press).

Evan, W. M. (ed) (1962) *Law and Sociology: Exploratory Essays* (Glencoe, Illinois: Free Press).

(1965) 'Law as an Instrument of Social Change' in A. W. Gouldner and S. M. Miller (eds) *Applied Sociology*, reprinted in Evan (ed) (1980) pp. 554–62.

(ed) (1980) *The Sociology of Law: A Social-Structural Perspective* (New York: Free Press).

(1990) *Social Structure and Law: Theoretical and Empirical Perspectives* (Newbury Park, Cal.: Sage).

Ewing, S. (1987) 'Formal Justice and the Spirit of Capitalism: Max Weber's Sociology of Law' 21 Law & Soc Rev 487-512.

Fahr, S. M. (1961) 'Why Lawyers are Dissatisfied with the Social Sciences' 1 Washburn Law Journal 161–75.

Feldman, D. (1992) 'Public Interest Litigation and Constitutional Theory in Comparative Perspective' 55 Mod L Rev 44–72.

Felstiner, W. L. F. (1974) 'Influences of Social Organization on Dispute Processing' 9 Law & Soc Rev 63–94.

(1975) 'Avoidance as Dispute Processing: An Elaboration' 9 Law & Soc Rev 695–706.

Fennell, P. (1982) 'Advertising: Professional Ethics and the Public Interest' in Thomas (ed) (1982) pp. 144–60.

(1986) 'Roberts v Hopwood: The Rule Against Socialism' 13 J Law & Soc 401–22.

Ferguson, R. B. (1980) 'The Adjudication of Commercial Disputes and the Legal System in Modern England' 7 Brit J Law & Soc 141–57.

Finkel, N. J. (1988) *Insanity on Trial* (New York: Plenum).

Fiss, O. M. (1984) 'Against Settlement' 93 Yale L J 1073–90.

Fitzpatrick, P. (1983) 'Marxism and Legal Pluralism' 1 Australian Journal of Law and Society No. 2.

Flango, V. E., Ducat, C. R. and McKnight, R. N. (1986) 'Measuring Leadership through Opinion Assignment in Two State Supreme Courts' in Goldman and Lamb (eds) (1986) pp. 215–39.

Fletcher, R. (1981) *Sociology: The Study of Social Systems* (London: Batsford).

Foucault, M. (1979) *The History of Sexuality*, vol 1, transl. by R. Hurley (London: Allen Lane).

(1980) *Power/Knowledge: Selected Interviews and Other Writings 1972-1977* (edited by C. Gordon) (New York: Pantheon).

Frank, J. N. (1930) *Law and the Modern Mind* (Garden City, NY: Anchor edn 1963).

(1949) *Courts on Trial: Myth and Reality in American Justice* (Princeton: Princeton University Press).

Freidson, E. (1970) *Profession of Medicine: A Study of the Sociology of Applied Knowledge* (New York: Harper and Row).

(1983) 'The Theory of Professions: State of the Art' in Dingwall and Lewis (eds) (1983) pp. 19–37.

(1986) *Professional Powers: A Study of the Institutionalization of Formal Knowledge* (Chicago: University of Chicago Press).

Fried, C. (1976) 'The Lawyer as Friend: The Moral Foundations of the Lawyer-Client Relation' 85 Yale LJ 1060–89.

Friedman, L. M. (1973) 'General Theory of Law and Social Change' in J. S. Ziegel (ed) *Law and Social Change* pp. 17–33 (Toronto: Osgoode Hall Law School, York University).

(1975) *The Legal System: A Social Science Perspective* (New York: Russell Sage Foundation).
(1985) *Total Justice* (Boston: Beacon Press edn 1987).
(1990a) *The Republic of Choice: Law, Authority, and Culture* (Cambridge, Mass.: Harvard University Press).
(1990b) 'Opening the Time Capsule: A Progress Report on Studies of Courts over Time' 24 Law & Soc Rev 229–40.
Friedman, L. M. and Ladinsky, J. (1967) 'Social Change and the Law of Industrial Accidents' 67 Col L Rev 50–82.
Friedman, L. M. and Percival, R. V. (1976) 'A Tale of Two Courts: Litigation in Alameda and San Benito Counties' 10 Law & Soc Rev 267–301.
Friedmann, W (1967) *Legal Theory* (5th edn, New York: Columbia University Press).
(1972) *Law in a Changing Society* (2nd edn, Harmondsworth: Penguin).
Fuller, L. L. (1971) 'Mediation: Its Forms and Functions' reprinted in Winston (ed) (1981) pp. 126–57.
(1978) 'The Forms and Limits of Adjudication' reprinted in Winston (ed) (1981) pp. 87–124.
Galanter, M. (1974) 'Why the "Haves" Come Out Ahead: Speculations on the Limits of Legal Change' 9 Law & Soc Rev 95–160.
(1983) 'Mega-Law and Mega-Lawyering in the Contemporary United States' in Dingwall and Lewis (eds) (1983) pp. 152–76.
(1986) 'The Day After the Litigation Explosion' 46 Maryland Law Review 3–39.
(1992) 'Law Abounding: Legalisation Around the North Atlantic' 55 Mod L Rev 1–24.
Galanter, M. and Palay, T. (1991) *Tournament of Lawyers: The Transformation of the Big Law Firm* (Chicago: University of Chicago Press).
Galligan, D. (1986) *Discretionary Powers: A Legal Study of Official Discretion* (Oxford: Oxford University Press).
(1987) 'Regulating Pre-Trial Decisions' in I. H. Dennis (ed) *Criminal Law and Justice: Essays from the W. G. Hart Workshop, 1986* pp. 177–202 (London: Sweet and Maxwell).
Gamble, A. (1988) 'Economic Decline and the Crisis of Legitimacy' in C. Graham and T. Prosser (eds) *Waiving the Rules: The Constitution Under Thatcherism* pp. 22–35 (Milton Keynes: Open University Press).
Garfinkel, H. (1956) 'Conditions of Successful Degradation Ceremonies' 61 Am J Soc 420–24.
Garland, D. (1990) *Punishment and Modern Society: A Study in Social Theory* (Oxford: Oxford University Press).
Geldart, W. M. (1911) 'Legal Personality' 27 Law Q Rev 90–108.

Genn, H. (1987) *Hard Bargaining: Out of Court Settlement in Personal Injury Actions* (Oxford: Oxford University Press).
Gerth, H. and Mills, C. W. (1954) *Character and Social Structure: The Psychology of Social Institutions* (London: Routledge and Kegan Paul).
Gibbs, J. (1978) 'Deterrence, Penal Policy and the Sociology of Law' in R. J. Simon (ed) *Research in Law and Sociology* vol 1, pp. 101–14 (Greenwich, Conn.: JAI Press).
Gibson, D. and Baldwin, J. K. (eds) (1985) *Law in a Cynical Society?: Opinion and Law in the 1980s* (Calgary: Carswell Legal Publications Western Division).
Gibson, J. L. (1989) 'Understandings of Justice: Institutional Legitimacy, Procedural Justice, and Political Tolerance' 23 Law & Soc Rev 469-96.
Gilligan, C. (1982) *In a Different Voice: Psychological Theory and Women's Development* (Cambridge, Mass.: Harvard University Press).
Gilmore, G. (1974) *The Death of Contract* (Columbus: Ohio State University Press).
Gleizal, J.-J. (1981) 'Police, Law and Security in France: Questions of Method and Political Strategy' 9 Int J Soc L 361–82.
(1985) *Le désordre policier* (Paris: Presses Universitaires de France).
Glendon, M. A. (1981) *The New Family and the New Property* (Toronto: Butterworths).
Goff, C. H. and Reasons, C. (1978) *Corporate Crime in Canada* (Ontario: Prentice-Hall).
Goldman, S. and Lamb, C. M. (eds) (1986) *Judicial Conflict and Consensus: Behavioral Studies of American Appellate Courts* (Lexington: University Press of Kentucky).
Goode, R. M. (1982) *Commercial Law* (Harmondsworth: Allen Lane).
Goode, W. J. (1957) 'Community Within a Community: The Professions' 22 Am Soc Rev 194–200.
(1969) 'The Theoretical Limits of Professionalization' in A. Etzioni (ed) *The Semi-Professions and Their Organization* pp. 266–313 (New York: Free Press).
Goodrich, P. (1987) *Legal Discourse: Studies in Linguistics, Rhetoric and Legal Analysis* (London: Macmillan).
(1990) *Languages of Law: From Logics of Memory to Nomadic Masks* (London: Weidenfeld and Nicolson).
Goody, J. (1977) *The Domestication of the Savage Mind* (Cambridge: Cambridge University Press).
Gordon, P. (1983) *White Law: Racism in the Police, Courts and Prisons* (London: Pluto Press).

Gray, J. C. (1921) *The Nature and Sources of the Law* (2nd edn, Boston: Beacon Press rep. 1963).

Greenberg, D. I. (1980) 'Easy Terms, Hard Times: Complaint Handling in the Ghetto' in Nader (ed) (1980) pp. 379–415.

Greenberg, D. I. and Stanton, T.H. (1980) 'Business Groups, Consumer Problems: The Contradiction of Trade Association Complaint Handling' in Nader (ed) (1980) pp. 193–231.

Greenberg, J. (1959) *Race Relations and American Law* (New York: Columbia University Press).

Greenhouse, C. (1986) *Praying for Justice: Faith, Order and Community in an American Town* (Ithaca, NY.: Cornell University Press).

Griffith, J. A. G. (1991) *The Politics of the Judiciary* (4th edn, London: Fontana).

Grossman, J. B. and Grossman, M. H. (eds) (1971) *Law and Change in Modern America* (Pacific Palisades, Cal.: Goodyear).

Gunningham, N. (1974) *Pollution, Social Interest and the Law* (London: Martin Robertson).

Gurvitch, G. (1947) *Sociology of Law* (London: Routledge and Kegan Paul).

Gusfield, J. R. (1963) *Symbolic Crusade: Status Politics and the American-Temperance Movement* (Urbana: University of Illinois Press).

Gutteridge, H. C. (1933) 'Abuse of Rights' 5 Cambridge Law Journal 22–45.

Habermas, J. (1976) *Legitimation Crisis*, transl. by T. McCarthy (London: Heinemann).

(1986) 'Law as Medium and Law as Institution' in Teubner (ed) (1986) pp. 203–20.

Hagan, J. (1982) 'The Corporate Advantage: The Involvement of Corporate and Individual Victims in a Criminal Justice System' 60 Social Forces 993–1022.

Haines, C. G. (1930) *The Revival of Natural Law Concepts: A Study of the Establishment and of the Interpretation of Limits on Legislatures with Special Reference to the Development of Certain Phases of American Constitutional Law* (New York: Russell and Russell edn, 1965).

(1932) *The American Doctrine of Judicial Supremacy* (2nd edn, New York: Da Capo rep. 1973).

Hale, A. R. and Pérusse, M. (1977) 'Attitudes to Safety: Facts and Assumptions' in J. Phillips (ed) *Safety at Work*, pp. 73–86 (London: Social Science Research Council).

Halliday, T. C. (1989) 'Legal Professions and the State: Neocorporatist Variations on the Pluralist Theme of Liberal Democracies' in Abel and Lewis (eds) (1989) pp. 375–426.

Hallis, F. (1930) *Corporate Personality* (Aalen: Scientia Verlag rep. 1978).
Hall Williams, J. E. (ed) (1988) *The Role of the Prosecutor* (Aldershot: Avebury).
Hamilton, W. H. (1931) 'The Ancient Maxim Caveat Emptor' 40 Yale LJ 1133–87.
Handler, J. (1978) *Social Movements and the Legal System: A Theory of Law Reform and Social Change* (New York: Academic Press).
Harlow, C. (1982) *Compensation and Government Torts* (London: Sweet and Maxwell).
Harrington, C. B. (1985) *Shadow Justice: The Ideology and Institutionalization of Alternatives to Court* (Westport, Conn.: Greenwood).
Harris, D., MacLean, M., Genn, H., Lloyd-Bostock, S., Fenn, P., Corfield, P. and Brittan Y. (1984) *Compensation and Support for Illness and Injury* (Oxford: Oxford University Press).
Hart, H. L. A. (1961) *The Concept of Law* (Oxford: Oxford University Press).
Hartzler, H. R. (1976) *Justice, Legal Systems and Social Structure* (Port Washington, NY: Dunnellen).
Hasselbach, O., Neal, A. C. and Victorin, A. (1982) *A Perspective on Labour Law* (Stockholm: Almqvist and Wiksell International).
Hawkins, K. (1984) *Environment and Enforcement: Regulation and the Social Definition of Pollution* (Oxford: Oxford University Press).
Hay, D. (1975) 'Property, Authority and the Criminal Law' in D. Hay et al. *Albion's Fatal Tree* pp 17–63 (London: Allen Lane).
Hayden, R. M. (1989) 'Cultural Context and the Impact of Traffic Safety Legislation: The Reception of Mandatory Seatbelt Laws in Yugoslavia and Illinois' 23 Law & Soc Rev 283–94.
Hayek, F. A. (1982) *Law, Legislation and Liberty* (revised edn, London: Routledge and Kegan Paul).
Heinz, J. P. and Laumann, E. O. (1982) *Chicago Lawyers: The Social Structure of the Bar* (New York and Chicago: Russell Sage Foundation and American Bar Foundation).
Held, D. (1984) 'Power and Legitimacy in Contemporary Britain' in McLennan, Held and Hall (eds) (1984) pp. 299–369.
(1987) *Models of Democracy* (Cambridge: Polity).
Hepworth, M. and Turner, B. (1982) *Confession: Studies in Deviance and Religion* (London: Routledge and Kegan Paul).
Hewart, Lord (1929) *The New Despotism* (London: Benn).
Hinkle, R. C. (1980) *Founding Theory in American Sociology 1881–1915* (London: Routledge and Kegan Paul).
Hirschman, A. O. (1970) *Exit, Voice and Loyalty: Responses to Decline in Firms, Organizations and States* (Cambridge Mass.: Harvard University Press).

Hirst, P. (1979) *On Law and Ideology* (London: Macmillan).
(ed) (1989) *The Pluralist Theory of the State: Selected Writings of G. D. H. Cole, J. N. Figgis, and H. J. Laski* (London: Routledge).
Hoebel, E. A. (1954) *The Law of Primitive Man* (Cambridge: Harvard University Press).
Holdaway, S. (1983) *Inside the British Police: A Force at Work* (Oxford: Basil Blackwell).
Hollis, M. and Lukes, S. (eds) (1982) *Rationality and Relativism* (Oxford: Blackwell).
Holmes, Jr, O. W. (1897) 'The Path of the Law' 10 Harv L Rev 457–78.
Horowitz, D. L. (1977) *The Courts and Social Policy* (Washington DC: Brookings Institute).
Horton, C. and Smith, D. (1988) *Evaluating Police Work: An Action Research Project* (London: Policy Studies Institute).
Horwitz, M. J. (1985) 'Santa Clara Revisited: The Development of Corporate Theory' 88 West Virginia Law Review 173-224.
Hughes, E. C. (1958) *Men and Their Work* (London: Greenwood Press rep. 1981).
Hughes, H. S. (1959) *Consciousness and Society: The Reorientation of European Social Thought 1890–1930* (St Albans: Paladin edn 1974).
Hunt, A. (1990) 'Rights and Social Movements: Counter-Hegemonic Strategies' 17 J Law & Soc 309–28.
(1991) 'Marxism, Law, Legal Theory and Jurisprudence' in P. Fitzpatrick (ed) *Dangerous Supplements: Resistance and Renewal in Jurisprudence* pp. 102–32 (London: Pluto).
Hurst, J. W. (1970) *The Legitimacy of the Business Corporation in the Law of the United States 1780–1970* (Charlottesville: University Press of Virginia).
Hutchinson, A. C. (1988) *Dwelling on the Threshold: Critical Essays on Modern Legal Thought* (Toronto: Carswell; London: Sweet and Maxwell).
Hutter, B. M. (1988) *The Reasonable Arm of the Law? The Law Enforcement Procedures of Environmental Health Officers* (Oxford: Oxford University Press).
Irvine, R. (1979) 'Legal Socialisation: A Critique of a New Approach' in D. Farrington et al. (eds) *Psychology, Law and Legal Contexts* pp. 69–89 (London: Macmillan).
Jacob, H. (1969) *Debtors in Court: The Consumption of Government Services* (Chicago: Rand McNally).
(1983) 'Courts as Organizations' in Boyum and Mather (eds) (1983) pp. 189–215.
(1984) *Justice in America: Courts, Lawyers and the Judicial Process* (4th edn, Boston: Little, Brown).

Jefferson, T. (1988) 'Race, Crime and Policing: Empirical, Theoretical and Methodological Issues' 16 Int J Soc L 521–39.

Jeffery, K. and Hennessy, P. (1983) *States of Emergency: British Governments and Strikebreaking Since 1919* (London: Routledge and Kegan Paul).

Jessop, B. (1982) *The Capitalist State: Marxist Theories and Methods* (Oxford: Martin Robertson).

Johnson, T. J. (1972) *Professions and Power* (London: Macmillan).

Kagan, R. A. (1978) *Regulatory Justice: Implementing a Wage-Price Freeze* (New York: Russell Sage).

Kahn, P., Lewis, H., Livock, R. and Wiles, P. (1983) *Picketing: Industrial Disputes, Tactics and the Law* (London: Routledge and Kegan Paul).

Kahn-Freund, O. (1967) 'A Note on Status and Contract in British Labour Law' 30 Mod L Rev 635–44.

(1969) 'Industrial Relations and the Law: Retrospect and Prospect' 7 British Journal of Industrial Relations 301–16.

Kamenka, E. and Tay, A. E-S. (1975) 'Beyond Bourgeois Individualism: The Contemporary Crisis in Law and Legal Ideology' in E. Kamenka and R. S. Neale (eds) *Feudalism, Capitalism and Beyond* pp. 127–44 (London: Edward Arnold).

(1978) 'Socialism, Anarchism and Law' in E. Kamenka,' R. Brown and A. E-S. Tay (eds) *Law and Society: The Crisis in Legal Ideals* pp. 48–80 (London: Edward Arnold).

Kaplan, J. (1971) *Marijuana: The New Prohibition* (New York: World Publishing).

Keane, J. (1988) 'Despotism and Democracy: The Origins and Development of the Distinction Between Civil Society and the State 1750-1850' in J. Keane (ed) *Civil Society and the State: New European Perspectives* pp. 35–71 (London: Verso).

Keedy, E. R. (1951) 'A Remarkable Murder Trial: Rex v. Sinnisiak' 100 University of Pennsylvania Law Review 48–67.

Keeton, G. W. (1952) *The Passing of Parliament* (London: Benn).

Kelley, D. R. (1990) *The Human Measure: Social Thought in the Western Legal Tradition* (Cambridge, Mass.: Harvard University Press).

Kelsen, H. (1945) *General Theory of Law and State*, transl by A. Wedberg (New York: Russell and Russell edn, 1961).

Kephart, W. M. (1957) *Racial Factors and Urban Law Enforcement* (Philadelphia: University of Pennsylvania Press).

Kessler, F. (1943) 'Contracts of Adhesion: Some Thoughts About Freedom of Contract' 43 Col L Rev 629–42.

Kiernan, V. G. (1990) *The Duel in European History: Honour and the Reign of Aristocracy* (Oxford: Oxford University Press).

King, M. and Piper, C. (1990) *How the Law Thinks About Children* (Aldershot: Gower).
Kirchheimer, O. (1961) *Political Justice: The Use of Legal Procedure for Political Ends* (Princeton: Princeton University Press).
Kirk, H. (1976) *Portrait of a Profession: A History of the Solicitor's Profession 1100 to the Present Day* (London: Oyez).
Klepper, S. and Nagin, D. (1989) 'Tax Compliance and Perceptions of the Risks of Detection and Criminal Prosecution' 23 Law & Soc Rev 209–40.
Klockars, C. B. (1985) *The Idea of Police* (Beverly Hills: Sage).
Kolakowski, L. (1972) *Positivist Philosophy: From Hume to the Vienna Circle,* transl. By H. Guterman (revised edn, Harmondsworth: Penguin).
Kolko, G. (1963) *The Triumph of Conservatism: A Reinterpretation of American History 1900–1916* (New York: Free Press).
Kommers, D. P. (1969) 'The Federal Constitutional Court in the West German Political System' in J.B. Grossman and J. Tanenhaus (eds) *Frontiers of Judicial Research* pp. 73–132 (New York: Wiley).
Kritzer, H. M. (1981) 'Studying Disputes: Learning from the CLRP Experience' 15 Law & Soc Rev 503–24.
Kurtines, W. and Greif, E. B. (1974) 'The Development of Moral Thought: Review and Evaluation of Kohlberg's Approach' 81 Psychological Bulletin 453–70.
Kutchinsky, B. (1973) 'The Legal Consciousness: A Survey of Research on Knowledge and Opinion About Law' in Podgorecki et al. (1973) pp. 101–38.
Lachmann, L. M. (1970) *The Legacy of Max Weber: Three Essays* (London: Heinemann).
La Fave, W. R. (1965) *Arrest: The Decision to Take a Suspect Into Custody* (Boston: Little, Brown).
Larson, M. S. (1977) *The Rise of Professionalism: A Sociological Analysis* (Berkeley: University of California Press).
Lempert, R. O. (1966) 'Strategies of Research Design in the Legal Impact Study: The Control of Plausible Rival Hypotheses' 1 Law & Soc Rev 111–32.
(1978) 'More Tales of Two Courts: Exploring Changes in the "Dispute Settlement Function" of Trial Courts' 13 Law & Soc Rev 91–138.
(1981) 'Grievances and Legitimacy: the Beginnings and End of Dispute Settlement' 15 Law & Soc Rev 707–15.
Lerner, M. (1937) 'Constitution and Court as Symbols' 46 Yale LJ 1290–319.
Lester, A. and Bindman, G. (1972) *Race and Law* (Harmondsworth: Penguin).

Lévy-Bruhl, H. (1961) *Sociologie du droit* (6th edn, Paris: Presses Universitaires de France).
(1964) *La preuve judiciaire: Étude de sociologie juridique* (Paris: Rivière).
Lewis, N. and Harden, I. (1983) 'Privatisation, De-regulation and Constitutionality: Some Anglo-American Comparisons' 34 Northern Ireland Legal Quarterly 207–29.
Lieberman, J. K. (ed) (1984) *The Role of Courts in American Society: The Final Report of the Council on the Role of Courts* (St. Paul: West Publishing).
Lipset, S. M. (1960) *Political Man* (London: Heinemann).
Lipstein, K. (1959) 'Reception of Foreign Law in Turkey: Conclusions' 9 International Social Science Bulletin 70–81.
Livock, R. (1979) 'Science, Law and Safety Standards: A Case Study of Industrial Disease' 6 Brit J Law & Soc 172–99.
Llewellyn, K. N. (1940) 'The Normative, the Legal, and the Law-Jobs: The Problem of Juristic Method' 49 Yale LJ 1355–400.
(1960) *The Common Law Tradition: Deciding Appeals* (Boston: Little, Brown).
(1989) *The Case Law System in America*, transl by M. Ansaldi (Chicago: University of Chicago Press).
Los, M. (1981) 'Law from a Phenomenological Perspective' in Podgorecki and Whelan (eds) (1981) pp. 187–200.
Lovenduski, J. and Outshoorn, J. (eds) (1986) *The New Politics of Abortion* (London: Sage).
Luhmann, N. (1979) *Trust and Power: Two Works by Niklas Luhmann*, transl. by H. Davis, J. Raffan and K. Rooney (Chichester: John Wiley).
(1981) 'Communication about Law in Interaction Systems' in K. Knorr-Cetina and A. V. Cicourel (eds) *Advances in Social Theory and Methodology* pp. 234–56 (London: Routledge and Kegan Paul).
(1982) *The Differentiation of Society*, transl. by S. Holmes and C. Larmore (New York: Columbia University Press).
(1985) *A Sociological Theory of Law*, transl. by E. King-Utz and M. Albrow (London: Routledge and Kegan Paul).
(1986) 'The Self-Reproduction of Law and Its Limits' in Teubner (ed) (1986) pp. 111–27.
(1988a) 'The Unity of the Legal System' in Teubner (ed) (1988) pp. 12–35.
(1988b) 'Closure and Openness: On Reality in the World of Law' in Teubner (ed) (1988) pp. 335–48.
Luker, K. (1984) *Abortion and the Politics of Motherhood* (Berkeley: University of California Press).

Lundman, R. J., Sykes, R. E. and Clark, J. P. (1978) 'Police Control of Juveniles: A Replication' 15 Journal of Research in Crime and Delinquency 74–91.

Lustgarten, L. (1986) 'Racial Inequality and the Limits of Law' 49 Mod L Rev 68–85.

Lyotard, J.-F. (1984) *The Postmodern Condition: A Report on Knowledge*, transl. by G. Bennington and B. Massumi (Manchester: Manchester University Press).

Macaulay, S. (1963) 'Non-contractual Relations in Business: A Preliminary Study' 28 Am Soc Rev 55–67.

(1979) 'Lawyers and Consumer Protection Laws' 14 Law & Soc Rev 115–71.

McBarnet, D. (1981a) 'Magistrates' Courts and the Ideology of Justice' 8 Brit J Law & Soc 181–97.

(1981b) *Conviction: Law, the State and the Construction of Justice* (London: Macmillan).

(1982) 'Legal Form and Legal Mystification' 10 Int J Soc L 409–17.

McClintock, F. H. (1981) 'Some Aspects of Discretion in Criminal Justice' in Adler and Asquith (eds) (1981) pp. 185–99.

McConville, M. and Mirsky, C. L. (1987) 'Criminal Defense of the Poor in New York City' 15 New York University Review of Law and Social Change 581–964.

McCormick, A. E. (1979) 'Dominant Class Interests and the Emergence of Anti-trust Legislation' 3 Contemporary Crises 399–417.

MacCormick, D. N. (1974) 'Law as Institutional Fact' 90 Law Q Rev 102–29.

McDonald, P. (1979) 'The Legal Sociology of Georges Gurvitch' 6 Brit J Law & Soc 24–52.

McDonald, W. F. (ed) (1983) *The Defense Counsel* (Beverly Hills: Sage Publications).

McLennan, G., Held, D. and Hall, S. (eds) (1984) *State and Society in Contemporary Britain: A Critical Introduction* (Cambridge: Polity).

Maine, H. S. (1861) *Ancient Law* (London: Dent, edn 1917).

Mann, M. (1970) 'The Social Cohesion of Liberal Democracy' 35 Am Soc Rev 423–39.

(1984) 'The Autonomous Power of the State: Its Origins, Mechanisms and Results' reprinted in J. A. Hall (ed) *States in History* pp. 109–36 (Oxford: Basil Blackwell, 1986).

Manning, P. K. (1977) *Police Work: The Social Organization of Policing* (Cambridge Mass.: MIT Press).

Mark, Sir Robert (1977) *Policing a Perplexed Society* (London: George Allen and Unwin).

Marshall, T. R. (1989) *Public Opinion and the Supreme Court* (Boston: Unwin Hyman).

Marx, K. and Engels, F. (1888) *Manifesto of the Communist Party*, transl. by S. Moore, reprinted in *Collected Works* vol 6, 1976 (London: Lawrence and Wishart).

(1974) *The German Ideology,* transl. by W. Lough, C. Dutt and C. Magrill, (student edn, 2nd edn, London: Lawrence and Wishart).

Mathiesen, T. (1980) *Law, Society and Political Action: Towards a Strategy Under Late Capitalism* (London: Academic Press).

Mayer, J. P. (1956) *Max Weber and German Politics: A Study in Political Sociology* (2nd edn, New York: Arno rep. 1979).

Mayhew, L. H. (1968) *Law and Equal Opportunity: A Study of the Massachusetts Commission Against Discrimination* (Cambridge Mass.: Harvard University Press).

(1971) 'Stability and Change in Legal Systems' in B. Barber and A. Inkeles (eds) *Stability and Social Change* pp. 187–210 (Boston: Little, Brown).

Merry, S. E. (1990) *Getting Justice and Getting Even: Legal Consciousness Among Working-Class Americans* (Chicago: University of Chicago Press).

Merryman, J. H. (1985) *The Civil Law Tradition: An Introduction to the Legal Systems of Western Europe and Latin America* (2nd edn, Stanford: Stanford University Press).

Merton, R. K. (1968) 'Manifest and Latent Functions' in R. K. Merton *Social Theory and Social Structure* pp. 73–138 (3rd edn, New York: Free Press).

Mesher, J. (1990) 'The Legal Structure of the Social Fund' in M. D. A. Freeman (ed) *Critical Issues in Welfare Law* pp. 35–57 (London: Stevens).

Miliband, R. (1969) *The State in Capitalist Society* (London: Quartet Books edn 1973).

Miller, D. (1976) *Social Justice* (Oxford: Oxford University Press).

Millerson, G. (1964) *The Qualifying Associations* (London: Routledge and Kegan Paul).

Mills, C. W. (1951) *White Collar: The American Middle Classes* (New York: Oxford University Press).

(1956) *The Power Elite* (New York: Oxford University Press).

(1959) *The Sociological Imagination* (Harmondsworth: Penguin edn 1970).

Mnookin, R. H. and Kornhauser, L. (1979) 'Bargaining in the Shadow of the Law: The Case of Divorce' 88 Yale LJ 950–97.

Moody, S. R. and Tombs, J. (1983) *Prosecution in the Public Interest* (Edinburgh: Scottish Academic Press).

Moore, S. F. (1978) *Law as Process: An Anthropological Approach* (London: Routledge and Kegan Paul).

Moore, W. U. and Sussman, G. (1931) 'Legal and Institutional Methods Applied to the Debiting of Direct Discounts VI: The Decisions, the Institutions, and the Degrees of Deviation' 40 Yale LJ 1219–72.
Morgan, J. B. (1990) *The Police Function and the Investigation of Crime* (Aldershot: Avebury).
Morison, J. and Leith, P. (1992) *The Barrister's World and the Nature of Law* (Milton Keynes: Open University Press).
Morrow, C. J. (1940) 'Warranty of Quality: A Comparative Survey' 14 Tulane Law Review 327–60, 529–72.
Muir, W. K. (1967) 'Under What Circumstances Can Law Bring About Attitude Change?' reprinted in Grossman and Grossman (eds) (1971) pp. 48–52.
Murphy, W. F. (1964) *Elements of Judicial Strategy* (Chicago: University of Chicago Press).
Murphy, W. T. (1991) 'The Oldest Social Science? The Epistemic Properties of the Common Law Tradition' 54 Mod L Rev 182–215.
Murray, T., Dingwall, R. and Eekelaar, J. (1983) 'Professionals in Bureaucracies: Solicitors in Private Practice and Local Government' in Dingwall and Lewis (eds) (1983) pp. 195–220.
Nader, L. (1980) 'Alternatives to the American Judicial System' in Nader (ed) (1980) pp. 3–55.
(ed) (1980) *No Access to Law: Alternatives to the American Judicial System* (New York: Academic Press).
Nader, L. and Shugart, C. (1980) 'Old Solutions For Old Problems' in Nader (ed) (1980) pp. 57–110.
Nelken, D. (1982) 'Is There a Crisis in Law and Legal Ideology?' 9 J Law & Soc 177–89.
Nelson, R. L. (1988) *Partners with Power: The Social Transformation of the Large Law Firm* (Berkeley: University of California Press).
Nenner, H. (1977) *By Colour of Law: Legal Culture and Constitutional Politics in England 1660–1689* (Chicago: University of Chicago Press).
Neumann, F. (1949) 'Introduction' to Montesquieu's *The Spirit of the Laws,* transl. by T. Nugent (New York: Hafner).
Newman, R. A. (1973) *Equity in the World's Legal Systems* (Brussels: Bruylant).
Newton, K. (1982) 'Is Small Really So Beautiful? Is Large Really So Ugly? Size, Effectiveness, and Democracy in Local Government' 30 Political Studies 190–206.
Niederhoffer, A. (1967) *Behind the Shield: The Police in Urban Society* (Garden City NY: Doubleday).
Nisbet, R. (1975) *Twilight of Authority* (New York: Oxford University Press).

Nonet, P. and Selznick, P. (1978) *Law and Society in Transition: Toward Responsive Law* (New York: Harper and Row).
Norrie, A. and Adelman, S. (1989) '"Consensual Authoritarianism" and Criminal Justice in Thatcher's Britain' 16 J Law & Soc 112–28.
Northrop, F. S. C. (1950) 'Underhill Moore's Legal Science: Its Nature and Significance' 59 Yale L J 196–213.
O'Donovan, K. (1985) *Sexual Divisions in Law* (London: Weidenfeld and Nicolson).
Offer, A. (1981), *Property and Politics: Landownership, Law, Ideology and Urban Development in England* (Cambridge: Cambridge University Press).
Ogus, A. I. and Veljanovski, C. G. (1984) *Readings in the Economics of Law and Regulation* (Oxford: Oxford University Press).
Olsen, F. (1984) 'Statutory Rape: A Feminist Critique of Rights Analysis' 63 Texas Law Review 387–432.
Parsons, T. (1939) 'The Professions and Social Structure' reprinted in Parsons (1954a) pp. 34–49.
(1954a) *Essays in Sociological Theory* (revised edn, Glencoe: Free Press).
(1954b) 'A Sociologist Looks at the Legal Profession' in Parsons (1954a) pp. 370–85.
(1960a) *Structure and Process in Modern Societies* (Glencoe, Illinois: Free Press).
(1960b) 'Durkheim's Contribution to the Theory of Integration of Social Systems' in Wolff (ed) (1960), reprinted in Parsons (1967) pp. 3–34.
(1962) 'The Law and Social Control' in Evan (ed) (1962) pp. 56–72.
(1964) 'Evolutionary Universals in Society' 29 Am Soc Rev 339–57.
(1967) *Sociological Theory and Modern Society* (New York: Free Press).
(1977) Book Review, 12 Law & Soc Rev 145–49.
Pashigian, B. P. (1982) 'Regulation, Preventive Law and the Duties of Attorneys' in W. J. Carney (ed) *The Changing Role of the Corporate Attorney* pp. 3–46 (Lexington: D. C. Heath).
Pashukanis, E. B. (1978) *Law and Marxism: A General Theory* transl. by B. Einhorn (London: Ink Links).
Paternoster, R. (1989) 'Decisions to Participate in and Desist from Four Types of Common Delinquency: Deterrence and the Rational Choice Perspective' 23 Law & Soc Rev 7-40.
Paterson, A. (1982) *The Law Lords* (London: Macmillan).
(1983) 'Becoming a Judge' in Dingwall and Lewis (eds) (1983) pp. 263–85.
Paterson, A., Farmer, L., Stephen, F. and Love, J. (1988) 'Competition and the Market for Legal Services' 15 J Law & Soc 361–73.

Pattenden, R. (1990) *The Judge, Discretion and Criminal Litigation* (2nd edn, Oxford: Oxford University Press).
Patterson, E. W. (1951) 'Historical and Evolutionary Theories of Law' 51 Col L Rev 681–709.
Paulus, I. (1974) *The Search for Pure Food: A Sociology of Legislation in Britain* (London: Martin Robertson).
Peay, J. (1989) *Tribunals on Trial: A Study of Decision-Making under the Mental Health Act 1983* (Oxford: Oxford University Press).
Pennock, J. R. and Chapman, J. W. (eds) (1974) *The Limits of Law*, Nomos XV (New York: Lieber-Atherton).
Petrazycki, L. (1955) *Law and Morality,* transl. by H. W. Babb (Cambridge, Mass.: Harvard University Press).
Phillips, R. (1988) *Putting Asunder: A History of Divorce in Western Society* (Cambridge: Cambridge University Press).
Piliavin, I. and Briar, S. (1964) 'Police Encounters with Juveniles' 70 Am J Soc 206–14.
Piven, F. F. and Cloward, R. A. (1972) *Regulating the Poor: The Functions of Public Welfare* (London: Tavistock).
Plamenatz, J. (1963) *Man and Society: A Critical Examination of Some Important Social and Political Theories from Machiavelli to Marx*, vol 2 (London: Longman).
Podgorecki, A. (1973) 'Public Opinion on Law' in Podgorecki et al. (1973) pp. 65–100.
(1974) *Law and Society* (London: Routledge and Kegan Paul).
(1985) 'Aspects of Public Opinion About Law in Poland' in Gibson and Baldwin (eds) (1985) pp. 128–34.
Podgorecki, A., Kaupen, W., Van Houtte, J., Vinke, P. and Kutchinsky, B. (1973) *Knowledge and Opinion About Law* (London: Martin Robertson).
Podgorecki, A. and Whelan, C. J. (eds) (1981) *Sociological Approaches to Law* (London: Croom Helm).
Podmore, D. (1980) *Solicitors and the Wider Community* (London: Heinemann).
Poggi, G. (1978) *The Development of the Modern State: A Sociological Introduction* (London: Hutchinson).
Polanyi, M. (1951) *The Logic of Liberty: Reflections and Rejoinders* (London: Routledge and Kegan Paul).
Pollock, F. (1929) 'Judicial Caution and Valour' 45 Law Q Rev 293–306.
Poulantzas, N. (1972) 'The Problem of the Capitalist State' in R. Blackburn (ed) *Ideology in Social Science* pp. 238–53 (London: Fontana).
(1978) *State, Power, Socialism,* transl. by P. Camiller (London: New Left Books).

Pound, R. (1917) 'The Limits of Effective Legal Action' 27 International Journal of Ethics 150–67.
(1954) *Introduction to the Philosophy of Law* (revised edn, New Haven: Yale University Press).
Powell Jr, L. F. (1976) 'What the Justices are Saying' 62 American Bar Association Journal 1454–55.
Prausnitz, O. (1937) *The Standardization of Commercial Contracts in English and Continental Law* (London: Sweet and Maxwell).
Prosser, T. (1983) *Test Cases for the Poor: Legal Techniques in the Politics of Social Welfare* (London: Child Poverty Action Group).
Punch, M. (1985) *Conduct Unbecoming: The Social Construction of Police Deviance and Control* (London: Tavistock).
Rabin, R. L. (1979) 'Impact Analysis and Tort Law: A Comment' 13 Law & Soc Rev 987–96.
Radcliffe, Lord (1961) *The Law and its Compass* (London: Faber and Faber).
(1968) 'The Lawyer and His Times' in A. E. Sutherland (ed) *The Path of the Law From 1967* pp. 9–19 (Cambridge, Mass.: Harvard Law School).
Reasons, C. E. and Rich, R. M. (eds) (1978) *The Sociology of Law: A Conflict Perspective* (Toronto: Butterworths).
Redfield, R. (1941) *The Folk Culture of Yucatan* (Chicago: University of Chicago Press edn 1961).
Rehbinder, M. (1971) 'Status, Contract, and the Welfare State' 23 Stanford Law Review 941–55.
Reichstein, K. J. (1965) 'Ambulance Chasing: A Case Study of Deviation and Control Within the Legal Profession' 13 Soc Prob 3–17.
Reiner, R. (1985) *The Politics of the Police* (Brighton: Wheatsheaf).
(1991) *Chief Constables: Bobbies, Bosses or Bureaucrats?* (Oxford: Oxford University Press).
Reiss, Jr, A. J. (1971) *The Police and the Public* (New Haven: Yale University Press).
Reiss, Jr, A. J. and Bordua, D. J. (1967) 'Environment and Organization: A Perspective on the Police' in D. J. Bordua (ed) *The Police: Six Sociological Essays* pp. 25–55 (New York: Wiley).
Renner, K. (1949) *The Institutions of Private Law and Their Social Functions*, transl. by A Schwarzschild (London: Routledge and Kegan Paul).
Rex, J. (1979) 'The Right Lines for Race Research' New Society, 5 April, pp. 14–16.
Rhodes, G. (1981) *Inspectorates in British Government: Law Enforcement and Standards of Efficiency* (London: George Allen and Unwin).

Richardson, G. with Ogus, A. and Burrows, P. (1983) *Policing Pollution: A Study of Regulation and Enforcement* (Oxford: Oxford University Press).
Roche, J. P. (1964) *Shadow and Substance: Essays on the Theory and Structure of Politics* (London: Macmillan).
Rock, P. (1973) *Making People Pay* (London: Routledge and Kegan Paul).
(1974) 'The Sociology of Deviancy and Conceptions of Moral Order' 14 Brit J Crim 139–49.
Rosenthal, D. E. (1974) *Lawyer and Client: Who's in Charge?* (New York: Russell Sage Foundation).
Ross, H. L. (1960) 'Traffic Law Violation: A Folk Crime' 8 Soc Prob 231–41.
(1984) *Deterring the Drinking Driver: Legal Policy and Social Control* (revised edn, Lexington, Mass.: Lexington Books).
Rottleuthner, H. (1989) 'The Limits of Law: the Myth of a Regulatory Crisis' 17 Int J Soc L 273-85.
Rueschemeyer, D. (1973) *Lawyers and Their Society: A Comparative Study of the Legal Profession in Germany and in the United States* (Cambridge Mass.: Harvard University Press).
(1989) 'Comparing Legal Professions: A State-Centered Approach' in Abel and Lewis (eds) (1989) 289–321.
Sacks, H. (1972) 'Notes on Police Assessment of Moral Character' in D. Sudnow (ed) *Studies in Social Interaction* pp. 280–93 (New York: Free Press).
Sajo, A. (1981) 'Why Do Public Bureaucracies Follow Legal Rules?' 9 Int J Soc L 69–84.
Sampson, R. J. and Cohen, J. (1988) 'Deterrent Effects of the Police on Crime: A Replication and Theoretical Extension' 22 Law & Soc Rev 163–89.
Santos, B. de S. (1982) 'Law and Community: The Changing Nature of State Power in Late Capitalism' in R. L. Abel (ed) *The Politics of Informal Justice. Vol. 1: The American Experience* pp. 249–66 (New York: Academic Press).
(1985) 'On Modes of Production of Law and Social Power' 13 Int J Soc L 299–336.
(1987) 'Law—A Map of Misreading: Toward a Postmodern Conception of Law' 14 J Law & Soc 279–302.
Sarat, A. (1975) 'Support for the Legal System: An Analysis of Knowledge, Attitudes, and Behaviour' 3 American Politics Quarterly 3–24.
(1977) 'Studying American Legal Culture: An Assessment of Survey Evidence' 11 Law & Soc Rev 427–88.

(1990a) '"...The Law is All Over": Power, Resistance and the Legal Consciousness of the Welfare Poor' 2 Yale Journal of Law and the Humanities 343–79.

(1990b) 'Off to Meet the Wizard: Beyond Validity and Reliability in the Search for a Post-Empiricist Sociology of Law' 15 L & Soc Inq 155–70.

Sarat, A. and Felstiner, W. L. F. (1988) 'Law and Social Relations: Vocabularies of Motive in Lawyer/Client Interaction' 22 Law & Soc Rev 737–69.

(1989) 'Lawyers and Legal Consciousness: Law Talk in the Divorce Lawyer's Office' 98 Yale L J 1663–88.

Savigny, F. K. von (1831) *Of the Vocation of Our Age For Legislation and Jurisprudence*, transl. by A. Hayward (New York: Arno Press edn 1975).

(1867) *System of the Modern Roman Law*, transl. by W. Holloway, vol 1 (Westport: Hyperion Press edn 1979).

Sawer, G. (1965) *Law in Society* (Oxford: Oxford University Press).

Schaffer, E. B. (1980) *Community Policing* (London: Croom Helm).

Schiff, D. (1981) 'Law as a Social Phenomenon' in Podgorecki and Whelan (eds) (1981) pp. 151–66.

Schubert, G.(1963) 'Judicial Attitudes and Voting Behavior: The 1961 Term of the United States Supreme Court' 28 Law and Contemporary Problems 100–42.

Schur, E. M. (1965) *Crimes Without Victims: Deviant Behavior and Public Policy* (Englewood Cliffs: Prentice-Hall).

Schwartz, B. (1987) *Lions over the Throne: The Judicial Revolution in English Administrative Law* (New York: New York University Press).

Schwartz, R. D. and Miller, J. C. (1964) 'Legal Evolution and Societal Complexity' 70 Am J Soc 159–69.

Scott, C. (1990) 'Continuity and Change in British Food Law' 53 Mod L Rev 785-801.

Seagle, W. (1941) *The Quest For Law* (New York: Knopf).

Seidman, R. B. (1965) 'Witch Murder and *Mens Rea:* A Problem of Society Under Radical Social Change' 28 Mod L Rev 46–61.

Selznick, P. (1969) *Law, Society and Industrial Justice* (New York: Russell Sage Foundation).

Serber, D. (1980) 'Resolution or Rhetoric: Managing Complaints in the California Department of Insurance' in Nader (ed) (1980) pp. 317–43.

Shapiro, M. (1981) *Courts: A Comparative and Political Analysis* (Chicago: University of Chicago Press).

Shapland, J. and Vagg, J. (1988) *Policing by the Public* (London: Routledge).

Shils, E. (1975) *Center and Periphery: Essays in Macrosociology* (Chicago: University of Chicago Press).
Silbey, S. S. (1991) 'Loyalty and Betrayal: Cotterrell's Discovery and Reproduction of Legal Ideology' 16 L & Soc Inq 809–33.
Simitis, S. (1987) 'Juridification of Labour Relations' in Teubner (ed) (1987) pp. 113–61.
Sinclair, A. (1962) *Prohibition: The Era of Excess* (London: Faber).
Skolnick, J. (1975) *Justice Without Trial: Law Enforcement in Democratic Society* (2nd edn, New York: Wiley).
Smigel, E. O. (1969) *The Wall Street Lawyer: Professional Organization Man?* (revised edn, Bloomington: Indiana University Press).
Smith, C. (1975) 'Judicial Attitudes to Social Security' 2 Brit J Law & Soc 217–21.
Smith, D. J. (1977) *Racial Disadvantage in Britain: The P.E.P. Report* (Harmondsworth: Penguin).
Smith, D. J. and Gray, J. (1983) *Police and People in London IV: The Police in Action* (London: Policy Studies Institute).
Spangler, E. (1986) *Lawyers for Hire: Salaried Professionals at Work* (New Haven: Yale University Press).
Stevens, R. (1979) *Law and Politics: The House of Lords as a Judicial Body 1800–1976* (London: Weidenfeld and Nicolson).
Stone, C. (1980) 'The Place of Enterprise Liability in the Control of Corporate Conduct' 90 Yale LJ 1–77.
Stone, J. (1966) *Social Dimensions of Law and Justice* (Sydney: Maitland).
Stone, K. (1981) 'The Post-War Paradigm in American Labour Law' 90 Yale LJ 1509–80.
Stone, L. (1990) *Road to Divorce: England 1530-1987* (Oxford: Oxford University Press).
Stone, O. M. (1982) *The Child's Voice in the Court of Law* (Toronto: Butterworths)
Sugarman, D. (1981) 'Theory and Practice in Law and History' in B. Fryer, A. Hunt, D. McBarnet and B. Moorhouse (eds) *Law, State and Society* pp. 70–106 (London: Croom Helm).
(ed) (1983) *Legality, Ideology and the State* (London: Academic Press).
Summers, R. S. (1971) 'The Technique Element in Law' 59 California Law Review 733–51.
(1977) 'Naive Instrumentalism and the Law' in P. M. S. Hacker and J. Raz (eds) *Law, Morality and Society* pp. 119–131 (Oxford: Oxford University Press).
Sumner, W. G. (1906) *Folkways* (New York: New American Library edn 1960).
Tapp, J. L. and Kohlberg, L. (1971) 'Developing Senses of Law and Legal Justice' 27 Journal of Social Issues No. 2, 65–91.

Tapp, J. L. and Levine, F. L. (1974) 'Legal Socialization: Strategies for an Ethical Legality' 27 Stanford Law Review 1–72.

Taylor, M. (1982) *Community, Anarchy and Liberty* (Cambridge: Cambridge University Press).

Teubner, G. (1984) 'Autopoiesis in Law and Society: A Rejoinder to Blankenburg' 18 Law & Soc Rev 291–301.

(1986) 'After Legal Instrumentalism?: Strategic Models of Post-Regulatory Law' in Teubner (ed) (1986) pp. 299–325.

(1987) 'Juridification: Concepts, Aspects, Limits, Solutions' in Teubner (ed) (1987) pp. 3–48.

(1988a) 'Evolution of Autopoietic Law' in Teubner (ed) (1988) pp. 217–41.

(1988b) 'Introduction to Autopoietic Law' in Teubner (ed) (1988) pp. 1–11.

(1989) 'How the Law Thinks: Toward a Constructivist Epistemology of Law' 23 Law & Soc Rev 727–57.

(ed) (1986) *Dilemmas of Law in the Welfare State* (Berlin: de Gruyter).

(ed) (1987) *Juridification of Social Spheres: A Comparative Analysis in the Areas of Labor, Corporate, Antitrust and Social Welfare Law* (Berlin: de Gruyter).

(ed) (1988) *Autopoietic Law: A New Approach to Law and Society* (Berlin: de Gruyter).

Thomas, P. A. (ed) (1982) *Law in the Balance: Legal Services in the Eighties* (Oxford: Martin Robertson).

Thompson, E. P. (1975) *Whigs and Hunters: The Origin of the Black Act* (Harmondsworth: Penguin).

(1978) *The Poverty of Theory and Other Essays* (London: Merlin Press).

Thompson, G. (1984a) 'Economic Intervention in the Post-War Economy' in McLennan, Held and Hall (eds) (1984) pp. 77–118.

(1984b) '"Rolling Back" the State? Economic Intervention 1975-82' in McLennan, Held and Hall (eds) (1984) pp. 274–98.

Timasheff, N. S. (1939) *An Introduction to the Sociology of Law* (Westport: Greenwood Press edn 1974).

Tittle, C. R. (1969) 'Crime Rates and Legal Sanctions' 16 Soc Prob 409–22.

Tittle, C. R. and Rowe, A. R. (1974) 'Certainty of Arrest and Crime Rates: A Further Test of the Deterrence Hypothesis' 52 Social Forces 455–62.

Tomasic, R. (1980) 'The Sociology of Legislation' in R. Tomasic (ed) *Law and Society in Australia* pp. 19–49 (Sydney: Law Foundation of New South Wales and George Allen and Unwin).

(1985) 'Cynicism and Ambivalence Toward Law and Legal Institutions in Australia' in Gibson and Baldwin (eds) (1985) pp. 89–106.

Tönnies, F. (1957) *Community and Society*, transl. by C. P. Loomis (East Lansing, Mich.: Michigan State University Press).
Turk, A. T. (1976) 'Law as a Weapon in Social Conflict' 23 Soc Prob 276–91.
Turpin, C. (1989) *Government Procurement and Contracts* (Harlow: Longman).
Tyler, S. A. (1969) 'Introduction' in S A. Tyler (ed) *Cognitive Anthropology* pp. 1–23 (New York: Holt, Rinehart and Winston).
Tyler, T. R. (1990) *Why People Obey the Law* (New Haven: Yale University Press).
Tylor, E. B. (1913) *Primitive Culture: Researches Into the Development of Mythology, Philosophy, Religion, Language, Art and Custom* (5th edn, London: John Murray).
Unger, R. M. (1976) *Law in Modern Society: Toward a Criticism of Social Theory* (New York: Free Press).
Vago, S. (1988) *Law and Society* (2nd edn, Englewood Cliffs: Prentice-Hall).
Vennard, J. (1982) *Contested Trials in Magistrates Courts* Home Office Research Study No. 71 (London: Her Majesty's Stationery Office).
Vincent-Jones, P. (1989) 'Contract and Business Transactions: A Socio-Legal Analysis' 16 J Law & Soc 166–186.
Vogel, D. (1986) *National Styles of Regulation: Environmental Policy in Great Britain and the United States* (Ithaca, NY.: Cornell University Press).
Von Hirsch, A. (1976) *Doing Justice: The Choice of Punishments: Report of the Committee for the Study of Incarceration* (New York: Hill and Wang).
Vorenberg, J. (1981) 'Decent Restraint of Prosecutorial Power' 94 Harv L Rev 1521–573.
Wacks, R. (1989) *Personal Information: Privacy and the Law* (Oxford: Oxford University Press).
Waddington, P. A. J. (1991) *The Strong Arm of the Law: Armed and Public Order Policing* (Oxford: Oxford University Press).
Waldo, G. P. and Chiricos, T. G. (1972) 'Perceived Penal Sanction and Self-Reported Criminality: A Neglected Approach to Deterrence Research' 19 Soc Prob 522–40.
Warburton, C. (1933) 'Prohibition' in E. R. A. Seligman and A. Johnson (eds) *Encyclopedia of the Social Sciences* vol 12, pp. 499–510 (New York: Macmillan).
Weber, M. (1930) *The Protestant Ethic and the Spirit of Capitalism* transl. by T. Parsons (London: Allen and Unwin).
(1949) *The Methodology of the Social Sciences* transl by E. Shils and H. Finch (New York: Free Press).

(1954) *On Law in Economy and Society,* transl. by E. Shils and M. Rheinstein (Cambridge, Mass.: Harvard University Press).

(1958) *The Rational and Social Foundations of Music,* transl. by D. Martindale, J. Riedel and G. Neuwirth (Carbondale, Illinois: Southern Illinois University Press).

(1978) *Economy and Society,* edited by G. Roth and C. Wittich (Berkeley: University of California Press).

Werner, W. (1981) 'Corporation Law in Search of its Future' 81 Col L Rev 1611–666.

Westley, W. A. (1970) *Violence and the Police: A Sociological Study of Law, Custom and Morality* (Cambridge, Mass.: MIT Press).

Whelan, C. (1990) 'Small Claims Courts: Heritage and Adjustment' in Whelan (ed) (1990) pp. 207–34.

(ed) (1990) *Small Claims Courts: A Comparative Study* (Oxford: Oxford University Press).

White, G. E. (1982) *Earl Warren: A Public Life* (New York: Oxford University Press).

Wigmore, J. H. (1894) 'Responsibility for Tortious Acts: Its History' 7 Harv L Rev 315–37.

Wilkinson, P. J. (1981) 'The Potential of Functionalism for the Sociological Analysis of Law' in Podgorecki and Whelan (eds) (1981) pp. 67–90.

Williams, P. J. (1991) *The Alchemy of Race and Rights: Diary of a Law Professor* (Cambridge, Mass.: Harvard University Press).

Willis, C. F., Macleod, J. and Naish, P. (1988) *The Tape-Recording of Police Interviews with Suspects: A Second Interim Report* (Home Office Research Study 97) (London: Her Majesty's Stationery Office).

Wilson, J. Q. (1968) *Varieties of Police Behaviour: The Management of Law and Order in Eight Communities* (Cambridge, Mass.: Harvard University Press).

Winston, K. I. (ed) (1981) *The Principles of Social Order: Selected Essays of Lon L. Fuller* (Durham, NC.: Duke University Press).

Witmer, T. R. (1941) 'Trade Union Liability: The Problem of the Unincorporated Corporation' 51 Yale LJ 40–63.

Wolff, K. H. (1979) 'Phenomenology and Sociology' in Bottomore and Nisbet (eds) (1979) pp. 499–556.

(ed) (1960) *Essays on Sociology and Philosophy by Emile Durkheim et al.* (New York: Harper Torchbook edn 1964).

Wright, E. O. (ed) (1989) *The Debate on Classes* (London: Verso).

Yeazell, S. C. (1987) *From Medieval Group Litigation to the Modern Class Action* (New Haven: Yale University Press).

Yngvesson, B. (1988) 'Making Law at the Doorway: The Clerk, the Court, and the Construction of Community in a New England Town'

22 Law & Soc Rev 409–48.
Zweigert, K. and Kötz, H. (1987) *An Introduction to Comparative Law,* transl. by T. Weir, vol 1 (2nd edn, Oxford: Oxford University Press).

Index